REVISITING THE EMPOWERMENT CONTROVERSY

BLACK POWER AND UNITARIAN UNIVERSALISM

Mark D. Morrison-Reed

Skinner House Books
BOSTON

Copyright © 2018 by Mark D. Morrison-Reed. All rights reserved. Published by Skinner House Books, an imprint of the Unitarian Universalist Association, a liberal religious organization with more than 1,000 congregations in the U.S. and Canada, 24 Farnsworth St., Boston, MA 02210–1409.

skinnerhouse.org

Printed in the United States

Cover design by Suzanne Morgan
Text design by Jeff Miller

print ISBN: 978-1-55896-819-6
eBook ISBN: 978-1-55896-820-2

6 5 4 3 2 1
21 20 19 18

Library of Congress Cataloging-in-Publication Data

Names: Morrison-Reed, Mark D., 1949– author.
Title: Revisiting the empowerment controversy : black power and Unitarian Universalism / Mark D. Morrison-Reed.
Description: Boston : Skinner House Books, 2018. | Includes bibliographical references and index.
Identifiers: LCCN 2018010463 (print) | LCCN 2017057096 (ebook) | ISBN 9781558968196 (pbk. : alk. paper) | ISBN 9781558968202
Subjects: LCSH: African American Unitarian Universalists. | Unitarian Universalist Association—History.
Classification: LCC BX9833.48.A47 M67 2018 (ebook) | LCC BX9833.48.A47 (print) | DDC 289.1/3208996073—dc23
LC record available at https://lccn.loc.gov/2018010463

Contents

Preface	ix
Introduction	xv
Abbreviations	xix
Chronology	xx
Before and After Selma [1964–1966]	1
The Emergency Conference on the UU Response to the Black Rebellion [August 1966–November 1967]	22
The Formation of the Black Unitarian Universalist Caucus [November 1967–May 1968]	68
The Cleveland General Assembly and Its Aftermath [May–December 1968]	102
Prelude to Controversy [January–July 1969]	135
Boston General Assembly [July 1969]	158
The Black Affairs Council Disaffiliates from the UUA [1970]	198
The Washington D.C. General Assembly [1971]	253

Deadlocked [1972–1975]	286
Black Power Was the Trigger, Not the Cause	309
Endings and Beginnings	345
Notes	357
Index	395

Acknowledgments

I NEED TO ACKNOWLEDGE that some individuals made a significant emotional sacrifice in agreeing to correspond with me about how they experienced the era this book discusses. They were reluctant to talk about those painful years. When participants did share there was a consistency to their reflections. One wrote, "It wasn't one of our best periods of history. I find myself with mixed reviews of how I handled myself during that chaos." Another said, "It raises a whole series of memories that I am not sure I really want to deal with." And still another said, "I am simply not inclined to comment. That is simply not where I am in this *Radiant Twilight of My Life* as I approach my 89th birthday." He was not alone in declining my invitation. Yet despite the discomfort, some shared deeply and thoughtfully with me. For that I am humbled and grateful.

I am thankful to people from earlier projects, such as Max Gaebler and Jack Mendelsohn, whom I interviewed while collecting materials in 1985 for the adult program *How Open the Door? The African American Experience in Unitarian Universalism*, and Henry Hampton and David Eaton, whom Carol Dornbrand interviewed for the same project. I had already begun corresponding with Donald S. Harrington about BAWA in 1982. I interviewed and corresponded with Mwalimu Imara in 2009, while doing research for *Darkening the Doorways*.

Among those who over many years corresponded with me, spoke to me about the era, shared documents they had collected, or read sections of the manuscript were: Marsh Agobert, Wayne Arnason, George Kimmich Beach, Mark Belletini, Ann Black, Richard Boeke, David Bumbaugh, Victor Carpenter, Barbara Coeyman, John Cummins, Denny Davidoff, Alan Deale, Nancy Doughty, Charles Eddis, Robert Eller-Isaacs, Kathy Ellis, Dorothy Emerson, J. Ron Engel, Marvin Evans, William J. Gardiner, John Gibbons, Gordon D. Gibson, Richard S. Gilbert, Nina Grey, W. Edward Harris, Carol Henderson, A. Phillip Hewett, James A. Hobart, Harry Hoehler, Hugo Holleroth, C. Leon Hopper, David A. Johnson, Richard Kellaway, Larry Ladd, Richard Leonard, David H. MacPherson, Gretchen Manker, Dan McKanan, Donald W. McKinney, Orloff W. Miller, Orloff G. Miller, Maura S. O'Brien, Clark Olsen, David B. Parke, Norma Poinsett, Christopher G. Raible, Ann Holmes Redding, Robert Reed, Eugene Reeves, Alan Rosenthal, William G. Sinkford, William F. Schulz, Neil Shadle, Bette Sikes, Betty Reid Soskin, Bruce Southworth, Ralph Stuztman, Del Tweedie, Ione Vargus, Grant Delbert Venerable II, David Weissbard, Leslie Westbrook, Jeffery Wilson, John Wolfe, Clemmie R. Wylie, plus members of Restoration Church in Philadelphia, as well as the congregations in Champaign-Urbana and Albany, and the Community Church of New York. There were other participants I knew and wish I could have spoken with, but they died before I began writing. During the three and a half years it took to write this book, nearly a dozen of those that I had communicated with died.

I am grateful to the archives and archivists who assisted me. These included the General Assembly of Unitarian and Free

Christian Churches in London; the Canadian Unitarian Council in Toronto; Community Church of New York, and Unitarian Church of All Souls in New York; First Unitarian Congregational Society in Brooklyn; Unitarian Universalist Congregation at Shelter Rock, New York; First Unitarian Universalist Society of Albany, New York; The Unitarian Society of Germantown and Restoration Church in Philadelphia; University Unitarian Church in Seattle; the Unitarian Universalist Fellowship of Athens, Georgia; the University of Michigan, where the Ann Arbor and Detroit congregational records are held; and the City of Ottawa Archives, which hold the records of the First Unitarian Congregation of Ottawa.

A special thanks to Deborah Rice, who reviewed the holdings of First Unitarian Church of Los Angeles for me; Meadville Lombard Theological School's Sankofa Collection and John Leeker; Andover-Harvard Theological Library and Jessica Saurez and Gloria Korsman; First Unitarian Church of Des Moines, Iowa, and Bob Glass; All Souls Church Unitarian in Washington D.C., and its archivist Molly Freeman; Cedar Lane Unitarian Universalist Church in Bethesda, Maryland, and Glenis Bellais; West Shore Unitarian Universalist Church in Cleveland and Gaile Schafer; First Unitarian Universalist Church of Richmond, Virginia, and Pat Vaugh; Bob Brzozowski of the Unitarian Universalist Society of Oneonta, New York; Sally Babbitt of the Unitarian Universalist Church of Urbana-Champaign, Illinois; Janet Nichols of First Parish in Framingham, Massachusetts; and Betty Boone of the First Unitarian Universalist Church of San Diego.

I am thankful to Linda Simmons, Sara Dennis, Beth Robbins, and Ann Holmes Redding, who allowed me to use their unpublished manuscripts that covered various aspects of this era; to Iska Cole for giving me a copy of *An Oral History of the Consolidation of the American Unitarian Association and the Universalist Church of*

America and the Creation of the Unitarian Universalist Association, and also to Lisa Ward, Ronald Cortes, and Betty Bobo Seiden who read and commented on major portions of the manuscript.

I am grateful to the students who took my course, *African Americans and the Universalists, Unitarians and Unitarian Universalists*, at Meadville Lombard Theological School and who over the last ten years scoured the archives of their teaching congregations.

The Unitarian Universalist Funding Program supported this work with three sequential grants beginning with the research, then the writing, and finally the editing and production. I am grateful not just for its support in this work but for supporting me in editing *Voices from the Margins* and *Darkening the Doorways: Black Trailblazers and Missed Opportunities in Unitarian Universalism* and in writing *The Selma Awakening: How the Civil Rights Movement Tested and Changed Unitarian Universalism*.

I appreciate Shoshanna Green's editorial acumen and hold Mary Benard, Editorial Director of Skinner House Books, in high regard for her skill at literary midwifery. She for the fifth time shepherded me through the process of writing a book, and I am indebted to her. At every step of the way my wife, Donna, has supported me: challenging my ideas and tightening my prose, cheerleading and hugging, tolerating the invasion of boxes of documents that spread out and sometimes took over our small apartment. From the beginning she was convinced this book had to be written and now was the time. I am happy, thankful, and grateful to her and to all those who have helped me.

Preface

REV. DR. MWALIMU IMARA, whom I had known as Rennie, sat behind his desk. I was happy to see him. This was the first time since before he graduated from Meadville Lombard Theological School in 1968. Since then he had served as senior minister in Champaign-Urbana and at the Arlington Street Church in Boston, and now was minister-at-large to the Benevolent Fraternity of Unitarian Churches (now Unitarian Universalist Urban Ministries). While at Meadville, he had served as an advisor to the Liberal Religious Youth (LRY) group at the First Unitarian Society of Chicago, of which I was president. Back then, I was a seventeen-year-old seeking role models, and as our one African American youth advisor, he was especially important to me.

Eleven years had passed since he had spent nearly every Sunday evening with that sixty-member LRY group in the Garden Room at Chicago First. As I sat across from him at the "Ben Frat," I was looking for help and information.

I wanted to know how the UU ministry had been for him. I also wanted to hear his take on the conflict over Black Power that had shaken the Unitarian Universalist Association (UUA) ten years earlier. As he denounced how the UUA had betrayed the Black Caucus during those years, his jaw clenched, his nostrils flared, and his finger jabbed. My pleasure dissolved into dismay.

Going through theological school, I sought out my black predecessors whenever the chance arose. By 1978, I had spoken with Marshall Grigsby, David Eaton, Lewis McGee, and Thomas Payne. By the time I sat down with Mwalimu, I had made up my mind that someone ought to unpack the acrimony from which we had just emerged. It would be the topic of my doctor of ministry thesis.

Mwalimu's outrage convinced me otherwise. After witnessing his fury, I shook my head and said, "No way." I wanted nothing to do with those tumultuous years between 1967 and 1974 in the UUA.

I was away at college when, in October 1967, over my father's protest, my mother flew to New York City to participate in the Conference on the Unitarian Universalist Response to the Black Rebellion held at the Biltmore Hotel. She and Mwalimu were among those who withdrew from the conference to form a black caucus, and soon after returning to Chicago, she took a lead in preparing for the first National Conference of Black Unitarian Universalists, which was to be held in Chicago in February 1968.

Being eighteen years old I thought anything my mother was involved in was suspect. As she zealously insisted that I come with her to the National Conference I objected, but eventually I caved in. She dragged me there and rightaway marched me up to Jesse Jackson and introduced me. His size and presence left me feeling small. I was sent into the meeting hall, where I listened briefly, and as soon as possible I fled. It was pure chance that I had come home from college that weekend; I was there to see friends and smoke weed, not to listen to adults harangue one another.

That might have been the end of my engagement with Unitarian Universalism's most divisive controversy if I hadn't decided to enter the UU ministry. In spring 1977, during a practice interview

PREFACE

in preparation for the real Ministerial Fellowship Committee interview, I was asked if I would have walked out of the Boston General Assembly in 1969. All I can remember is the feeling of dread at being asked. I have no memory of what I said, except that I was less than honest. What I knew, and did not say, was that I would have felt torn in an unbearable way.

During my ministerial internship in the fall of 1977, Paul Carnes, the newly elected president of the UUA, was visiting Cedar Lane Unitarian Church, and we fell into a conversation during which he asked me about the Empowerment Controversy. I said, "It's another generation's fight and we need to get over it and move on." A couple of weeks later, Dalmas Taylor, an African American member of the UUA Board, called to report that Carnes had referred to our conversation during the UUA Board meeting. Taylor said, "You'd better be careful."

Six months later I met with Mwalimu Imara. After witnessing his fury, I decided it would be wiser to write my thesis about two black Unitarians who were ministers during the first half of the twentieth century.

It was too soon to write about the late sixties. The hurt and anger were still fresh and deep. But although I retreated from the topic, my concern and confusion, fascination and trepidation remained. In 1989, early in our ministries, Rob Eller-Isaacs and I naively tried to convince our very senior colleagues Jack Mendelsohn and Donald Harrington that their reconciliation would be healthy for the UUA. They refused. In 1993, I led a history workshop on Diversity Day at General Assembly. When I began discussing the Empowerment era, a verbal fight erupted right there.

My experience in reading and listening to people reminisce—and argue—about that era is that there have been few honest retellings. The accounts have been largely polemic, and attentive listening

xi

rare. I have endeavored in this book to tell the story of the Empowerment Controversy from all sides. It is a story that can be reconstructed by reading UU publications but I filled in the details and captured the emotional response by accessing sermons, newsletters, and correspondence from over a dozen archives and through correspondence with the archivists from an additional dozen. During the last three decades I have also interviewed over a dozen individuals and several groups, corresponded with at least fifty people, and received permission to quote from their emails and interviews. There were also a few who declined to participate, a desire that I understand. Nonetheless, when combined, a full array of positions is represented.

My own involvement in these events was peripheral. Nevertheless I was affected. Thus what I write, which I hope is fair, is neither detached nor dispassionate. It reflects my interpretation and opinion. Therefore, there are a few things the reader should know in order to understand what lies behind my point of view.

From the age of three, I grew up in one of the UUA's most integrated congregations. At age eight, I began rehearsing in that church's junior choir, which would grow into the city-wide, multicultural, and interracial Chicago Children's Choir. Interracial settings are the water in which I swim; I find them natural but not always easy. I have lived outside the United States for over half my life, and since 1995 I have held both U.S. and Canadian citizenship. I relate to America as an ex-pat, but one who has served almost continuously since 1981 on UUA committees, task forces, and commissions. I also served for twenty-six years as co-minister in Rochester, New York, and Toronto, Canada, with my wife, Donna. I am, at heart, a parish minister, and my perspective is first and foremost pastoral. Therefore, the story I tell explores how the events of those years played out in UU congregations.

Finally, for me this book represents unfinished intellectual and emotional business, and the completion of the historical arc I have followed since 1978, when I began writing *Black Pioneers in a White Denomination*. It is my effort to become reconciled with a past that also lives within myself.

Introduction

It was the middle of July, 1969. In Boston, Monday was 77 degrees and comfortable, but as the days passed, it grew hot and then hotter. On Tuesday, the temperature and the humidity both reached 84. Wednesday, the mercury hit 94, and it remained there on Thursday. On Friday, it was still 90. In the Statler-Hilton Hotel, where the Unitarian Universalist Association was holding its annual General Assembly, the meeting began normally, grew heated, then exploded.

On Monday, immediately following the opening ceremonies and greetings, the Black Unitarian Universalist Caucus (BUUC) commandeered the mikes until a motion to reorder the agenda was debated. The motion was defeated. Tuesday morning, as the Assembly was about to hear from the candidates in the upcoming UUA presidential election, a motion was called to reconsider BUUC's motion from the day before. This motion to revisit the first motion passed. However, the motion itself was once again defeated. As the vote was close, 692 to 687, a recount was called. But another motion, to table the recount until after the presidential candidates' forum, carried easily.

Before the presidential candidates had a chance to address the gathering, it was pointed out that the members of BUUC had left the hall. The candidates went ahead with their presentations, but immediately afterward, Rev. Jack Mendelsohn, minister of the nearby Arlington Street Church, went to the procedural microphone. Calling this walkout "one of the most serious events in the history of our movement,"[1] he asked to address the Assembly. After a brief deliberation, it was announced that Mendelsohn and Dr. Glover Barnes, the African American co-chair of Black and White Action (BAWA), would each speak. Mendelsohn announced that he could not remain and carry on business as usual. He was going to the Arlington Street Church, and anyone who wished could join him. Without waiting to hear Barnes, he left. Many white BUUC supporters rose and followed him. Mendelsohn said that as he made his way up the aisle, his colleague Horace Westwood rose from his seat and spat in his face.[2]

A mile away and nine years earlier, more than 25 hundred Universalists and Unitarians had gathered at Symphony Hall on Massachusetts Avenue to celebrate the vote to consolidate the American Unitarian Association (AUA) and the Universalist Church of America (UCA). Hundreds of robe-clad ministers had processed down the aisles. The entire body had risen to sing, "As tranquil streams that meet and merge and flow as one to meet the sea, our kindred fellowships unite to build a church that shall be free." They kept singing it over and over again. The sound was thunderous, the mood triumphant; even staid New Englanders shed tears of joy and hope. Four years later, Rev. Dana McLean Greeley, the UUA's first president, boasted, "The course has been charted, and we are out beyond the shoals."[3]

He was wrong. During that week of July 13, 1969, the days were hot, passions were enflamed, and the situation was dire. Now, as the dissidents marched out of General Assembly, their departure was met with catcalls and hissing. Such was the turmoil that it was impossible to continue.

How had it come to this?

The General Assembly of July 1969, the UUA's eighth, marked the end of Greeley's term. Because he was slated to step into the presidency of the International Association for Religious Freedom (IARF), the IARF's twentieth congress was being held in Boston in conjunction with the UUA General Assembly.[4] Seven male Euro-American ministers were vying to become the next president of the UUA. One layperson, G. Robert Hohler, had dropped out before the serious campaigning began, and so had the favored candidate, Rev. Harry Scholefield. The war in Vietnam garnered some attention at that General Assembly, but there were also pressing budgetary issues and contentious matters of governance that needed to be debated. The UUA was clearly not beyond the shoals. But all other business was overshadowed by "the Walkout."

How had the hope that filled Unitarians and Universalists in 1960 so quickly dissipated? How could this happen, after they had shown such solidarity and courage in the 1965 civil rights campaign in Selma, where two Unitarian Universalists, Viola Liuzzo and James Reeb, were martyred in the cause of racial justice? What of the $1 million the General Assembly had voted to commit to black concerns just one year earlier, at its meeting in 1968?

Julius Lester's book *Look Out, Whitey! Black Power's Gon' Get Your Mama!* had recently come out—a rallying cry for Black Power that critiqued white liberalism and laid bare its underlying racism. It had a catchy title and an accurate assessment of the situation in which Unitarian Universalists found themselves as their hallowed values of individualism, pluralism, and democracy came under fire.

Black Power triggered the upheaval but was not its cause. The story of the Empowerment Controversy related here is a tale of honorable people pursuing dreams of racial justice, while battered by historical forces beyond their control and social circumstances not of their making, circumstances that forced them to choose between dearly held but conflicting values. It was a collision of worldviews and loyalties in which every decision was colored by the partakers' humanity: noble intentions alongside inflamed passions; egocentrism masquerading as activism; susceptibility to self-delusion, defensiveness, and as tragedy requires, hubris. The members of the Black Unitarian Universalist Caucus, its white allies, contesting integrationists, and the institutional loyalists who saw themselves as fighting for the financial survival of the fledgling Unitarian Universalist Association all misconstrued and racialized a broader range of tensions. Cultural and denominational pressures that had been mounting along several fault lines were increased by the urgency of the late sixties and then released by the *cause de jour*. Underlying it all were competing needs for power and control.

A British Unitarian observer at that General Assembly said, "One can only hope that out of the heart-searching, the agony, and tears, love and justice will emerge triumphant."[5] Tragedy rarely leads to triumph. But perhaps wisdom can be gleaned from the pain and upheaval of those years, a wisdom that will be of use today in a new era of turmoil and polarization.

Abbreviations

AUA—American Unitarian Association
BAC—Black Affairs Council
BAWA—Black and White Action
BIC—Black Affairs Council Investment Corporation
BUUC—Black Unitarian Universalist Caucus
BUUR—Black Unitarians for Radical Reform
CORE—Congress of Racial Equality
FFR—Fellowship for Renewal
FULLBAC—Full Recognition and Funding of the Black Affairs Council
GA—General Assembly of the Unitarian Universalist Association
IRC—Interdenominational Racial Caucus
IFCO—Interreligious Foundation for Community Organization
LRY—Liberal Religious Youth
SCLC—Southern Christian Leadership Conference
UCA—Universalist Church of America
UUA—Unitarian Universalist Association

Chronology

AUGUST 1967—Black Unitarians for Radical Reform (BURR) is formed in the Los Angeles area.

OCTOBER 1967—At the Emergency Conference on Unitarian Universalist Response to the Black Rebellion, a caucus of black Unitarian Universalists (eventually to be called the Black Unitarian Universalist Caucus or BUUC) demands the formation and funding of a Black Affairs Council (BAC).

NOVEMBER 1967—The UUA Board of Trustees rejects the black caucus's proposal for BAC and votes instead to reorganize the Commission on Religion and Race. The caucus calls on congregations to withhold support from the UUA's annual program fund until the next General Assembly. Supporters of Black Unitarians for Radical Reform (SOBURR) is formed to organize white support of black empowerment.

FEBRUARY 1968—BUUC is officially formed at the National Conference of Black Unitarian Universalists and votes to establish BAC.

MARCH 1968—The UUA Board of Trustees forms the Fund for Racial Justice Now and the Commission for Action on Race.

APRIL 1968—Full Recognition and Funding of BAC (FULLBAC) is created.

MAY 1968—Black and White Alternative, later Black and White Action (BAWA), is formed. General Assembly votes to meet BUUC's demands for funding BAC.

JUNE 1968—The UUA Board of Trustees grants BAC affiliate status.

MAY 1969—The UUA administration recommends to the Board of Trustees that it not reduce BAC funding but require annual reaffirmation. The Board votes to include $50,000 for BAWA in the budget.

JULY 1969—Hundreds walk out of General Assembly in protest.

NOVEMBER 1969—The new UUA administration's plan to deal with inadequate funding to continue its current operations is approved by the Board of Trustees.

DECEMBER 1969—BAC begins a campaign to persuade congregations to convert half of their investment portfolios into BAC bonds.

JANUARY 1970—The UUA Board reaffirms its decision to reduce BAC annual funding and pay out the total over a longer time frame.

FEBRUARY 1970—BAC disaffiliates from the UUA.

JUNE 1970—BUUC/BAC boycotts General Assembly and a motion to restore BAC funding is defeated.

MARCH 1972—BAC and BAWA are granted associate organization status as part of the arrangement to receive Veatch funds. Of these funds, $180,000 is allocated to BAC and $45,000 to BAWA.

FEBRUARY 1973—BUUC splits into factions, one of which reorganizes as the Black Humanist Fellowship.

1979—BAC's status as a UUA associate organization comes to an end in 1979 and BAWA's in 1981.

Before and After Selma

[*1964–1966*]

"SELMA WAS A TRANSFORMING EXPERIENCE," said G. Robert Hohler, the executive director of the Unitarian Universalist Laymen's League. In March 1965, he had dropped everything and flown from Boston to Atlanta with James Reeb and a dozen others, in response to Dr. Martin Luther King Jr.'s call to join with the African American citizens of Selma in the March to Montgomery. "Some of us would call it religious," Hohler said, "others would call it radicalizing. Again, we would differ on our definitions, after all we are UUs. But no matter how we would parse and define it, Selma changed our lives."[6] Hohler was radicalized; indeed, everyone who went to Selma spoke of how they were changed. The Unitarian Universalist Association, however, was not so much changed as redirected.

Social Justice, UU Style

During the Eisenhower presidency (1952–1960), the concerns of the Universalist Church of America and the American Unitarian Association were largely internal. In 1953, the two denominations formed the Council of Liberal Churches (CLC); through it they cooperated in the areas of religious education, publications, and youth programming. When that effort to harmonize their programs faltered, the UCA and AUA began a process that led, in 1959, to a vote to begin planning for consolidation. In 1961, following a vote to implement that plan, the new Unitarian Universalist organization's first election was held. In 1963, the release of *The Free Church in a Changing World* provided a blueprint for its future. The process that led to merger overlapped with the fellowship movement, which had fueled the growth of Unitarianism beyond New England after the Second World War. Throughout these years, issues of social justice were not ignored, but of necessity, internal affairs predominated.[7]

Soon after consolidation, Unitarian Universalists began to more fully engage the world. In 1962, the UUA established the Unitarian Universalist United Nations Office (UU-UNO); in 1963, the Department of Overseas and Interfaith Relations was formed, and General Assembly mandated the formation of the Commission on Religion and Race. The Commission's first major effort led to nearly 16 hundred UUs participating in the March on Washington for Jobs and Freedom in 1963. In 1964, the Department of Social Responsibility was established and several dozen Unitarian Universalist college students and clergy participated in the Mississippi Summer and Mississippi Delta Projects. And by February 1965, the first four Unitarian Universalists of what would swell to hundreds arrived in Selma.

In April 1965, following the March to Montgomery, the Commission on Religion and Race mailed a questionnaire to all 1,108 Unitarian Universalist congregations, inquiring whether and how each had responded to the events in Selma. The response rate was 10 percent from a balanced mix of congregations; 111 replied. Their answers were fairly uniform. The vast majority had commemorated James Reeb's life. Some did so during a Sunday service, while others held a special memorial service; many sent contributions to the James Reeb or Freedom Funds; a number sent telegrams of protest to their congressional representatives. Some members participated in local marches, and many ministers went to Selma, Montgomery, or the memorial services held in Washington D.C. or Boston.

The congregation in Chico, California, went further than most. Members participated in the local Hour of Concern, a community protest during which they marched, prayed, and sang. Their minister, Rev. Arthur Wilmot, had been among those who responded to Dr. King's initial call and went to Selma. The white minister of Grace Baptist Church preached against these "marching ministers." Denouncing the Selma march, he proclaimed that it was "contrary to the Scriptures, provided Communists with propaganda, and fostered lawlessness."[8] In response, a group of fifty gathered at the Unitarian church and, after a heated discussion about how to respond, decided to hold a vigil at Grace Baptist Church to demonstrate their belief in the brotherhood of all. Nearly 150 people participated in the vigil and were condemned in a local newspaper for picketing. That led to Wilmot receiving hate calls. The action also resulted in the formation of a community group interested in solving Chico's civil rights problems. It is perhaps not coincidental that Wilmot had been preceded in the Chico pulpit by Rev. Lewis A. McGee. Chico had been the first predominantly Euro-American UU congregation to call an African American as its senior minister.

Organizing seems to be the quintessential Unitarian and Universalist response to injustice, going back as far as 1790, when Benjamin Rush co-founded the Society for the Abolition of Slavery. Across the country in the forties, fifties, and sixties, Unitarians and Universalists organized Human Relations Councils and local chapters of the NAACP, the Urban League, and the Congress of Racial Equality (CORE). In 1963, the Unitarian Church of

Harrisburg played a lead role in forming the Human Relations Council of Greater Harrisburg. In 1965, the minister of the First Unitarian Church in Albany, New York, Rev. Nick Cardell, had met with a community committee to establish a local Urban League, and in Rochester earlier that year Rev. Robert West had preached that it was time for a branch of the League in that city as well. In 1967, Hayward Henry and others would found the Black Unitarian Universalist Caucus (BUUC). And the advice of Rev. Stephen Fritchman to the dissenters who walked out of the 1969 General Assembly was the same: "Organize! Organize! Organize!"

School Integration

School integration, open housing, and equal access were the race relations issues that garnered the most attention from Unitarian Universalists in the mid-sixties. Since Unitarian Universalists expected to live, eat, and send their children to school where they wished, these were concerns with which they identified. Such discrimination was a particular affront to UU individualism and sense of entitlement.

During the sixties, Unitarian Universalism was politically more diverse than it is today. When the 1964 Civil Rights Act was ratified by the U.S. Senate, Roman Hruska (R., Nebraska) and Leverett Saltonstall (R., Massachusetts) voted for it, as did Joseph S. Clark Jr. (D., Pennsylvania) and Paul Douglas (D., Illinois), all UUs. Earlier, when the bill had come before the House of Representatives, the UUs William R. Poage (D., Texas) and William H. Harrison (R., Wyoming) had voted against it. In 1966, when Unitarian Universalists were asked, "Which political party do you support?" 34 percent answered "Republican" and 56 percent "Democrat."[9] In no way was it unusual to be Unitarian and Republican. William

Howard Taft, the Republican president of the United States and later chief justice of the Supreme Court, had also been the moderator of the American Unitarian Association. Harold Burton, a Boston-bred Unitarian, had been mayor of Cleveland and a U.S. senator as a Republican, and was later appointed to the Supreme Court by Democratic president Harry Truman. Burton is credited with convincing the conservative justices on the Supreme Court to support the 1954 *Brown v. Board of Education* decision.

A strong conservative vein ran through Unitarianism. Although Unitarians were not opposed to civil rights, many drew a line at civil disobedience. Indeed, UUs in white suburbs were buffered from issues of access, while New England and rural UUs saw civil rights as a Southern and urban problem and were indifferent to the issue.

It was in this context that the 1965 UUA General Assembly received the report of the Commission on Religion and Race and voted for the Commission's continuance. Following that vote, Jack Mendelsohn, Robert Hohler, Connie Burgess (executive director of the Unitarian Universalist Women's Federation), and Jack Zoerheide (director of the Community Relations Department of the UUA Massachusetts Bay District) put forward a resolution entitled "To Bear Witness." The resolution was a call to condemn the ongoing racial segregation in Boston's public schools. Earlier protests had taken the form of a school boycott in February 1964, which was followed by a lawsuit filed in the state supreme court against the Boston School Committee. James Reeb had been a plaintiff in the case, and the GA resolution invoked his name in inviting the delegates to march to the School Committee headquarters and stand in silent vigil. A lengthy debate ensued, after which a vote counted 531 in favor and 256 against. Thus, with the backing of 67 percent of the Assembly, the Unitarian Universalists marched.[10]

The public school situation in Seattle mirrored that in Boston. Eight schools in the central area of Seattle were more than 85 percent nonwhite. A lawsuit had been filed in federal court in Seattle in 1961 on behalf of African American schoolchildren. When the remedies implemented by the school board proved largely ineffective, another lawsuit followed in March 1966. After the school board dismissed proposals put forward by CORE, the NAACP, and the Urban League, Seattle CORE proposed boycotting Seattle public schools. The school superintendent was notified in February 1966 of the boycott and of the Freedom Schools that would run in parallel; among the three co-signers of that notice was John Cornethan, the African American chair of Seattle CORE and member of University Unitarian Church. The Board of Directors of the Greater Seattle Council of Churches supported the boycott, as did Rev. Peter Raible, minister of University Unitarian. Raible called a congregational meeting in order to engage his congregation and hear their views on what position the church should take. By a vote of 141 to 19, the congregation passed a resolution calling upon "the Seattle School Board to take steps as may be necessary to end racial imbalance at the earliest possible date," but they balked at supporting the boycott itself. Nevertheless, UUs did participate when the boycott took place, and both Raible and Rev. Ralph Mero of East Shore Unitarian Church taught in the Freedom School.[11]

In Chicago in 1963, where a recalcitrant school board and superintendent were committed to keeping the system segregated, a group of parents had hired an attorney and sued. The settlement established the Advisory Panel on Integration of the Public Schools, which reported that 84 percent of black students and 86 percent of white students attended essentially segregated schools. When no progress was made in implementing the Advisory Panel's recommendations, a boycott was called, and 200 thousand children boycotted the public schools on October 22. In the lead-up to the boycott, the minister of the First Unitarian Society of Chicago organized a forum for congregation members to weigh in. It was a contentious meeting in which people spoke passionately for and against the protest. Toward its end, Lee Reed spoke. She was African American and had just returned from Switzerland, where her husband had been on sabbatical. She recounted that when Europeans asked her about racial discrimination in the United States, she had spoken proudly of the headway being made. But according to one report of her speech, she was dismayed to discover "the white liberals in her own church rationalizing and equivocating about a course of action that was aimed at achieving equality. With tears in her eyes, she asked the people in the room to support the school boycott."[12]

School integration was a cause in which UU congregations were engaged before and after the spotlight fell on Selma, but their responses were not monolithic. Some were progressive and bold, many sympathetic but cautious, and a few opposed. Even after the deaths of Viola Liuzzo and James Reeb in 1965, conservatism was reflected at the 1965 General Assembly by the 33 percent who voted against the "To Bear Witness" resolution.

Opposition existed to civil rights. It was evident in the Unitarian church in Melrose, Massachusetts, where its Board refused to hold a collection for the James Reeb Fund and the congregation "in no way" marked his death. In Shreveport, Louisiana, the editor of the church's newsletter delivered a hateful sermon that denigrated Reeb. Among those who opposed the march on the Boston School Committee was James Madison Barr, the minister in Memphis, who had also opposed the March to Montgomery and who opined that Dr.

King was partly to blame for Reeb's death. In Boston, he declared, "I don't like to be pressured into attending a march in the name of James Reeb."[13]

Urban Ministry

The UU congregations most engaged in the fight for racial justice were urban. In Brooklyn Heights, New York, the co-chair of the Community School Committee was Rev. Donald McKinney, minister of the First Unitarian Church. In 1965, the church hired Rev. Duke T. Gray as assistant minister, specifically to address urban issues. Early in 1966, the congregation established the Fulton Street Center and Gray, together with the church's Social Action Committee, led the congregation through a process of deciding how best to engage the low-income area surrounding the Center. After beginning with a "ministry of *listening*," they joined with local residents in creating the Central Brooklyn Citizens Union as a vehicle for self-help and community action.[14]

When Gray began his work in Brooklyn, his inspiration was the UU Center for Urban Ministry in Chicago. There he had worked under the supervision of Rev. Ron Engel and Rev. Neil Shadle, with whom he had attended Meadville Lombard Theological School. Over time, the influence of urban-focused ministry would grow within Unitarian Universalism and eventually find institutional expression in the Urban Church Coalition and the Society for Community Ministries.

The Center for Urban Ministry had been founded in 1964 on Chicago's near north side, in the Forty-Third Ward neighborhood, "deliberately located precisely at the point of confrontation of black and white." That urban mishmash included, as was often the case, school administration chicanery aimed at keeping the schools segregated and white flight fanned by real estate agents. "Fear, panicky-selling . . . mixed with an honest desire to rebuild a racially integrated, quality neighborhood."[15]

In 1963, James Reeb had been serving as associate minister at All Souls Church Unitarian in Washington D.C. and as president of the University Neighborhood Council, and Engel had worked with him as an intern. Shortly thereafter, Reeb left All Souls to more fully immerse himself in the concerns of the African American community. He moved to Dorchester, a black neighborhood in Boston, enrolled his children in local schools, and became the community relations director of Boston's Metropolitan Low Income Housing Program of the American Friends Service Committee.

Following in Reeb's footsteps, Engel and Shadle moved their families. They sent their five children to the predominantly African American Mulligan School and walked about the neighborhood talking to their neighbors and hearing their concerns. They partied with them as well. By establishing a stake in the community, they were creating conditions of mutuality from which collaboration could flow. They were doing together *with* their neighbors rather than doing *for* them.

Reeb, Shadle, and Engel deliberated over what it meant to be authentically present. They were part of a cadre of young ministers that also included James Hobart, Duke Gray, and George K. ("Kim") Beach. They saw themselves as urban pioneers following in the tracks of Rev. Joseph Tuckerman and Rev. Robert Collyer, nineteenth-century Unitarians committed to working with the disinherited and downtrodden,[16] and they followed the lead of the Catholic Workers in being grounded in a community.

By January 1965, Shadle and Engel had rented space above a bar. One Meadville Lombard professor mockingly called their vision "the bar-brothel-slum bit." The effort was helped a great deal when they joined up with Dick Brown, a well-regarded black leader from the neighborhood. "Dick had lots of friends in the Movement but there was a good deal more to it," said Engel. "We walked into—and helped assemble—a mixed race community center composed of persons who really liked and enjoyed one another—we had fun together! This was the best of the 60s!!"[17]

They used a corridor model that linked inner city, middle city, and suburban UU congregations to Chicago's north side. These included Near North Fellowship in Old Town, the Second Unitarian Church of Chicago (where Shadle and Engel were the co-ministers), and the Lake Shore Unitarian Universalist Society in Wilmette and Glenview. Congregations sent laypeople to the Center to help with its various projects. The lay-led Lake Shore Society, which co-sponsored the Center with Meadville Lombard, was the most engaged, and the UUA Central Midwest District was also supportive. They hoped that this coordinated action would overcome the silo effect that resulted from the UU tendency to prize autonomy over relationship building.

In Philadelphia in 1961, Roger and Hershel Gordon became the first African American members of the Church of the Restoration. Describing her first visit, Hershel said, "No one talked to me. I took a seat in an empty pew, and no one sat next to me the entire time."[18] But having been members of the Community Church of New York before moving to Philadelphia, they were committed and stayed. Like Restoration, the East Mount Airy neighborhood in which it was located was overwhelmingly white. After Rev. Rudi Gelsey became its minister in 1964, he noticed that the demographics of the neighborhood were changing. Real estate agents were leafleting the area, "warning white owners not to be the last to sell."[19] On one street a few blocks from the church, seventeen of eighteen houses changed owners from white to black in six months.

An activist to his core, Gelsey had been among those who had gone to Selma. As white flight accelerated, he acted. In January 1966, the East Mount Airy Neighborhood Association was founded. With Gelsey serving as its first president and church members as its backbone, it began working to racially stabilize the community and to fight off the efforts of unscrupulous real estate agents to scare white homeowners into panic selling. Additionally, as chair of the Program Committee for the Joseph Priestley District's annual meeting in Philadelphia, Gelsey saw to it that the meeting's theme was "Urban Ministry."

Gelsey was succeeded as president of the neighborhood association by Richard Traylor, an African American who was chair of Restoration's Social Concerns Committee. Within two years, Traylor would be one of the leaders of the Black Affairs Council, and Gelsey, along with Don McKinney and Duke Gray, would be among its staunchest white allies. However, dissension within Restoration would lead to Gelsey's departure by early 1969, and a year later Traylor would take his leave as well.

Consensus on Racial Justice

At the fifth UUA General Assembly, held in Hollywood, Florida, in 1966, the UUA Commission on Religion and Race submitted its third annual report, describing its work over the past year in lobbying in support of the 1965 Voting Rights Act, hiring someone to fill the recently created position of James Reeb Civil Rights Worker (to represent the UUA "where the action is"), interacting with national civil rights organizations, and pressing the UUA to integrate its ministry. The Commission had also developed a Consensus on Racial Justice that was to be tabled at GA. It pledged Unitarian Universalists to "work to eliminate all vestiges of discrimination and segregation in their churches and fellowships and to encourage the integration of congregations and of the Unitarian Universalist ministry, and work for integration in all phases of life in the community."

The resolution ran six pages. Its sections were titled "Segregation and Discrimination," "Racial Violence and the Administration of Justice," "The Franchise," "Education," "Housing," "Employment," "Public Accommodations and Facilities," "Federal-Aid Programs," "Demonstrations and Civil Disobedience," "Inter-racial Marriage and Adoption," and "Personal Associations and Integration of the Churches and Ministry." Among the resolution's concerns were social issues with which UUs were currently engaged, namely the need to "curb police brutality," ensure "equal protection of the law," and protect the "right to vote." It suggested that congregations striving for integration as a "continuing goal" should examine the content of religious education curricula, consider the makeup of their leadership, and begin an exchange program with black churches. But although its preamble called on the UUA to pledge "to eliminate all vestiges of discrimination" from its congregations, its call to action focused almost entirely on government and other non-UU institutions. In other words, UUs saw the problems as located elsewhere.

The reality it did not address was that *de facto* housing patterns meant the majority of Euro-American UUs lived in isolation from African Americans. Indeed, the Consensus conveyed no sense that UU institutions or culture needed to change. Nor did it give any hint as to what "stopping being prejudiced" might involve, or charge UUs to examine their own lives in a deep way. There was no analysis of the systemic depth of the issue, nor of how UUs, through their everyday choices, perpetuated racism. It avoided reckoning with the ways racism existed and was perpetuated within the UUA and its congregations. Finally, it made no reference to anything akin to Black Power, a phrase that in less than a month would rock the nation. Indeed, there were only a handful of UUs attuned enough to the African American community to sense what was stirring.

Don't Sleep Through the Revolution

On May 18, 1966, three days before the Consensus was to be debated and voted upon, Rev. Dr. Martin Luther King Jr. delivered the Ware Lecture to the fifth UUA General Assembly. His speech was entitled "Don't Sleep through the Revolution." Delegates were eager to embrace his call, for "it felt like we were in the midst of a revolution and that Unitarian Universalists were important actors."[20]

"There are those wonderful moments in life when you speak before a group that is so near and dear to you that you don't feel like you have to engage in the art of persuasion," King began. "You don't feel like you are in the midst of strangers. You know that you are with friends."[21] He went on to hold up the many connections he had to Unitarian Universalism. He mentioned James Reeb and thanked all UUs for being so stalwart in their support of civil rights efforts. Then using the story of Rip Van Winkle, he introduced his theme: Don't sleep through the revolution: "Too many individuals and institutions find themselves in a great period of change and yet fail to achieve the new attitudes and outlooks that the new situation demands." It seemed as if he were about to call UUs to something new. "The idea whose time has come today is the idea of freedom and human dignity, and so all over the world we see something of freedom explosion, and this reveals to us that we are in the midst of revolutionary times. An older order is passing away and a new order is coming into being"[22] He continued, "I would like to suggest some of the things that the church must continually do in order to remain awake through this revolution. First, we are challenged to instill within the people of our congregation a world perspective.... Secondly, it is necessary for the church to reaffirm over and over again the essential immorality of racial segregation.... It is necessary to refute the idea that there are superior and inferior races." And thirdly, he said, "the church must engage in strong action programs to get rid of the last vestiges of segregation and discrimination." His listeners all nodded, for there was nothing among these admonitions that the vast majority of UUs would not affirm.

King elaborated,

> If we are to have a truly integrated society, white persons and Negro persons and members of all groups must live together, not merely because the law says it but because it's natural and because it's right. But that does not make legislation less important. It may be true that you can't legislate integration, but you can legislate desegregation. It may be true that morality cannot be legislated, but behavior can be regulated. It may be true that the law cannot change the heart, but it can restrain the heartless. The law cannot make a man love me, but it can restrain him from lynching me, and I think that's pretty important also. And so, while the law may not change the hearts of men, it does change the habits of men. So it is necessary for the church to support strong, meaningful civil rights legislation.[23]

Although some of his listeners may have expected to hear that Negros were seeking an "integrated society," that was not mentioned until he was halfway through. The goals with which King began were freedom, human dignity, and justice. He mentioned *freedom* twelve times, *dignity* five times, and *justice* seven times. By comparison, he used the word *discrimination* seven times and *segregation* or *segregated* seventeen times. These words described what had to be confronted and ended. The words *integrated* and *integration* were used eleven times in total, and *desegregation* twice. Sometimes he named these as goals, but more often they were identified as the means of achieving other goals. This function of integration as a means was obfuscated, not because he identified integration as an end in itself but because he so vividly and powerfully evoked the image of an integrated society.

Euro-American UUs could not really envision integration. What they visualized was the domination of white norms and African Americans *assimilating*. That, as Stokely Carmichael and others would soon tell them, was not the goal.

"Since we are working for an integrated society as an end," King continued, "we must work on an integrated basis on our staffs and civil rights organizations so that we don't get to racial justice and integration through the means of Black Nationalism."[24] This position was one with which the delegates were in full accord, as they were with the familiar imagery he drew upon as he built toward his conclusion: "We will be able to transform the jangling discords of our nation into a beautiful symphony of brotherhood, and speed up that day when all of God's children all over our nation and the world will be able to walk the earth as brothers and sisters, and then we can sing in the words of the old Negro spiritual, 'Free at last, free at last, thank God almighty we are free at last.'"[25]

Bill Sinkford, who was then the president of Liberal Religious Youth, recalls tears streaming down his face and the faces of many others as they rose in ovation. But a minister who had heard King deliver both "I Have a Dream" at the March on Washington and Reeb's eulogy in Selma said the Ware Lecture lacked their "passion."[26]

Of course, the Ware Lecture was marked by King's ever-present Baptist cadence, and he quoted John Donne, Martin Buber, Paul Tillich, William Cullen Bryant, Margaret Meade, Thomas Jefferson, even Bob Hope—but not a single African American. He mentioned Jimmie Lee Jackson twice, quoted the prophet Amos and Jesus of Nazareth, and ended with a line from a spiritual. He talked about discrimination and the momentous struggles African Americans faced in housing, education, and employment. These were issues many in the audience had worked to improve. Yet in emphasizing integration, he did not challenge these white liberals to think about privilege, systemic racism, power, or identity.

What is surprising is that, while he did mention the Voting Rights Act, he did not mention the Watts Riot, the first major urban rebellion, which erupted on August 11, five days after the act was signed. The Watts Riot left thirty-four dead and nearly four thousand arrested. King himself had visited Los Angeles on August 17. But while he did not mention Watts, he did allude to the danger presented when people have no stake in society and "feel that they have nothing to lose." He used this as a springboard for one of his major thrusts—a defense of nonviolent protest: "I think we can offset the long, hot, violent summer with the long, hot, nonviolent summer." If such an outlet for legitimate discontent "isn't provided, they are going to find it through more irrational, misguided means."[27]

Stephen Fritchman, minister of the First Unitarian Church of Los Angeles, saw the challenge for UUs more accurately than King did. In a sermon reporting on the headway that had been made since the Watts Riot, he said, "The greatest project in social action is *self understanding* in rooting out deeply embedded prejudice about Negro Americans and ending the grip of out-moded policies by business, government and churches." (This can be understood as a reference to "institutional racism," a concept that did not enter the social action vernacular until 1967.) "Millions of white church people need to be quiet and listen to a long-postponed monologue from the black American. It is time for a lot of us to listen. . . . Only then will many of us be ready for a dialogue of significance."[28]

Rather than challenge UUs not to sleep through the revolution, King offered up the kind of intellectual palaver that put them at ease. "No one present there . . . denied the King premise. America was a racist nation. We all agreed," said Farley Wheelwright. "Everyone in America [was racist] except us Unitarian Universalists."[29]

What King needed to say, and did not say until a year later (in *Where Do We Go from Here: Chaos or Community?*), was, "Whites, it must frankly be said, are not putting in a similar mass effort to re-educate themselves out of their racial ignorance. It is an aspect of their sense of superiority that the White people of America believe they have so little to learn."[30] This was doubly true of intellectually haughty UUs, but as Wheelwright said, they wanted "desperately to deny it."[31] Indeed, King's Ware Lecture left them self-satisfied, and therefore unprepared for the events that were bearing down upon them.

Three days after King's address the General Assembly voted on the Consensus on Racial Justice and on a resolution to secure a cease-fire in Vietnam. Both passed by greater than a two-thirds majority. But the consensus reached by UUs was, in fact, broader than a single vote at a General Assembly. Six months later, in November 1966, the Committee on Goals, which had been established in January 1965, delivered to the UUA Board of Trustees the findings of its survey of Unitarian Universalists. When asked, "How important is it to you that liberal religion be involved in education and action" concerning social problems, fully 94.4 percent said that racial integration was either "very" or "somewhat" important. Alongside that, 62.3 percent approved of "civil disobedience when laws are unjust." Asked about "planning denominational activities" in "areas of social controversy," 90.6 percent "approved" or "strongly approved" of such activities in the context of "civil rights (race relations)."[32] Combined, the passage of the resolution at GA and the *Report of the Committee on Goals* seemed to indicate that UUs had reached a consensus on race.

Two realities undercut the achievement.

First, the Goals Committee survey had asked, "If you were a member of the pulpit committee seeking a minister for your church, which of these statements would best describe how you would feel about a Negro candidate?" Fully 26.6 percent of the respondents chose "His race might hamper his effectiveness." The dismal record the UUA had in settling African American ministers was evidence that the actual resistance was greater than that percentage indicated. Unitarian Universalists were not open to the changes they were urging upon others.

Second, the consensus that Dr. King extolled in his Ware Lecture was no longer the consensus among civil rights groups. In fact, urban American riots were about to supplant nonviolent protest. UUs were deluded. Everything was about to change; the consensus would prove irrelevant and UUs unprepared.

The Meredith March

James Meredith set out on the March against Fear on June 6, 1966, planning to walk from Memphis, Tennessee, to Jackson, Mississippi. The next day he was shot. What ensued revealed a split in the Civil Rights Movement, and like Dr. King, Unitarian Universalists would soon be pushed to make a choice.

Meredith had not invited the major civil rights organizations to join him, but with Meredith in the hospital, they swooped in and decided the march had to continue. Meredith had only invited black men to march, and that changed too.

Ron Engel went at the urging of Dick Brown, a black Mississippian and a member of CORE, who was working with Engel at the Center for Urban Ministry. Engel says that he also went because he felt guilty. He had not gone to Selma for the march to Montgomery, while his friend and mentor, James Reeb, had gone to Selma and been killed.

Four guys stuffed themselves into a VW Beetle and set out in the middle of the night for Jackson. Brown and his friend were black; Engel and the activist who owned the car were white. A mixed group was a dead giveaway that they were radicals from up north. "I was scared," recalled Engel, "very scared given what had happened to Jim." He had no experience protesting in the deep South; all he knew about was marching in Chicago. And although he and Shadle had once been arrested in Grant Park, they had asked "to be arrested by deliberately walking into a nearby police van."

"The drive through Mississippi was more memorable than the march itself," Engel said. "From the moment we crossed the state line Dick insisted that we never allow both White and Black guys to be visible in the car together—this was just too dangerous!" So they took turns lying down on the back seat and the floor. "I looked up and out of the back seat at daybreak and [saw] lines of Black folks male, female and children bent over picking cotton. I had seen pictures of this kind of thing before (it is a kind of iconic image for Americans), but there it really was in real life, a scene out of the antebellum South."[33]

After Meredith was shot, the March against Fear became the media event he had hoped to avoid. During the throes of those days, an undercurrent that had been gaining strength in the movement captured the public's attention. With protestors streaming in and the press present, Willie Ricks, an organizer for the Student Nonviolent Coordinating Committee (SNCC), first used the term *Black Power*.[34] The SNCC chairman, Stokely Carmichael, quickly picked up the phrase, and when he gave his "Black Power" speech on June 16, ten days after Meredith was shot, he became the person most strongly identified with it.

It was less than a month since King had delivered the Ware Lecture, which barely hinted at the depth of the schism. Now it was out on the table, and King and Carmichael (who had the support of Floyd McKissick, the executive director of CORE) went at it head to head. King said that, with "the implications of violence" the press had attached to the phrase, "it carried the wrong connotation." Carmichael replied that the question of violence versus nonviolence was irrelevant. The real issue was the need for black people to consolidate their political and economic resources to achieve power. "Power," he said, "is the only thing respected in this world, and we must get it at any cost."

"Yes, we must work to build racial pride and refute the notion that black is evil and ugly. But this must come through a program, not merely a slogan," said King.

"How can you arouse people to unite around a program without a slogan as a rally cry?" retorted Carmichael.

"But the words *black* and *power* together give the impression that we are talking about black domination rather than black equality," said King.

"Martin," Carmichael told him, "I deliberately decided to raise this issue on the march in order to give it a national forum, and force you to take a stand for Black Power."[35]

Eventually they arrived at a compromise. For the rest of the march, they would chant neither "Black Power," the preference of the SNCC and CORE, nor "Freedom Now," the phrase the Southern

Christian Leadership Conference (SCLC) preferred. This was the closed-door prelude to June 26, the day when Engel, Brown, and 15 thousand others arrived for the final day of the march. Ron Engel said, "It was rumored that some had not wanted the march to be integrated." But he didn't experience any hostility from black marchers. In fact, "there were not many Whites there so I was proud of myself to be one of the few who were."[36]

On that day in Jackson, Mississippi, Engel missed the signs. Others, however, had already taken note. In 1964, Robert McKersie, a white member of the First Unitarian Society of Chicago who was closely involved with black activists, told his minister, Rev. Jack Kent, "I see a growing cleavage between the militants in the civil rights movement and many White liberals with whom I associate."[37] And in 1965, at a meeting in Boston of the After Selma Committee, Joe Barth, director of the Department of Ministry, told his colleagues, "Negroes have pulled out of interracial activities—since Selma attitudes have changed [and] often offers of help are resented."[38]

The Emergency Conference on the UU Response to the Black Rebellion

[*August 1966 – November 1967*]

IN SEPTEMBER 1963, a month after the March on Washington for Jobs and Freedom, Rev. Peter H. Samson, minister of West Shore Unitarian Universalist Church in Cleveland, preached a sermon entitled "If I Were a Negro." It was unusual in that Samson, while progressive, was neither an activist nor engaged in the African American community. Nonetheless, it was prophetic, and fifty years later it remains so.

> The new demand upon the white man everywhere, and especially America, is that he knows himself to be no more than a man among men in a largely colored world; no longer master or natural leader, no longer automatically superior, but one among many—and unfortunately, one who has been especially favored by history so long that he has come to regard these favors as his right, thus giving him much in himself to undo.[39]

This glimpse into the future was precipitated by the evolution of black consciousness rather than white. For African Americans, it signified a shift in mood and means. Those of Samson's Euro-American colleagues who were deeply involved in the African

American community sensed the change, but none foresaw the magnitude of the consequences it would have for the UUA.

The Debate over Black Power Begins: Stephen H. Fritchman vs. Donald S. Harrington

The phrase *Black Power* shook America just as Carmichael had hoped and King had worried. During the March against Fear, now often called the Meredith March, *Time* magazine, the *New York Times*, and the television networks amplified the new rallying cry and Unitarian Universalist preachers preached about it. The most prominent of these were Rev. Stephen H. Fritchman in Los Angeles and Rev. Donald S. Harrington in New York City. They served congregations located on the opposite ends of America, and over the decades, they had opposed one another on many issues; however, in fall 1966 there was no significant distance between their responses to Black Power.

"Is There an Alternative to Black Power for the American Negro Today?" was the title of the sermon Fritchman preached to the First Unitarian Church of Los Angeles on August 7, 1966. Then on October 3, "What's the Matter with Black Power?" was preached by Harrington to the Community Church of New York.[40] The titles do convey a difference in tone. Fritchman began by asking whether there was an alternative to Black Power, and answered with a definitive "No." Harrington's question initially sounded as if he were questioning the efficacy of Black Power. He was not. Rather, he was asking why the public reaction, which he called the "White backlash," was so strong.

Situated in dynamic metropolitan centers that defined American culture in different ways, Fritchman and Harrington served two of the largest and most integrated congregations in the Unitarian Universalist Association.[41] The Community Church of New York had begun the process of integration in 1910, when Harrington's predecessor, Rev. John Haynes Holmes, who was one of the founders of the NAACP, told the church, "I do not want to be the minister of a lily-white congregation." The First Unitarian Church of Los Angeles began to integrate after Fritchman arrived in 1947. Finding there were no African American members, he proposed to the Board that the bylaws be changed to welcome "men and women of all races and national origins." One trustee resigned, and the change was made.[42]

Both congregations went on to call African American ministers. Rev. Maurice A. Dawkins came to Community Church in 1948 as its minister of education; ten years later, First Unitarian called Rev. Lewis A. McGee to serve as its associate minister. By 1963, a tenth of that congregation was African American, while at Community, the figure was a full third, making it the UUA's most integrated congregation.

It is not surprising that these two Unitarian titans addressed the issue of Black Power. Fritchman had been the editor of the *Christian Register* in the forties, while Harrington, who served as chair of the Liberal Party of New York State for nearly twenty years, had preached "Unitarian Universalism: Yesterday, Today and Tomorrow" at the Celebration Service at Boston's Symphony Hall for the 1961 consolidation. They were comfortable having and wielding power, their commitment to racial justice was of long standing, and their connections to African Americans were extensive.

When Fritchman became editor of the *Register* in 1942, articles about race became a regular feature. He met Paul Robeson for the first time the following year, and not only got him to write two columns but also began a lifelong friendship with him and his wife. "How often I have blessed Paul and Eslanda Robeson," he later wrote, "for teaching me how to let my feelings show with unfeigned candor." In 1965, he flew from Los Angeles to Selma for James Reeb's memorial service, and five months later, when Watts erupted, he was taken "behind the police-lines ... by the Black chairman of C.O.R.E., to see the devastation."[43] He was fully engaged in responding, as were many others in his congregation. In March 1966, he preached about his activities in "The Churches and Watts: A Report Seven Months Later." That summer he met with the Citizens Alert Patrol, which was organized as observers to protect Negro men and women from police harassment.[44] When he delivered "Is There an Alternative to Black Power for the American Negro Today?" in praise of Black Power in August, the sermon was both challenging and wholly aligned with his earlier commitments.

Harrington was also well connected to the black community and understood its concerns. In 1946, he had delivered a sermon entitled "The White Problem," in which he said that the race problem was created and sustained by whites and concluded, "Until white people are ready to face the white problem, beg forgiveness for their crimes against humanity and God, turn and make amends for past errors and follies, no white man in this land can live a healthy spiritual life."[45] In 1952, he was among the founders of the American Committee on Africa, which supported African colonies' struggles for independence. In 1965, he and his wife Vilma were the third and fourth UUs to visit Selma in the weeks preceding Bloody Sunday, when Alabama State Troopers attacked the city's peacefully protesting black citizens. He credited Maurice Dawkins for helping him "to discover how many valuable Black members we already had in our congregation." Harrington made it his "business to know them personally in their homes, and to steer them into leading positions in our Church Boards, Groups and Committees." He recalled that he and Dawkins were once going through the mailing list when Dawkins stopped at a name:

"Does [Cornelius McDougald] belong here?" he exclaimed. "Don't you know him? My! He is a big man uptown, a prominent lawyer and manager of the huge HMO centered at Harlem Hospital!" Neil became one of my dearest and closest friends, served 3 terms as Chair of our Board of Trustees, came with a delegation to bail me out when I was arrested at the NY World's Fair and got me an invitation to join his Black Greek Letter Fraternity, Sigma Pi Phi. I was the second white member of this all-black professional Fraternity, which turned out to be the most interesting group of men I ever belonged to![46]

That Harrington, a white man, was invited into membership in Sigma Pi Phi (also known as the Boulé), an organization of African American elite, was remarkable and rare, and signaled the regard in which he was held among black movers and shakers in New York City.

Fritchman opened his 1966 sermon by saying there was no alternative to Black Power, and declared, "The phrase 'Black Power' has truly shaken White America—every sector, every class, as nothing else has been able to do since... Selma."[47] Echoing him, Harrington denounced that "horrid hurricane of fear and hate which we call the White Backlash, smashing its way across this broad American land." He cited a Gallup poll indicating "that 52% of all adult Americans believe that the Administration is going too fast with this business of integration. Only 10% of the whole, the percentage that is the minority itself, felt that the Administration was not going fast enough."[48]

Why Black Power? Because "integration has become mere pie in the sky for the great majority of Negroes in this country," said Fritchman—or, as Harrington put it, "there is a deep ambivalence in the Negro Spirit today with respect to the long-range goal of integration"[49]

"'Black Power' is no sinister term," said Fritchman. "It is a long overdue assertion that the power of free nations must be justly shared by all sections of the people or there will inevitably follow a just and inescapable explosion. The Italians, the Irish and Jews have passed through such periods of building their own communities in America ... and if the Negroes choose to do the same thing it is their prerogative to do so"[50] Harrington concurred: "Surely there is nothing very strange about the word *Power*.... Fifth Avenue is tied up all day long in the Pulaski Day Parade, a demonstration of Polish power. And what is the Steuben Day Parade, the Columbus Day Parade, the St. Patrick's Day parade, but demonstrations of German, Italian and Irish solidarity and power? We are familiar with Jewish power, organized through the American Jewish Committee and American Jewish Congress.... All such organisations exercise power through social solidarity of their minority status."

Harrington then asked, "So what's the matter with *black* power? Why should not the Negro seek the same social solidarity and resultant power that other groups have successfully sought and wielded for their advancement ... ? Why should the call for black power have evoked the furies of the white backlash?"[51]

Speaking to the white liberal, Fritchman said,

> The past six weeks of American reaction to the concept of *Black Power* have been a very alarming revelation of the subconscious mind and the unconscious mind of many of those in the white community who describe themselves as fighters for brotherhood and equality. We who are white, radical, liberals and conservatives, are much sicker, much more infected with racism than we have allowed ourselves to suppose. Large sections of the Unitarian-Universalist Church, of NAACP, of CORE [the Congress of Racial Equality], of SCLC [the Southern Christian Leadership Conference] believe in *brotherhood*, but by that they

mean that big white brother takes care of little brother ... and gets thanked for it. Many white liberals in CORE and other groups have felt very virtuous in recent years in encouraging Negroes to run their own movement.... But all too often the liberals did not mean to have it taken so seriously. The idea of freedom-loving white liberals actually being governed by black legislators, judges and sheriffs in various parts of the nation had never been thought of as a live option.... [What] we really were talking about [were] a few well-scrubbed, "right-thinking," "white-thinking" Negroes scattered in appointive [sic] office but never enough of them ... to make any significant difference.[52]

Harrington also addressed white liberals about the effect of their efforts. It has "not been wholly good," he said, because it "has tended to rob the Negro of the opportunity of doing for himself, and of the satisfaction of fighting his own fight and winning his own battles. We have not often been content to remain behind the scenes, to shout our support from the sidelines, to run interference.... We have far too often said that if we cannot run the show, we won't give the money."

Harrington spoke less politically than Fritchman and spent more time analyzing the white frame of mind:

The answer ... lies in the depth of the white psyche, the white, Western soul, and it is high time that we began to explore the deep, unconscious basis of prejudice in the white spirit. We have to do here with a deep, philosophical, religious and linguistic problem, which stems from our Western, Judeo-Christian, dualistic philosophy, which divides the universe into two parts, one dominated by God and the other by the Devil, which divides men into two categories, the Children of Light and the Children of Darkness.... Inevitably, the imagery was transposed and the symbolism applied to the dark-skinned children of God.... Light was good and dark was evil.... White man went so far as to project upon the black man all of his fears of the flesh, and to see him somehow as more capable of feeling, more capable of fierceness and anger, more capable of love, of sex, of all the rejected side of the self that he called "flesh." Even our language ... is full of it ... full of derogation of dark-skinned people. We speak of a "dark day," a "black mood," a "blackguard"—by which we mean a villain.[53]

Drawing toward the conclusion of his sermon, Fritchman said,

The clock cannot be turned back.... The Negro revolution is here.... *Black Power* may try to isolate itself and go it alone, which will only make it harder for an eventual sharing of power, black and white, at all levels; but this may be the avenue that will have to be taken for a while. The decision lies not with black Americans alone. It is primarily with those of us who are white, and who can, if we will, make long overdue changes in acceptance of the Negro in political, economic, social and cultural areas of American life.[54]

Harrington framed this same point as a question: "Why are white Americans unable to accept black people as fully human, fellow men, fellow Americans?"[55]

The conclusion Fritchman arrived at was prophetic. "The future will be hard, stormy, and unpredictable. Our own hearts will often have to change, our subconscious minds must be cleansed. Our own value system must be shaken up. And we must not run away from it because we grow weary in the struggle."[56] Tempestuous times did loom for America and the Unitarian Universalist Association. That tempest would upend the Unitarian Universalist value system.

Those, black and white, who aligned themselves with Black Power saw the issue as a political one and relied on gaining power rather than grappling with the spiritual challenge required to change hearts and minds. Absent that change, Unitarian Universalists would grow weary of the struggle and run away from Black Power. It was not a full-scale retreat from a commitment to justice but rather a diversion of their energies toward other justice concerns, which for them, as Euro-Americans, felt more pressing and more personal: the draft and the war in Vietnam, feminism, abortion reform, and gay rights.

The timeliness of Harrington's and Fritchman's responses and the depth of their understanding reflected their involvement in and commitment to the black community. They both had long-standing friendships with African Americans and thus were connected to the black community in ways most of their colleagues were not. These two sermons represent variations on a theme rather than a debate; indeed, it is difficult to discern a significant difference between them in anything other than tone. But in less than two years, the Unitarian Universalist Association would become polarized between Black Unitarians for Radical Reform (BURR) and Black and White Action (BAWA), organizations that sprang from Fritchman's and Harrington's congregations, respectively.

Prelude to the Long Hot Summer of 1967

"The tinder is there because we all have failed to take it away," said Fritchman in March 1966.[57] He and Harrington were both aware that the price of inaction would be more eruptions, but the differences in how they spoke of this conveyed the difference between a radical and a liberal. As Fritchman unequivocally asserted, the "double standard that expects a turning of the other cheek by every

Negro, under great or small provocation...is over," while Harrington offered an understatement: "Many of the riots have arisen because of the lack of confidence of minority groups in the police."[58]

The tinder was there, and it exploded.

A riot erupted in Cleveland's Hough neighborhood on July 18, 1966, half a mile from the Unitarian Society of Cleveland.

In Chicago, a series of marches for open housing culminated on August 5. Dr. Martin Luther King Jr. and seven hundred demonstrators were marching on Gage Park when they were attacked by whites. Sixty-nine were sent to hospitals and Dr. King was struck by a hurled rock. He said, "I've been in many demonstrations all across the South and I can say that I have never seen, even in Mississippi and Alabama, mobs as hostile and as hate-filled as I've seen in Chicago."[59]

In Albany, New York, that same August, "the Brothers" held their first meeting. They were young, unemployed African American construction workers who, day after day, were being turned away from job sites while hundreds of white laborers were hired. They decided to begin picketing construction sites. As their protests expanded to include poverty, schools, and police brutality, they began picketing the mayor's home. Police routinely harassed them, taking surveillance photos, tapping their phones, and arresting them on trumped-up charges that were later dropped. On November 8, thirty of the Brothers were arrested for picketing outside two polling stations, carrying signs that read "Don't Sell Your Soul for $5."[60]

In all three cities, Unitarian Universalists showed support. On July 31, 1966, in Chicago, Robert McKersie, a white member of the First Unitarian Society of Chicago, took part in one of the open housing marches. He later wrote that as they approached the "white community, I could hear loud jeers and commotion toward the front of the line. Matters turned ugly, and to put it mildly, I was scared.

Fairly soon, I saw bottles and rocks being thrown at the leaders and before I knew it, those missiles were coming at us."[61]

In Albany on March 3, 1967, seven months after the Brothers was founded, Rev. Nick Cardell, minister of the First Unitarian Church of Albany, was one of six ministers who came out in support of the Brothers. Subsequently, Cardell received hate mail: a picture of two leaders of the Brothers with Cardell pasted in between them. His face was blackened. Scrawled across the top was written, "THIS IS WHERE YOUR PICTURE BELONGS." "Come downtown," it continued, "go in the stores and you will open your eyes [to] all the black thieves.... if I belonged to your church I would put you in your place."[62] Cardell, who had been a POW during the Second World War, was not fazed. In November 1967, when the next election came around, Cardell and members of the church picketed city hall carrying signs with the same wording the Brothers had carried the year before.[63] This time there were no arrests.

In Cleveland, Peter Samson had departed and the West Shore ministerial search committee sought out an activist minister to replace him. They found one in Rev. James Curtis. At his first Board meeting, which took place in August 1966, just weeks after the Hough Riot, Curtis suggested that West Shore join with the three other UU congregations in greater Cleveland to establish an innercity ministry. The next month, the ministers and lay members of the four congregations gathered, along with representatives of the UUA Ohio-Meadville District. Over the following month, each congregation voted to support and finance an urban social justice ministry, and in the fall of 1967, two ministers were hired and the work of the Cleveland Unitarian Universalist Parish (CUUP) began.

These local efforts notwithstanding, the 1967 General Assembly revealed the extent to which most Unitarian Universalists were oblivious to the mounting tension. It was held in Denver, far from the urban tumult, and none of the general resolutions directly addressed the mounting revolt. A year after Stokely Carmichael popularized the term, Black Power did not even garner enough support in the pre-GA parish poll to merit its inclusion. The war in Vietnam occupied most Unitarian Universalists' attention. A resolution calling for a "new comprehensive national policy for the American Indians" was adopted unanimously. But one censuring the director of the Department of Social Responsibility for not being militant enough in his efforts failed, while a resolution to support conscientious objectors who practiced civil disobedience passed by the small margin of 256 to 215, after a long debate.

What set the Assembly abuzz was the 1967 Ware Lecture by Saul Alinsky. Ever the provocateur, he called on the Unitarian Universalist Association to support FIGHT (Freedom, Independence, God, Honor, Today) in challenging the Eastman Kodak Company's discriminatory hiring practices. The motion, amended by the First Unitarian Church of Brooklyn to call upon the UUA Board to "cooperate with FIGHT," passed.[64] Leon Hopper observed that Alinsky gave the Assembly a framework in which to understand "the process of social change." Max Gaebler remembered Alinsky saying, "The way to get something accomplished is to polarize the issue. If you [can] somehow frame the questions ... in such a way that you can demand an up or down vote, no amendments, yes or no ... If you can get it framed that way, even if you start out with only 10% of the people—no, even 5%—you can win the day. You can get there." From Gaebler's perspective, it was Alinsky who defined the modus operandi for the conflict that would overtake the UUA.[65]

The Denver General Assembly met during the first week of May. A race riot began in Tampa Bay on June 11, and another in Cincinnati the next day. Ultimately "the long hot summer of 1967," as it came to be known, would be marked by 159 riots. Yet as urban

America was about to erupt, the Assembly was largely mute concerning the realities African Americans lived with and Unitarian Universalist inner-city churches were facing. And while Dana Greeley, the UUA's president, had appointed a Task Force on the Urban Church and Inner City Ministry, its report was not due to be submitted until October or November.

Black Unitarians for Radical Reform

In August 1967, at the First Unitarian Church of Los Angeles, a group of black members of that and other local Unitarian Universalist congregations began meeting. Their meetings were closed to whites, something many whites found distressing. The meetings were led by lay members Jules Ramey of First Unitarian and Louis Gothard of Throop Memorial Universalist Church in Pasadena. The discussions led to the formation of Black Unitarians for Radical Reform (BURR).

Later that month, after Fritchman returned from vacation, BURR invited him to its meeting. He described that meeting in *Heretic: A Partisan Autobiography*:

> I received a warm reception, though it was not an easy session. I was asked sharp and sometimes critical questions. At long last they were leveling with a white minister, with courtesy, not in anger, but in a "speak bitterness" meeting—about experiences that had bothered them which they had not brought to me lest they might injure the work of our church, an institution they knew was desperately needed as a catalyst in the community. There was not one criticism raised of my words or work that did not have some legitimacy. They endured slights, rudeness, rejection, all their lives, as any black person will tell Mr. Charlie if he will listen, and one of the places where they endured all this was

their own church. So the smothered anger boiled over and got expressed. It was one of the most productive conversations I had ever had in my ministry.[66]

Subsequently, BURR issued a statement entitled "The New Black Revolution":

The New Black Revolution is an awakening of the black man to the fact that he is a man. He cannot and will not endure the shackles of prejudice any longer. Prejudice, the progeny of slavery, propagated by history and perpetuated by the white man in his daily thoughts and deeds has so permeated his heart and mind, that neither love nor reason reaches the root cause, his own moral decadence, which has rot-gutted his soul and paralyzed his mind.

The black man likewise has been affected by the effect of history and the white man's thoughts and deeds by virtue of having been reared in the white man's culture and inculcated consciously or subconsciously with the white man's values.

He is now unloosing the shackles of such values with an awareness of his own black values, and his own black worth, not because he is black, but because *he is.*

This awareness breeds pride and this pride breeds a further awareness of the intolerable condition of societal servitude to which the black man has been relegated.

The Black Revolution is a clash between the awareness of dignity and the societal servitude imposed by a history of disabled morally decadent whites. Recognizing that *love* has not and cannot work, because a rot-gutted soul cannot pull itself up by its own bootstraps, recognizing that reason cannot work, since reason ultimately is the slave of the total being, therefore other force must be applied with sufficient impact to overcome.

There is no power greater than a man's self-respect. Therein lies the meaning of the Black Revolution.[67]

BURR's statement was a striking wake-up call for Unitarian Universalists. It explicitly critiques the major tenets of Universalism (love) and Unitarianism (reason) and finds them wanting. An honest appraisal of their experience in the church led these African Americans to say that the values white Unitarian Universalists espoused were not matched by their deeds. BURR members had endured intolerable white behavior long enough. If love and reason were not up to the task of rectifying the situation, there had to be another "force" that was, and they turned to "self-respect." We cannot know but must suspect that this was a repudiation not only of Universalism but also of love as Martin Luther King Jr. meant it in speaking of *agape*, which he described as "understanding, creative, redemptive goodwill for all men, an overflowing love which seeks nothing in return."[68] Yet wasn't the "self-respect" BURR extolled a form of love? That is, love directed toward oneself is empowering, and power is what these revolutionaries were seeking.

Within weeks, BURR's statement would be adopted *in toto* by the Black Caucus that formed at the Emergency Conference on the Unitarian Universalist Response to the Black Rebellion and used as the preamble to its report. BURR had not known about the upcoming conference until Rev. Roy Ockert brought it to their attention.

Ockert arrived at First Los Angeles that September to serve as its assistant minister. The newly ordained former union economist enthusiastically supported the revolutionary ferment he found there. On October 1, he delivered a sermon entitled "Conflict: Function and Dysfunction." The sermon began with a clarification in which he spoke directly to the congregation's white members. He confessed that, like them, he was disturbed when black militants appeared, brushed aside integration, and dismissed the efforts of white liberals and radicals.

THE EMERGENCY CONFERENCE ON THE RESPONSE TO THE REBELLION

Referring to his experience in the union movement, he drew a parallel. Since labor and management have different experiences and priorities, they look "from different angles [and] see different pictures." Likewise, "black militants ... recognize that there are differences between being white, and being black." White segregationists, however, see these differences as "evidence of natural racial 'superiority,'" while white liberals see the differences as a matter "of white cultural superiority." We favor integration, he said, "because we have been trained from infancy by everything around us to feel, deep in our bones, that *white* culture is better than *black* culture." Therefore, the integration "we have been working so hard for ... threatens to destroy ... black culture." And unless white liberals and radicals realize this and honor the desire of black people to have and develop their own black culture, and also understand that black people are increasingly taking pride in being black, they will not be able to comprehend what black radicals are telling them.

He drew a second example from the labor movement. When the labor organization that would become the American Federation of Labor was founded in 1881, alongside factory workers and miners it included as full members "socialist *middleclass* businessmen, lawyers, clergymen and others who sympathized with the objectives." They were dedicated to the cause of union recognition and better working conditions in the same way "white liberals and radicals worked in recent years for the objectives of the black freedom movement." And the middle-class unionists were dismayed when they were eventually told they could no longer join the union but should instead work to change the attitudes of the many who were anti-union.

But one can imagine this personal dismay, grief and frustration, *hurt* even better if one has been a white liberal or ... radical risking position, and sometimes life, for black freedom and is told he can no longer be a member of black organizations—some of which he helped organize and gave his life's blood for—but that he should now go into his own white communities and seek to re-educate his neighbors, most of whom are *violently anti-black.*

Ockert pointed out that this is exactly what happened with the Congress on Racial Equality (CORE), setting up his next point.

It does not mean that we must withdraw from the fight for black freedom. It only means that our method and procedures will inevitably be different. And, possibly, if we undertake to re-educate ourselves, we white liberals and white radicals, like the black militants, might find means of being more effective.

Halfway through the sermon, he shifted from a general analysis to address the situation at First Los Angeles:

Recently, when we white religious liberals and radicals—we Unitarians—heard that black members ... had formed an organization which they call "Black Unitarians for Radical Reform," many of us were ... severely disturbed.
"What! Black Unitarians separating from us whites? Shades of segregation! of Bilbo! of Wallace! ... How can they be so un-Unitarian?!"
We refused to accept them; we refused to admit they could have a separate organization; we refused to acknowledge that they—the blacks—might have a more accurate view of their needs than we whites.

Toward the end of the sermon, he proffered two specific invitations to the members of the congregation. The first was an urgent call for financial contributions to BURR:

THE EMERGENCY CONFERENCE ON THE RESPONSE TO THE REBELLION

BURR makes it possible for us to find a place where white Unitarians and black Unitarians can meet face to face, can talk across the bargaining table as human being to human being, can argue and fight and dispute and disagree—and still be Unitarians searching for humanness, questing for answers to our whys, and our hows.

Beginning this Friday, October 6 . . . white and black Unitarian Universalists will be doing just that in New York City. The Commission on Religion and Race of the Unitarian Universalist Association has called for an "Emergency Conference on the Response to the Black Rebellion"—largely because of the militancy of Black Unitarians this will not be a conference of white religious liberals, sprinkled by a few middleclass black religious liberals, talking about matters they know only from a distance.

If the money can be raised, Black Unitarians from this area are going to that emergency conference in New York. Many of them are experts on the "Black Rebellion." It is essential that they go because there will be no chance for an intelligent, reasonable, compassionate [response] unless militant Black Unitarians are there.

Ockert asked for financial support to send three members of BURR to the conference and then moved on to his second invitation. He invited white members to join him in a small group to read about and discuss the racial situation in America from the black militant perspective, in a program that would run up to twelve weeks. "If this runs counter to all you believe and you 'see red' then you should register," he stated. His hope was that it would lead participants to a deeper understanding of African American culture and its new militancy, and in addition that they would begin to see how they themselves "think white" and evaluate everything in terms of "white values."

We are so close to ourselves, so enveloped in the white shroud woven about us since infancy that we cannot hear them when they try to point out that there is such a thing as "thinking white." . . .

I suspect that they are not finding it easy—and neither will we. Many old ways of doing and acting and thinking will have to be overthrown. . . . We—and they—have a lot of rethinking to do.⁶⁹

Seattle CORE President John Cornethan Deposed

The history of Unitarian interaction with the Congress of Racial Equality [CORE] dates back to that civil rights organization's inception in 1942. Rev. Homer A. Jack, while still at Meadville Lombard training for ministry, was one of its co-founders, and in 1947, he was among the first wave of freedom riders it sent to the border states. In 1961, the organizing meeting of the Seattle chapter of CORE was held at University Unitarian Church. Its organizing secretary was Ken Rose, a nineteen-year-old member of Liberal Religious Youth, and among its leadership were members of University Church, including John Cornethan. When CORE established a chapter in Denver, Unitarian Ruth Steiner was a founding member. In 1962, Rev. Charles Blackburn, the minister in Hayward, California, had founded a chapter. The UUA's Committee on Goals reported that 4.3 percent of the respondents to its survey identified themselves as members of CORE or the Student Nonviolent Coordinating Committee.⁷⁰

In his October 1967 sermon, Roy Ockert had said, "They tell us to get out of CORE. . . . They run their own demonstrations—and tell us whites to stay out of the way." He was on target.⁷¹

THE EMERGENCY CONFERENCE ON THE RESPONSE TO THE REBELLION

The issue of whether or not to include whites had been a part of the debate Floyd McKissick, the new leader of CORE, and Stokely Carmichael had had with Dr. King during the Meredith March in June 1966. A year later, McKissick moved to change CORE's constitution. He proposed that, rather than a multicultural organization concerned with integration, it become an "organization to implement the concept of Black Power for black people" and that its membership be restricted to African Americans. His attitude toward whites was evident in a comment he reportedly made during a visit to Seattle: "Dealing with white people is like holding a bag of snakes. Only one of them might be poisonous, but if you reach your hand in the bag, you don't know what you're gonna get."[72]

This shift in purpose and of constituency was on the agenda when CORE held its national conference in July 1967 in Oakland, California. Four members of the Seattle chapter attended. Two were black, two white, and John Cornethan, one of the black delegates, was chapter president. The two white delegates gave their votes to the other black delegate, who voted for the change; Cornethan voted against it.

When Seattle CORE met on July 27, Cornethan supported Black Power specifically in regard to economic development but refused to implement the new national policy. The reaction was decisive. "Twenty-two blacks and sixteen whites were in attendance, along with the West Coast regional director.... [He] made it clear that Seattle CORE could not reject national policy and retain the CORE name."[73] A few spoke in opposition, but in the end they voted to accept national policy. At the August meeting, Cornethan's resignation was called for, and in September he was impeached.

At over six feet tall, Cornethan was a big man with the build of a football player. He had grown up in Alabama as the thirteenth of fourteen children and served in the Army during the Second World War. He moved to Seattle in the early fifties and joined University Unitarian Church. Employed by City Light, he worked his way up to lineman. A friend described him as easygoing but persistent and said that he did not let racism directed at him bother him. While being voted out left him sad and disappointed he moved on. He joined Black and White Action (BAWA) after it was founded in 1968; in 1994 he attended General Assembly in Fort Worth, and he was still a Unitarian Universalist when he died in 1999.[74]

For a while, Seattle CORE continued to work interracially on projects in which it was already engaged, but as one member recounted, the "white members were stunned and disbelieving that such a change applied to them."[75] The period of transition came to an end with the March 1968 edition of *Corelator*, the Seattle CORE newsletter. One article was headlined "CORE All Black" and said, "In order for CORE to function in the community it must be an all black organization." Another article began, "Notice to All White CORE Members and Friends of CORE." It was an invitation by Jean Adams, a white member, to come to a meeting to plan how they could "combat white racism." The meeting was set for the end of the month, but no one came.[76]

Adams continued to try to organize whites to confront racism, but without success. That fight did not generate the excitement and commitment that civil rights efforts had generated, and after months of effort, she abandoned the attempt.

Instead, Adams's attention and that of "other white CORE members, turned to the antiwar movement, the grape boycott, the women's movement and the environmental movement."[77] Inevitably white Unitarian Universalists would follow a similar path. To avoid asking themselves self-incriminating questions about race, they turned to other causes.

Preparing for the Emergency Conference

During the summer of 1967, riots spread like wildfire: June 12–15 in Cincinnati; June 26–July 1 in Buffalo; July 12–18 in Newark leaving twenty-three dead; July 14 in Plainfield, New Jersey; July 19 in Minneapolis; July 23–27 in Detroit with forty-three dead; July 24 in Cambridge, Maryland; July 25 in New York City; July 30 in Milwaukee. On July 28, President Lyndon Johnson appointed the National Advisory Commission on Civil Disorders.

Homer A. Jack, the director of the Unitarian Universalist Association's Department of Social Responsibility, was at a loss as to what a constructive Unitarian Universalist response might be. On a hot night early in August, the Commission on Religion and Race gathered at his Boston apartment. Two years earlier, an After Selma Committee had convened, at which Jack had wondered whether Unitarian Universalists of both races shouldn't gather together and "have a real brainstorming session."[78] With so many cities now erupting, the idea became urgent.

Benjamin F. Scott was new to the Commission. An African American chemist, he had been one of fewer than two dozen black scientists who worked on the Manhattan Project. He and his wife Joyce were members of the Arlington Street Church. Looking back, he said,

> I was against ["a real brainstorming session"] because I had no confidence that any assemblage of white liberals would really do anything but rationalize and maybe pass a resolution of support. I had become increasingly radicalized by events since 1954, not the big national events so much, though they had obviously had an effect, but by lesser events which I had become involved in in Chicago, in Evanston and in Boston. I was angry and disgusted at what this country was, and I felt that a large part of the reason

for the state of the country was to be laid at the feet of people like those who had gathered that night and that included me.[79]

At that August 1967 meeting, the Commission decided to sponsor the Emergency Conference on the Unitarian Universalist Response to the Black Rebellion. The word *rebellion* was chosen because the upheaval in urban America was more than merely riots, yet less than a revolution.

Homer Jack was responsible for organizing the Emergency Conference. In order to make it broadly representative, he asked not only the twenty-one UUA districts but also eight urban centers to send delegates, and that extra effort be made to ensure there was a significant African American presence.

Invitations to speak went to Unitarian Universalists Whitney M. Young Jr., executive director of the National Urban League, and Dr. Kenneth Clark, a child psychologist; long-time civil rights activist Bayard Rustin was also approached. In the context of the time, all of them would have been thought of as strong but moderate voices by liberal whites and as "Uncle Toms" by black militants. When none of the three was available, Floyd McKissick of CORE was asked to deliver the keynote. McKissick, who was at the center of the promotion of Black Power, ended up setting a very different tone than any of the original invitees would have.

Over the Labor Day weekend, Homer Jack was an observer at the National Conference on New Politics in Chicago; there he saw a black caucus in action. Whitney Young was there as well and felt that "the white radicals fell all over themselves trying to comply with the ridiculous demands of the blacks."[80]

Jack said that he "did not really believe that a Black Caucus would develop at our Conference." But on September 30, a week before the Emergency Conference, Jack received a letter from

THE EMERGENCY CONFERENCE ON THE RESPONSE TO THE REBELLION

BURR. It called for a black caucus and told him it was sending three representatives.[81]

Jack expanded the number of delegates invited from Southern California and several other districts. In an effort to include more African Americans, Hayward Henry Jr., a member at Second Boston, was invited, although the organizers knew little about him. Seeing only a bright doctoral student in microbiology, they had no idea that he was a member of SNCC, had attended the inaugural national conference on Black Power in Newark that July, worked with McKissick, and was well connected to the emerging militants.

It must be noted that the two African American ministers who had been in fellowship the longest, Rev. Jeffrey Campbell and Rev. Lewis A. McGee—who was seventy-four years old and had retired in 1966—did not attend.[82] Also absent were any representatives of All Souls First Universalist in Chicago. Following the conference, its president, Jesse A. Reed, wrote to Jack, "Although we do not share in all the tenets, etc. of the so-called black caucus, it seems to us that as the church with the highest percentage of non-white membership in the whole association, we should have been invited."[83] In his response, Jack blamed the oversight on the district. But given that he had preached there earlier in the year, it seems the oversight was his as well.

The Commission on Religion and Race provided travel subsidies, but for some, neither the lack of an invitation nor money was at issue. Lee Reed, the chair of the church council at the First Unitarian Society of Chicago, was invited to attend by her minister, Rev. Jack Kent. When she told her husband she was going to the Emergency Conference, his response was "Absolutely not." The day of the conference, after he left for work, she packed her bag and left for New York City. He and their three children—ages seventeen, fourteen, and eight—would have to take care of themselves.

45

The Emergency Conference and the Birth of the Black Affairs Council

The night before the conference began, two BURR leaders came to Homer Jack. They wanted a room made available for a black caucus and an additional registration table, which they would staff, so that they could register the African Americans who wished to participate in the caucus. Both were provided.

Conference attendees arrived from across the country—34 conference leaders, 139 participants, and 4 observers in total.[84] All but two UUA districts were represented. Of forty clergy, half had been in Selma, and five represented the UU urban ministry efforts in Chicago, Brooklyn, Cleveland, and Boston. The Unitarian Universalist Service Committee (UUSC), the Laymen's League, the Unitarian Universalist Women's Federation (UUWF), Liberal Religious Youth (LRY, representing high school–age youth), and Student Religious Liberals (SRL, for those of college age) sent representatives. There were thirty-six women and nine youth. McGee and Campbell were not present, but the other two African American ministers in fellowship, Eugene Sparrow and William R. Jones, were. Four African Americans preparing for the ministry were also in attendance.[85] African Americans made up over a third of the conference's leadership, including its chair, Cornelius McDougald. They made up over 20 percent of the total conference in a denomination of which they comprised 1 percent, and they hailed largely from the urban churches in a faith community that was becoming more and more suburban.

On October 6, when Ann Redding walked into the Biltmore Hotel, she had no idea what to expect or what to do. She was an LRY member, not quite sixteen years old, and one of the few African Americans active in LRY at a national level. That was why she

THE EMERGENCY CONFERENCE ON THE RESPONSE TO THE REBELLION

came to the attention of those making decisions about who would represent young people.[86]

As Friday evening's opening plenary session was beginning, Henry Hampton, an African American and the UUA's director of information, heard one white UU muse, "I have the uneasy feeling that it just isn't going to be enough to simply be here unprejudiced."[87] "The racial tension was palpable," recalled Redding. "The atmosphere vibrated with the same discontent that had erupted in the streets of black communities all over the country in recent months."[88]

The session began with a welcome and address on the purpose of the conference by Unitarian Universalist Association president Dana McLean Greeley. He put it bluntly. Notwithstanding the "martyrdom of James Reeb," Unitarian Universalists had offered "too little, much too late." The UUA's "basically segregated ministry" was one example, and lack of financial support for civil rights efforts was another. Greeley reported, "Our Unitarian Universalist Freedom Fund is four years old. While we raised in several months more than $100,000 for the James Reeb Memorial Fund, in four years we have raised less than this amount for our more inclusive Freedom Fund. In an affluent denomination in an affluent society, this is embarrassingly small."[89] In 1964–1965, the Freedom Fund had raised $72,400; in 1965–66, $19,300; and in the first seven months of 1966–1967, $4,405. While Unitarian Universalists proclaimed a commitment to brotherhood, this revealed an obvious lack of concern for the black community.

Despite Greeley's call to mobilize a "massive assault on our problem,"[90] African American concerns do not appear to have been among his priorities either. Following the release of the *Report of the Committee on Goals* in spring 1967, a discussion guide was issued to assist congregations in exploring its findings. In it race was barely mentioned, and in Greeley's own list of twenty possible goals, both race and integration are absent.⁹¹ This was yet another indication that, although Greeley was able to rise to the occasion and speak about civil rights with a prophetic flourish, his real priorities were growth, internationalism, and peace.

That evening, Floyd McKissick gave an address entitled "The New Black Rebellion." When the time came to form discussion groups, Ann Redding later recalled, she saw a taut, lean black woman striding "into the middle of the crowd in the electrified silence following the address." The woman said something like, "Why are we still here with these people? We got to go! Are you coming with me?" Redding watched as most of the African Americans present followed her out of the room. But Redding heard her father's voice rising within her and saying, "This is nothing but self-imposed segregation!" She yearned to join them, but loyal to her upbringing by staunch integrationists, she stayed put.⁹²

Among those who walked out was Ben Scott. "I had no idea what would come out of it but it was at least different from what we had been doing," he said. "Well, what came of it was BAC [the Black Affairs Council] and a total immersion of the people of the UUA in the fury and the glory of the Black Power Movement."⁹³

"The idea of being in an all-black meeting," said Henry Hampton, "was incomprehensible to me.... It was simply not part of my experience to walk into a room where the only reason you could be there is because you are black. And it upset me. I had to really think about whether I was going to stay or not."⁹⁴ But he found that "Very quickly it simply became clear what could happen in a meeting of all black people." He learned things he hadn't known and found himself speaking about things he had rarely mentioned before—some he had never, ever talked about. It was invaluable just to be able to hear "other black people talking about themselves and about the turmoil and pain and isolation ... especially those of us who had grown up in predominantly white institutions."[95]

To the degree they had accepted the integrationist approach, black delegates found the process of forming a black caucus wrenching. When Hampton saw Ann Redding, who had cried all morning of the second day, he gently comforted her and assured her that the caucus members wouldn't "lock her in." Then he said, "I think you should check it out; I think you'll like it."[96]

Within the Caucus, people began to see themselves as black people in relation to other black people. Examining their relationship to one another, rather than fixating on white people, was new to most of them, and also entirely outside the realm of white understanding. So the Caucus met late into the night. They talked about why they were Unitarian Universalists and what it was like to be one of a few; and as they talked, with unusual openness, they tapped into raw emotion hidden behind middle-class reasonableness. Theirs was a search for an authentic identity in place of the futile attempt to be "carbon copies of white people."[97] They saw white liberalism's emphasis on integration as a one-way street that elevated white people and debased black. Civil rights had changed the law but proven ineffective at remedying black poverty. Liberal religion had failed to address the experience of blackness, settle black ministers, or welcome African Americans into the national committees and boards where decisions were made. Nor had it committed significant resources in any meaningful way to the black community.

The imposing figure of seminarian Thomas E. Payne guarded the entrance to the Black Caucus room and shooed away white interlopers. For three days, Caucus members participated in the main sessions but withdrew to discuss and do their own work during the meetings of the three commissions that were to develop recommendations. The longer they were huddled together, the stronger their group identity grew.

The white conference participants were confused. "I knew not what was going on," said Hobart, "until it became apparent that most of the Black participants had withdrawn into a caucus group."[98] Homer Jack said that some blacks stopped talking to their white friends at the conference. "Some no longer smiled," said Harrington, "some were serious, often grim, even secretive."[99] The point of being close-lipped was to maintain a solidarity that would enable the caucus to develop its own consensus before disclosing it to the conference. When they spoke, they would speak with one voice.

Sitting in discussion groups, white conferees felt shocked and puzzled, then hurt. Hadn't they been working, black and white together, through the hard years up to today? Hadn't they been breaking down the color line? Now they felt chagrined to be talking about the black rebellion without African American participation when the primary reason they had come was to confer with black people.

While the Caucus met elsewhere, speaker after speaker "castigated the blindness and apathy of 'white liberals' in a society rampant with racism"—and "justly" so, said Rev. Tony Perrino, the minister in Schenectady.[100] Roy Ockert, who had made sure BURR was represented, described the speeches as "traumatic for an awful lot of whites."[101]

After a restless, sleepless Saturday night, the white chair of the commission that was to outline action priorities as a step toward a denominational program announced, "I have no wish to participate in a ritual dance of black demand and white obsequiousness." On Sunday morning, she wrote a report that called the exercise a charade, resigned, and left.[102]

THE EMERGENCY CONFERENCE ON THE RESPONSE TO THE REBELLION

The agenda in the Black Caucus meeting was twofold. First was introspection, in which people began a process of redefining themselves. The experience led Lee Reed to declare, "For the first time in my life I feel black," and another participant to say, "I'm not a Unitarian now; I'm a black woman now."[103] Second was to answer the question, How do we make this predominantly white denomination address our problems in a way that we, as black people, see as important? This was easier to answer for those who had maintained connections to the black community and were not primarily concerned with Unitarian Universalism. Personal and institutional battles took place over how each person identified their primary concern and how they balanced it with competing ideologies, principles, and relationships. In these battles, personal loyalties, whether to the black community, racial integration, or the Unitarian Universalist Association as an institution, would prove pivotal.

At the final session of the conference, the various commissions were to offer recommendations, which would then be crafted into a resolution by the Commission on Race and Religion. The UUA Board would then adopt these at its November meeting. The meeting agenda was altered so that the reports of the three commissions would follow those of the Youth Caucus (which had also formed at the conference) and of the Black Caucus.

Before the Black Caucus's report was delivered, Louis J. Gothard, its chair, instructed that all tape recorders be turned off. Three Caucus members then presented reports on national, local, and denominational affairs. Among the recommendations they made were supporting Black Power organizations and withholding support from organizations that were not black-controlled; resisting the war and aiding conscientious objectors; supporting black cooperatives; organizing black Unitarian Universalists across the country in local groups like BURR; placing black people at all levels of the

Unitarian Universalist Association, with special attention to settling black ministers; and urging Beacon Press to publish black authors and the Department of Religious Education to publish curricula about black history and achievements.

Two further recommendations would become contentious. The first was the call for the creation of a Black Affairs Council (BAC) made up of Unitarian Universalists, a clear majority of whom would be black. BAC members would be elected at a general meeting of black UUs and would be charged with implementing the program of a reconvened Black Caucus. The second was for the Unitarian Universalist Association to commit $250 thousand a year for four years, to be directed toward black community development and managed by BAC.

Finally, Gothard made the following motion: "That these proposals of the Black Caucus be given unqualified and total endorsement by this Conference to be transmitted directly to the Board of Trustees of the Unitarian Universalist Association through the Commission on Religion and Race. Any discussion of changes or revisions will only take place between the U.U.A. Board and the Steering Committee of the Black Caucus."[104] This strategy was straight from Alinsky, but it confused David Parke, who would later become an important ally. "Who are you," he wanted to ask the Caucus members, "and why are your demands non-negotiable?"[105]

The plenary veered into outraged haggling over parliamentary procedures, as whites accustomed to wielding power reacted to finding it reversed. "There was a huge uproar on the plenary floor," said Hobart. "Confusion, anger, conviction, accusations, all rolled into one as the 'discussion' went forth.... In this context [a] professionally-dressed, tall and beautiful Black woman walked into the aisle, paced up and down, and addressed the group with passion and anger. I recall her saying something like 'I'm sick of liberalese.

I'm tired of UUese. We demand the endorsement of this group with no modification of the demands we will take to the UUA Board of Trustees. That is where the power of change lies, not here.'"[106]

Rev. Duke T. Gray and others called on the conferees who opposed the resolution to have faith in the consensus the Black Caucus had developed, just as African Americans had shown faith in a liberal religious movement despite the fact that it had consistently fallen short in living out its principles in regard to race.

The Black Caucus insisted that its agenda be voted up or down without debate, and it was carried by more than a two-thirds majority. Caucus members then withdrew again, this time to elect a Steering Committee and make plans.

Thirty-one people registered for the Black Caucus. Among them were those who would emerge as its leaders: Gothard, Hayward Henry (who would become chair of its Steering Committee, and later of BUUC, the Black Unitarian Universalist Caucus), Ben Scott, Richard Traylor, Jules Ramey, and Renford Gaines. Except for Scott, who was forty-five, these emerging leaders were in their twenties and thirties and exasperated with the status quo. There was a generational divide, although it was nuanced rather than absolute.[107]

Among the African American conferees who did not register with the Black Caucus were Rev. William R. Jones, age forty-one; Cornelius McDougald, fifty-five; and Joseph Jenkins, sixty-one. Jenkins, a professor at Virginia State University and the immediate past president of the First Unitarian Church of Richmond, Virginia, attended with his minister, Rev. William Gold. Two days after the conference, they reported on it to their church Board, and when nearly two hundred black UUs met in Chicago in February, no one from Richmond was there.

Forty-six-year-old Rev. Eugene Sparrow had been in fellowship since 1949. Soon after the Emergency Conference, he sent a letter to Homer Jack expressing his thankfulness that "it provided an opportunity to see myself as I am and not as others cast me," and then invited Jack to send him any suggestions Jack might have about how he might "make some positive contribution."[108] He did not attend the subsequent gathering in Chicago.

Thomas Payne attended the Chicago meeting but did not remain a member of the Caucus. Instead, he tried to remain in relationship to it while staking out a middle ground. As positions polarized that became impossible.

The responses of black Unitarian Universalists to the events of the Emergency Conference were mixed. Max Gaebler, a white minister from Madison, Wisconsin, reported that one African American member who was at the Biltmore voted for the proposal, and said afterward, "Any program worth its salt should be able to be defended in open discussion and not be rammed through by this kind of tactic."[109] Winnifred Norman, a Black Caucus member and third-generation Unitarian Universalist, had represented the Community Church of New York at the Emergency Conference and come away supporting the Black Caucus.[110]

The conference sent shockwaves through the Unitarian Universalist Association. Ten years later, Ben Scott described it as "traumatic." "I am not the only UU who was irreversibly shaped by it. Thousands were born again. They came to a thrilling sense of the awesome potential of human society and [yet] lifelong friendships crumbled, marriages dissolved, careers were ended and congregations factionalized."[111] But at that moment, no one imagined what lay ahead.

Taking It Home

Among the seven members of the Black Caucus Steering Committee were two women, Marjorie Jordan and Lee Reed.

Jordan was a member of the well-integrated First Unitarian Church of Cincinnati, and her husband, Cornelius (usually called Van), had served as its president. She knew how desperate the situation in black America was. She was the first executive director of Housing Opportunities Made Equal, which was concerned with fair housing. In June 1967, in response to ongoing police harassment, a riot had erupted in Cincinnati's Avondale neighborhood, a mile north of the church.

Upon returning from the Emergency Conference, both Marjorie and Van Jordan became strong advocates for BAC. Ann Black, a white member, said, "Van was very good at trying to pull us out of our 'white think' by challenging our perceptions."[112] Van taught English at the University of Cincinnati, and challenging people in this way was one of his talents. There were also integrationists in the congregation, black and white, who were not supportive of BAC. Among them was Kathryn Sinkford. Her son Bill was the first African American president of Liberal Religious Youth, and he recalled that they had long arguments about the issue.

Lee Reed traveled back to Chicago with George Sikes, her white co-representative from the First Unitarian Society of Chicago. Realizing his role was to support rather than to lead, he said, "You're going to have to carry the ball," and she did.[113]

An essential part of the Black Caucus proposal adopted at the Emergency Conference was the establishment of local black caucuses. Reed called a meeting of African American Unitarian Universalists in the Chicago area, to which forty came. Alex Poinsett was elected chair of the newly formed Chicago Area Black UU Caucus (CABUUC), and the group began preparing for a national gathering of African American Unitarian Universalists.[114] Eight other caucuses also formed soon after the conference, joining CABUUC and BURR.[115]

The minister of Chicago First, Jack Kent, was supportive of the plan for a national black gathering, and twenty-three members of his congregation joined CABUUC. But there were others—both black and white—who dissented. Indeed, when Sikes, in reporting to the congregation, said the Caucus was for blacks only, there was an uproar. Some said having such a caucus was "divisive, racist and militant."[116] It was a meeting at which some spoke openly for the first time.[117]

Hoping to help congregation members to better understand Black Power and to open up communications with those who disagreed, the church council sponsored an all-day gathering, calling it "A Black and White Retreat." It was held in January 1968 and drew 120 participants. As he listened to the conversation, George Reed, Lee Reed's husband, felt it was going in circles and Euro-American members kept saying things that "just didn't ring true." Growing exasperated, then annoyed, he finally stood up and said, "Listen, when you all walk out of here you're white and you can go do whatever you want. We all walk out of here and we are still black and we can't change that. You can do whatever you want but we can't." Years later, in describing that day, he said,

> I was upset by the cavalier attitude that many whites took about the kind of problems we were dealing with. Their attitude was, "it is no big thing we can take care of it." But they couldn't. When they left they were white and they didn't really have to be burdened with the sort of thing that blacks were complaining about. It was amazing. A lot of them simply weren't aware of the subtle ways in which bigotry played a role in determining black people's lives, not just jobs but health-wise, house-wise and otherwise. Everything, every aspect of life was controlled by people who were unsympathetic to and not committed to dealing in an equitable way with people who were not the same color as themselves.

THE EMERGENCY CONFERENCE ON THE RESPONSE TO THE REBELLION

So something did happen. Blacks decided no more of this accommodation stuff. Let's get our own act together.[118]

CABUUC was one of the largest caucuses in the Unitarian Universalist Association. But some African Americans could not reconcile its existence with their understanding of Unitarian Universalism, and at least one such couple resigned.

In Cincinnati, Chicago, and elsewhere, congregations were confronted with this challenge. Members disagreed. Some saw the formation of black-only groups as a betrayal of their long-held commitment to integration. Others saw it primarily as an issue of black solidarity and self-determination. In the meantime, many whites were self-servingly naive. And while the issue of white privilege was pointed out, the phrase would not enter the social justice vernacular for another twenty years, when the most widely recognized essay on the topic, "White Privilege: Unpacking the Invisible Knapsack" by Peggy McIntosh, was published.[119]

As well as spurring the formation of black caucuses and preparation for a national meeting, the Emergency Conference also had repercussions for those engaged in urban ministry.

Ron Engel and Neil Shadle had established the UU Center for Urban Ministry in 1964 and its community development agency, the Neighborhood Commons Corporation (NCC), in 1966. Shadle attended the Emergency Conference on behalf of these community organizations. For him, the decisive moment was the prophetic witness of the African American woman who, striding up and down the aisle, electrified the debate with her summary of what had been wrong with white support. He went back to Chicago ready to turn over the reins to the already emerging African American leadership. Late in 1968, he and Engel relinquished their staff roles. "We were in the awkward position of feeling that we should leave but wanting to stay and the membership reflected this as well, both wanting us to stay and to get out," said Shadle. "It was a poignant, sad, but seemingly necessary transition."[120] Dick Brown, a local leader, NCC staff member, and longtime activist, became the director of the Center. Among its subsequent accomplishments was the development of the Neighborhood Commons Corporation, a low- and moderate-income 168-apartment complex in North Side Chicago.

Kim Beach and James A. Hobart also attended the Emergency Conference. They had just arrived in Cleveland to staff the CUUP ministry. The Unitarian Universalist Association had assigned George T. Johnson, the James Reeb Civil Rights Worker, to Cleveland for the summer, and he had oriented Hobart to the Cleveland scene before moving on to become the director of the East Bay Project in Oakland, California.

CUUP was conceived as Cleveland's equivalent of Chicago's Neighborhood Commons Corporation, but Beach and Hobart were unsure what that would now mean. They were "troubled and excited," said Beach. "I shuddered in dawning recognition that racism cut much deeper than any of us had thought, and we hardly had a clue about how to respond." "I went back to Cleveland aware that the social ground had shifted under our feet," said Hobart. "No longer was it workable for two white guys to direct a white-supported program in the urban ghetto, which was the concept the Cleveland UU churches had bought into."[121]

Four congregations had united to form CUUP, but the strength of their commitments varied. At West Shore, the vote to support the project was 105 for and 73 against. Behind this weak endorsement lay unhappiness with the minister, Jim Curtis. Many members were displeased with his emphasis on civil rights, even though the congregation had expressly said it wanted the new minister to be more of an activist. The division in the congregation led to West

Shore's not providing the funding for CUUP that it had promised, and by March 1968, the situation had become so tense that Curtis resigned.

It was a tumultuous beginning for CUUP, and more tumult was to follow.

The Black Affairs Council vs. the UUA Board of Trustees—Round One

The expression *Black Power* gained traction during the Meredith March in June 1966. *Black* and *Afro-American* became the preferred terms, and *Negro* was avoided except when used as a put-down. But the transformation of black consciousness had begun long before.

In 1963, Afro-American campus groups were springing up. A gathering of the northeastern groups in December 1966 included three hundred delegates from thirty schools.[122] Already in July 1966, the National Committee of Negro Churchmen had issued a statement that said, "We must not apologize for the existence of this form of group power, for we have been oppressed as a group, not as individuals."[123]

The Unitarian Universalist Association was not alone in trying to figure out how to respond to the urban rebellion in the context of shifting black consciousness. The National Council of Churches held a conference on September 27–30, 1967, a week before Unitarian Universalists. Entitled "The Church and the Urban Crisis" and attended by a hundred people from seventeen denominations, it divided into black and white caucuses.[124] But Unitarian Universalism's constituency meant that Unitarian Universalists were, despite a few exceptions, less well connected to black communities. Indeed, many were far removed from them. Therefore, the reaction to the Emergency Conference was as disparate as it was swift.

On October 11, three days after the conference ended, Samuel Beecher, a white Unitarian Universalist Association Board member and an attorney, wrote to Joseph Fisher, the UUA's moderator, "We are faced with a new situation in the Civil Rights Movement which is different than that with which we have had to deal . . . in the past." He said the Board would need help to prepare for its meeting with the Black Caucus Steering Committee in November. "Although some of the [Caucus's] proposals show the usual lack of understanding of the financial position of the Denomination, I have come to believe that their desire for 'self-determination' is a valid one and deserves serious consideration." The insight offered in his final paragraph was predictive:

> This is a situation which will not improve by temporizing and trying to put it off to a later meeting of the Board. This is a matter which needs to be dealt with promptly in order that it may be handled creatively long before the May meeting of the General Assembly where, I believe, if it came up for the first time it would cause very serious divisions within the Denomination because of the lack of understanding on the part of persons of good will on both sides.[125]

On October 19, Dan Ackron, a Liberal Religious Youth delegate, wrote to Homer Jack to share his take on the "weird" questions he was being asked: "The only reason . . . for so many white Unitarians being upset now, and at the conference, is that they have no black friends; if they had they would have known what was happening."[126]

On October 26, Robert Reed, the chair of the Central Midwest District's Social Action Committee, sent out a memorandum about the Emergency Conference, in which he noted that it had "generated a good deal of interest in our own and other districts." He reported on what had happened and then offered, "Needless to say, there is a good deal of Monday morning quarterbacking.... We will see more of the Black Caucus in the future here and there. It is not possible to say where or to what degree. There are some very good reasons for it."[127]

Homer Jack had consulted with Kenneth B. Clark, the African American psychologist who had testified as an expert witness in *Brown v. Board of Education* in Topeka, Kansas. On November 2, Clark responded in a letter outlining his concerns about the Black Caucus. He said that he remained committed to the struggle to make America a racially integrated society, and that segregation harmed both Negroes and whites. The Caucus, on the other hand, had come to the conclusion that integration was impossible to achieve. He understood the depth of their frustration but judged the emerging separatism to be "self-defeating." He said, "I personally question the validity of pride based on color of skin, whether it be white or black. Such a pride seems to be at best tenuous and at worst destructive." He called on the Unitarian Universalist Association Board to use the same standards in judging the Caucus proposal as it would in judging that of any other group.[128] This letter was distributed to the Board prior to its meeting with the Black Caucus Steering Committee and published in the May 1968 *Register-Leader*.

On November 3, Lee Reed wrote Jack from Chicago, saying, "The confrontation was necessary and long overdue."[129]

The November 4 Commission on Religion and Race meeting in Arlington, Virginia, endorsed many of the recommendations that had come out of the Black Caucus at the Emergency Conference. But it modified one that had been put forward by both the Black Caucus and the Emergency Conference's third commission, which was on "Action Priorities For Unitarian Universalists." Both those groups considered it "the highest priority" that the Unitarian Universalist Association back "existing Black Power organizations" like CORE. Because the UUA had seminal and longstanding relationships with the NAACP and the Urban League, and an ongoing one with SCLC, the Commission added these organizations to the original recommendation. And it was unable to reach consensus on the recommendation to establish and fund a Black Affairs Council.[130]

On November 5, William R. Jones, who was teaching at Howard University, responded to the sermon Duncan Howlett, minister at All Souls Unitarian in Washington D.C., had delivered on October 14 that was critical of the Black Caucus. The title of Jones's sermon was "Black Power and Unitarianism: A Personal View." In it, he explored the nature of power and then asked whether the Caucus had subverted the democratic process, as Howlett had alleged. His answer was no. "The only force employed was the implied threat of a withdrawal and its consequent embarrassment for Unitarians.... The decisions of the Conference which are criticized should be interpreted as the injudicious choice of the majority—not the subversion of the democratic process by the minority, i.e. the Black Caucus."[131]

On the same day, at the Arlington Street Church in Boston, Jack Mendelsohn delivered his sermon "Black Power and the Liberal Church":

> I don't care how devotedly integrationist and equality-minded whites may be, they cannot bestow upon Black people a sense of their own identity. Whatever else Black Power may be or may come to be, however constructively, destructively, or stagnantly it may develop, its soul is a revolutionary attempt by Black People to define at last for themselves who they are, what they are worth,

and what they want. It is more than a militant revulsion against the hollow promises and moral betrayals of affluent white America. At its heart it is an unprecedented, trailblazing quest for Black self-acceptance, Black assertiveness, Black accomplishment, and Black pride.[132]

The Unitarian Universalist Association Board would meet with the Black Caucus Steering Committee on November 12. The Commission on Religion and Race covered the Committee's travel expenses from the Freedom Fund. While the Board held its regular meeting on November 10–11, the Steering Committee met to determine its compromise position and "strategy for the confrontation with the Board on Sunday."[133]

Horace Westwood said that before the Board meeting began, he and the other trustees were given reams of sermons representing a multitude of views. They had also read Kenneth Clark's letter discussing his misgivings. For most of them, it was their first exposure to, and opportunity to discuss, the proposals that had arisen from the Emergency Conference.[134]

Two hours were spent on Sunday debating procedure. The Steering Committee wanted an up or down vote on its proposals; as at the Emergency Conference, some people recognized its use of Alinsky's tactics. The Board position was that it could not say how it would act until it heard the proposals and the reasons for them. The debate went on until federal court judge Wade H. McCree Jr., an African American and vice-moderator of the Association, said that "if they didn't stop he would leave or they could." Finally an understanding was reached that it was the Board's intention, if possible, to act positively or negatively on the proposals, and the meeting continued. Westwood said he felt the members of the Steering Committee were sincere and that what they wanted was to be heard and have their wishes acted upon. When asked about the size of their following, they said they did not know but thought it would grow once they had a program. They asserted that the program they proposed should be judged on its merits rather than the size of its constituency.[135]

From the outset, the Unitarian Universalist Association Board was divided and would remain so. Some members wanted to support a separate organization for Black Unitarian Universalists; others were opposed to having a group in the Association that was defined along racial lines. In addition, there was the problem of how to finance any new initiative. The unrestricted capital reserves were extremely low, and the Board had just made the last of $400 thousand in budget cuts. Both unwilling and unable to fully endorse the Steering Committee's four proposals, the Board settled instead on a proposal made by McCree to reorganize the Commission on Religion and Race with more nonwhite members and to invite the Steering Committee to participate in that reorganization.

To make sense of the Board's response, it helps to consider who was in the room. The Steering Committee was led by Hayward Henry, a twenty-five-year-old graduate student who had been introduced to Unitarian Universalism in New Orleans and was on the Board of the Second Unitarian Church of Boston. Louis F. Gothard was a thirty-year-old activist and the chair of BURR. Richard Traylor was thirty-three and had belonged to the UU congregation in Flint, Michigan, before joining Restoration in Philadelphia. Marjorie Jordan and Ben Scott, both in their mid-forties, were longtime Unitarian Universalists, she in Cincinnati and he in Evanston, Illinois, and Boston. All were professionals. On the Board were McCree, several ministers who had gone to Selma, and Samuel Beecher, whose experience at the Emergency Conference had turned him into an advocate for the Black Caucus. Staff member

THE EMERGENCY CONFERENCE ON THE RESPONSE TO THE REBELLION

Homer Jack had been advocating for the Steering Committee. Cornelius McDougald was there as well. What can be discerned is a generational split. On one side of the divide were the three most respected African Americans in the Unitarian Universalist Association, the veterans—McCree, Clark, and McDougald, who were respectively forty-seven, fifty-two, and fifty-five—and on the other a younger more radically inclined group.[136]

Given these circumstances, it is hard to imagine the Board giving an unequivocal assent; indeed, it thought of the meeting as only the beginning of its deliberations. On the other hand, the Steering Committee assumed that the Board was familiar with its proposals and would be ready to deliver a decision. Jack had forewarned the Steering Committee of the likelihood that the Board would want discussion rather than closure, and he was correct. Immediately after the Board recessed, its response was conveyed to Hayward Henry by Greeley and Fisher.

The next day, the Black Caucus Steering Committee called a press conference at which Hayward Henry said, "A group of Black Unitarians were scorned and rejected in favor of a conservative reform proposal.... If this is their response, it's too little and too late." The Committee saw the Board's response as "white backlash," and it encouraged congregations to withdraw their financial support from the Unitarian Universalist Association and send it instead to the Black Caucus Fund.[137]

In response, Greeley issued a statement at a press conference of his own which said, in part,

> The number one domestic problem facing the United States today is the absence of racial justice. We agree with the members of our recently formed Unitarian Universalist Black Caucus that we must demonstrate our knowledge of this by finding ways to make immediate progress that will be meaningful to an anguished

segment of our society. However, the problem of bringing racial justice has never been seen by Unitarian Universalists as a black problem. It is, if [anything,] more a problem for our white members than for the black ones. We have long advocated an integrated society.

We understand the frustration that painful and continuing delay has caused to all who seek progress in race relations.... Even so we have taken some exception to the procedures of the Unitarian Universalist Black Caucus. Their policies of separation, exclusiveness and abrogation of what we have always considered essential democratic procedures are perhaps understandable. We understand, but we have difficulty in concurring.[138]

Two days later, an article appeared in a Vermont paper, the *Bennington Banner*, under the headline "Negroes Consider Breaking Away." It quoted James Carter, a member of the Steering Committee, as saying that the caucus was "seriously considering a complete break" from the Unitarian Universalist Association and that "many Negroes have already withdrawn their financial support."[139]

Two days after that, Bob Jones, director of the UUA's office in Washington D.C., wrote a letter to Jack excoriating the Black Caucus Steering Committee's "shameful and shabby treatment of Dana Greeley and the denomination in its press conference." He argued that it should not be allowed to participate in the reorganization of the Commission on Religion and Race because it did not have the interests of the Association at heart but rather wished "to disrupt and to wreck this liberal religious movement":

> If it is the intention of the Black Steering Committee to form its own church then I say let them go their way. They will soon find themselves wandering off into the wilderness with no following. I for one am not going to aid and abet them in their plans to

subvert this denomination which has consistently been on the line for racial justice and brotherhood.... Homer, it pains me a great deal to differ with you on this issue.... But, I think there are values at stake here which are so overriding that I must speak out.[140]

The battle had begun. Sermon upon sermon was preached—some soul-searching, some polemic; flurries of letters were sent and countless meetings held. Episodes of collaboration followed by vitriolic condemnation left many feeling betrayed and still others conflicted. The political skirmishing intensified as the 1968 General Assembly approached.

The Formation of the Black Unitarian Universalist Caucus

[*November 1967–May 1968*]

IN THE WAKE OF THE November Unitarian Universalist Association Board meeting, it seemed unlikely that the program advanced by the Black Caucus at the Emergency Conference would come to fruition. But the formation of the Black Unitarian Universalist Caucus (BUUC) in February 1968, societal upheaval beyond the Association, and political machinations within the denomination set the scene for a surprising outcome.

Seizing the Association's Attention

One of the recommendations of the Black Caucus report adopted by the Emergency Conference in October 1967 was to convene black Unitarian Universalists. On November 13, following the press conference in which Unitarian Universalist Association president Dana Greeley responded to the Steering Committee's description of the UUA Board as "paternalistic" and of its inaction as a "traumatic blow to Black people," he met privately with four Steering Committee members. During that meeting, Greeley indicated that he would take its request for funds for a national conference of black Unitarian Universalists "under sympathetic advisement," which Hayward Henry saw as a "conciliatory gesture."[141]

On November 29, the Commission on Religion and Race, with Henry attending as an observer, affirmed the right of black Unitarian Universalists to form a caucus and agreed to help fund the gathering with a contribution of $4,100 from the Freedom Fund. And to give the Association's Board a free hand in restructuring the Commission, all its members submitted their resignations. The Midwestern UU Conference soon contributed $1,000 to the Black Caucus Fund as well. On December 15, the Black Caucus Steering Committee met and set February 23–25 as the date of a National Conference of Black Unitarian Universalists in Chicago.

A group of fifty white allies gathered in the Pacific Southwest District. Calling themselves Supporters of Black Unitarians for Radical Reform (SOBURR), they gave the Black Caucus their full backing, including endorsing a plan to divert congregational contributions from the Unitarian Universalist Association's Annual Program Fund to the Black Caucus Fund. Roy Ockert, associate minister at the First Unitarian Church of Los Angeles, composed a resolution for the church Board that fully supported the Black Caucus but not the call to redirect the congregation's UUA contribution to the Black Caucus Fund. Meanwhile, the Arlington Street Church's Prudential Committee voted to recognize the Boston Black Caucus as an official church organization and to provide $1,200 to send delegates to Chicago.[142]

On February 10, 1968, a dozen black Unitarian Universalists from seven Bay Area congregations gathered at the First Unitarian Church of Oakland to discuss the Black Caucus proposals and the upcoming meeting in Chicago and to form a local caucus. Among them was Betty Bobo Seiden, a long-time member of the Berkeley church. She said,

I was so excited! I had not realized how much I had missed the companionship of other Black congregants! It was going to be fun getting to know this room full of [Black] people, none of whom I had seen before this meeting.

The meeting was a long one because some of us were unaware that there had been a previous meeting; everything from the previous meeting had to be repeated. We also learned that an influential member of the San Francisco Church, Charles Patterson, had attended the first meeting, rejected the proposals and decided to abstain from further participation ... but I was still excited about the possibilities for a Black Caucus and the creation of our local BUBA, Black Unitarians of the Bay Area. I looked forward to attending the meeting in Chicago.[143]

Four days later, a similar meeting took place at All Souls Church Unitarian in Washington D.C. Letters of invitation were sent to over a hundred African American Unitarian Universalists in the metropolitan Washington area, and about thirty attended. Richard Traylor came from Philadelphia. His invitation to support the Black Caucus in its "affirmation of blackness" led critics to accuse him of "inverse racism." A stormy debate followed, full of shouting, accusations, and interruptions, but eventually a majority voted to establish the Greater Washington Association of Negro Unitarian Universalists Concerned with Race.[144]

Late in January, Rev. Dwight Brown and Rev. Philip Giles, two white Unitarian Universalist Association district executives, had sent a memo to the other district executives. Assessing the publicity that had circulated to be largely supportive of the Black Caucus, they felt it necessary to offer a contrary opinion. They charged, as had others, that the rules of open discussion had been abrogated at the Emergency Conference and people intimidated, and went on to say that they personally knew "a substantial number" of Negro Unitarian Universalists who did not support the Caucus's position. Canadian Unitarians were more concerned about the separatists in Quebec and the treatment of First Nations People.[145]

In the meantime, Homer Jack was responding to missives coming from all sides. Writing to a member of SOBURR, he said he regretted they had so readily agreed with Louis Gothard's characterization of the Board when it did not "rubberstamp" the Caucus's proposals. Given that he had warned them of the Board's likely attitude, Jack felt Gothard's response was overblown. He listed what the Commission on Religion and Race had done, including paying for the Emergency Conference and the Steering Committee's travel to meet with the Board. What would happen, he asked, if every group that disagreed with the Association about an issue withdrew its contribution? Such a withdrawal had already been threatened in regard to the war in Vietnam. His bottom line was that yes, the urban situation was dire but it would take time for religious liberals to come to a consensus that would lift them to "a much higher level of involvement." Having been deeply engaged with issues of race since the forties, he knew how long it had taken to bring the Association to the depth of commitment that made its response to events in Selma so quick and emphatic. And in response to Brown and Giles, he wrote, "I myself am strongly suggesting that every Black or Negro Unitarian Universalist ... go to Chicago. ... The more Blacks who attend, the better for them and for the denomination."[146]

Black Unitarian Universalist minister Jeffrey Campbell shared a newsletter column with Jack in which he had written, "I have never lost my distrust of caucuses. Basically they affirm that an organized minority can and should sway a multitude that cannot be trusted to make up its mind." Nevertheless, he asked for Jack's advice. Jack replied that it was very important for Campbell to attend, "whatever your present feeling about this technique."[147]

Caucuses formed in Los Angeles, Chicago, Boston, the Bay Area, the Washington D.C. area, the New York area, Denver, Des Moines, the Twin Cities, and Toronto. The Black Caucus found an active ally in SOBURR and outspoken white champions in Roy Ockert and Jack Mendelsohn. Meanwhile, Homer Jack, the seasoned activist, was fighting a rearguard action fending off naysayers while trying to moderate the Caucus's expectations. There were also African Americans, like Charles Patterson and Kenneth Clark, who were opposed to the organization of caucuses, and others, like Jeffrey Campbell and Thomas Payne, who were skeptical participants. In addition, white Unitarian Universalist Association staff members like Brown, Giles, and Bob Jones (of the Washington office) began mounting an active resistance.

These people were paying attention. Many others were not. However much controversy there was about the emerging Black Caucus among some Unitarian Universalists, the concern was not universal; indeed, many gave it no thought at all.

Founded in 1959 as part of the fellowship movement, the Unitarian Universalist Fellowship of Bozeman, Montana, was still meeting in members' homes. Interviewed later, a longtime member could say only, "Oh, yes, I do remember there was a flap in the UUA about that—something to do with GA."[148] The only mention of race in the records of the Olympia Brown congregation (Racine, Wisconsin) for 1967–1968 is that members of the Social Concerns Committee were involved in influencing the city's Fair Housing Ordinance; across the country, fair housing was something for which UUs typically crusaded. In other congregations with no black members (including Oneonta, New York; Oklahoma City; Fort Myers, Florida; and Athens, Georgia), nothing about either conference appears in congregational records. The same was surely the case throughout New England. In 1970, across the birthplace of Unitarianism and Universalism in America, the percentage of African Americans in the population was minuscule; in Vermont, Maine, New Hampshire, and Massachusetts, it was respectively 0.2, 0.3, 0.3 and 3.1 percent. In Canada, meanwhile, the First Unitarian Congregation of Ottawa drew up a "Plan for a Unitarian Universalist Social Responsibility Office in Ottawa," which stated that "Civil Rights, however much a *good thing*, is just not an issue in Canada."[149] This was not true, but it did reflect Canadian and Unitarian Canadian beliefs in a context in which blacks made up 0.2 percent of the population. What mattered most to Canadians were the separatists in Quebec, multiculturalism, and the treatment of First Nations people.

Black Unitarian Universalists Gather

In February of 1968, the black delegates met at Chicago's Windermere Hotel. Two blocks east on Lake Michigan, the ice coverage was mounting as the winds swept in from the northwest. The temperature dipped below zero degrees Fahrenheit two days before the National Conference of Black Unitarian Universalists began. But about two hundred black Unitarian Universalists endured whatever they had to in order to be at this first-ever gathering.

"I got to Chicago," said Joseph B. Samples Jr. of Detroit, "and I didn't know there were so many black Unitarians."[150] They came from San Diego, Los Angeles, and the Bay Area; from New York, Boston, and D.C.; from Cincinnati and Syracuse; from the Twin Cities and Toronto. There was someone from Texas, but few from the South. Of those attending this inaugural meeting, fifty were from the Chicago area, and while twenty-five states were represented, the delegates were largely, though not exclusively, from urban America.

Joe Samples said, "Man, I was also surprised at the wide range of professions. We had an oceanographer and a guy who owned an electronics company."[151] "To say we were an uncommon assemblage would be an understatement," said Grant Venerable II, "for we represented a dazzling cross-section of talents, of backgrounds, of educational preparation."[152] "They were lawyers and judges and doctors and teachers and writers. They were social workers, defense contractors, managers, scientists, business men," reported Ben Scott, "strictly middle class.... They were people who can play successfully under the present rules, but who want the rules changed for the benefit of others."[153]

There were many more men than women, who made up about a fifth of the attendees. Most were legal members of a Unitarian Universalist congregation; they had to be in order to vote at this caucus. Of thirty-seven observers, two represented foundations and three represented denominations. Among those not present were the veterans Wade McCree, Cornelius McDougald, Eugene Sparrow, Charles Patterson, and Lewis McGee.

The announced goals of the conference were:

To foster and develop a sense of Black consciousness, Black Unity and Black self-determination within the denomination.

To create a mechanism by which the denomination can be made more relevant to the Black community through the unity of its Black constituency.

To assist in the continuing distribution to the denomination of information on the political, social and economic status of Black people in the United States.

To advance those institutions and approaches which are unifying and power generating in the Black community.[154]

On Friday evening, the first address was delivered by Hayward Henry. "There is nothing more tragic than an institution or nation which sleeps through a revolution," he began. Nine months earlier, in his Ware Lecture, Dr. Martin Luther King Jr. had said, "There is nothing more tragic than to sleep through a revolution." That Henry's words echoed Dr. King's is undeniable, yet Henry made no explicit reference to King or his speech.

Henry continued, "Who would have thought but one year ago that black Unitarian Universalists would have dared to form into a caucus from which whites were excluded?" Indeed, there was not a whiff of this idea in the Unitarian Universalist Association Board minutes from January 1967 and, in general, little mention of the state of race relations in America.

Unitarian Universalists, Henry said, "have long articulated a religious ideology which insists that we believe in the brotherhood of man. We believe in the creative worth and dignity of human personality. In fact, we say we are committed to an interracial and integrated society.... We say we are an integrated society, but until this day, there are only two black men holding full-time pulpits in our church."[155] In fact, the situation was worse than Henry described it as being. At that moment, there was not a single African American in a full-time Unitarian Universalist pulpit. Jeffrey Campbell was the only one serving a parish, and he was part-time; Lewis McGee had retired; William R. Jones was teaching at Howard University; Eugene Sparrow was the executive director of the Grand Rapids Human Relations Council; George Johnson, a Methodist, was the director of the East Bay Project of the Association's Pacific Central District; and there were five black seminary students. The Association's record of settling African American ministers was terrible.

The Commission on Religion and Race had approached the Unitarian Universalist Association's Department of Education in 1964 about updating its materials. The department had responded that for financial reasons, it could not "scrap its present stock of books despite the fact the texts and illustrations are 'pure white' but that new materials will reflect intercultural and interracial situations. The issues of city life, multi-ethnic groups and poverty, will be featured in contemplated new materials."[156] The only material the Association had published about African American achievements was four chapters about the life of George Washington Carver in *Worshipping Together with Questioning Minds* (1965). The Department of Adult Programs produced a study guide entitled "The Negro Protest."[157] Otherwise the few programs that existed were developed by individual congregations and made available through the monthly Religious Education Action Clearing House packet.

"Yes, we are integrated," said Henry. "We have tokens everywhere—one on the Board, one on the Laymen's League Board, . . . one on the Board of the Women's Federation and one on the Board of the Service Committee."[158] There were no African Americans on the Nominating Committee, the Commission on Appraisal, the Program Committee, or the Business Committee—whose memberships were all elected—and only one black commission chair, Cornelius McDougald, chair of the Commission on Religion and Race. Of thirty-two people nominated for denomination-wide elected positions in 1967, one was a member of the Urban League, two belonged to Human Relations Councils, and five to the NAACP—and they were all white.

"What is more tragic about the whole Unitarian experience is the fact that we don't see the concrete expression of blackness as a liturgical form," Henry said.[159] In 1964, the Unitarian Universalist Assocation published *Hymns for the Celebration of Life*, in which there was not a single hymn or reading by a black person or reflective of African American culture.

African Americans' expectations had been built upon decades of General Assembly resolutions and the Unitarian Universalist engagement in Selma, and bolstered by the Association's 1966 Consensus on Racial Justice, which committed the Association to eliminate discrimination in its congregations and to encourage the integration of the ministry and of all phases of community life. The Association's failure to bring about timely and significant change invited Henry's indictment. The institutional reality in regard to ministry, religious education, governance, and worship—the institution's values in practice—did not begin to approach its espoused values but rather supported white supremacy. In the face of the awakening black consciousness, *liberalese* was revealed to be all talk, no action. For all the resolutions, and despite the internal prodding of the Commission on Religion and Race, the will was fleeting and progress scant.

Henry briefly talked about inequality in America and the crisis in the black community before circling back to the situation within Unitarian Universalism. "So, when you talk about integration in the church and integration in the society, you're not being honest. It does not exist."

"The major difference in social philosophy, it seems, between us is that the white Unitarian is still talking about liberal reform and black Unitarians are talking about radical transformation."[160] This tension within Unitarian Universalism between radicals and reformists is long-standing and somewhat fallacious. Prophets hold up a vision and the behavior of radicals garners attention, but to sustain a movement, one must not only have vision but also organize and reform. Unitarian Universalists, regardless of race, are usually highly educated and middle class; the social status this gives them means they are more often reformers than radicals. Their proclivity has been to create and maintain institutions that embody and transmit values into the public sphere for generations to come, rather than to obliterate a status quo in which they have figured out how to succeed. In regard to race, the problem was neither reformation nor transformation—little of either was evident within the Association. Too many Unitarian Universalists, preferring order to the discomfort of change, chose inaction and acquiesced exactly where they had the most influence—in their own congregations.

Henry called on white Unitarian Universalists to deal with the fact that theirs was a racist society, and on black Unitarian Universalists to build "strong black communities [and] strong black institutions." He concluded with, "For those who don't want to join us in this effort, all we ask is that you don't obstruct us."[161] After Henry had finished, the Honorable Richard G. Hatcher, mayor of Gary, Indiana, delivered the keynote. The next day, the conference heard from Floyd McKissick and Jesse Jackson. It was a sign of the time that Jackson was accompanied by a contingent of Black Stone Rangers—a young, black nationalist, uniformed honor guard.

Much of the rest of the conference was dedicated to problem-solving sessions focused on goals, structures, and programs, the Commission on Religion and Race, the relationship that the proposed Black Affairs Council should have to other civil rights groups, and the relationship of black Unitarians to Black Power.[162] "What we wanted to do," said Joe Samples, "was get together and decide our destiny by ourselves. It was not about separating ourselves or anything like that. You can't empower people, people have to empower themselves."[163]

Reports on the conference from attendees were varied. An anonymous one said that while many delegates "were critical of the Black caucus or were even hostile to it, . . . all points of view were heard."[164]

That was not Betty Seiden's experience. "It was not a feel good meeting to me. People were very strident [and] divisive. It was one of those if you're not gung-ho with us you're against us."[165] Lillian W. Jenkins's report to the Unitarian Universalist Women's Federation incorporated both sides: "From the amount of discussion and controversy, one could observe much divergence of opinion, however the dominant 'Theme' of the 'movers of the caucus' seemed to win out over those of 'Conservatives' by a vote of two to one."[166] Afterward, the press release issued about the founding of BUUC called the vote "overwhelming." But Betty Reid Soskin mentioned "power plays" in her report,[167] and Jenkins alluded to such struggles as well. Ben Scott, one of the driving forces behind BAC, described the conference as "combat," and the word captures its tone.[168] In the long run, such efforts to assert control provoked a reaction.

As well as taking control of Unitarian Universalist Association programming on race, the conference had another goal. Scott also said, "The first job of a black caucus is to combat 'Negro racism' and Negro middle class paternalism and most of [the Black Caucus's] early efforts must go into this. We're ridding ourselves of racial prejudice . . . against ourselves." He was talking about what is now called *internalized racism*, the tendency of an oppressed people to take on the prejudice of the dominant society, which encourages them to present a "pseudo-self."[169] In the case of African Americans, internalized racism elevated whiteness—its capabilities and standards of beauty—while demeaning blackness. In 1968, the idea existed but not the term; Scott found the phrase "Negro racism" brought a helpful clarity.[170] *Uncle Tom* and *Oreo* were the commonplace, and harsher, terms.

For some, attending that meeting began a process of transformation. "Many Blacks found themselves," said the anonymous report, while others "who had reservations were converted."[171] But Jenkins warned, "I see the division, the separativeness.... Blacks for me: whites for you—Blacks for blacks; whites for whites. Ultimately, such intense chauvinism could lead to the disastrous philosophy of 'My brother, right or wrong!'" While abhorring that attitude, she came to the conclusion that "it would be a great thing...if the UUA would help the BAC. It would be daring; it would announce to the world the faith of the denomination in its black members."[172] The sentiment was echoed by Grant Venerable II when he said, "Unitarian Universalists will derive new-found social relevance and vitality."[173]

Among the meeting outcomes were agreements that BUUC would meet annually, support the immediate formation of BAC as an affiliate organization of the Unitarian Universalist Association whose makeup would be two-thirds black, petition the Association to fund BAC at $250 thousand a year, demand the termination of the Commission on Religion and Race, and annually commemorate Malcolm X on the date he was assassinated. The gathering elected Hayward Henry as chair of BUUC, regionally balanced the Steering Committee, and expanded its membership to ten but included only one woman, Marjorie Jordan. This gender imbalance needs to be understood in context. In the face of racism, "there was a resistance [among black women] to stepping up in front of our men or to compete for power," said Betty Reid Soskin.[174]

Responses to the formation of BUUC were mixed. Betty Seiden, who had been sent to oppose the idea of a national black caucus, reported to her congregation that it "was going to go through because there were very few voices against it."[175] Reporting back to the Flushing church, Bill Kurlew said, "They are a bunch of radicals...but let's support them."[176] Betty Reid Soskin wrote in a letter to Hayward Henry that "many [were] traumatized by their experience," but that she also watched "the new pride rise suddenly, causing black muscles to ripple under black, *newly* black skin, with a resulting swagger and strut."[177] "In the end," said Ben Scott, "we wound up more black, that is freer from racism, than we were and more Unitarian Universalist than we were."[178] A proposal was even made to withdraw from the church, but it was soundly rejected, and it would be again a year and half later when it was repeated by those who walked out of the 1969 General Assembly. Nonetheless, some held onto the idea.

A month after the conference, Jeffrey Campbell wrote to Dana Greeley to share his response to the conference. As a fifty-seven-year-old, fair-skinned black Unitarian Universalist minister, raised Universalist in Nashua, New Hampshire, by his white mother, he was uniquely situated to observe a room full of middle-class black liberals wrestling with survivor's guilt:

> I have fought the peculiar complex called the American race relations struggle all my life, but it has been as an individual and not as representative of a group with which I felt no identity. I cannot enter into any "mystique," Black or otherwise so far as complexion is concerned....
>
> At Chicago I saw some two hundred very middle class and able people caught up in the struggle to achieve an identity. They reminded me of similar types who in the thirties were attempting the same effort in relation to the "class struggle." There was the same aura of guilt for not being "workers" as I saw here for not being "black inside" (many had to rely on the inside for their blackness).[179] The whole mystique strikes me as artificial....
>
> Positively, I see this development as a magnificent opportunity to educate our Liberal Religious fellowships in a way that they simply have never been educated before. The demands of the Caucus should, in my opinion, be met. The very form of their presentation, the arrogance, rudeness and rejection of the parliamentary procedures should be shown as a measure of the deep, soul-searing

wounds which the insensitivity and blind stupidity of the majority have inflicted throughout the history of our church. I realize fully that a great measure of the impetus for the Caucus is drawn from the plight of America's largest minority outside our U.U. members, but the Caucus is adequately reflecting this. . . .

I realize that the vast majority of our fellowship is not ready for the eventualities suggested in this letter. It is intensity, not time, that matures liberals to the extent that they do mature. Be this as it may, I suggest history has already granted us all the time it is going to grant.[180]

The Black Affairs Council vs. the UUA Board of Trustees — Round Two

Black Unitarian Universalists were not alone in mounting a revolution within a denomination. On February 8, 1968, seventeen African American Episcopal priests had met in New York City and founded the Union of Black Clergy and Laity to take on the issue of racism within society at large and their own church.[181] Black United Methodists and Lutherans were doing likewise, and fifty black Catholic priests had called their Church "primarily a racist institution."[182]

On February 29, four days after BUUC's inaugural meeting ended, the National Advisory Commission on Civil Disorders, which had been established by President Lyndon Johnson the summer before, released its report, commonly called the Kerner Report. It found that riots were a result of black frustration over the lack of economic opportunities, and warned, "Our nation is moving toward two societies, one black, one white—separate and unequal." The report simply confirmed what black Americans already knew, but it alerted the rest of the nation to just how bad the situation was and made the Unitarian Universalist search for relevance that much more urgent.

"BUUC will stimulate the holding of metropolitan workshops to brief Black and white delegates to the General Assembly," said one post-conference report.[183] Some conferees began this as soon as they arrived home. The very next Sunday, Richard Traylor preached a sermon entitled "Black Caucus" at the First Unitarian Church of Philadelphia, and Victor Carpenter followed soon after with one entitled "The Black Caucus and Black Rebellion: A White Perspective." Grant Venerable, seeing First Chicago "rent apart by the Black Caucus," felt compelled to compose an essay "to speak to the terrifying emotions tearing at persons of all racial backgrounds." He entitled it "The Black Caucus: Racism or Not?"[184] And before the next General Assembly, Jack Kent, the minister in Chicago, sent out a letter to delegates outlining his reason for endorsing BAC.

The March meeting of the Unitarian Universalist Association Board hammered out a new proposal, which was rejected by BAC as an insult. To Homer Jack, it revealed that the Board did not understand Black Power, and on March 17, he circulated a detailed memorandum to Dana Greeley and all UUA vice presidents and division directors that explained the shortcomings of the proposal, warned that a storm was mounting, and accurately predicted it would be overturned at the coming General Assembly.

Jack outlined three problems with the Board's plan:

- the Board's continuing equivocation over whether it could grant BAC affiliate status because its membership was structured to ensure that black people made up the majority
- the establishment of a competing locus of authority to BAC, in regard to race, by replacing the Commission on Religion and Race with a Commission for Action on Race
- relying on donations to a new UU Fund for Racial Justice Now to fund BAC rather than guaranteeing funds from denominational

sources. The unpredictability of the donations to such a fund, alongside the paltry contributions to the UUA Freedom Fund it was to replace, made it utterly unrealistic.[185]

The following weekend, at the annual Social Responsibility Washington Seminar, Homer Jack unexpectedly ceded his time to Hayward Henry. This action, along with Henry's and subsequently Jack's criticism of the Unitarian Universalist Association Board, so outraged Phil Giles that he wrote to Greeley, "I think it is time to dispense with his services on the continental staff."[186] Giles, no champion of the Black Caucus, had actively discouraged African American Unitarian Universalists from attending the gathering in Chicago. Now he was upset by what he saw as Jack's sleight of hand. Giles also argued that as a member of the Association's staff, Jack should have defended rather than criticized the Board's position. Four days later, Jack wrote to Greeley, explaining again what he had done and why, and offering to shoulder the consequences.

> If anything, I have written too many position papers and vacillated too often. I have been battered, if not bloodied, at different times and occasionally at the same time, by the Black Caucus and by certain of its opponents. I understand my role as kind of a middleman....
>
> This role is not easy. The pressures are extreme. I am sure I have made mistakes of judgement and strategy.... However, if I am in any way an embarrassment to your relations with the Board, the Black Unitarian Universalist Caucus, or any other constituencies, I shall be glad to resign and on short notice. If so, I will neither be the first casualty of the Black caucus controversy nor the last.[187]

Greeley did not accept Homer's offer.

THE FORMATION OF THE BLACK UNITARIAN UNIVERSALIST CAUCUS

. . .

SUPPORTERS OF BLACK UNITARIANS for Radical Reform (SOBURR) was organized in Los Angeles on November 19, 1967, and by Thanksgiving Day, it had mailed a letter denomination-wide calling on congregations and ministers to support the demands of the Caucus. In early March, following the initial BUUC gathering and the Kerner Report, it circulated another letter, aiming to rally support for BAC at the upcoming General Assembly in Cleveland by setting up local groups, analogous to SOBURR, that would form a national alliance.

BAC wrote to Rudy Gelsey asking him to create a national white support organization. Gelsey accordingly called David Parke, minister of the nearby Unitarian Society of Germantown. Parke said that Gelsey told him, "The Blacks, there are too few of them. They cannot possibly prevail at the General Assembly on their own.... The only hope they have ... is the formation now immediately across the continent of a white support group." Jack Mendelsohn, a BAC member, offered two other reasons: "It was a response to the accusation that the BUUC people were separatist. We wanted to demonstrate another point of view. We did not consider them to be separatist at all. [And] we wanted to make clear that there was strong white support for BAC." But the bottom line was "political motivation. We had to win votes."[188]

Right before the founding meeting of FULLBAC (Full Recognition and Funding of the Black Affairs Council), Mendelsohn received a letter from the Massachusetts Bay District. It announced that on March 30, a "White Caucus" to support BAC and fight white racism had been formed. Its members were largely members of the Massachusetts Bay District Social Action Committee. This was typical. A study entitled "Unitarian Universalism and Black

Empowerment in the United States: A Nationwide Survey of UU Attitudes toward Black Power and Participation in Militant Civil Rights Activities" showed that those post-traditionalists for whom social activism was central to their religious life were the most likely to support Black Power.[189] The list of the ninety-five initial FULLBAC sponsors bears this out.[190]

One of those sponsors was Orloff Miller, district executive of the Mountain Desert District. In February, he had sent out an open letter on district letterhead encouraging Unitarian Universalists in the region to support the Black Caucus, and at the upcoming General Assembly, there would be buttons reading, "Mountain Desert Delegates Give FULLBAC support to BAC." This Selma veteran was even more radical than Homer Jack. Naturally, Jack was also a FULLBAC supporter, as was Harvard Divinity School professor James Luther Adams. Jack had sent Adams a copy of his memorandum "Black Power and the White Liberal." In his response, Adams told Jack he had given a report on the Black Caucus at First Parish Cambridge and taken a position that the church Board should contribute to "paying the expenses of Negro delegates to the May Meetings" of the Unitarian Universalist Association.[191] Meanwhile, Phil Giles, another district executive, continued to press Greeley to fire Jack for insubordination.

Dr. King's Assassination

On the evening of April 3, as he drew toward the conclusion of his sermon at Mason Temple in Memphis, Tennessee, Martin Luther King Jr. said,

> Like anybody, I would like to live a long life. Longevity has its place. But I'm not concerned about that now. I just want to do God's will.

And he has allowed me to go up to the mountain. And I've looked over, and I've seen the Promised Land. I may not get there with you, but I want you to know tonight that we as a people will get to the Promised Land.

So I'm happy tonight. I'm not worried about anything—I'm not fearing any man. Mine eyes have seen the glory of the coming of the Lord.[192]

The next day, April 4, at the Unitarian Society of Germantown in Philadelphia, the organizers of FULLBAC held a meeting with the BUUC leadership—about a dozen people altogether. Mendelsohn remembered, "We were having dinner together when a black woman burst into the room wailing 'They killed him. They've killed Dr. King.' It was like a thunderbolt had hit the parish hall and we immediately separated. The blacks in the group said, 'We have to be by ourselves. We have to go off.' So we whites went off to be by ourselves."[193]

Dr. King had been in Memphis supporting the striking African American sanitation workers. Around 6 PM, as he stood on the balcony of the Lorraine Motel, he was shot dead. James Earl Ray was later convicted of the killing.

In Cambridge, Massachusetts, about seventy-five people had come to a meeting that night at First Parish to discuss the Black Caucus. Greeley had accepted an invitation to speak to the issue; he planned to discuss both his objections to the Unitarian Universalist Association's recognition of the Caucus and what he found positive in it. Word of King's murder arrived during his talk. Silent prayer was followed by a spoken prayer offered by Rev. Ralph Helverson, the minister, and remarks by Greeley.

James Luther Adams was there, but over the next years, he and his wife, Margaret, a member of the Massachusetts Bay District Social Action Committee, grew increasingly unhappy with the congregation's conservatism. Eventually they would resign and join the Arlington Street Church.

In Chicago, seventeen-year-old Rob Isaacs, a Liberal Religious Youth leader who had grown up in the First Unitarian Society of Chicago, did not know what to do when he learned of King's death, but he couldn't sit at home. He went down the apartment building's stairs and out onto the street. Not knowing why, he walked west. Now the spire on that neo-Gothic church edifice was in sight, and when he pulled on the great oak sanctuary doors, which were usually locked, they opened:

> Almost blinded by my tears I walked into the dim, cool sanctuary, turned left up the steps into the gallery, then right through the gallery and into the bell room. In the empty, silent church I took hold of the rope. Though we'd been taught from early childhood not to touch that rope, I had to do something. So I began to toll the bell. For what seemed like forever I tolled that bell and wept. Finally, exhausted and drained, I stopped. As the sound of the bell died away I heard voices coming from the sanctuary. I left the bell room, walked into the chapel, turned toward the stairs which led down to the sanctuary and there they were. A thousand people, maybe more, holding one another, weeping and singing. Not knowing what to do I tolled the bell. Not knowing where to turn the neighborhood turned to the church.[194]

Just a half mile south, in the impoverished African American Woodlawn neighborhood, windows were being broken, stores looted, and calls for revolution spread along Sixty-Third Street. Eventually, as rioting erupted on Chicago's West Side as well, the National Guard was called out and Mayor Daley issued the order "Shoot to kill."

In Washington D.C., rioting engulfed Columbia Heights, the neighborhood in which All Souls Church was located. Decades were to pass before it would be rebuilt. There were more than a hundred riots in the days following King's death.

On April 5, at Coretta Scott King's request, Homer Jack flew to Memphis. She asked him to accompany her and Dr. King's body back to Atlanta. There Jack served as an honor guard, and on April 9, he represented the Unitarian Universalist Association at King's funeral.

In Kansas City, Missouri, on Sunday, April 7, Lewis McGee delivered a eulogy for Dr. King. He began by saying a white friend of his daughter's had called her and offered condolences, as if only black people had suffered a loss. His audience was certainly predominantly white, and he wanted them to understand that this was a shared loss. Shared it was. Many Unitarian Universalists were close to King. Indeed, he was scheduled to speak that day at the installation of Rev. Farley Wheelwright as minister of the Unitarian Society of Cleveland.

But as grief-stricken as the nation and Unitarian Universalists were, grief was not universal, and the event was not felt the same way by African Americans and Euro-Americans.

On April 15, Jack wrote to Greeley, saying he wished to be relieved of his responsibilities in the field of race relations. "The funeral of Dr. Martin Luther King, Jr. must be the last time that I represent the Association in such an event." That position, he said, should be held by a black man. "I feel sensitive enough to the trends of our time not to want—as a white man . . . to represent our denomination's racial concerns. . . . Now is the time for at least this white liberal to bow out from this particular role." For the second time, he offered his resignation[195] and again Greeley declined.

The Community Church of New York and the Birth of Black and White Action

On Sunday, April 7, 1968, the Community Church of New York held a memorial service for Dr. Martin Luther King Jr. The opening hymn was followed by the reading of President Lyndon B. Johnson's proclamation declaring the day a national day of mourning. Immediately after that, the congregation recited its affirmation, as it did every Sunday:

> Unto the Church Universal, which is the depository of all ancient wisdom and the school of all modern thought; which recognizes in all prophets a harmony, in all scriptures a unity, and through all dispensation a continuity; which abjures all that separates and divides, and always magnifies brotherhood and peace; which seeks truth in freedom, justice in love and individual discipline in social duty; and which shall make of all sects, classes, nations and races, one fellowship of men—unto this Church and unto all its members, known and unknown throughout the world, we pledge the allegiance of our hands and hearts. Amen.

Eventually, a bust of King would join those of the congregation's other saints: Albert Schweitzer, Margaret Sanger, and Mahatma Gandhi. The affirmation had been written by Keshab Chandra Sen, a nineteenth-century Brahmo Samaj leader, and arranged by John Haynes Holmes, the minister of the congregation from 1907 until 1949.

Holmes was one of the five founders of the NAACP. He began integrating the congregation in 1910, and it took twenty-five years to become well integrated. In 1924, the theme of its annual conference was "Inter-racial Harmony and Peace"; in 1925, J. Rosamond Johnson, the composer of "Lift Every Voice and Sing," offered a program of Negro spirituals and W. E. B. Du Bois praised the congregation's stance on race, which he declared "was not merely sentimental, or a matter of personal charity."[196] In 1946, toward the end of his ministry, Holmes wrote, "No church is a true church which does not have whites and Negroes, like rich and poor, sitting side by side." The Community Church of New York, he said, "rejects and repudiates segregation in every form."[197]

Community was the first church in which a young poet named Langston Hughes was invited to read his poetry; among its members was Ida Cullen Cooper, wife of black author and poet Countee Cullen. In 1948, it called Rev. Maurice A. Dawkins, an African American, as minister of religious education. In 1950, Community Church members were among the founders of the Committee on Civil Rights in East Manhattan. In 1952, the American Committee on Africa, the first anti-apartheid organization in America, was founded and housed at the church, and Donald S. Harrington, Holmes's successor, was its first chair. In 1965, Donald and Vilma Harrington were among the first Unitarian Universalists to visit Selma prior to Bloody Sunday. The longtime chair of the church's Board was well-known Harlem lawyer Cornelius McDougald, and the congregational leadership was thoroughly integrated. Since about a third of its membership was black, it was by far the most integrated congregation in the Unitarian Universalist Association.

Community Church served as the entry point for many African Americans who later joined other congregations. Errold Collymore, for example, went on to join White Plains in 1927 and later became its Board chair. Hershel and Roger Gordons, who joined Restoration in Philadelphia, were first drawn to Unitarian Universalism by Community Church. Betty Seiden, who grew up in the thirties in an integrated Pentecostal church, discovered Community in 1955 when she was attending Columbia University. Seeing that it offered a comparative religion course, she thought to herself, "This is what religious education should be," and when she had children, she joined the First Unitarian Church of Berkeley.

The congregation was also heavily Jewish and celebrated the Jewish holidays, as it did Diwali and American Indian Sunday. Its three hundred–student Sunday School was thoroughly intercultural in its constituency and program, devoting a year at a time to different countries and cultures, learning their music, their alphabets, their food, their dances, and their dress. Malcolm X had spoken at its Community Forum. Its bookstore promoted books by and about African Americans. The congregation donated office space for the National Committee for Free Elections in Mississippi.

Community Church's senior minister in 1968, Donald S. Harrington, was a well-known and controversial activist, chair of the Liberal Party of New York, and candidate for lieutenant governor. He called Congressman Adam Clayton Powell Jr. his friend and preached from Powell's pulpit at Abyssinian Baptist. He served as chair of the American Committee on Africa until he realized it didn't make sense for a white man to be the chair, so he persuaded A. Philip Randolph to co-chair with him.[198] And he was one of the few white members of Sigma Pi Phi (the Boulé), an organization of the African American elite.

Community Church saw itself as the embodiment of the Church Universal. Having eschewed assimilation, it reached for true integration, and not only in regard to race; it also strove to be culturally inclusive and theologically diverse. Since it had begun the process of integration fifty years earlier, many of its senior members were black. Harrington had first preached about racism being a "white problem" in 1946. The chair of its Board, Cornelius McDougald, was an established figure in Harlem and chair of the UUA Commission on Religion and Race. This was not tokenism. Both Harrington and McDougald were smart and savvy, and neither was out of touch with what Black Power meant; nor was Harrington unsympathetic, as his sermon "What's the Matter with Black Power?" showed.

But the Emergency Conference at the Biltmore Hotel in October 1967 had shocked both men. Harrington had a long history of collaborating with Homer Jack and naturally followed his lead. Their relationship had begun in 1941, the year Jack entered Meadville Lombard Theological School and Harrington began his ministry at Beverly Unitarian Church on Chicago's South Side. As pacifists, civil rights and peace activists, and anti-Communists, they naturally found that their concerns overlapped.

As anti-Communists, Jack and Harrington were both part of the group that had orchestrated the departure of Stephen Fritchman from his position as editor of the *Christian Register*. In a 1953 letter to Fritchman, Jack wrote, "Do you think I have opposed you in the denomination, and outside, all these years just for fun? I feel your communism, and I use the word carefully, is hurting Unitarianism, America, world peace, and all humanity. As such, I have no inhibitions whatsoever to oppose you in any context."[199] Harrington's sentiments were the same; indeed, Fritchman alleged that Harrington gave the FBI the materials that Fritchman was questioned about when he was called before the House Un-American Activities Committee.

In regard to the Emergency Conference, Jack advised Harrington that it was wise to follow the young people, and at first he did. Harrington was also extremely busy during the fall of 1967 with the New York State Constitutional Convention. Meanwhile McDougald, as chair of the Commission on Religion and Race, chaired the Emergency Conference. From the beginning, an attempt was made to accommodate the emergence of the Black Caucus. A Steering Committee was established and empowered to make adjustments as necessary. Again McDougald was chair, and the Committee was careful to include Louis Gothard, the chair of Black Unitarians for Radical Reform. But Gothard skipped the meetings.

When time finally permitted, McDougald joined the Caucus meeting. As chair of the entire event, however, he was juggling many demands on his time. After a while, he excused himself to go to an event he was hosting. At this point, one of the BURR leaders challenged him, declaring that he would have to choose who to be with. McDougald never returned.

Afterward, Harrington blamed the debacle on Homer Jack. "I think [Jack] suspected the plan to immediately polarize the conference racially, but he didn't warn McDougald, who would have refused to chair it, had he known. [McDougald] felt he had been used, and betrayed. We both had been! We had been maneuvered into having to make a choice between race and democratic process. We both refused. But it was very unpleasant."[200]

As soon as the Emergency Conference concluded, the Commission on Religion and Race met. McDougald was there, as was Ben Scott, a member of the Caucus's Steering Committee. Tired and quarrelsome, the group wasn't ready to do business.

McDougald later told Harrington he was "disgusted" and would not attend the next General Assembly. Indeed, he thought that Community shouldn't send anyone; he felt the Unitarian Universalist Association "was going the way of separatism which would turn out to be only another kind of segregation, self-segregation."[201]

Two weeks after the Emergency Conference, McDougald received a letter from Clifton Hoffman, the Southeast District district executive, expressing his admiration and urging him not to resign as chair of the Commission on Religion and Race.

Around the same time, Harrington heard that Rev. Donald McKinney, his colleague at the First Unitarian Church of Brooklyn, had expressed support for the Black Caucus. Harrington called him to inquire if this was true, and McKinney shared his enthusiastic support. "Enlightening" him, Harrington was unequivocal in saying he would do all he could to stop this "radical, dangerously divisive perversion of our honored commitment to an integrated approach to full equality and racial justice."[202]

On November 2, 1967, Kenneth Clark, the African American Community Church member whom Homer Jack had consulted after the Emergency Conference, wrote a letter that was published in *Readout* and later in the *Register-Leader* under the title "Racism for the UUA?" It was widely circulated. On February 18, the Sunday prior to the Chicago meeting, excerpts from Clark's letter appeared in the *Community News*, Community Church's newsletter. The introduction to the piece said, "Some of the black Unitarian Universalists are making every effort to set up a separate movement." This was an exaggeration. A couple of people had suggested breaking off, and there was fanciful speculation about entering a discussion with black Methodist, Lutheran, and United Church of Christ members (i.e., those in predominantly white denominations) about forming a United Black Church, but the claim was not true for the vast majority of African American Unitarian Universalists. It was alarmist and reinforced by Clark's assertion that "the demands made by the Black Caucus are a specific manifestation of a new racist thrust."[203]

The following week, as African American Unitarian Universalists gathered in Chicago, Harrington shared an editorial from the NAACP *Crisis* magazine that took aim at the National Conference on New Politics that had taken place in Chicago. Calling that conference misguided, the *Crisis* editorial maintained, "Had these same proposals been advanced by any group other than Negro, these liberals would have disdained to consider them. In ratifying [them] these particular white liberals reveal themselves for what they really are—patronizers of black folks."[204]

McDougald did not travel to Chicago for the black Unitarian Universalist gathering at the Windermere, but one Community Church member who did returned enthusiastic. Although she tried, Winnifred Norman could not sway Harrington or McDougald. For his part, Harrington found her disagreement with him unacceptable, and he let her know it. She would eventually leave Community Church, but she did not let herself be run out of Unitarian Universalism and went on be elected to the Board of Trustees of the Unitarian Universalist Association.

There was a short-lived effort to form a black caucus within Community Church. A meeting was called to plan the effort, chaired by Bob Grier, who had married a German woman while in the army. Harrington recalled, "We met at [Grier's] apartment. Right at the outset, Clayton Flowers, a Black married to a White, said that only the Blacks could speak or vote, or officially attend the meeting. Bob said, 'Clayton, do you mean that my wife and your wife cannot take part in this, or any of our work?' Clayton said, 'Yes. They are not African.' 'In that case,' Bob said, 'you're looking for a new chairman! I want no part of this!' "[205]

Maude Jenkins, a longtime African American Board member of Community, said that they had to straighten Harrington out when they saw him tilting toward Black Power. The actions he took later never reflected only his opinion; as the matter evolved, he was taking his lead from his members, both black and white. The position of Jeannette Hopkins was clear. She had chaired one of the commissions of the Emergency Conference; she was the one who called it a charade and left in protest. Harrington knew where Kenneth Clark and McDougald stood, but Norman and Flowers, who'd been at both the Emergency Conference at the Biltmore and the black gathering in Chicago, saw things differently. Nowhere was the generational divide within the black community more evident than in Community Church, with its deep and long-standing ties to the black community.

On April 23, 1968, in response to a letter and Harrington's "Minister's Corner" column in the church newsletter, Homer Jack wrote Harrington to defend the Black Caucus. Answering a point Harrington had raised about democratic process, Jack asked rhetorically, "Isn't it interesting that no other group of Blacks in our denomination has organized since October to speak against the Caucus?"

Harrington may have taken that as a challenge. His April 26 reply to Jack proposed forming an organization of "Blacks and Whites Together, for a radical program." Jack responded that he saw BUUC and FULLBAC as an example of "working closely together." This was not what Harrington had in mind, and the next day he wrote back, asking Jack to send materials for a meeting to be held May 3–5, and also for a description of exactly what the UUA had done to promote integration in its congregations. This last was necessary, he explained, because some at Community did not trust Jack or the Social Action Department, feeling they had done too little in this regard.[206]

With General Assembly approaching, the Community Church Board called a special congregational meeting for May 12, to consider the position of the church on the Black Caucus and Black Affairs Council, and whether it should recognize an official Black Caucus in the Unitarian Universalist Association. Seventy members attended, and the meeting ran for three hours. Harrington recalled,

> A white member, Chairman of our Social Action Committee, stood up and suggested that the congregation divide into two groups, one Black one White, and talk for ten minutes to each

other, and then come back together and tell each other what we had said.... One of our Black members, Thomas V. Challenger, who had been a member since 1918, stood up and made a little speech in which he said ..., "I didn't join this church forty years ago in order to be segregated or to segregate myself, but to be just one human being among many.... If we are now going to separate along racial lines in this church, I am going out that door and I will never come back again.... That settled that.... The church members simply were not willing to turn their back on all those years of fellowship with each other."[207]

The following motions were made and voted upon in the meeting, as recorded in the church newsletter:

1. The Community Church continues as an integrated church in *all* official activities, working together to correct *all* aspects of social inequity.
2. The alternative proposal presented by Co-Chairmen Cornelius McDougald and Donald S. Harrington for an independent denominational agency in which those Black and White Unitarian Universalists who desire to pursue a radical program of action for equality within the Unitarian Universalist Church and our American society at large can work together as equals be accepted. (7 members opposed)
3. Delegates would continue to have freedom of vote at the General Assembly.
4. The congregation officially opposes recognition of the Black Affairs Council, responsible to the Black Caucus, as an affiliate of the UUA. (40 in favor, 7 opposed, 8 abstentions)[208]

The Community Church members who tried to form a black caucus protested being shut out, and led by Hayward Henry, they picketed the church before a Sunday service.[209] After the service started, they marched in and occupied a row. They remained seated when the congregation stood for the hymn, and after about ten minutes they marched out again. Harrington said, "That was the last we heard of BUUC-BAC or FULLBAC at Community Church."[210] Winnifred Norman found that she was left out of activities she had once been included in, was no longer asked to represent the church, and was cold-shouldered by other members who would speak with her only surreptitiously. She left the church and became a member of the Fourth Universalist Society of New York.

Black and White Action (BAWA) was born at the Community Church of New York in May 1968.[211] Its founding was an effort to affirm the congregation's understanding of itself as the Church Universal, its long-standing commitment to racial equality, and its decades of relationship building. In August 1967, the First Unitarian Church of Los Angeles had been the birthplace of BURR, which reflected Fritchman's outspoken, left-leaning radicalism; the devastation of Watts; and an emerging black consciousness and militancy. Situated in two great American urban centers that were themselves iconic, both congregations had large memberships—among the largest in the Unitarian Universalist Association. Their buildings were imposing, with worship spaces more like auditoriums than traditional sanctuaries. Both congregations had been established in the nineteenth century and had long-tenured senior ministers; Fritchman and Harrington had held their positions for more than twenty years. They were twelve years apart in age; Fritchman was in his prime, while Harrington had entered his during the Second World War. Like their congregations, these two ministers were in many ways alike—tall, imposing, self-possessed white men who cared deeply about the institutional church and felt it important that it embrace people of different races and ethnic origins.

Indeed, they had dedicated themselves to this effort since the forties and had been crusaders for racial justice.

Both were also unwilling to set aside long-standing animosity.

Both were well connected and well known in their communities, and both were forces within the Unitarian Universalist Association. They were also opinionated orators with forceful styles and outsized egos who often felt compelled to battle for principle whatever the cost. Among their church members, both had a reputation for being hard on their associates. Members of Community pointed to the high turnover of associate ministers[212] and Fritchman, himself, wrote, "of the difficulty of any man or woman to work with me without great tolerance and patience... previous associates and secretaries... can testify to this..."[213] Their relationship to members was different. Harrington was pastoral, stood up for his people and, in general, was supportive of their efforts; Fritchman was described as warm and friendly. However both, displaying the paternalism of that era, called the shots, possessed little humility, and shared a fatal flaw—unyielding moral certitude.

Indeed, Fritchman's self-regard was such that when he reviewed his papers in writing his memoir, *Heretic: A Partisan Autobiography*, he said he found nothing he would recant. But the claim in his memoir that the Los Angeles church had a higher percentage of non-whites than any Unitarian Universalist church in the country except First Chicago was not true. Community Church had more African American members in absolute numbers and percentage, and percentage-wise, so did All Souls First Universalist in Chicago. Since Community stature, in this regard, was widely known and undisputed, Fritchman's omission had to have been a conscious one.

In the month leading up to the Emergency Conference, another of their clashes was on display in the May edition of the *Christian Register*. Harrington had earlier published an article in which he had offered a defense of Christian terminology (words like *prayer*, *grace*, and *salvation*). Now Fritchman struck back under the heading "Are Unitarians Christian?," a question he answered with a definitive "No." Harrington had asked that Unitarian Universalists not be captives of "religious literalism"; Fritchman called this "doubletalk."

The ongoing conflict between these Unitarian Universalist titans raises questions: What role did personality play in the denominational upheaval? How much was the conflict about principle and how much due to a personality style that manifested itself in displays of posturing and a sense of prerogative, verbal aggression in defense of honor, and relationships sacrificed to principle? Other key figures in the conflict, both black and white, were of the same mold. How much did this exacerbate tension and ill will, and thus amplify the polarization?

The Cleveland General Assembly and Its Aftermath

[*May–December 1968*]

IN MAY 1968, at the Unitarian Universalist General Assembly in Cleveland, delegates voted to recognize the Black Affairs Council and to give it $1 million over a period of four years. This is what the Black Caucus had proposed during the Emergency Conference in October 1967. As they had in Selma, enough Unitarian Universalists proved themselves to be stalwart allies that the denomination briefly placed itself in the forefront of religious communities' response to the crisis in urban America.

"We Shall Wrestle with Many Problems"

In the three months between the founding of the Black Unitarian Universalist Caucus in Chicago and General Assembly in Cleveland, some Unitarian Universalists found themselves wrestling with their feelings and moral principles, while those who had made up their minds organized.

In March, Rev. Bob Zoerheide, minister of Cedar Lane Unitarian Church in Bethesda, Maryland, preached a sermon entitled "Black Power and the White Liberal." In it he struggled with how he and the congregation should respond:

I know that as a white minister I have brought but a molehill of civil rights activity to the mountainous problems of racial discrimination in our society and in our church life. I must determine, as you must, I believe, how far special privilege for exceptional grievances of the black community can go with my support, and, I hope, with yours, without jeopardy to our organizing principles of democracy. We need to take a new look, as we safeguard our principles, and we try to act responsibly toward black power.[214]

By mid-April, FULLBAC had an initial list of sponsors and had begun distributing materials. Its flyers were headed "Cleveland and Beyond—A Summons to Unitarian Universalists" and called for recognizing and fully funding BAC's activities. Its supporters included those engaged in urban ministry: Kim Beach, Duke Gray, Ron Engel, Jim Hobart, and Neil Shadle; the ministers in the Philadelphia area: Rudi Gelsey, Victor Carpenter, and David Parke; Harrington's junior colleague Dick Leonard; Stephen Fritchman and Roy Ockert; Leona Light, the executive secretary of SOBURR; Homer Jack and Unitarian Universalist Association district executives Theodore Webb and Orloff Miller; James Luther Adams, the foremost Unitarian Universalist theologian; Malcolm Sutherland, the president of Meadville Lombard Theological School; and Harry Scholefield, the minister of the First Unitarian Church of San Francisco and presumptive candidate in the 1969 UUA presidential election. The list would grow to a thousand names.

Impressive as the original list was, there was a notable absence. It included almost no ministers of note who had been Universalists. Indeed, the former general superintendent of the Universalist Church of America, Phil Giles, was outspoken in his opposition to BAC and BUUC. There were many dynamics at work seeding Universalists' ambivalence, and their complexity defies a simple answer, but it had as much to do with the feeling of buyers' remorse following the Universalists' consolidation with the Unitarians (which we will explore later) as it did with creating a Black Affairs Council.

In early May, with General Assembly bearing down upon them, BUUC and FULLBAC continued to line up endorsements, while others agonized over the decision that lay ahead.

Rev. John Wolfe, the white minister of All Souls Unitarian Church of Tulsa, shared his struggle in a sermon entitled "Black Power Comes to Unitarianism." "I am forced to choose between two rights ... democratic procedure ... [and] the redress of grievances of an oppressed minority," he said. At GA, the Black Caucus would present proposals that he considered "in effect an ultimatum." "My reaction again and again has been to say that this is not Black Power, this is Black Fascism." He quoted Martin Luther King's words about those "more devoted to order than justice." "I have finally decided," he said, "that it is not a question of right against wrong or of right against right, the issue is wrong against wrong." Coming to his conclusion, he said, "I have weighed the wrongs—wrong against wrong—and there being no other choices left I have decided to change my former position and to vote for the Black Affairs Council."[215]

The political maneuvering accelerated. In mid-May, Greeley met Ann Raynolds at the Harvard Club in New York City. She was co-chair of FULLBAC with Meldelsohn, Parke, and Light. The tone of the letter he sent her afterward suggests it was a testy exchange:

> I am almost conscientiously unable to withhold from the Southern Leadership Conference and other groups our moral support, which the Black Caucus seems to request us to withhold.
>
> I want us to support the Black Affairs Council as generously and vigorously as we can and the whole cause that it represents;

but if my ears serve me adequately, Hayward Henry and others have said in my presence many times that they desire or demand a kind of exclusive right which it seems to me we cannot grant. I had some question at the very outset about the Black Caucus and some of my close associates persuaded me to buy the idea on the basis of our pluralism denominationally—and that seemed right—but how can we now deny that pluralism and concur with the thought that only the Black Caucus knows the answers or can give us the answers as to how to deal with the urban situation or the race questions?[216]

Four days later, Greeley heard from black Unitarian Universalist Association Board member Wade McCree. "I have your letter about the meeting with representatives of the BAC and FULLBAC and I, too, regret that I could not be with you," McCree wrote. "As sympathetic as I am and as much as I am identified with the expressed goal of the BAC representatives to eradicate racism from our Association and the great society of which it is a part, I cannot approve their vehicle of a racially exclusive body within our institutional framework.... I feel so deeply about this that I am seriously considering resignation as I would feel obliged to in the event of action by the board to establish a White Affairs Council."[217]

Alfred Weissbard, white president of the First Unitarian Society of Albany, also opposed BAC. Throughout that spring, he returned to the issue in his weekly newsletter column. Where he and the congregation stood on racial justice is clear. The congregation had a close relationship with local black activists, the Brothers. Congregation members had marched with them, and Brothers had taught in the church school, worked with the youth group, and spoken in the church and in nearby Schenectady. The congregation's minister, Nick Cardell, supported BAC, but Weissbard could not be persuaded. "I will oppose the resolution in Cleveland," he said, "because

I don't think we can afford the luxury of kidding ourselves.... A million [dollars] won't solve the Black man's problems."[218]

For months, congregations and districts had been sending letters to the Unitarian Universalist Association endorsing BAC. A resolution passed at the May Pacific Southwest District annual meeting by a vote of 102 to 8, with 10 abstentions, called for the Association to recognize BAC and guarantee it $300 thousand a year for four years. The First Unitarian Church of Louisville also sent a resolution to the Association in support of BAC, proposing that it be given $250 thousand a year for four years, to be raised as the Association thought appropriate. The Louisville vote was closer, however: 33 for, 19 against, and 8 abstentions.

As required by the UUA's bylaws, a parish poll was carried out to determine what general resolutions should be considered by the General Assembly. A resolution on the war in Vietnam topped the list. With a weighting of 2,455, it surpassed the 2,070 for "Black Self Determination and Racism." Close behind that was "Equal Opportunity in Housing," at 1,974; this was a concern that had been part of the Consensus on Racial Justice adopted in 1966. It was followed by "Right of Dissent/Peaceful Protest" and "Abortion," at 1,797 and 1,670 respectively.

When the Unitarian Universalist Association Board convened on Thursday, May 23, prior to the opening of GA, the first item on its agenda was a resolution on draft resistance. The second was a report on the Arlington Street Church, which had become a sanctuary congregation and been raided by U.S. marshals to arrest a draft resister. Then after some housekeeping items, another war-related endorsement was discussed. The issues that had significant financial impact, including support for BAC, were last on the agenda of a marathon meeting that began at 2 PM and did not end until after 2 AM. And in the end, the Board's position on BAC changed only slightly. It rescinded its earlier proposal to form a Commission for Action on Race and made a minor adjustment to the financial offer.[219]

That Vietnam ranked so highly in the parish poll and came first on the Unitarian Universalist Association's Board agenda was not surprising. The North Vietnamese Tet offensive had begun in January, the My Lai Massacre took place in February, President Johnson decided in March that he would not run for another term, and the Paris peace talks began on May 10. These developments pushed BAC and the Association's financial problems, for which the Board had no good solutions, to the back of the agenda, and as the Assembly began they were still unresolved.

In the introduction to the program guide for the Seventh Annual General Assembly, Dana McLean Greeley foretold that the "Assembly is bound to be controversial ..." and that "We shall wrestle with many problems through these days and nights."[220] So it was to be.

One Million Dollars

The seventh General Assembly began on Thursday, May 23, and ran until May 30. It drew 1,350 delegates—the highest attendance ever—from 364 Unitarian Universalist societies representing about a thousand congregations and 175 thousand adult members. About 8 percent of the delegates were African American, a little more than a hundred of an estimated 1,500–1,750 black Unitarian Universalists.

Many Unitarian Universalists, particularly New Englanders, were shocked at the number of African Americans who came as delegates. A few white delegates asked whether they were interlopers "trying to *use* the denomination and its funds."[221] As this question was murmured and spread, it suggested to many that black Unitarian Universalists were outsiders and recent arrivals. This misapprehension could thrive because of the long-standing blindness of the American Unitarian Association, the Universalist Church of America, and their successor, the Unitarian Universalist Association. They had disseminated almost no representations of African American religious liberals. There were few religious education materials, no worship materials reflective of the black cultural experience, and no scholarship that explored African American involvement in the movement. Regardless of which side delegates took in regard to BAC, few knew any of the long history of black involvement in Unitarianism and Universalism.

From the beginning, black founders and leaders were making their mark on Unitarianism and Universalism.

- (1785) Gloster Dalton, a black man who had been born in Africa, was a signatory at the founding of John Murray's Universalist congregation in Gloucester.
- (1801) Amy Scott was one of the incorporators of the First Universalist Society of Philadelphia.
- (1860) Rev. William Jackson testified to his conversion to Unitarianism at the fall conference of the American Unitarian Association in Bedford, Massachusetts, but was turned away.
- (1871) Six years after the founding of the National Unitarian Conference, Peter H. Clark attended, representing the First Congregational Unitarian Church of Cincinnati.
- (1887) John Bird Wilkins founded the People's Temple Church (Colored Unitarian) in Chicago.
- (1892) Joseph Jordan founded a Universalist Church in Norfolk, Virginia.

- (1908) Lewis Latimer was a founder of the Unitarian Church of Flushing, New York.
- (1908) Rev. Powhatan Bagnall was granted fellowship by the AUA and established a community ministry to "colored people" in Greater Boston.
- (1920) Rev. Ethelred Brown founded the Harlem Unitarian Church.
- (1932) In Cincinnati, William H. G. Carter founded the Church of the Unitarian Brotherhood.
- (1948) Lewis A. and Marcella Walker McGee helped to found the predominantly African American Free Religious Fellowship on South Side Chicago and Lewis McGee served as its first minister.
- (1955) James Cunningham, MD, was the founding president of a fellowship in Sitka, Alaska.
- (1956) Errold D. Collymore was elected to the American Unitarian Association Board.
- (1960) Sylvia Lyons Render was a founding member of the Eno River congregation and first secretary of its Board.

In the nineteenth century, there were several prominent African American Unitarian abolitionists; for nearly a hundred years, a black Universalist mission existed in Suffolk, Virginia; in 1956, 10 percent of Unitarian congregations had African Americans in positions of leadership. By the sixties, nearly two dozen urban UU congregations had substantial numbers of African American members and leaders, and these numbers had been growing since the forties.

Why did no one know? Would knowing have changed what happened? Unitarian Universalists' embrace of white cultural hegemony led them to assume there was nothing to know. Their ignorance had consequences, and as they debated the future, most did so without any sense of the past.

The opening Business Session of the Assembly took place on Friday morning, May 24, and that afternoon, the debate on the UUA's response to BAC's proposals began with reports.[222] The Board presented its position; Hayward Henry spoke for BAC, David Parke for FULLBAC, and Cornelius McDougald and Donald Harrington for BAWA.

At that point, Black and White Action was nothing more than its co-chairs Harrington and McDougald, its recognition by the Community Church of New York, and a circular, sent out two weeks prior to General Assembly, that outlined the purpose and program of what was initially called "Unitarian Universalists for a Black and White Alternative." The flyer proposed a program of action for equality in which blacks and whites would work together. Its goals were modest and focused on both the Unitarian Universalist Association and American society. Once General Assembly began, an ad hoc committee was formed and BAWA scrambled to get organized.

Glover Barnes, an African American microbiologist at the University of Buffalo Medical School, had earlier been asked to support BAC, and he had introduced such a resolution at the annual meeting of the St. Lawrence District. Once he saw how things stood in Cleveland, he began to feel he had been misled by the member of BAC who had originally approached him. His anxiety changed to indignation when he was told that his white wife was not welcome at BUUC meetings "unless she declare herself black." He went to McDougald and Harrington with his concern, and they asked him to take a lead role in BAWA.[223] Soon afterward, Max Gaebler, the minister in Madison, appeared at the ad hoc meeting of several hundred BAWA supporters. He said he was "commandeered" and asked if he would serve as co-chair with Barnes.[224]

Gaebler said he soon realized that BAWA was "ill-equipped to oppose the discipline" of BUUC. He had run into a colleague and friend of long standing who was supporting BAC. After a brief conversation in which they tried to find common ground, his friend said, "I should not be having this conversation with you. We've been told to maintain a tight common front, no individual talks."[225] Indeed, a memo had circulated to BUUC members emphasizing internal discipline, loyalty, and the need for unity; in the same vein, FULLBAC had tried to exclude all non-FULLBAC members from its meeting in Cleveland.[226]

When BAWA's proposal was added to the business meeting agenda, BAC felt betrayed. It wanted its proposal to be considered on its own merit and not in competition with others. It was predictable that alternative resolutions would emerge, so what was behind BAC's expectation? This was parallel to BAC expecting the UUA Board to vote on its proposal when it met with them in November. Did inflated expectations serve a strategic purpose? Did frustration help fuel indignation? Why decry a pluralistic approach given that pluralism had buttressed BAC's argument that it be given a chance in the first place? Indeed, BAC's appeal to UU pluralism had helped convince Greeley. Dismissing pluralism now suggested that its original appeal was tactical, a way of gaining leverage rather than a sincere belief.

BAC's indignation seems overblown. Signs of ambivalence and resistance were readily apparent. As to the UUA Board making space for BAWA on its agenda and working it into a subsequent proposal, it was unlikely that the Board would ignore overtures from Harrington, minister of the UUA's largest congregation and someone who had known Greeley since they were youth; McDougald, the former chair of the Commission of Religion and Race; and Gaebler, the founding director of the UUA Department of Overseas and Interfaith Relations.

• • •

ON FRIDAY EVENING OF MAY 24, the Honorable Carl B. Stokes, the first African American mayor of the city of Cleveland, was the Ware Lecturer. Quoting from Martin Luther King Jr.'s address two years earlier, he said, "There is nothing more tragic than sleeping through a revolution.... An old order is passing away and a new order is coming into being."[227]

Meeting on Sunday morning, May 26, while Assembly participants attended the five local Unitarian Universalist congregations, the Association Board met and once again tried to come up with a proposal that responded to BAC's demands while accommodating BAWA. It remained hesitant about giving BAC what they wanted. Supporters of BAWA were arguing that BAC was separatist, while BAC, it would turn out, was tacitly seeking the exclusive right to set the Association's racial agenda to the exclusion of BAWA. In doing that it had to backtrack on affirming pluralism in the context of black liberation. This undermined relationships in which the trust level was already low. Moreover, there was no room to negotiate, since BAC/BUUC was unwilling to entertain a compromise; given the momentum of the Assembly, they did not need to.

When the Assembly Business Session resumed at 2 PM, Hayward Henry spoke for BUUC: "We have missed a very simple question and it is: Who will the Black community follow—those who believe in its own participation and right to self-determination as our caucus have attempted to investigate or those who offer paternalism?"[228] Everyone agreed that he was a gifted orator. Norma Poinsett's observation that "he was one of the brightest people"[229] she had ever met was echoed by Rev. Vincent Silliman, who wrote home that he was an "outstanding person—very young—black—brilliant."[230] Fritchman called him a "magnetic, forceful leader."[231]

"He just swept everybody off their feet," said Miriam Barnes, wife of BAWA co-chair Glover Barnes.[232]

A tempestuous debate over BAC's proposal lasted four hours. Marcia McBroom, a college student who was raised in Community Church, spoke about her pride in being a black woman and added, "People have never been known to start accepting and respecting each other before they know each other so if we don't make up our minds that we are going to start working together as Americans with a common goal we will drive each other to irrevocable alienation and eventual destruction."[233]

People's positions shifted. Jeffrey Campbell, who had been on the fence, declared, "A magnificent alchemy is at work here. The quality of confrontation is great. It can be a rebirth of this denomination if rooted in the experience of BAC.... Churches do not mature until they face the opportunity before them."[234]

The issue of where to find the $1 million to be given to BAC over four years was raised but not reported upon in *UUA Now*, nor did the magazine mention how dire the Unitarian Universalist Association's financial situation was. Bob West said the Board did not reveal the difficulties to the Assembly, and that those who suggested finances as a reason for voting no "were considered to be against the high ideals of an admirable cause."[235] The numbers that backed the argument for caution were available in the complete treasurer's report that was provided to the attendees. However, the way they were presented was misleading. Instead of separating out the restricted endowment from the unrestricted and giving separate totals for each, the report listed their sum as the bottom-line total—the number to which one's attention naturally goes. So even though the unrestricted total was inadequate to cover the expenses to which General Assembly was about to commit, the consolidated bottom line made it appear that the Association had several million dollars readily available.²³⁶ The reality was that there was no way to fund the $250 thousand a year for BAC, much less the additional hundreds of thousands voted to support the Unitarian Universalist theological schools and the Association's districts, without increasing the deficit.

That Sunday, as afternoon turned to evening and the end of the Assembly Business Session approached, two final arguments were made. James Luther Adams was passed up to the head of the line at the "pro" microphone. He argued that BAC "has sensitized this denomination so it can march into a new period of American history."²³⁷

Meanwhile, Greeley came down off the dais and was being passed to the "con" microphone when a twenty-eight-year-old colleague, Gordon Gibson, walked up to him and said, "My God, Dana, you have spoken on this three or four times. We know what you have to say. Why don't you let somebody else talk?" Gibson recounted that the response of the normally unflappable Greeley, whose magnanimity was legend, was to shove him out of the way. Gibson said, "It was painful having that level of antagonistic energy in that room."²³⁸ Meanwhile Greeley made his final appeal, saying, "I cannot believe that BAC is the one route for redemption" and calling for the recognition of both BAC and BAWA.²³⁹

When the vote on BAC's proposal was taken, it was 836 for and 327 against, and the Assembly erupted in cheers and rejoicing. When the noise died down, Henry led them in singing "We Shall Overcome."

BAWA supporters did not walk out, as they had threatened, but some were disheartened. Harrington and most of the Community Church delegation returned to New York before the end of the Assembly. Harrington charged that the Unitarian Universalist Association was being used by a "small extremist black minority," and Barnes said the decision was "injustice and a tragedy," and that a "racially exclusive caucus" had violated the Association's "commitment to the brotherhood of man."[240] In Cleveland, however, the remaining delegates who supported BAWA got down to work. They changed the meaning of the second "A" in BAWA from "Alternative" to "Action" in an effort to cease defining itself in opposition to BAC, elected officers, collected contributions, scheduled a meeting of the Board, and left General Assembly energized.

Alfred Weissbard, who came from Albany to vote no, voted yes in the end; once home, he struggled to explain his change of heart in his church newsletter column:

> When we arrived at the convention headquarters in Cleveland on Wednesday afternoon I almost immediately detected a new sense of purpose, an intoxicating fragrance, almost an *air* of wonder that one might experience when crossing the threshold to what may be a new era. This is UUA in living black and white—on the air day and night.
>
> I tried to fight it. As many of you know, I have been upset for months by what I had been reading about the Black Caucus. The many attempts . . . to change my position didn't sway me. I didn't (and still don't) buy many of the "guilty white conscience" and "we *owe* it to them" and "we must help them to mature" stuff. I don't swallow the "black is beautiful, white is wicked" line anymore than I'd subscribe to the KKK ideology.
>
> Why then, in spite of some reservations that I still have, did I vote with the majority to recognize and provide financial support to B.A.C.? I haven't room enough to give you all of the reasons, and there are many, but I can, I hope, give you some idea. I met and spoke with men and women whom I judge to be honest, intelligent, dedicated, inspired and dignified INDIVIDUALS. They indeed have a program—it just isn't the kind you can, at this stage, submit to a board for review and approval. They want to

bring a truly Unitarian message to the ghettos of America. They expect to have the people in the ghettoes formulate the programs. There was dialogue. There was confrontation. There was, and is, the promise of hope, of faith in the future of our denomination and of our country. I was swayed. I deliberately voted yes.

Now the denomination needs your help. You'll have to help me "put *our* money where *my* mouth was." With more love than ever—Al Weissbard[241]

For some BAC members, the rejoicing was short-lived. The black women who had remained in the background, doing the grunt work, planned a celebration of their victory. But as Betty Reid Soskin writes, that is not what happened:

The hour came for our victory party. We found ourselves sitting in small groups chatting nervously whatever nonsense came to mind as the clock ticked mercilessly on as we anxiously waited for male friends, co-conspirators, and husbands to join us. I remember the heavy unspoken feelings of embarrassment as the ice melted in the punch, the brie began to melt into formless blobs, and the icing on the brownies grew sticky and stale. Unfortunately, our men had opted for the "white" parties in other places in the hotel where the young white women they'd charmed during the week were waiting.

That evening just before leaving the conference, I participated in an encounter group session called by the emotionally-bruised women. There was a highly volatile confrontation with the men. It was one of the most intensely-charged meetings I've ever experienced. I cowered in a dark corner next to my friend, the late Henry Hampton . . . who, along with several other men, shared the outrage of the tearful sistahs. The men were petulant, defensive in the face of the brutal honesty of the women, and on an ego-centric high from their conquests. Little of value was achieved that fateful night, and it was a prelude to the many break-ups of relationships and marriages over the following decade.[242]

"Healing within the denomination will be difficult," Homer Jack said.[243] Indeed, for many the wounds never healed.

The Aftermath of Cleveland

While the seventh General Assembly was taking place in Cleveland, the Poor People's Campaign was mired in mud on the National Mall and in the politics of Washington D.C. A week after General Assembly, Senator Robert F. Kennedy was assassinated while campaigning to be the Democratic nominee for president of the United States. In August, antiwar protestors and Youth International Party members (Yippies) swept into Chicago ahead of the Democratic National Convention. In the middle of a rally, they were attacked by "Chicago's Finest," a police riot that transformed chants of "Peace now" and "Hell no, we won't go" to roars of "Fuck you, Daley" on the streets and chaos on the convention floor. It was a time of turmoil.

After the jubilation of BAC's triumph in Cleveland, Hayward Henry, speaking from the dais, offered this caution: "Let us not leave here divided; and let us not leave here with hate, because it is hard sometimes to decide what is a victory and what is a defeat."[244]

How deep was the divide?

Many Community Church delegates left Cleveland in despair. At a congregational meeting soon after General Assembly, the congregation voted to remain a member of the Unitarian Universalist Association but to reduce its contribution to the minimum necessary to retain membership.[245] It shifted its support and budgeted $7,500 for BAWA.

Delegates from Main Line Unitarian Church in Devon, Pennsylvania, also left General Assembly divided and in shock. Most were shocked that the Assembly had promised $1 million to BAC without concrete knowledge of what it would be used for and without holding BAC accountable to the Unitarian Universalist Association, while several were dismayed that some of their own had voted against granting the money.[246]

On Sunday, June 9, Ralph Helverson, the minister at First Parish in Cambridge, Massachusetts, spoke on why he had voted no and James Luther Adams spoke on why he had voted yes. The next day, Helverson wrote in his diary, "I feel that in . . . defending integration and the togetherness of the blacks and whites . . . my actions may get me in good with the conservative whites, but I may have lost the young radicals. I don't know, but I worry about it, and wonder what the future will bring."[247]

On June 13, speaking to the Unitarian Universalist Association staff, Homer Jack emphasized that from then on, BAC, supported by BUUC and FULLBAC, would be the denomination's primary "agency in race relations." He owned, "It is surely no secret that I personally feel that Black Power in our denomination is welcome, necessary, and overdue." But he went on to make a plea for pluralism and BAWA and asked that BAWA be judged by results rather than prejudged as "paternalism" or "co-optation." For the Department of Social Responsibility, the most pressing question was what its new role should be, and for that he proposed options like maintaining its relationships to the Poor People's Campaign and the National Urban Coalition or creating a task force to take action on white racism.[248]

On Sunday, June 16, Rev. Walter Donald Kring, the minister at the Unitarian Church of All Souls in New York, preached a sermon in which he expressed alarm about BAC, full support for

Harrington, and outrage that the Assembly had taken steps to change Article III of the UUA Constitution so that dues to the Unitarian Universalist Association would be assessed and mandatory.[249] The proposal to make dues mandatory proved so contentious that the UUA Board would eventually vote not to recommend it to the 1969 General Assembly.

On June 21, the Board met and admitted both BAC and BAWA into affiliate status. In the case of BAC, five Board members voted against and one abstained; in the case of BAWA, three abstained. The GA vote had not put the conflict to rest.

Although BAC was integrated, with three of nine member positions designated for non-blacks, admitting it to affiliate status required a review of the Unitarian Universalist Association rules by an outside legal counsel. The rules pertaining to affiliate membership that forbade segregation by race or color were accordingly amended to say that they did not "preclude those affiliates designated to benefit specific interest groups whom past exclusion from the larger society warrants organizing around a 'special interest' of race or color." The Board also appropriated $250 thousand for BAC, of which $150 thousand would be disbursed on July 1. The Board did not commit to support beyond the 1968–1969 fiscal year. BAWA received no funding.

BAC was upset by two parts of the Board motion. First, it was surprised to discover that the commitment was for only one year and would need to be revisited. Second, it objected that BAWA had also been granted affiliate membership. In responding, the Unitarian Universalist Association treasurer said that the Board, having ultimate fiduciary responsibility, had to review the entire budget and recommendations from General Assembly every year. Greeley also wrote, explaining that the Board had no basis to deny BAWA's application for affiliate status and that it interpreted the GA resolution as giving BAC the lead role in black affairs, but not an exclusive one.

On June 28, five of BAWA's officers met in New York. Reporting on the meeting in a letter to supporters, Max Gaebler said the organization's purpose was "to forward the cause of integration." Its goals were modest: to develop a leaflet outlining its purpose and program, to do a survey to discover what congregations were doing locally in regard to racial justice, and to grow its membership and contributions. It decided not to form chapters but to work through local congregations. It also foresaw working with Bob Jones, director of the Unitarian Universalist Association's Washington office, so that it could address legislative issues.[250] Turning to Jones was natural, not just because of his position but also because, since the Emergency Conference, he had been among those most opposed to BAC.

On July 16, in response to a letter from Harrington, Greeley wrote, "I trust it is not a futile hope that all of us can work together effectively in the months ahead and for our own sake as well as for the sake of the program can heal the division among us." After owning that he had misgivings, he said he had come to believe that "this movement represents a group which is striving for self-identity and self-realization and ultimately for a kind of integration in which you and I both believe."[251]

In September 1968, Donald Harrington and Walter Kring exchanged pulpits for the first time in either of their long pastorates. It was the first such exchange between Community Church and All Souls since 1917, when Harrington's predecessor, John Haynes Holmes, a pacifist, had withdrawn from Unitarian fellowship during the First World War.[252] For years, Harrington had exchanged pulpits with Donald McKinney, the minister of the First Unitarian Church of Brooklyn, but now that McKinney was the co-chair of FULLBAC, Harrington brought an end to that tradition.

Between May and October, BAC had met three times—in New York, Washington D.C., and Denver. Besides electing officers and establishing administrative procedures, it developed funding guidelines and began awarding grants.[253] Among the initial causes it supported were a revolving capital fund for former gang members starting small businesses, to be administered in Philadelphia by a group called Young Afro-Americans; efforts to advance community control of schools in Boston and Cincinnati; and a black labor union in San Francisco. Grantees needed to focus on unifying the black community, promoting self-determination, and developing black leadership; they also had to be ineligible for funding from government agencies or traditional grant-giving agencies. BAC relied on local black caucuses to initiate and screen programs; it met in and funded programs in cities that had strong ones. To support BUUC in this work and to help it prepare for its second annual meeting, BAC awarded BUUC a grant of $40 thousand.[254]

BAC faced several challenges. One was the number of proposals. As the only black-controlled funder in America, BAC was a groundbreaking source of support for black-developed programs. Already at its October meeting, BAC reviewed eighteen proposals. As well as awarding grants, it began seeking additional sources of funding.[255] Another challenge was responding to speaking invitations from Unitarian Universalist congregations. Following the Denver meeting, BAC and BUUC members presented at seven congregations in the Mountain Desert District, and invitations arrived from elsewhere as well. The demand for speakers was such that there was an urgent need for a speaker's bureau.[256] This educational role was an unanticipated demand on BAC's time and money, drawing the group away from its primary mandate, to serve the black community rather than the needs of white Unitarian Universalists.

Following BAC's October meeting, Richard Traylor reported,

> Many middle-class Black Unitarian Universalists are rediscovering themselves in their new attempts to relate to the grass roots. In addition, we know that we have stimulated a new level of interest and participation in the denomination generally as a result of our radical posture. We are fully aware of the fact that much of this participation is in opposition to our efforts, but at least it is the hope that even though many are not willing to concur with our position that they will be elevated to significant levels of concern and activity.[257]

. . .

FROM THE BEGINNING, BAC's most resolute white ally was Roy Ockert, the assistant minister at First Unitarian in Los Angeles. He supported BURR, alerted it to the Emergency Conference, and solicited funds so its leaders could attend. Later he organized the study group from which SOBURR emerged and authored resolutions supporting the Black Caucus's demands. It was natural that he was asked to serve as one of the three white members of BAC.

His place as a white ally was secure, but his job was not. On July 12, 1968, a letter to First Unitarian members from the congregation's president announced that Fritchman, the senior minister, found it "impossible to maintain a working relationship with our Associate Minister" and the congregation's finances were in "desperate" shape. Hence the Board had voted to immediately terminate Ockert's services.[258] The letter caused an uproar.

Three days later, in advance of a congregational meeting, Fritchman sent out a letter of his own. It opened with a confession. He wrote that it was common knowledge he was a difficult person with whom to work: "[If] Mr. Ockert can be stiff and ornery, so can I." Fritchman recognized that Ockert had given much attention to the "black rebellion" and "draft resistance," but while both of them "rejoiced in militant" activism, Fritchman's "professional ego" was hurt because Ockert had not acknowledged the fact that he had prepared the way. He also found Ockert wanting as a pastoral presence and wondered if that lack reflected his union background. Still, he admitted that, while he did not find Ockert's way of working with people acceptable, others in the church and denomination did.

Fritchman concluded, "I find I cannot tolerate a major division in our church which seems to be rising" and suggested that they all needed a "cooling off" period. Therefore, he was going out of town. "This church has fought too many battles with very real foes of progress and humanism to endure splits and antagonism within our ranks."[259]

In the end, Ockert's contract was extended until the end of 1968, and Fritchman's own ministry finished a year later when he retired. In 1972, after several years of ministry elsewhere in California, Ockert returned to union work. Indeed, several of the most high-profile white supporters of BAC would move on to new ministries—Jack Mendelsohn and Rudi Gelsey in 1969 and David Parke in 1970. Striking the balance between prophetic and pastoral ministry is a challenge, and perhaps even more so during an era when Black Power and war resistance were front and center in UU congregations and feminism and gay rights were quickly emerging concerns.

Fundraising and Other Travails

The relationship between BAC and the Unitarian Universalist Association grew more collaborative in the fall of 1968. As challenges sprang up, ad hoc administrative groups were formed and the issues addressed. Fundraising, however, became increasingly difficult due to distrust, acrimonious relationships, conflicting interests, and a lack of clarity on all sides. BAC wanted autonomy, but Dayton T. Yoder, the Association's vice president for fundraising and development, bore overall responsibility. When Henry discovered that BAWA was doing independent fundraising, he became upset, concerned that BAWA was breaking the Association's rules and diluting its ability to raise money for BAC. Yoder told him that since BAWA was an unfunded affiliate, he had no power to stop it from raising its own money.[260] When Yoder's office expressed the need for more cooperation with BAC, BUUC, and FULLBAC, Greeley brought them together and a new Task Force on the Black Affairs Council was formed.

Yoder and BAC both reported that not much came out of the Task Force's monthly meetings. The blame for that depended on which side of the divide one stood. FULLBAC member Gordon Gibson said little got done because the person the Association used "was slow, not very imaginative and on top of that was a BAWA supporter" who was not committed to raising funds for BAC.[261] Yoder said, "To induce more generous giving we needed information about interesting and useful BAC projects." But that was exactly what BAC, fearing "UUA officials would negate them," were reluctant to disclose.[262] The distrust ran deep.

A number of potential donors responded to BAC solicitations with hostile letters; at one meeting, fifty such letters were reported. BAC had to develop literature to address potential donors' concerns and sometimes send representatives to speak to them. There were also decisions to be made about approaching non-UU donors and foundations. The underlying issue, since BAC naturally insisted on maintaining its independence, was that of control of information and approach.[263]

The underlying challenge for fundraising had little to do with the UUA administration or BAC. When Al Weissbard returned to Albany and announced that, to his own surprise, he had voted to give $1 million to BAC, he warned that Unitarian Universalists would now have to "put *our* money where *my* mouth was."[264] Later, Rev. Paul Carnes felt remorse because he had not done that. "I voted in Cleveland to give the million dollars," he said. "Like a lot of Unitarian Universalists we went there and the democratic process was used in its most legalistic way. As a consequence, most of us, and I'm one of them, went home and did not do our bit to try to raise the money."[265] It was completely predictable that the Unitarian Universalists would respond to fundraising appeals for BAC with the same meager donations that had flowed into the Association's Freedom Fund. Although those who were in Cleveland felt a brief passion, most Unitarian Universalists simply were not connected enough to African Americans or informed enough about white racism to care.

Later that fall, the UUA Board's Executive Committee asked Greeley to present the Board with a program directed at white racism. He went for support to the Task Force on BAC, which formed a subcommittee to develop such a program. The mandate of the Task Force II on White Racism was to explore how the denomination should address white racism, both internally and externally. It considered developing religion education curricula, tracking the experience of black ministers, and having the Board and later the staff participate in a one- or two-day workshop on white racism. The Commission on Religion and Race had begun addressing both education and ministry in 1965, but its subsequent preoccupation with the Emergency Conference—which then led to the Commission's demise—meant these concerns were not addressed for over a year.[266] Collaboration between the UUA's administration, BAC,

BUUC, and FULLBAC seemed to be working and progress was being made, but there was an undercurrent that did not bode well.

Following the November 4 Task Force on BAC meeting, Homer Jack summarized the problem in a memo: "Within the denomination, the discussion about Black Power and BAC versus BAWA continues. Some persons on both sides are still angry, but it appears that the role of BAC is increasingly accepted.... Some individuals are still strongly pro-BAWA and the controversy is likely to continue for many more months."[267]

Prior to that meeting, Hayward Henry had written to Jack saying that while BAWA and BAC, BUUC, and FULLBAC might be able to cooperate in attacking white racism, there was a fundamental divide on the issue of black empowerment. So Henry advised against forcing the other groups to work with BAWA as he believed it would prove counterproductive.[268] Task Force on BAC meetings were filled with heated exchanges, and no action was taken. The Unitarian Universalist Association Board had made it known that it preferred for BAWA to be included but would not insist upon it.[269]

. . .

IT'S TEMPTING TO OVERSIMPLIFY what caused the tension between BAWA and BAC/BUUC by distilling it down to a conflict between Black Power and integration; it was more complex.

On October 20, 1968, while BAC was fully engaged with the Unitarian Universalist Association, Harrington preached a sermon at Community Church entitled "Is Integration Dead?" Up front, he conceded that black patience had run out and that he understood why. He also understood why, in the face of white recalcitrance, black people turned to Black Power. He decried the fact that "integration was one-directional, always Black into White." He explained why it was necessary to reconstruct black history, spread knowledge of African heritage, and reinforce a black sense of identity. And he admitted that it was painful for those who thought they "had thrown off any supposed inferiority or superiority feelings in race relationships" to find themselves confronted with what looked like a step backward into separation.

Why, then, was he opposed to BUUC?

"My primary reason for opposing the Black Unitarian Universalist Caucus tactic in the Unitarian Universalist Association," Harrington said, "was my feeling that it was an inappropriate tactic for this particular situation. The Unitarian Universalist Association is, I am sorry to say, 99.8% White. To talk about Black empowerment in this situation is almost ludicrous." He argued that, given this reality, the emphasis needed to be on integrating UU congregations and building relationships from which a deep, continuing concern for real racial equality could grow. "My plea is that we work, Black and White together, first to integrate our ... movement."[270]

What does his sermon tell us? Harrington was not opposed to Black Power in general but rather in the context of the Unitarian Universalist Association. It tells us that he saw BUUC as separatist and that he believed Unitarian Universalists should first work to integrate their congregations.

The conflict between BAWA and BAC/BUUC was, in part, over tactics and priorities. But in labeling BUUC separatist, Harrington and others had to ignore the intense collaboration that was taking place between blacks and whites in BAC, BUUC, and FULLBAC. BUUC member Harold Wilson said, "While everyone was talking about separatism, there was more honest, decent, wholesome relationship between Black People and White people than ever appeared in the church before."[271] Calling this separatism was not only inaccurate; it was misleading. But earlier comments by James Carter and

Jerry Jones about breaking away from the Unitarian Universalist Association had fed this anxiety.

The truth was that the primary focus of each group was different. BAWA saw its constituency as the whole denomination and its goal as the denomination's transformation. BAC's goal was to address the needs of a black community that was in distress, not those of white Unitarian Universalists. Indeed, requests from Unitarian Universalist congregations were proving to be a diversion from its purpose.

Hayward Henry conceded that both had a common interest in attacking white racism. The minutes of the white racism task force noted that BAWA was working with the Department of Ministry. Clearly, a faction on the Unitarian Universalist Association Board wanted to have BAWA involved. BAC had appealed to pluralism when it wanted a seat at the table, only to argue against a diversity of approaches once it was largely in control of the UUA's racial agenda. BAC saw the granting of affiliate status to BAWA as a betrayal of the General Assembly's intention and a means of undermining BAC, and it protested the Board's action. The fact that BAC blocked BAWA at every occasion only served to strengthen the latter's resolve.

BAC and BAWA each felt that the other was blocking it, and so the frustration and anger grew. BAC felt BAWA was "insincere" and was spreading negative and untrue claims about BAC, misinformation it then had to counter. BAWA felt BAC was not honoring the Unitarian Universalist pluralism it had appealed to in establishing its own legitimacy. Moreover, BAWA felt that injustice had prevailed after it was politically outmaneuvered in Cleveland. Finding itself shut out of Unitarian Universalist Association committees verified for BAWA BAC's undemocratic tendencies and validated its mistrust. Each felt called to defend its principles against an adversary that was making false claims to delegitimize its position. As the battle continued, the inflated rhetoric left each feeling that its integrity and goodness were being impugned.

The Way Forward

In regard to race, there were several signs that the Unitarian Universalist Association was entering a process of transformation and institutional reform.

On July 4, 1968, John Hendrik Clarke's *William Styron's Nat Turner: Ten Black Writers Respond* was released by Beacon Press. Beacon was on the leading edge of progressivism in the Unitarian Universalist Association and in the country at large, as it had been since Mel Arnold became its editor in 1946. Among the books Beacon published in these years by African Americans or about their concerns were King's *Where Do We Go from Here: Chaos or Community?* (1967); Arnold Schuchter's *White Power, Black Freedom* (1968); John Hope Franklin's *Color and Race* (1968); Arna Bontemps's *Great Slave Narratives* (1969); Joseph Washington's *Black and White: Power Subreption* (1969); and *The Coming of the Black Man* (1969), by BAC member Benjamin Scott. One of BAC's initial demands, made during the 1967 Emergency Conference, was for more black authors. Considering the number of books published, two questions arise: How much was BAC's demand based in feeling and impression rather than fact? Or given that it urged Beacon to cooperate with CORE, was it seeking to promote a more radical ideological bent?

In August 1968, a number of newly graduated black seminary students were settled. Renford G. Gaines, who had just graduated from Meadville Lombard Theological School, was settled as the minister of the Unitarian Universalist Church of Urbana-Champaign. Harold A. Wilson, who had just graduated from Starr King School for the Ministry, was settled as the associate minister at Mt. Diablo Unitarian Universalist Church in Walnut Creek, California. And Thomas E. Payne, with a BD from the Howard University School of Divinity, was working part-time as an assistant to Dana Greeley while pursuing a graduate degree at Harvard Divinity School. John Frazier, having graduated from Crane Theological School, was studying at Cambridge University, supported by a scholarship provided by the First Unitarian Congregation of Ottawa.

At the November 1968 Unitarian Universalist Association Board meeting, the decision was made to purchase $10 thousand in M-REIT (Mutual Real Estate Investment Trust) shares, in "symbolic support of racial integration."[272] M-REIT was among the first corporations to develop integrated housing.[273] Among the members of its Advisory Committee were Unitarian Universalists Donald Harrington, Homer Jack, Whitney M. Young Jr., and Senator Joseph S. Clark Jr.; among the institutions that had invested were the Arlington Street Church in Boston; the Community Church of New York; First Unitarian of Los Angeles; Mt. Diablo Unitarian Universalist Church in Walnut Creek, California; North Shore Unitarian Universalist Society in Plandome, New York; Meadville Lombard; and Starr King. These were the people and institutions that one would expect to be involved. However, Unitarian involvement went back to 1959, when M-REIT founder Morris Milgram had tried to build integrated housing in all-white Deerfield, Illinois, and been blocked by the township.[274] Subsequent efforts, however, did succeed, and across the country, M-REIT went on to build and manage integrated housing for twenty thousand people.

During that same Unitarian Universalist Association Board meeting, five African Americans were placed on three UUA committees. Renford Gaines sat on the Division of Communication and Publications Advisory Committee, Dr. Charles Pinderhughes and Thomas E. Payne on the Social Responsibility Advisory Committee, and Dalmas A. Taylor and William R. Jones on the Advisory Committee for the Association's office in Washington D.C. At the next meeting, Vincent Harding was voted onto the Beacon Press Board.

Among the Unitarian Universalist Association staff, however, after Henry Hampton resigned from his position to found Blackside, Inc., a film production company, there were no African Americans filling management positions. In June 1969, BAC wrote a letter to Greeley inquiring about equity in staffing. In his response, Greeley confessed, "We do not have anywhere near as many as we ought to have or as I would like to have." He went on to say that a black man had turned them down for an executive position; Payne was working part-time for Greeley; and Thomas Haley was the part time social responsibility officer for the Canadian Unitarian Council in Ottawa. Also, he said, the Unitarian Universalist Association employed three African Americans as janitors and six as secretaries, not one in each role as BAC had understood.[275]

Progress on employment equity and growth of black membership within the Unitarian Universalist Association was modest and faltering, in part because following normal departmental practices led to squandered opportunities. In December 1968, for instance, Cliff Hoffman, the district executive for the Southeast District, sent a polite reply to Dr. Amrit Lal, an associate professor at the Tuskegee Institute in Alabama, who had asked for assistance in founding a black Unitarian Universalist congregation. Hoffman followed the standard policy; he offered $25 to help with advertising and the rental of a room for a public meeting. Beyond that, he explained, no funds were available. Hoffman, who had already heard that a group from Tuskegee had approached BAC, said that he would put them in direct touch with the BAC administrator, Richard Traylor. The problem was that Tuskegee fit neither the UUA extension model nor BAC's mandate. BAC would have argued that extension was the responsibility of the Association; indeed, it did so six months later, when it was approached about funding a "ghetto ministry" in Cleveland's Hough neighborhood. On the other hand, Tuskegee was not in the kind of area the extension department would have chosen. However, it was a college town, the kind of environment in which fellowships had sprung up in the past. A presence at a renowned African American institution of higher education could have served as a UU vanguard. Such a congregation, drawing in black academics and professionals while reaching out to Tuskegee's student body, would have had a long-term and far-reaching impact on the diversity of Unitarian Universalist membership. However, once BAC made itself the center of the black Unitarian Universalist agenda, it was easy for white Unitarian Universalists to abdicate any responsibility by simply handing over such issues to BAC. Given the mistrust between BAC and BAWA, approaching BAWA would surely have provoked a reaction, even though the proposed congregation fit comfortably into BAWA's goal of integrating Unitarian Universalism. Since a Tuskegee fellowship is not listed among the projects BAC funded, it seems that the opportunity passed by. This was a significant failure of vision—another in a string of squandered opportunities to support liberal religion in African American communities that dated back to Rev. William Jackson, the Baptist convert whose testimony to being converted to Unitarianism was brushed off by the American Unitarian Association in 1860.

. . .

BUUC, WHICH WAS EMBEDDED IN but autonomous from the Unitarian Universalist Association, was evolving as well. Its second annual meeting took place in Detroit on the weekend of February 14–16, 1969. It was attended by 165 delegates, all members of Unitarian Universalist congregations. Its theme was "Beyond 'Black Is Beautiful,'" and its agenda reflected BUUC's need to accomplish basic organizational work, including adopting a constitution, formalizing its administrative structure, and making a decision about its position in the upcoming UUA presidential election.

BAC reported to the delegates on its activities since General Assembly and outlined its funding guidelines. In assisting other black groups "to move beyond the rhetoric of the ebonization process," it had reviewed eighty-two proposals and funded twenty-six of them. These included the Black "P" Stone Nation in Chicago, which returned dropouts to school and engaged them with economic development ventures; the Welfare Rights Organization; the Third Annual National Black Power Conference, which drew more than four thousand delegates; and the National Alabama Democratic Party. The party, founded and led by Unitarian John Cashin, supported black candidates and had contested the seating of the regular Alabama Democratic Party delegates at the Democratic National Convention in Chicago in 1968.[276]

Alongside the reports and plenary sessions, workshops were offered. Among these was one for women. On Friday evening, during the women's workshop's first session, its chair proposed the formation of a BUUC Women's Caucus. Men were invited to the Saturday workshop session, and some, including Traylor and Scott, attended. There the decision was made to recommend a conference for African American Unitarian Universalist women. When the proposal was reported out at BUUC's final plenary session, a poll of the female delegates tallied eighteen for and ten against, with a few abstentions.

Lillian Jenkins, reporting on the proceedings to the Unitarian Universalist Women's Federation, wrote, "I began to see a problem emerge that so many things were 'bugging' the black women delegates . . . that it would be good to have a get-together for the purpose of communication and for the purpose of resolving their anomalous relationship to BUUC.[277]

Prelude to Controversy

[*January–July 1969*]

It turned out that the Cleveland General Assembly was just a beginning and resolved less than some had thought. Now as the spring of 1969 progressed, many could feel the crisis mounting. On March 6, 1969, Robert Reed delivered a sermon in which he strove to help his predominantly white congregation in Louisville, Kentucky, understand the relationship between racism, Black Power, and "the struggle for racial justice."

> Do we agree as to the point of this? That the thoughts which crowd a Black mind in the moment of fresh experience and the form and intensity of feeling which accompanies them are often *markedly different* from what occurs in white minds, even in those white minds which are particularly sympathetic to the Black?
> It is true, I think, and it makes a difference, too. It makes it hard for persons, Black and white, to work together. We don't really know each other when it comes to intense reactions. And it makes it all the more difficult because, having shared the same events, it seems natural to think that our experience has really been the same.[278]

What began as a Unitarian Universalist search for how to respond to the black rebellion became an opportunity to forthrightly deal with issues of race and the place of youth in Unitarian Universalist congregations. It was a time of soul-searching, transition, and conflict that saw the eight-year-old Association descend into an existential crisis.

The Fast

On April 3, 1969, an announcement was posted in the elevator at Unitarian Universalist Association headquarters announcing that on the next day, which would be Good Friday and also the anniversary of the death of Rev. Martin Luther King Jr., there would be a "service of reconciliation and re-commitment in memory of Martin Luther King Jr. and Jesus. At that time, Bob Hohler will deliver a personal statement to be followed by a non-violent act of witness and conscience."[279] When G. Robert Hohler, the executive director of the UU Laymen's League, delivered his sermon, the second-floor chapel was packed. Protesting the policies that governed the investment of the $27 million in the UUA's General Investment Fund (its endowment and the funds of related organizations), he said, "I feel that I must visibly demonstrate public remorse for the institution of which I am a part and stand witness until my denomination takes steps to reconcile its beliefs and its actions. Therefore, I intend to remain here at 25 Beacon Street until positive unequivocal action is taken . . . and during that time I will fast." Thus, Hohler began his sit-in and fast.

Hohler's protest was widely covered in the local press. Greeley responded with a press release that listed the changes to the investment policy that had been made in November 1967, together with other actions the Unitarian Universalist Association Board had taken. The day after Hohler began his fast, Homer Jack wrote to him, noting that the changes Greeley had listed had been made at the prodding of the old Commission on Religion and Race, long before Hohler began using his position with the Laymen's League to push for change. Jack, while admitting the Association should have acted faster, upbraided him for being uninformed and missing an important step in Gandhian resistance, which was to negotiate first and fast only if negotiation produced no results.[280]

On Monday, April 7, Greeley met with the entire Investment Committee, and on Wednesday, Hohler ended his fast, saying he did so "not because all of the demands have been met, but because the administration shows a new understanding of the problem and a willingness to move swiftly."[281]

In June, the Social Implication Subcommittee of the Investment Committee met with representatives of the American Metal Climax Corporation and the Chemical Bank New York Trust; the former did substantial business in South Africa and the latter was part of a consortium that gave credit to the South African government. The Unitarian Universalist Association, which held over $350 thousand in shares in each, was there to protest their policies on South Africa. Members of BAC, FULLBAC, and BAWA were invited to attend. (The Association had already sold its shares in two similar banks, as well as the six thousand shares it had held in Dow Chemical, the maker of napalm used in the Vietnam War. In these initiatives, it lagged far behind the Community Church of New York. Several years earlier, Community's Board had decided to sell all the church's stock in Dow Chemical and give the profit "to agencies serving children in Vietnam."[282])

Mandatory Contributions?

In the lead-up to the 1968 Cleveland General Assembly, David Pohl, the minister in Ottawa and a member of the Continental

Committee on Development and Fundraising, used the Ottawa church's newsletter to highlight what issues the Assembly would address. He focused first on the Unitarian Universalist Association's financial situation, saving the BAC for last. Some congregations, he wrote, did not pay their fair share of UUA dues, and he had "seen the inequities and insufficient giving of the present voluntary system." Although some argued that making dues mandatory would infringe on congregational autonomy, he had concluded "that mandatory giving by churches is probably the only fair and reasonable way to achieve the kind of support needed to pull our denomination out of its financial crisis."[283]

After General Assembly passed a motion to consider implementing mandatory contributions, Walter Donald Kring, the minister at All Souls New York, called it a "monstrosity" and said his congregation would never accept a compulsory assessment. He also tied the proposal to the Assembly's decision to fund BAC. This accusation was unfair; the money given to BAC only exacerbated a difficult long-term financial situation. The American Unitarian Association, and then the Unitarian Universalist Association, had exceeded its income year after year. The motion to consider mandatory contributions was placed on the GA agenda independently of the proposal to fund BAC.

As Kring conceded, this was not the first time mandatory dues had been proposed. Rev. William E. Gardner had done so prior to consolidation, when he chaired the Interim Study Committee on Fund Raising. At its first meeting, he made the proposal that the newly consolidated denomination raise funds by imposing a mandatory assessment on all member societies. He said, "It seemed to me that starting a new association would give us a good opportunity to change the whole system from a voluntary contributory system to a mandatory one.... My proposal was rejected out of hand almost within five or ten minutes of my making it."[284]

Following the Cleveland General Assembly, the Unitarian Universalist Association Board asked the Department of Fundraising and Development to study how mandatory dues might be implemented, and at its November meeting, it decided it wanted a survey. On January 31, 1969, in response to that survey, 17 ministers circulated a letter to 596 colleagues asserting that such a change would threaten Unitarian Universalist values and that mandatory dues were not enforceable. Ultimately, it said, the proposed change was an issue not of money but of governance and power: Consolidating such power in the administration would undermine congregational polity. So overriding was the alarm that Stephen Fritchman and Donald Harrington were both signatories.

Condemnation of the proposal was broad-based. On March 9, in a sermon entitled "The UUA *Still* in Crisis," Rev. Paul Beattie, minister of All Souls in Indianapolis, tagged it as the second major issue, after the election of a new president, coming before the 1969 General Assembly in Boston. He argued that "the most distinctive thing about Unitarianism is radical congregational polity," which was what had allowed it "to continue to become liberal." "The great challenge our movement faces today," he said, "is to resist adopting the denominational pattern of church organization, by seeking a form of church organization that uniquely expresses our tradition of individual freedom and radical congregational polity."[285] He identified these as bedrock UU principles. The idea of mandatory contributions was ultimately defeated. And even though funding for BAC would be affirmed for a second time at the Boston General Assembly in 1969, BAC, BUUC, and FULLBAC did not seem to understand that no matter how groundbreaking the vote for funding, winning a vote was not enough to prevail in an association of autonomous congregations.

Well before General Assembly began in mid-July, it was clear that mandatory contributions would never make it into the Unitarian Universalist Association bylaws. The Commission on Appraisal, the UUA's internal critic, rejected it. The response rate to the survey about mandatory contributions was 19.1 percent. The first question in the survey asked whether the formula proposed to calculate contributions was fair, and 61.6 percent of respondents said it was. But when asked if they were for or against mandatory contributions, 77.4 percent were opposed.[286] At the 1969 General Assembly, the proposal was overwhelmingly defeated. But the fact that it was on the agenda in both 1968 and 1969 meant that it was linked with BAC in many people's minds; viewing the controversy from afar, some came to believe that the $1 million commitment to BAC had caused the Association's financial woes.

The Signs Were There

Surveying the wreckage of the ninth annual meeting of the Unitarian Universalist Association, Homer A. Jack wrote, "The 1969 General Assembly included a group of delegates expecting, if not seeking, a confrontation. We on the staff at 25 Beacon Street realized this expectation, but we honestly didn't know whether the confrontation would be from youth, Blacks, the Radical Caucus or some unexpected source—women, ministers, women ministers, divorced ministers' wives.... In the end, we felt that the confrontation would most likely come from James Forman since he was hitting, it seemed at the time, almost a denomination a week."[287]

On May 4, 1969, James Forman, a long-time activist who had worked with the Student Nonviolent Coordinating Committee and the Black Panthers, had taken over the Sunday worship service at Riverside Church in New York City and delivered the Black Manifesto that had been adopted a week earlier at the National Black Economic Development Conference (NBEDC). The NBEDC was sponsored by the Interreligious Foundation for Community Organization (IFCO), and BAC was one of its funders. Three Unitarian Universalists were members of the IFCO Board of Directors: Hayward Henry, Richard Traylor, and Rev. James Brewer, who was white; Joe Samples was later a member as well. Louis Gothard, one of the founders of BURR and a member of BAC, was IFCO's associate director. The manifesto demanded that white churches and synagogues pay $500 million (about $15 for each black person in the United States) in reparations for the exploitation and oppression of African Americans. The money was to be used to forward black economic development in a variety of ways.

On May 8, the Black Manifesto was on the agenda when a Continental Conference [288] organized by Homer Jack met at a retreat center in Punderson State Park, thirty miles east of Cleveland. Mary Lu MacDonald, who was there representing the Canadian Unitarian Council, said that she had thought they were going to discuss the "fundamental principles . . . underlying our denominational commitments." Instead, she found "people arrived girded for battle" and that BAC's supporters "had come to refight last year's battle with the rival Black and White Action group." She said they were "ritualistically crucifying the leading BAWA supporter present," Max Gaebler. Moreover, "the Youth Caucus had come to try out on us the tactics they planned to use to demand and get a $100,000 budget allocated to them by the General Assembly." [289]

The Youth Caucus's agenda was inspired by BUUC's empowerment philosophy, tactics, and insistence on self-determination. In a sermon entitled "The Youth Agenda 1969," Larry Ladd, the president of Liberal Religious Youth, described the situation as a "time bomb." "Liberalism has failed," he said, "because it has promised much, while its lack of action perpetuated the conditions that created the bomb."[290] He put forward the demands that LRY's Executive Committee had developed: that funding for youth programs be increased by $35 thousand (to $100 thousand), that these programs be administered by the youth, and that there be greater youth representation on the Unitarian Universalist Association Board and committees.

Wayne Arnason, a conference participant and LRY member, said that many pressing issues of social concern came together at the Punderson conference, "a national UU conference that was smaller and whose agenda would be easier to disrupt and change."[291] And according to Kim Beach, one of the two ministers running the Cleveland UU Parish urban ministry program, "the entire program of the conference was in fact thrown into the grinder and re-formed." The Youth Caucus, he said, told the gathering that "'liberals' are not the vanguard, but the defenders of established institutions (church, university, democracy). The radical initiative lies with blacks and youth—both groups confronted us at Punderson."[292]

The confrontation over the Punderson conference began during the planning stage when the FULLBAC Steering Committee refused to participate in any way and urged its members not to attend. When the Social Action Department expressed its dismay, David Parke, the FULLBAC co-chair, responded that the meeting was "irrelevant" and "that the hoped-for denominational consensus would retard rather than advance the denomination's work."[293] In the end, BUUC members Richard Traylor, Hayward Henry, and Renford Gaines also decided not to go, but Harold Wilson, a member of the BUUC Steering Committee, did.

During the conference, a Black Caucus formed. Friday evening, when the conference broke into small groups, its members drafted a statement. It said, in part,

> We see you ... caught up in the vortex of your rhetoric which you use to protect your own vested interest in the very system that oppresses us and our brothers and sisters. White Unitarian Universalists are the theoreticians and technicians of the establishment: Lawyers, accountants, engineers, physical scientists, computer engineers, ministers, politicians, etc.
>
> We feel deeply within ourselves the force of your dishonesty pushing us into desperate alternatives in our church and community....
>
> We ask you [to] confront your own complicity and to move your agenda to a discussion [of] the basis for your own inability to place human values before your own vested interests, so that you can in fact contribute to the struggle for liberation.[294]

The phrase "white racism" does not appear, but the concept is implied. The statement makes clear that this group found it unconscionable that in the nineteen months since the Emergency Conference, white UUs had examined neither their own racism nor their culpability in systemic racism. The youth delegates Ann Redding and Marsh Agobert were among its signatories, as were Thomas Haley (from Ottawa) and Thomas Payne.[295] They weren't radicals but were nonetheless frustrated.

• • •

THE UNWILLINGNESS OF WHITE LIBERALS in the Unitarian Universalist Association to confront their own racism would have looked familiar to Jean Adams, the white member of the Congress of Racial Equality who, when CORE expelled its white members in

July 1967, had called the other former members of the Seattle chapter to a meeting to discuss combating "white racism"—a meeting to which no one came. Within the Association, there was talk of having a national conference on white racism, and the UUA Board also explored the idea of a day-long workshop for itself and a later one for staff. The Task Force II on White Racism discussed it, Homer Jack sent letters seeking models to use, and there were a couple of local efforts, but little actually happened until the first annual FULLBAC conference was held in Philadelphia on March 21–23, 1969.

One of FULLBAC's goals was "to enable white people to achieve a non-oppressive identity," and the theme of the conference was "What Does It Mean to Be a White Racist?" FULLBAC's field director, Duke T. Gray, provided a two-page definition of racism that explained the difference between racism and prejudice. Prejudice was personal, racism cultural. Racism was built into and maintained by institutions in a way that was advantageous for white people and disadvantageous for blacks.

The problem with the conference, as one participant reported, was that "none of the ministers or staff were prepared to deal with the theme question in a realistic way in spite of a number of indications from the participants that they, at least, would like to."[296]

Unlike the white members of Seattle CORE, who simply had not shown up, Unitarian Universalists came to Philadelphia ready to engage with the issue. But the program failed them. While white radicals and reformers were eager to align themselves with moral goodness, the conference leaders seemed to have lacked the will, the courage, or the means to explore their own racism.

Dr. Nathan Wright Jr., a black Episcopalian who had participated in the Unitarian Universalist Association's Emergency Conference, wrote that for white people to assist the black community, they needed to become self-aware by honestly addressing how they themselves and all American life were infected with racism.[297] Both Dr. King and Roy Ockert described the task for the white liberal as one of reeducation; Fritchman spoke of cleansing the white subconscious; Homer Jack was seeking workshop models; and Duke Gray could intellectually explain the problem. Yet FULLBAC couldn't help those who came ready to explore what it meant to be a white racist.

At the Punderson conference, Kim Beach heard an idea from Robert Kimball, president of Starr King School for the Ministry, which put a different spin on the issues and pointed him toward another reason for engagement: "Black people have in many ways pointed up our spiritual emptiness, and we've begun to see this inward abyss. That white adults can't live vicariously from black souls any more than from youth spirit, so we'd better find our own. That our chief job, then, is to get back in touch with what may prove real and moving in us."[298] The breakthrough for African Americans participating in the Emergency Conference came when they sat down together and shared stories about the realities of black life in America, their struggles to succeed in a white world, and what these had cost them. White liberals and radicals needed to have their own version of that conversation. But such a conversation had not happened, and would not.

Mary Lu MacDonald, a Canadian, said that if there was a failure at the Punderson conference, it was that there were "insufficient opportunities for personal communication." She wondered whether "the UUA would still be around after this year's General Assembly." Her answer was a cautious "yes," if "delegates can be brought together on a one-to-one basis and the speech-making is kept to a minimum."[299] It was not to be.

MacDonald's insight and concerns were akin to those of Rev. David Hicks MacPherson, the minister in Towson, Maryland, who outlined them in a draft letter dated May 7, 1969, the day before Punderson began. In reading various Unitarian Universalist publications and flyers and a first-hand report on the FULLBAC meeting, MacPherson had been disturbed by calls for the Unitarian Universalist Association to become a "revolutionary movement." The FULLBAC conference working papers were unequivocal that the funding of the BAC and youth agendas must be first on the agenda at the upcoming General Assembly. He cited passages from the report on the FULLBAC conference, which read, "FULLBAC must fight to make non-negotiable certain priorities in our denomination" and "If we fail to get full funding for BAC next year, at that moment the denomination is destroyed."[300]

MacPherson discerned a coalition behind the fervor made up of FULLBAC, LRY, Student Religious Liberals, and the Laymen's League. A letter sent on April 4 following the FULLBAC meeting by LRY president, Larry Ladd, to David Parke seems to confirm MacPherson's belief. "My greatest single fear about FULLBAC at this point is the fact that it hasn't really been able to escape its 'white support group' syndrome. The decisions at Philadelphia clearly indicate to me that we are now the left-wing of the UUA, dealing with many areas of societal oppression. We must make that Philadelphia decision a reality."[301]

While MacPherson shared many of the concerns of these groups, he feared that the result of politicizing and polarizing tactics "can only be the end of the continental association of UU societies." Furthermore, he was not interested in forming another political faction within the Unitarian Universalist Association. His proposal was to disseminate as much information as possible about the issues to be considered at General Assembly. In addition to FULLBAC's plan and the youth agenda, this meant discussing the rumors that a walkout or a takeover of UUA headquarters was being planned and the tactics some groups were preparing to use.

On May 7, the day MacPherson drafted his letter, a group of thirty-two had met in Towson and formed C.O.N.C.E.R.N., and on May 16, its Steering Committee sent out a letter to "all UU societies," which concluded,

> We want no confrontation of intractable positions. Let every issue be faced in the context of our diversities. The most revolutionary contribution we can make is the example of a people giving serious attention to serious issues and arriving at pragmatic choices in a climate of unbroken mutual respect and fellowship. If we can do this we will find ways to be relevant to black revolution and white readjustment, to the fervor and frustration of youth, to war and peace, and every other challenge of these agonizing yet promise-filled times.[302]

On May 21, ten members of the Interdenominational Racial Caucus (IRC) "liberated" (i.e., occupied) 78 Beacon Street, the headquarters of the Unitarian Universalist Service Committee (UUSC). Among the IRC's leadership were Alex Jack, son of Homer Jack, and Victor Jokel, who was running for Unitarian Universalist Association president but (in an anti-establishment move) never filed nomination papers. Among the group's demands were "the immediate withdrawal of the UUSC from Vietnam (and other AID [Agency for International Development] programs)" and "a massive program of reparations for the Vietnamese and North American victims of the war in Vietnam." On May 28, the UUSC staff was locked out of their offices; on May 29, the occupiers gave shelter to "street people"; and on June 1, the occupiers and their guests were evicted. Meanwhile, two hundred people endorsed the "IRC

Manifesto." Among them were James Luther Adams, Stephen Fritchman, Homer Jack, Jack Mendelsohn, Leona Light, and Rhys Williams.[303]

That May, while others were protesting and strategizing, BAWA sent out its first newsletter. It reported that its Executive Board had met three time since the Cleveland General Assembly and offered a summary of its activities. These had been modest: a grant, a sponsorship, a scholarship, the authorization of a black ministerial recruitment plan, and the dissemination of its first project paper, entitled "Black History in Our Curriculum," and of materials about integration. In response to a note from a Unitarian Universalist minister asking about BAWA's projects and strategy, its executive secretary, Betty Seiden, responded, "As for strategy, I don't think we are planning any! We're just keeping the faith."[304]

Dear Brother Rennie

Renford Gaines graduated from Meadville Lombard Theological School and was called by the Unitarian Universalist Church of Urbana-Champaign, Illinois, in June 1968. It was a strong call, with a vote of 137 for and 3 against.

In mid-June, as the end of his first year approached, Gaines received a letter from Hayward Henry. "Dear Brother Rennie," it began. The 1969 Boston General Assembly was only a month away, and Henry had a problem he hoped that Gaines, as the minister of the Urbana-Champaign congregation, could solve.

Henry wrote that because of his own "moral position and because you are the first Black minister holding a full-time position in the denomination, and as I am leader of a National Unitarian Universalist group, I am compelled to seek membership in your church. I am willing to abide by the by-laws and constitution of the Unitarian Universalist Church of Urbana-Champaign and I hope that my petition for membership will be favorably received."[305]

Henry had been a member and on the Board of Second Church in Boston until he resigned first from the Board and subsequently the congregation after it chose to merge with First Church. A decision to build a new building had triggered his resignation. Henry called the plan an "irrelevancy and immorality at its highest" when the needs of deprived citizens in Boston were so pressing.

Gaines took Henry's request up with his Board.

The situation at Second Church in Boston that led to Henry's letter was more complicated and conflicted than his letter conveyed. On March 29, 1968, a fire gutted First Church in Boston, a historic congregation dating back to the founding of the city in 1630. Beset by deep grief, the church leadership gathered at the home of their minister, Rhys Williams. Williams recalled, "There was a knock on the door. A ministerial member of the staff of the Unitarian Universalist Association was there with advice. We should immediately join another Unitarian church and turn our money over to a relevant social project."[306] This was just the beginning of an effort to persuade First Boston to give away its endowment and insurance settlement to Boston's poor, an effort in which Henry, Jack Mendelsohn, Duke Gray, and others participated.

Discussion of a possible merger between First Church Boston and the Arlington Street Church, where Mendelsohn was serving, dated back to Rhys Williams's call to First in 1960. Talks now began again with Arlington Street and also with Second Church in Boston, this time in earnest. First was of the traditional New England mold, what Henry in his letter had described as a "conservative Unitarian Universalist Church." Williams, who would serve as its minister for forty years, was pastoral in style and his commitments institutional. Mendelsohn's ministry at Arlington Street was first and foremost one of social action, and the congregation was in the forefront in supporting BAC and providing sanctuary to draft resisters. Jack Hammond, the minister at Second, was a member of BAWA, which indicates he was a liberal rather than a radical.

Finally, on October 9, 1968, Second, which had a hundred members, made the decision to merge with First, which had three hundred. Second was to sell its property and join with First in rebuilding.

On October 19, Jack Mendelsohn wrote to Williams expressing his surprise and disappointment regarding the merger. "[We] must now view the future of liberal religion in Boston as having lost a great opportunity which I described to you in a letter some time ago, and with which I thought you agreed."[307]

Mendelsohn thought a merger between Arlington and First was desirable. Like Hayward Henry and later the New England Fellowship for Renewal (formed by local FULLBAC members), he saw the potential of what could be done in the community with First's assets. First's endowment and insurance settlement certainly would have enhanced Arlington Street's status and outreach while alleviating its "extremely painful financial problems."[308] Indeed, the finances at Arlington Street were such that on October 7, Mendelsohn had told the UUA that the church could not make a commitment to the Annual Program Fund. His letter extolled the congregation's community work and suggested the UUA consider awarding Arlington Street a subsidy, while failing to mention that its budget included $11 thousand for BAC. He also pursued the idea of a merger with First, despite the fact that uniting profoundly disparate congregational cultures was neither his style nor his interest. Being prophetic was his strength, and writing his talent.

Subsequently, in spring 1969, he announced he was leaving Arlington Street to become the minister of the First Unitarian Society of Chicago.

The pressure on First Church Boston continued. On February 20, 1969, Rev. Duke Gray, assistant minister at the First Unitarian Church in Brooklyn and field director of FULLBAC, wrote to Rhys Williams, "The purpose of the church is to serve the world and not its own institutional self-aggrandizement.... It would appear to me that this is a case wherein a gross and shameful travesty against all moral and theological sense is being perpetuated.... The choice is the simple one between faith and pride."[309] As the onslaught escalated, the congregation began a process of soul-searching about its identity and responsibility to the larger community.

This was the series of events and decisions that led Henry to resign from the Board and then the congregation of Second Boston. He was not alone. However, the number of members of First and Second who opposed rebuilding and favored bequeathing First's resources to charity instead was small.[310]

Henry's resignation left him with a major problem. He was no longer a member of a Unitarian Universalist congregation. If he was not a member, he could not be a delegate, and if he was not a delegate, he would not have the right to speak at the upcoming and pivotal General Assembly. How does one, at the last moment, go about joining a religious community solely for the purpose of being a delegate to General Assembly? And what congregation would accept such a proposition? For this reason, he turned to Renford Gaines. Gaines reminded the Urbana-Champaign board that they had met Henry when he participated in Gaines's ordination, and asked them to accept him as a member and make him one of the congregation's five delegates to General Assembly. They did.

Race for the UUA Presidency

In a letter sent to Aron Gilmartin on July 22, 1968, G. Robert Hohler told him he was about to announce his candidacy for president of the Unitarian Universalist Association. "My decision is prompted by the deep conviction that the ideas and ideals we fight for—black empowerment, participatory democracy, resistance to the war, new ministries and new programs—must be advocated for in this campaign."[311] Exactly two months later, he said that he had learned, while traveling across America, that his "basic impulse is to bring about revolution, not preside over it," and ended his run for the presidency.[312] His withdrawal opened the door for Gilmartin, whose constituency, like Hohler's, was the left wing of the Association.

Just prior to the 1969 General Assembly, Duke Gray sent a letter to the delegates announcing that the FULLBAC Steering Committee endorsed Gilmartin, as had BUUC and all the youth leaders. He also noted that another candidate, Carlton Fisher, had withdrawn and thrown his support to Gilmartin. Gray declared that Gilmartin, more than any other candidate, symbolized the progressive thrust needed to meet the challenges of the 1970s.[313]

Gilmartin had a strong social action pedigree. Upon graduating from Meadville Lombard Theological School in 1942, he was called to Fort Wayne, Indiana. Finding no NAACP branch in the city, he helped found one and became its first president. By the time he left Fort Wayne in 1951, he was president of the local Urban League. His involvement in the Urban League continued in his new settlement at University Church in Seattle.[314] When he settled at Mt. Diablo Unitarian Universalist Church in 1960, he took on housing discrimination, marched in Selma, and hired an African American, Harold Wilson, as associate minister. He attended the Emergency

Conference and was an unwavering supporter of BAC from the beginning.

Since April, Gilmartin had been pushing FULLBAC to make an endorsement. He saw it as politically unwise not to do so and said he would have encouraged them to make one even if he were not running. He and Carlton Fisher also negotiated an understanding that, when it became clear which way support was leaning, whoever was trailing would drop out and throw his support behind the other.

In addition to Gilmartin and Fisher, there were six other candidates in the race; that is, there were five plus Victor Jokel, the Arlington Street Church executive director, who never submitted nomination papers. Jokel thought FULLBAC should realign itself to support the IRC and the Black Panthers instead of BUUC, and he communicated through satire. The other candidates were John Ogden Fisher, J. Harold Hadley, Philip Larson, Deane Starr, and Bob West. They were all experienced white male ministers.

This would be the first change of UUA administration since consolidation, and the priority issues were governance, the budget, and BAC. Several candidates criticized the existing distribution of power and proposed alternatives. Carlton Fisher advocated decentralization and for the districts to hold power. This was akin to returning to the Universalist model, in which significant power had been held by state conventions. John Ogden Fisher said he would be a one-term president, after which the president would be appointed by the Board. That would require a bylaw change and was also a return to the Universalist model. Larson's proposals for putting the Unitarian Universalist "house in order" were decentralization, district autonomy, and holding General Assembly only every four years. In comparison, West's proposals were vaguer and emphasized better communication.

All the candidates acknowledged that the Unitarian Universalist Association had a budget crisis, although they varied in how central they considered the issue and how they proposed to address it. John Ogden Fisher offered a detailed account of how the Association had expended nearly $4 million in capital funds and depleted its unrestricted capital, a significant portion of which had come from the supposedly poor relations, the Universalists. Larson and Starr, the Association's vice president for field services, put out budgets. West admitted there was a budget crisis and went on to attack their proposals. Gilmartin said in a major *UUA Now* article, published before General Assembly, that he "took for granted that the UUA budget must be brought into balance in the shortest time possible," but the financial situation garnered no mention elsewhere in his writings or campaign literature.

In regard to BAC, the candidates spread across a continuum. On one end, Philip Larson said, "We have to turn the clock BACK. The goal, the vision, the dream of Martin Luther King Jr. was black and white together. We should transcend BAC."[315] On the other end, Gilmartin and Carlton Fisher were committed to the continued full funding of BAC from the UUA budget. In the middle was West. In Rochester, New York, he had been an early supporter of FIGHT (Freedom, Independence, God, Honor, Today) when it challenged Kodak; now in regard to BAC, he argued for pluralism and said he would raise the $750 thousand that remained to be awarded outside the UUA budget.

The issues of Unitarian Universalist Association governance and budget did not precipitate the crisis at the Boston General Assembly; nor did the funding of BAC. Signs indicated that there would be a confrontation, but its trigger was the UUA Board's decision to fund BAWA. BAC categorically rejected that decision, and its insistence on reordering the General Assembly agenda brought the meeting to a standstill.

Although the UUA administration advocated adhering to the pledge to BAC of $250 thousand in each of the next three years, the UUA Board Finance Committee, faced with a $650 thousand deficit, recommended at its May meeting that BAC receive only $200 thousand in 1969–1970. The Board approved this recommendation by a vote of seven for and five against. Immediately, a motion was made to also award $50 thousand to BAWA. It was carried, with thirteen for and five against. The six unrecorded abstentions on the first vote indicate how conflicted the Board was. Bringing BAWA into the budget eliminated the problem presented by BAWA's independent fundraising, which it would end. Henry had called it unfair that BAWA could fundraise and BAC could not, but the solution to that particular problem created another.

When Carlton Fisher sent a letter to the UUA Board protesting the BAWA allocation, Ralph Helverson responded with a memo to the Board recounting how the Board had committed to pluralism at a meeting in Cleveland that lasted nearly all night. However, the proposal it had agreed on then, which included funding for BAWA, never made it to the floor because of BAC's mastery of parliamentary procedure. Some on the Board had not changed their minds, and during the last year pluralism and the funding of BAWA had remained a topic of concern.[316]

Hayward Henry was outraged. Richard Nash, chair of Greater Boston FULLBAC, outlined his understanding of Henry's reaction in a memo to the FULLBAC Steering Committee. Henry, he said, wanted all the money for BAC: "In fact, he was ready to push the position that BAC should turn down the $250,000 if BAWA is given anything. In other words, he wants to make a head-on battle out of it." The Board's allocation to BAWA showed him that they had not accepted that "the BAC philosophy [is] the only legitimate one," as Henry maintained it was. He felt, said Nash, "that the argument of pluralism approached as support for BAWA funding, is a cover-up for funding an illegitimate group." Nash considered Henry's course of action "politically unwise" and believed he was "seriously misreading the political realities," but said dissuading him was difficult: "His determination is firm."[317]

Henry was about to challenge an attitude that was part of the liberal tradition's genius, its ability to hold opposing positions. "Our chief glory as Unitarians," Frederick May Eliot once said, is that "at every stage in our history, we have had conservatives and radicals, both in theology and in social philosophy...."[318] This required a respect for pluralism that must be seen as the extension of two fundamental Unitarian Universalist principles—congregational polity and individual freedom of conscience. Becoming a haven for people fleeing other religious traditions during the twentieth century reinforced these principles. How deeply held they were was apparent in 1963 when a change in the UUA bylaws was proposed that would have required UU congregations to include a non-discrimination clause in their bylaws. In the passionate three-hour debate, some argued for the primacy of congregational autonomy and others for non-discrimination. The latter lost, and ironically, Harrington and Mendelsohn were together on the losing side. Since the freedom of conscience and tolerance of differing points of view were nearly sacrosanct, dismissing pluralism, as Nash cautioned, was ill-advised.

Distrust of Henry was spreading, and it was not confined to BAWA supporters. In a letter to Gilmartin, Walter Royal Jones, former chair of the Commission on Religion and Race, and member of the C.O.N.C.E.R.N. Steering Committee, wrote, "Hayward

Henry frankly disavows concern for any pluralism except his own. So much for him. He is a significant Black leader, but not a significant liberal. I respect his achievements, despite his principle, which is sheer self-serving power politics, of a kind I have never trusted."[319]

Jones went on to explain that he had voted for funding BAC and expected to do so again, and that he questioned the wisdom of funding BAWA. But he disagreed with the assertion that support for an alternative of any sort diluted or confused support for BAC: "It is a complete non sequitur, and I am astonished to hear it from you."[320]

As General Assembly approached and the various camps began estimating the vote count, Rudi Gelsey conferred with Rev. John Wells, one of Deane Starr's campaign managers. Wells said he thought 15 percent of the vote would go to the far right, represented by John Ogden Fisher and Larson, and most of that to Larson, who was strong in the Northeast; 70 percent to the center (Bob West on the center-right and Deane Starr on the center-left); and 15 percent to Gilmartin. Wells also told Gelsey that he believed "that the swing of the pendulum is against black power and minority groups."[321]

Boston General Assembly

[*July 1969*]

IN JULY 1969, the General Assembly of the Unitarian Universalist Association took place in Boston for the first time since 1965. It had met since then in Hollywood, Florida; Denver; and Cleveland. Now the Assembly returned to Boston for the end of Dana MacLean Greeley's term as president. In the campaign of 1965, John Ogden Fisher had opposed Greeley, and Greeley had won by a ratio of four to one, with 1,360 delegates in attendance and 1,626 ballots cast in total. In 1969, however, the election was contested and its outcome uncertain. A British Unitarian newsletter reported, "The advance write-up of the Boston meetings of the American Unitarian Universalist General Assembly in *The Unitarian* last month hinted that the election of the new UUA President ... would not be the quiet formality that we are used to over here."[322]

Nonetheless, what the 1969 General Assembly is remembered for is not the presidential election. Grant Venerable II, a twenty-six-year-old African American Ph.D. candidate in chemistry, was a delegate from the First Unitarian Society of Chicago. Describing that GA years later, he said, "The assembly moments with Jack Mendelsohn were important and dramatic. I had never experienced anything like it before."[323] He was referring to what has come to be known as "the Walkout."

The Walkout

As General Assembly drew near, the Board of Main Line Unitarian in Devon, Pennsylvania, felt pressured to select delegates committed to one side or another. The Board was inclined to select delegates who were opposed to continuing the commitment to BAC, but after difficult discussions, it decided that fairness demanded appointing some delegates committed to the other point of view as well. It chose three Board members who opposed funding and two non–Board members who were for it.[324]

Within the Unitarian Universalist Association and across America, the tone of the era was set and the sides defined before the eighth General Assembly commenced at the historic Statler-Hilton Hotel in Boston. Already in November 1968, the Boston branch of BUUC had approached Boston FULLBAC and asked it to study the Statler-Hilton's hiring practices. FULLBAC found that the vast majority of the hotel's minority staff were in service jobs. It formed a coalition with Project Equality, the Massachusetts Council of Churches, the United Church of Christ, BUUC, and other groups that forced the uncooperative hotel to begin to hire minorities into its managerial, professional, and sales staff.

The 1969 Boston General Assembly was the first for Alan Rosenthal, a Board member of Cedar Lane Unitarian Church in Bethesda, Maryland. He came expecting to have an uplifting experience. Sitting in the ballroom in which the Assembly took place, he could not help but notice that because of "the enormous number of delegates and observers the air-conditioning simply was inadequate to provide sufficient cooling for that many people principally engaged in heated debate."[325] He was not alone in noticing; someone else said it felt like a steam room. Indeed, that week was so hot and humid that one British observer reported, "Most of us found an occasional cool bath a necessity in this humid atmosphere."³²⁶

Not only was an election to be held in a city rich with Unitarian Universalist history, but the International Association for Religious Freedom was holding its own conference there simultaneously, with more than 250 delegates from 19 countries. This made attendance the largest ever. The initial count indicated 15 percent more attendees than were in Cleveland the year before for the young Association's most highly attended General Assembly to date. There were 1,785 delegates plus observers in attendance in Boston. And the Boston General Assembly was also different in texture from Cleveland. BAC, BUUC, FULLBAC, and LRY were well organized; BAWA was more prepared; C.O.N.C.E.R.N. was attentive and attuned to the tone of the meeting; youth had joined the rebellion; and the drama was witnessed by the IARF delegates.

Notwithstanding the high attendance, some ministers who usually came could not, and still others did not come because they did not wish to participate in what was going on. Among them was John Cummins. He was minister of First Universalist of Minneapolis, and his father had served as the general superintendent of the Universalist Church of America. Cummins saw the struggle over Black Power as leaders of Unitarian Universalism and leaders of the black intelligentsia warring over power and money. He said, "I have always understood the liberal's dark side to be elitism." Seeing the conflict between BAC and BAWA as a struggle between Unitarians, he wanted no part of it and instead focused his energies on antiwar efforts.³²⁷

In fact, few Universalists were involved in the leadership of FULLBAC, BUUC, or BAC. Among the Universalists, Harmon Gehr at Throop Memorial Church in Pasadena was leery of BURR and SOBURR from the outset, and Phil Giles was an active opponent of BUUC and BAC. Ray Hopkins, the Unitarian Universalist Association's executive vice president, had to be nonpartisan. David MacPherson organized C.O.N.C.E.R.N. Their colleague Dick Gilbert, who was raised Universalist in small-town upstate New York, supported BAC but engaged with BAWA. The most prominent Universalist to support BAC was the presidential candidate, Carlton Fisher. In general, the denominational upheaval did not correspond with the cultural experiences of those who had been Universalist, a faith more attuned to class injustice than racial inequality. And two African American Universalist ministers tended toward opposite opinions: Thomas Payne, who had joined National Memorial Universalist in Washington D.C. as an adolescent, leaned toward BAWA, while Jeff Campbell was a skeptic and bystander whose appreciation of BAC had grown.

General Assembly opened on Monday, July 14, with the traditional greetings from visiting dignitaries, of which there were many because of the IARF's presence. In his opening remarks, Greeley ebulliently welcomed everyone. Then he shifted to a conciliatory note: "Let us not quarrel with any man. We need love; I need love, and Don Harrington needs it, and Jack Mendelsohn ... and Dick Traylor ... and Larry Ladd."[328]

At the start of the General Assembly business meeting, BAC made a motion to set aside the published agenda. Del Tweedie, chair of the Main Line Unitarian Church of Devon, Pennsylvania Board of Trustees, was surprised. He could not understand why a procedural item was so important; it seemed reasonable to him to get the routine items of business out of the way before addressing the main controversial issue. But Hayward Henry declared that unless the Assembly agreed to deal with the funding of BAC and BAWA "now, not Wednesday, the microphones will be possessed and the business of this house will come to a halt."[329] Tweedie, who was sitting right next to one of the floor microphones, said it was suddenly "surrounded by about 15 young men, both black and white." All the other mikes—pro, con, and procedural—were commandeered as well; BUUC and LRY would let no one else approach them, and they aimed to stack all the lines with pro-revision speakers. "Violent shoving matches occurred," said Tweedie, "and even a few fists were thrown."330 John Gibbons, a sixteen-year-old member of LRY from Chicago Third, ended up standing in line at one mike behind Max Gaebler, the BAWA co-chair. "For some reason, Gaebler left the line. When he returned, he assumed he would resume his previous position. I told him to move to the back of the line. He pushed me aside; I chest-bumped him back. As I recall that scrimmage, neither of us got to the front of the line."331 Consternation filled the ballroom as the takeover Homer Jack had anticipated began.

According to Stephen Fritchman, the atmosphere as Henry addressed the Assembly was electric. Fritchman paraphrased Henry's words: "The funding of B.A.W.A. is wrong. The commitment to fund B.A.C. and only B.A.C. must be honored.... What we seek is a reparational grant as is our due by the 1968 vote."332

Jules Ramey, a founding member of BURR and BUUC, reported, "As I stood with a liberated mike in my hand, I looked back at the gathering and I saw so much hatred it was hard to believe I was with Unitarians and not with the John Birchers or even the KKK.... There was no attempt to conceal the white racist's stance that was rampant at the General Assembly."333 Ramey saw hatred, but what Tweedie felt was resentment of behavior "which seemed totally out of place in what was supposed to be a democratically run organization."334

The prejudice in the room was palpable. Many thought, and some said, "Who are these black people and where did they come from?" The demographics of Unitarian Universalism were such that, while there were many more African American Unitarian Universalists than anyone imagined, they were largely clustered in metropolitan America in Boston, New York, Philadelphia, Washington D.C., Cleveland, Cincinnati, Detroit, Chicago, Denver, and Los Angeles. Delegates who came from Racine, Wisconsin, or Oneonta, New York, or especially from New England or Canada would have rarely met a black Unitarian Universalist. For most, their knowledge of African American history was scant, their grasp of the day-to-day challenges of being black in America minimal, and their understanding of institutional racism nonexistent. Stereotypes, ignorance, and annoyance, rather than experience, would have shaped delegates' reactions. That youth were allied with the groups staging the takeover contributed to the sense that they were all ungrateful children, so adultism blended with and reinforced racism—and classism too. For this was definitely not middle-class behavior.

In that hall it would have been impossible to distinguish racism, classism, and hatred from frustration, shock, and anger. Ramey's frustration and the frustration of Tweedie and others mirrored one another as it all intermingled in the heat of that moment.

Fritchman was among those who addressed the Assembly: "You all know how slow our progress has been. Now we have a chance to do something really significant, and you tell me to wait until Wednesday. I've waited for forty years, and I don't intend to wait until Wednesday."[335]

Nina Grey, a mother and full-time Sunday School teacher, was another first-time delegate. Although she was unaware of the issues before she arrived, she became outraged when she heard the charge that the Unitarian Universalist Association was backing away from the promise the General Assembly had made in Cleveland. At the same time, she learned about the Association's financial difficulties, which she also had known nothing about. But she thought, "Well that doesn't matter. Somehow we have to live up to our commitment to BAC."[336]

A vote on the motion to reorder the agenda was called and received a sizable majority (710 for and 536 against). But it fell short of the required two-thirds majority and was not carried. By this time, the hour was late and the meeting was adjourned.

This vote needs to be understood in context. On the one hand, it was normal practice to present the budget later in the meeting. It was placed there by the Business Committee, which was elected by the delegates and accountable to the Assembly, not to the administration. The majority of the delegates were there for the election and many, like Rosenthal and Grey, were new, uninformed, confused, and distressed. As one commentator wrote later, "There were several moments when it was not clear to the delegates ... what the fight was all about. ... The specific issues were complex and chimeric."[337] Indeed, it would not have been unusual if a third to half of them had never served as delegates before. One religious educator said, "It is obvious that many societies do not do a particularly good job of educating their delegates prior to the General Assembly."[338] Additionally, we can assume that a significant number of them knew little to nothing about BAC or BAWA, much less the controversy that precipitated the conflict they found themselves called to resolve. Nonetheless, they were required to make a decision.

On the other hand, there were some delegates who felt that the cries arising from the black community demanded swift action and who came, as Ramey said, "to redirect the energies and resources of the denomination to addressing itself in a relevant way to the massive problem that confronted the mass of black people on a 24 hour basis."[339] For them, the question of who controlled the General Assembly agenda and the Unitarian Universalist Association's resources was connected to what was happening in urban America. Feeling such urgency, they had little patience for the ponderousness of parliamentary procedure and the "failings of Robert's Rules of Order."[340]

On Tuesday morning, the Unitarian Universalist Association's moderator, Joe Fisher, introduced the idea of what he called "The Moderator's Rap." This would be "a noon meeting with any interested parties wanting to discuss any subject at all—to air controversies, compare recommendations, explore alternative procedures"[341] and to do so without the regular formalities. The delegates' response was enthusiastic.

But before the Assembly could proceed to the next item of business, Hayward Henry's voice rose above all others as he called for the moderator's attention. He urged that the Assembly take up the issues BAC had raised on Monday. He then again announced, "No further business should go on in this Assembly until questions of BAC and BAWA are settled. The $50,000 earmarked for BAWA should be added to the funds supporting BAC."[342] The Assembly could fund BAC or BAWA but not both, he insisted, and he demanded that the Assembly reconsider the motion from the night before.

A minister who had voted against changing the agenda the day before now made a motion for reconsideration, which was seconded. After an hour of heated debate, the vote was called and taken by show of hands, and the motion was defeated 692 to 687. Immediately a motion for a recount was made, to which the moderator acceded. But then, before the recount could commence, a motion was made to table the motion until after the presidential candidates delivered their addresses. This was what many delegates had waited for all morning, and it was now well after 10 AM. Indeed, it was the day of the election, and the polls would only be open from noon to 6 PM. The motion to delay the recount carried.

"We knew what we were going to do," said BUUC vice president Harold Wilson. "We had designed our walkout in advance.... It was strategy, not impulse."[343] As prearranged, BUUC walked out. There was silence and confusion. Then Greeley moved that the Assembly hear the candidates, at which point David Parke went to a mike and announced that the African American delegates had left the hall. There was disarray, but after a recess, the candidates went on to present their platforms.

During the recess, Mendelsohn, a white member of BAC, found the BUUC members and asked them to let him speak to the Assembly and tell them what he saw, which was that they were about to leave. The BUUC members agreed, and so Mendelsohn went to Fisher and Greeley and asked for a point of personal privilege. After some tense negotiation, they agreed that Mendelsohn would address the Assembly and, for fairness, would be followed by Glover Barnes, co-chair of BAWA.

Mendelsohn said, "The spirit of Cleveland has been diminished.... Yesterday, the Black Caucus, through Mr. Henry, tried to get this major issue re-established, and was defeated, and again this morning rejected."[344] In an attempt to explain how the members of BUUC felt, he said that being at the back of the agenda was like being told to go to the back of the bus, to which the crowd responded with thunderous cries of "No, no, no." He continued, "Therefore, they have left—and I must leave also, and will hope to be accompanied by as many as may wish to consult on these things with us."[345]

As Mendelsohn walked down the aisle, a colleague came up to him and spat in his face. Another told him later that if he had had a gun he would have shot him. Mary Jane Miller, the wife of Orloff Miller, was headed out of the meeting herself even before Mendelsohn finished speaking, and others rose and followed him.

Having agreed that both he and Barnes would speak Mendelsohn not only left but took a sizable portion of the Assembly with him. (Greeley was so aggrieved at this that he would not support Mendelsohn's 1977 bid for the UUA presidency, even though Mendelsohn had been his campaign chair in 1965.)

Fritchman and his wife Frances rose to depart, not knowing how many of Los Angeles's nine delegates would join them, but he was not surprised when all of them rose and followed him out of the hall.[346] "Let's go," said Richard Kellaway to his new wife, a Canadian from New Brunswick whose first marriage had been interracial. They too left.[347] For Rev. Victor Carpenter of First Philadelphia, "it was an easy decision to get up and walk out." As he left, he passed a delegate from his congregation, to whom he said, "I am going to have to go now." No one from the congregation joined him.[348] The Hartford church split the other way: "None of us Hartford delegates . . . said anything," said Nina Grey. "We just got up and joined the walkout. Nat Lauriat (the minister in Hartford) was sitting with us and didn't come."[349]

"As I was leaving my seat," said Rudi Gelsey, "next to me was a white colleague and he said 'Good riddance,' and he said it with real hate in his voice."[350]

"It was wrenching to be part of the group that walked off the floor," said Gordon Gibson. "Walking out with the sense that we may not be back. Maybe this is it. . . . I didn't have time to wrestle with that. There are people walking out the door. Am I? That was the time frame in which the choice was made."[351]

LRY leader Wayne Arnason sat paralyzed. Uncertain of what to do, he cried. As she came down the aisle, Margaret Blattman, the director of religious education at West Hartford, Connecticut, saw him sitting there sobbing. She put out her hand and asked him, "Do you want to go with me?" and he grabbed hold and went.[352]

"The children wept, all of us, over the hate, bitterness, and anger with which our black brothers and their supporters were treated," said Larry Ladd. "As we walked out in dismay, 'grownup' people leaped in delight, shouting 'Go! Go!' We left, not in anger, but in despair."[353]

"It was emotionally rending. I called for the youth walk out for that reason and none other," said Marsh Agobert, a black Chicagoan on the LRY Executive Committee who was also the LRY floor manager. "Young people were very stressed, breaking down, sobbing. Several LRY in our 'delegation' turned to me and implored me to *do* something; stating that they couldn't take anymore. I felt this pain and acted by calling a withdrawal from the floor. It wasn't until I walked past an adult, a *close* friend, who looked disparagingly toward me that I realized how this would look in the larger context."[354]

Others remained in the hall. Mendelsohn's associate minister at Arlington Street, W. Edward Harris, had been privy to the public arguments that had taken place in that congregation. He himself had been "radical and hot headed" in Birmingham earlier in the sixties. "I was deeply sympathetic with the Empowerment group but could not walk out," he said. "I believe in the church as a community of moral discourse. Hard to discourse if some of the parties are not present." At that time, Arlington Street was a church of nine hundred or a thousand, with a significant black membership. "Most were integrationist—but not all," said Harris. "I decided not to walk out in part because I wasn't comfortable with that strategy, but also to keep faith with that part of the church which was unsure of that course of action. My response was 'pastoral.' "[355]

Alan Deale told his colleague Brandy Lovely, "When I saw you walked out I hoped never to see you again, likewise for Jack Mendelsohn and a few others. I could not support the idea of 'non-negotiable demands' which I feel have no place in our religion."[356]

Gibson, Gelsey, Mendelson, Fritchman, and Gilmartin had all marched in Selma. Some others who had also done so chose not to leave but felt deeply wounded. Robert Reed, a member of FULLBAC, stayed seated and watched as other BAC supporters walked out because he feared that if he left he would never come back. Alan Rosenthal also feared that the diversity of views would tear the Unitarian Universalist Association apart.[357]

"Had I been a delegate," said Homer Jack, "I guess I would have walked out. Emotionally, I could have done no other, with so many close friends departing, and I would have found rational reasons later."[358]

As they marched out, there were shouts of reproach, charges of "blackmail," raised fists, and some racist jibes "directed at the departing white leaders."[359]

Those who had stayed were in dismay. "I couldn't believe it," said Betty Seiden, BAWA's African American executive secretary. "Without thinking I ran up to the dais. The only idea in my head was everybody isn't leaving. I'm here. I just stood there and cried as I watched people walk out."[360] Dana Greeley, who was seated on the podium, cried as well.

Meanwhile, hundreds of protestors had left the building. "Tearful, joyous, singing we went out and made our way to Arlington Street Church," said Rob Isaacs, who was soon to become the LRY president.[361] John Gibbons, another LRY member, recalled that they were "more than stunned.... It felt like we were leaving not a particular assembly or any mere meeting, but we were leaving an institution that had denied its heritage and broken its prophetic promise. The institution of Unitarian Universalism and our association of congregations seemed irreparably broken.... In a stream of departing delegates, forsaken and bereft, we made our exodus, crying and inconsolable. In the hotel lobby, I recall the glare of

TV lights and cameras. I recall the tears on my face, and I recall the wave of tears that carried us out of the hotel, down the sidewalk and across the street until we entered the sanctuary of Arlington Street."[362]

Around three hundred people had walked out, including presidential candidate Aron Gilmartin.[363] In their wake, Glover Barnes, co-chair of BAWA, delivered an impassioned speech in which he appealed for harmony and said he would rather forego the $50 thousand for BAWA than see the discord grow worse. Still, he rejected "the separatist way" and "asserted that not all groups who claim to speak for minorities actually represent minorities."[364] He pleaded, "Where is inclusiveness here?"[365] As he spoke, recalled Seiden, "a few of us stood crying behind him to demonstrate that there were many black Unitarians who were not going to walk out on the denomination."[366] Joe Fisher, the moderator, finally called a recess.

When those who remained reconvened on Tuesday afternoon, someone called for a count, to determine whether a quorum still existed. It was determined that one did. Jack Kent and Jeffrey Campbell proposed that a small delegation be formally sent to the Arlington Street Church to confer with the protestors, who had by then taken on the name Moral Caucus, and also with BUUC, to invite them back in the hope of negotiating a settlement. This proposal was quickly and almost unanimously adopted. Greeley was invited to lead a group that, since power was about to change hands, included Fisher and representatives of the two leading presidential candidates.[367]

The delegation hurried through the heat to the Arlington Street Church. As Hayward Henry noted, "When the black folks left, there was no crisis. When the white folks left there was a crisis."[368]

In the Arlington Street sanctuary, impassioned speeches went on interminably. Mendelsohn called for "a new church, for new men and women in a new world." David Parke said, "We are out from under the intransigence, which I now designate racist, of the Assembly we have left. Free at last."[369]

Clark Olsen, who had joined with those who followed Jack Mendelsohn there, sat in the back feeling more a sympathetic observer than an active player. As the day progressed, others came to see what was going on. Homer Jack dropped in briefly. Nat Lauriat from Hartford came to check on his congregants.

Leon Hopper, like many others, had gone to Selma and was a member of FULLBAC. Now he was a newly elected Mountain Desert District trustee on the UUA Board. He had walked out too and gone to the Arlington Street Church, but he quickly tired of what he heard as self-righteous bravado and left.[370] "I seem to live in a world of ambiguity not looking for hard lines [but] my practice of tolerance for ambiguity didn't seem possible. I was torn," he said. "As I walked by the Arlington Street Church they were singing hymns. I felt lost and alone, wandering the streets of Boston for twenty minutes or more. I finally decided to go back to the hall and participate in the work of the association and to greater serve our stated values."[371]

Addressing the renegades, LRY member Kathy Lazaras said, "I really think you're copping out. I'm tired of the rationalizations. Go back and talk to those people on a rational, intellectual level." And Fritchman told them, "Organize—no matter what else turns out.... We have failed if all we do is indulge ourselves, almost erotically, with what we have done."[372]

While some urged returning and conducting discussions according to regular parliamentary procedures, others argued that they should go back and use stronger tactics and, if necessary, break up the Assembly. A few proposed withdrawing from the Unitarian Universalist Association.

When the Greeley-led delegation arrived, Greeley was expected to get in line and wait his turn to speak, which he did. When his turn came, he stood in the pulpit of the congregation he had served for twenty-seven years and said,

> I was moved to join this group. I did—a little tardily. Most of them have stayed and done the kind of work which made us the most relevant religious movement in America today.... As many of you know, I opposed the funding of BAWA.... The Board in its wisdom or lack of wisdom funded it. And I support the Board until their decision is proven incorrect.
>
> Your conscience has to be your guide and if you can find an Association which will be more relevant than this one I will consider it with you.
>
> Come back in two weeks, two years or two hours if you can come back, but if you can't come back we'll respect you wherever you are.[373]

He told them, with firm but heartfelt insistence, that the Assembly, by a unanimous vote, invited them back. Rob Isaacs remembers that as he spoke, "tears streamed down his cheeks." "He called us to come home. He reminded us that we were part of a family and that families don't settle debates this way."[374]

Greeley's use of the words *home* and *family* give us a glimpse into his felt sense of the UUA. His words would have resonated with many longtime Unitarian Universalists, including those in rebellion. David Parke's grandparents were Unitarian ministers. Rob Isaacs had grown up in the First Unitarian Society of Chicago, and John Gibbons in Third. In Greeley's delegation, Chris Raible had two Unitarian Universalist ministers in his family, his father and brother; David Weissbard grew up in the Albany church, where his father was president of the congregation. Jeffrey Campbell had joined the Universalist Church in Nashua, New Hampshire, when he was ten years old. For them, the Unitarian Universalist Association was home. Unitarians had felt this way since the nineteenth century, when New Englanders moved west and founded Unitarian churches as a way of preserving New England culture. The May Meetings of the American Unitarian Association, which had drawn two hundred ministers and as many laypeople, had been as much a ministers' convocation as an annual meeting. Its presidents were patriarchs, and Greeley was of the same mold.

With the growth of the fellowship movement, this family feeling among Unitarians had begun to change. "Resistance to authority often extends to distrust of denominational leadership.... Many fellowship members express a mixture of disdain, ignorance, and indifference to the Unitarian Universalist Association," Holley Ulbrich writes in *The Fellowship Movement*.[375] These congregations, which were largely filled with people coming in from other faiths, had a more distant relationship to Boston than those founded by the earlier New England diaspora. The Universalists also felt ambivalent about the Unitarian Universalist Association. For them, the family unit, beyond the congregation, was the state convention. Since the Universalists were fewer than the Unitarians, we are not talking about large numbers. Nonetheless, the family expanded significantly with consolidation. Now it was a blended family, albeit of kissing cousins.

With the consolidation of the Unitarian and Universalist denominations, the combined Unitarian Universalist Association was larger, more bureaucratic, and less personal than the sum of its parts. General Assemblies also grew larger and no longer felt so much like family gatherings, nor did the delegates behave as one. Indeed, that was not the way Louis Gothard, a founder of BURR and associate director of the Interreligious Foundation for Community

Organization, saw it. He said of BUUC, "We see ourselves as a union of black people within the denomination," and likened the administration to management. He even implied, but did not say outright because Harrington was part of the conversation, that BAWA was "analogous" to a "scab."[376] Likewise, BAC member Roy Ockert, with his many years of experience in the union movement, talked about the "bargaining table," "each side in a situation of conflict," and "collective bargaining."[377] He, like others, described the world in adversarial rather than familial terms. Their inspiration was Saul Alinsky, who popularized the idea that the way to force people in power to negotiate was by organizing, disrupting, and polarizing.

This changing dynamic was, in part, why the 1969 General Assembly was so wrenching. Cultural shifts, along with the effort to accommodate Black Power and the youth rebellion, helped to disrupt the practices to which Unitarian Universalists were accustomed. They were debating with people they did not know, while Greeley, as he continued doggedly on, was presiding as a lame duck over the Unitarian Universalist Association—a patriarch out of step with the time.

There was another shift taking place; it was in where power resided and how it was exercised. Indeed, the configuration of power within the Unitarian Universalist Association had been in subterranean flux and in contention ever since consolidation in 1961.

It was after 4 PM when Greeley's delegation withdrew into a side room to negotiate the return of this ad hoc group. The Moral Caucus was represented by Jack Mendelsohn, Robert Hohler, and Ann Raynolds. Weissbard said he "was embarrassed by Greeley's naiveté and condescension. . . . He really did not 'get it.' He had no grasp of the situation or what it meant to the people who had walked out."[378] After that, the delegation met with Hayward Henry, Ben

Scott, and others in BUUC's suite. Those who had walked out struggled late into the night with what to do.[379]

The next morning, some four hundred dissident whites (not all of whom were delegates) returned to General Assembly as youth released balloons from the balconies. They were followed by about sixty members of BUUC.[380] Betty Seiden found the spectacle of "the great walk-back-in" ironic. As she explained, "All the white prodigals came in first through the front door. And the black ones came in later through the back. I'm sure it was not planned that way, but it happened just like that."[381]

Unexpected Outcomes

The outcomes of the Boston General Assembly of 1969 were many. Some were predictable, but others could not be foreseen, and their influence on the Unitarian Universalist Association would be significant.

Elections

Right before the return of the "prodigals" to General Assembly, the result of the presidential election was announced. With seven candidates running, there had been concern that no one would win an absolute majority on the first round. Because of this, voters cast two different ballots; the second one was preferential and asked the voters to rank order the candidates. But before the polls opened, the necessary amendment to permit preferential voting was defeated, and as it turned out, was not needed. Robert Nelson West, minister of the First Unitarian Church of Rochester, New York, won a narrow victory. Garnering 1,025 votes, he won just over 50 percent of the 2,031 votes cast; Deane Starr's 491 represented 24 percent; and Gilmartin received 364, or 18 percent. John Wells's prediction had been essentially correct: The political center had attracted most of the votes. It helped that Hadley had withdrawn during the candidates' speeches and thrown his support to West. Additionally, during those strife-filled days, West's campaign had emphasized that it was important to elect a president with a clear, absolute majority so that, whatever other decisions General Assembly made, he could move forward from a position of strength. Given the role West would play in salvaging the financial wreckage he inherited and the myriad of crises he would face, that affirmation was needed.

The other critical, long overdue, and consequential part of the election was the number of African Americans elected. BAC was dismayed that the Nominating Committee had not consulted with it in assembling its slate of candidates and had put forward only three African Americans. For that reason, it developed a supplemental slate. This resulted in Edna M. Griffin being elected to the Board of Trustees; Jack O. LeFlore, Henrietta McKee, Cornelius McDougald, and William M. Scott to the Nominating Committee; Joseph Samples and Harold Wilson to the Commission on Appraisal; Gwendolyn Thomas to the Business Committee; and Dr. S. J. Williamson Jr. and Raymond L. Wilkins to the Program Committee.[382] In all, ten of the thirty people elected to committees were African American. In addition, Althea Alexander was elected to the Board of the Unitarian Universalist Service Committee and Wesley S. William was elected president of the UU Laymen's League. And when the Board met in September, it appointed Griffin to its Executive Committee, Renford Gaines to the Ministerial Fellowship Committee (where he joined African American psychologist Nolan Penn), Margaret Williams to the Accreditation of Directors of Religious Education Committee, Jack O. LeFlore, Benjamin Scott, and Isaac McNatt to the Social Responsibility and Investment Committees, and Vincent Harding to the Beacon Press Board.

This was a major shift. In the decades that followed, governing bodies and Board committees of the Unitarian Universalist Association would never again be without a significant African American presence. Prior to 1969, the absence of blacks meant that any expertise, insight, or guidance African Americans might have contributed never made it to the table. African Americans had been largely without a voice in the administration's discussions and decision-making. And because they had not held positions of influence and power anywhere within the Unitarian Universalist Association during an era in which race was America's most pressing domestic issue, the Association was not attuned to that issue and not prepared to handle it. Without a doubt, this contributed to the crisis that engulfed the Association. Given the achievements of African American Unitarian Universalists and given their leadership roles in local congregations, their absence from the national levels of power was clearly the result of systemic racism and the blindness of whites to their own behavior and working assumptions. Greeley cannot escape accountability; the Nominating Committee consulted with him, and he sat on executive committees that for decades permitted this near vacuum to exist.

Either But Not Both

Once the dissidents had rejoined the Assembly, a motion was put forward to fund "either BAC or BAWA but not both." Hayward Henry said, "If you want to be relevant to the black movement in this country, you will vote affirmatively,"[383] while Glover Barnes spoke to the theme of inclusiveness. When the vote was taken, the motion passed by 798 to 737. BAWA then moved that it be funded for $50 thousand; however, a substitute motion by BAC, funding it again for $250 thousand, carried. The next day, Richard Traylor, on behalf of BUUC, moved that the Unitarian Universalist

Association make a reparations investment of $5 million but then withdrew it in the face of a substitute motion endorsing the plan the Board had already implemented and augmented after Hohler's fast at 25 Beacon Street. That plan specified that $500 thousand be invested during the 1969–1970 year in enterprises of high social value. On Friday, Guillermo Martinez, one of Fritchman's congregants, moved that the UUA budget allocate $50 thousand for Chicano empowerment. This motion passed, as did a general resolution supporting the Delano grape boycott. Finally, in regard to youth liberation, the UUA came to an agreement with Liberal Religious Youth and Student Religious Liberals that the two groups would form an independent, autonomous Board that would receive $100 thousand annually from the Unitarian Universalist Association and control its use. Support for this was nearly unanimous.

Afterward Hayward Henry wrote,

> Willing to support a Black self-determination movement, many of the same people were also willing to support a ridiculous and counter-productive movement. Preaching brotherly love, many attacked Blacks with the viciousness of the larger society. Claiming to be liberals and committed to social justice, conservatism and business as usual prevailed. One is left with the all but inevitable conclusion that the denomination is indeed a microcosm of the national society—racist to its roots.[384]

Whatever solidarity BAC, BUUC, FULLBAC, and the youth had found and whatever parliamentary triumphs they had achieved, the close vote (798 to 737) indicated that despite the votes of the 1968 and 1969 General Assemblies to fund BAC, no true consensus existed within the Unitarian Universalist Association about black empowerment.

Homer Jack called BAC's victory pyrrhic. Echoing Richard Nash, he said that BAC had made a major tactical mistake in its attack on BAWA, which was seen by many as an attack on pluralism. Jack identified pluralism as a "hallmark of the denomination," and the result was that BAWA gained even more support than it had in Cleveland. When Jack dropped in on its annual dinner, he found lifelong Unitarian Universalist friends attending: people who were "involved with [him] in social action battles before Hayward Henry (or Larry Ladd) were born," people whose integrity he trusted and of whose dedication to the UUA he was certain. The "banquet [was] a huge success. Buoyed by this strength through defeat, BAWA announced a $333,333 annual budget, and received $45,000 in cash, pledges, and loans on the spot. BAWA left Boston an 'empowered' organization." "And yet, and yet . . ." Jack also found BAWA to be an "anachronism."[385]

The Fellowship for Renewal

FULLBAC was dissolved at the 1969 General Assembly and merged with their compatriots who had walked out to form the Moral Caucus. The new group called itself the Fellowship for Renewal (FFR) and went about broadening its mandate. Supporting the black agenda remained one of its goals, but others included organizing the white community to fight racism, taking political action within the UUA, developing a program to promote socially responsible investment, and experimenting with expressions of worship. Regional committees were to gather and develop further plans. Duke Gray, the former FULLBAC field director, told the FFR membership that its "success or failure will depend upon the part you play in an organized effort to root out the sins of racism and oppression in your local church and community."[386] During that fall, five regional groups met and each, in an effort to build groups "free of the old institutional hang-ups," emphasized interpersonal relations and small group discussion.[387]

The FFR's co-chairs were Jack Mendelsohn and Ann Raynolds. Youth were represented by Larry Ladd and Wayne Arnason. And the acting director was G. Robert Hohler. After his brief candidacy for president of the Unitarian Universalist Association and his hunger strike, he had stepped down from leading the Laymen's League and now took on a new role consistent with his growing radicalism.

Following the November Unitarian Universalist Association Board meeting, at which the Board made a decision that would spread BAC's funding over five years instead of four, the FFR newsletter said, "It is up to us WHITE FOLKS to confront the white institution to which we belong on this issue."[388] The Midwest and New England FFR groups called for their members to demonstrate their concern by attending the January UUA Board meeting. Until then, they advised people to enter into dialogue with individual members of the Board. A discussion also began about whether congregations should place their Association dues in escrow.

While the national FFR was mobilizing for a January confrontation with the Board, the New England FFR began pressuring the First Unitarian Church of Boston to give away the money it had collected from the insurance payment after the fire, the sale of Second Unitarian, and membership donations, which it meant to use to replace its fire-gutted building. The plan was for a group of FFR members to march into the December 7 worship service and read a statement. However, following negotiations between Rhys Williams and the FFR, an agreement was reached that the FFR could pass out its statement during fellowship hour and then hold a forum. Its statement read, in part, "Friends, we know you are not the whole of rich fat America but news of your $2 million plan in this day and age cannot go unchallenged. . . . A beautiful cultural shell cannot mask the suffering and deprivation and desperation of our people.... YOUR MONEY IS YOURS IF YOU HAVE THE WILL TO EXERCISE YOUR OWN POWER; to act IMMEDIATELY in a humanitarian way, to provide housing for poor people."[389]

The Process

Before the 1969 General Assembly, in reporting on the Punderson Conference to Canadians, Mary Lu MacDonald had written, "If the purpose of it all was to see if the UUA would still be around after this year's General Assembly, the answer would seem to be yes—provided that the delegates can be brought together on a one-to-one basis and the speech-making is kept to a minimum."[390] The Unitarian Universalist Women's Federation (UUWF), judging the temper of the times as MacDonald had, less than a month before the General Assembly, proposed to the Unitarian Universalist Association Board and then the Program and Business Committees that they use "a process" at General Assembly "whereby all could share their concerns in small groups, raising their questions, and agreeing on primary concerns before taking up the actual business matters we were there to consider."[391] When none of these groups took up its suggestion, the UUWF made an attempt to raise the issue again at the Tuesday morning session of the Assembly. But when "Mrs. Alice Kimball of Winchester, the president of the UUA Women's Federation, moved that the assembly recess to allow discussion groups to ascertain priorities for the meeting," the motion was defeated.[392]

In reporting on General Assembly "from an educational point of view," religious educator Til Evans wrote,

> It seems incredible to me that in a denomination such as ours, which has many human resources available to it in the area of

human dynamics, that those people were not used in planning the whole Assembly, in view of the fact that it is impossible to educate a large number of people on the floor of the Assembly in a business session. I would estimate that a third of the delegates (and they were the third who made the difference) were unsure about the issues on which they were called to vote. It's obvious that many societies do not do a particularly good job of educating their delegates prior to the General Assembly.

The Woman's Federation motion for an alternative (small group discussions for part of a morning) was poorly presented, and came too late, as the intensity of the polarity showed at that point.[393]

The UUWF motion ran counter to the radicals' Alinsky-inspired strategy and the rampant polarization of the era. But the lessons born of the trauma of the 1969 General Assembly were taken in by Rev. Ralph Stuztman and Rev. David Weissbard. When, a couple of years later, they were on the General Assembly Program Committee, they saw an opportunity to implement needed changes. Stuztman said of the Committee, "All of us had been traumatized by the controversy and sought to change the atmosphere at GA, bringing some sanity to the GA process."[394]

A consensus quickly evolved. After experimenting with small groups in 1971, the Program Committee invented the mini-assemblies format, in which issues could be debated in small groups before coming to the general floor. The intent of these smaller gatherings was to give more delegates the opportunity to speak and thus to enhance the democratic process. The Program Committee, which Weissbard chaired, thought that in smaller gatherings people would be able to operate in a less emotional manner and in a less polemic style. In addition, they reintroduced worship services to GA, which had abandoned them, and later a meditation room with plants, art, and soft music where individuals could step away from the commotion into a space for centering themselves. Stuztman said, "It was our attempt to bring healing to a wounded movement."[395]

Local reports about the 1969 General Assembly delivered after the event offered starkly different assessments. In the Los Angeles congregation, one delegate decried the "Negro delegates who played the role of the Uncle Tom." Jules Ramey blamed the UUA and said the task before the congregation was "to stop the reactionary, fascist direction within the denomination."[396] Phillip Hewett, who was then chair of the Unitarian Universalist Association Program Committee, identified the threat very differently. In a sermon delivered in Vancouver, he compared the BAC/BUUC strategy to fascism point by point. He said it had "the same mystique of togetherness and of race," "the same intolerance of dissent, the same anti-intellectualism," and "the same name-calling to discredit the opposition."[397]

What fed such opposite views? The more reflective of those who walked out offer some answers. John Gibbons said the division gave them "the clarity of identities—*us* or *them*, and as far as *we* were concerned, the absolute certainty of the righteousness of *our* cause."[398] Richard Kellaway, when asked, "Why did BAC put so much energy into attacking BAWA?" answered, "They needed an enemy because it helped create group cohesion." Larry Ladd, writing immediately following the Assembly, said, "Within the UUA each side, for purposes of reform, has chosen to make the other into a group of sinister, conspiratorial demons. It's rather obvious really that BAWA, BUUC, FULLBAC, or any other group is not like it is pictured by its opponent. Charges of conspiracy are erroneous, but they do show the degree of mistrust in this institution. People become genuinely afraid of each other."[399]

Not every Unitarian Universalist was caught up in the acrimony. As the 1969 General Assembly was ending, Apollo 11 landed on the moon, and Neil Armstrong said, "That's one small step for [a] man, one giant leap for mankind." On Earth, an African American Unitarian Universalist scientist was awaiting the lunar soil samples the mission would bring back and had no time for and little interest in Unitarian Universalist political intrigue.[400]

The IARF and the CUC – The World Was Watching

The coming together of the Unitarian Universalist Association and the International Association for Religious Freedom at General Assembly was a unique occasion. The IARF was an organization founded in Boston on May 25, 1900, as the International Council of Unitarians and Other Liberal Religious Thinkers and Workers. Its inspiration came from the 1893 World Parliament of Religions, in which Universalists and Unitarians were intimately involved.[401] Its inaugural meeting was held in connection with the seventy-fifth anniversary of the American Unitarian Association, which was also the seventy-fifth anniversary of the British and Foreign Unitarian Association.[402] The creation of the Council marked the founding of the world's first international interfaith organization.

In 1969, the IARF once again met in Boston, in conjunction with the UUA General Assembly. This confluence had long been Dana MacLean Greeley's dream. Phillip Hewett said that Greeley wanted "to broaden the too nationalistic outlook of many Americans."[403] It could have been a celebration of liberal religion as a worldwide movement, but as Homer Jack said, "the vast majority of delegates and observers could not remove their attention from Black/white relations."[404] According to the British General Assembly of Unitarians, "the UUA Meetings were, in fact, so lively and at times explosive, that the IARF gatherings faded into comparative insignificance."[405] Amidst the upheaval, most IARF-sponsored gatherings were poorly attended: A reception that BUUC was to have sponsored for the IARF was canceled; the National Information Hour to meet liberal religious leaders from around the globe attracted few guests; and "visitors from Assam, Negros Orientale and Lagos, Nigeria walked the corridors, unknown and largely ungreeted."[406]

Not only did the IARF receive scant notice but little attention was paid to the war in Vietnam. In his final address, Greeley denounced American involvement in Vietnam as "the most morally offensive crime against the human race since ... the gas chambers." But Vietnam was never debated during the Assembly.[407] "With an exaggerated focus on its own internal affairs," said Max A. Kapp, director of the Unitarian Universalist Association's Office of Overseas and Interfaith Relations, "our movement seemed to be trending toward a new isolationism."[408]

Nonetheless, at its 1969 Congress, the IARF redefined itself in a way that in the long term would greatly affect its relationship to the UUA, a change that went largely unnoticed. Since 1932, it had been the International Association for Liberal Christianity and Religious Freedom; now it officially became simply the International Association for Religious Freedom. This was done to allow non-Christian groups into membership, specifically the Japanese lay Buddhist movement Rissho Kosei-kai, with its 3 million members, and the Konko Church of Izuo, a Shinto movement. This move toward greater inclusivity made the IARF a truly interfaith organization, and over time this would have wide-ranging consequences—although its significance was not grasped at the time.

Following the IARF Congress, there was a gathering of leading European delegates at UUA headquarters. Canadian Phillip Hewett said, "These visitors expressed their feelings very strongly. They had felt totally marginalized, but more seriously, were indeed aghast at . . . the unfolding of events that reminded them all too vividly of what they had witnessed in Europe during the rise of Nazism—not only the totalitarian procedures but also the impotence of liberals to act on behalf of their avowed principles when these were being so directly challenged."[409] Such a small, marginalized group as those who walked out of General Assembly could never amass the power of fascism. But many of the European visitors had seen their style before.

When the IARF Executive Committee met after the meeting, it made the decision that for the foreseeable future, no further joint meetings should be held.

BAC was an issue in Canada, but a very small one. A fifth of the cover page of the December 1968 *Canadian Unitarian* was given to the announcement that BAC grants were available to blacks and people of other ethnic origins in the U.S. and Canada. However, the lead article introduced Thomas L. Haley, newly appointed as the social action representative of the Canadian Unitarian Council (CUC) in the nation's capital, Ottawa. Haley was Afro-Canadian, and although that was one of the reasons he was hired, nowhere in the article was this mentioned.

In May 1969, BAC was discussed at the CUC's Annual General Meeting. The feeling was "that BAC would not be qualified to decide on . . . possible Canadian projects" with "Eskimos" or "Indians."[410] BAC claimed that it embraced all oppressed peoples with the term *Black*, and it did support the allocation of $50 thousand to Chicano empowerment. However, there is no indication that it awarded any grants to a Canadian project. While inquiries were made of BAC and Hayward Henry came to Toronto later that year to deliver the Workman Lecture,[411] it is possible that no Canadians applied. If that is so, it too is indicative of distance and disconnection.

At the CUC meeting, the main issue in contention was not BAC but the CUC's relationship to the UUA. "Signs of Unitarian Separatism in Canada" was the headline in the spring 1969 edition of the *Canadian Unitarian*. During the workshops at the CUC Annual General Meeting, the future of the CUC was discussed, and people uniformly expressed a yearning for a stronger Canadian Unitarian identity. When the meeting turned to the business agenda, a resolution was proposed calling for the CUC to reconstitute itself as a national body paid for by Canadians. It failed twenty-one to twenty-nine. However, both this and a subsequent resolution[412] that did pass communicated Canadian dissatisfaction with the UUA, and Greeley and Homer Jack were there in Montreal to hear it.

The issues were not new, but the specific event that led to the call for reconstitution of the CUC was an earlier meeting of Ontario representatives, who had complained that they had difficulty communicating with the UUA, that the materials sent out by the UUA were not appropriate for the Canadian context, and that they wanted better intra-Canadian ties. Also, in regard to social action, the UUA did not speak to Canadian concerns. A review of the resolutions passed by the CUC shows a focus on the treatment of First Nations people. Another cause of friction was the UUA's continued blocking of CUC membership in the IARF. In fact, the UUA had not consulted Canada when choosing a Canadian delegate to attend the IARF Congress in Boston.[413] Yet another issue was that, in dealing with the UUA budget crisis, the Greeley administration proposed cutting back on the already meager amount it provided to run the volunteer office the CUC maintained in Toronto. In 1964, when the CUC's total budget was $4,700, it requested $3,500 from the UUA and was allocated $3,100; now the UUA proposed cutting its contribution by $1,800, despite the fact that Canadian congregations contributed over $25 thousand a year to the UUA's Annual Program Fund.[414]

In his memoir, *25 Beacon Street*, Greeley noted, "Our Canadian brethren think that we are preoccupied with national problems."[415] He was right, and it was never clearer than it became at the 1969 General Assembly.

It wasn't until Thursday of that General Assembly that the Canadians had an opportunity to make a resolution regarding the CUC's relationship to the UUA—and just as the president of the CUC gained the floor, he was cut off by a point of order. It took an impassioned appeal to convince the Assembly to reverse its procedural decision and hear the Canadian resolution. It began, "The Canadian delegates at this assembly have suffered and rejoiced and been involved throughout.... many items of business before us. Some, however, have little or no relevance to the Canadian scene.... Minorities in Canada, for the information of this assembly, are, in order of percentage of population, French speaking, Indian, Eskimo, Oriental, and Black. Whether French and English speaking Canadians can learn to live together with love is the point on which the future of our country depends."[416] The resolution that called for improved CUC-UUA relations received near unanimous approval.

Reporting on General Assembly to his church's Board, Ottawa's assistant minister said that the delegates had been upset to hear about the breakaway vote at the CUC annual meeting and wanted the UUA's relationship with Canadian Unitarians to improve. But American Unitarian Universalist publications that reported on the CUC's annual meeting focused not on Canadian Unitarians but on the CUC's disenchantment with the UUA.

Meanwhile, Canada was in the grip of its own crisis. In February 1969, the Front de libération du Québec (FLQ) had bombed the

Montreal Stock Exchange, and in October 1970, it would kidnap and murder Pierre LaPorte, the deputy premier of Quebec. The existential threat that Canada faced was not mentioned in American UU publications, nor did American Unitarian Universalists understand it. Canadians could not help but feel that the UUA was evolving into a national rather than continental organization, while they were looking to have their identity affirmed and their own needs met. They wanted control of their own resources—just what BAC and BUUC were seeking. To put this in context: About 4 percent of the UUA congregations and total membership were Canadian, meaning that there were three times as many Canadians as African Americans. Why, then, did the engagement with BAC garner most of the UUA's attention and resources? Canadians were beginning to confront a kind of quasi-colonialism, a form of Unitarian Universalist American-centric imperialism in which both black and white American Unitarian Universalists were implicated.

Just as the delegates to the 1969 General Assembly did not appreciate the significance of the transformation of the IARF, neither did they understand that this Assembly marked the beginning of the end of the UUA as a continental movement. "My thinking too is swinging," wrote Phillip Hewett. "I don't want to be nationalistic in my religion but the issue is being forced."[417] *UUA Now* said that the resolution at the CUC annual meeting had failed for economic reasons: The delegates did not feel the CUC could manage the financial burden of going it alone. It would be another thirty years before the CUC finally separated from the UUA, but there can be no doubt that the UUA's self-absorption in responding to Black Power reinforced the Canadian apprehension that separation was necessary.

Commission on Religion and Race (1963). From left, facing camera: Homer A. Jack, Howard Harris, Clifton Hoffman, Cornelius McDougald, Dana McLean Greeley, Walter Royal Jones, Matilda Moore, unknown woman, Robert Jones, Ken Marshall, Sid Freeman, Alfred W. Hobart, Greta Crosby. Not visible: William Rice and Howard Thurman. Photo by JET Commercial Photographers. Commission on Religion and Race File, bMS 15033/2 (63-64), Andover-Harvard Theological Library, Harvard Divinity School, Cambridge, Massachusetts.

Ware Lecture at UUA General Assembly in Hollywood, Florida (1966). From left: Clifton Hoffman, Martin Luther King Jr., Dana McLean Greeley, Homer A. Jack. Dana McLean Greeley Minister File, bMS 1446/77, Andover-Harvard Theological Library, Harvard Divinity School, Cambridge, Massachusetts.

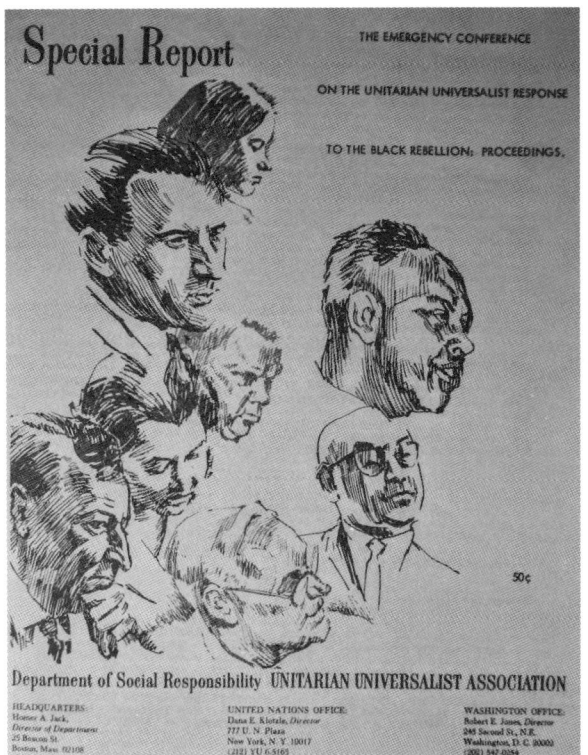

Cover of *Special Report: The Emergency Conference on the Unitarian Universalist Response to the Black Rebellion: Proceedings*, from the Unitarian Universalist Association's Department of Social Responsibility, October 23, 1967.

Front page of *UUA Now* news supplement, June 1968, *UUA Now*/UUA Archives, Andover-Harvard Theological Library, Harvard Divinity School, Cambridge, Massachusetts.

Supporters of the Black Affairs Council commandeer the microphones and demand a new agenda at the 1969 General Assembly. Photo by Steven H. Hansen. *UUA Now*/UUA Archives, Andover-Harvard Theological Library, Harvard Divinity School, Cambridge, Massachusetts.

Stephen Fritchman (at microphone) speaks out for the BAC at the 1969 General Assembly. Hayward Henry stands to his left. Photo by Steven H. Hansen. *UUA Now*/UUA Archives, Andover-Harvard Theological Library, Harvard Divinity School, Cambridge, Massachusetts.

BAWA leaders during General Assembly 1969 press conference. From left: Max Gaebler, Betty Seiden, Glover Barnes. Photo by Dan Bernstein. *UUA Now*/UUA Archives, Andover-Harvard Theological Library, Harvard Divinity School, Cambridge, Massachusetts.

Protesting white delegates to the 1969 General Assembly, led by Jack Mendelsohn, march to Arlington Street Church after the BUUC walk-out. Photo by Steven H. Hansen. *UUA Now*/UUA Archives, Andover-Harvard Theological Library, Harvard Divinity School, Cambridge, Massachusetts.

BAC supporters on day of either-or vote for BAC or BAWA, 1969 General Assembly. From left: Althea Alexander, Carroll Williams, Harold Wilson, Aron Gilmartin. Hayward Henry sitting in front on right. Photograph by Forrest Speck. *UUA Now*/UUA Archives, Andover-Harvard Theological Library, Harvard Divinity School, Cambridge, Massachusetts.

Dwight Brown (left) and Donald Harrington (right) speak for BAWA at 1969 General Assembly. Photo by Forrest Speck. *UUA Now*/UUA Archives, Andover-Harvard Theological Library, Harvard Divinity School, Cambridge, Massachusetts.

Supporters celebrate when the 1969 General Assembly approves funds for BAC while denying them to BAWA. Hayward Henry is in the center right, facing the camera with his arm raised. Benjamin Scott is sitting to his right, clapping. Photo by Dan Bernstein. *UUA Now*/UUA Archives, Andover-Harvard Theological Library, Harvard Divinity School, Cambridge, Massachusetts.

Newly elected UUA president Bob West addresses the 1969 General Assembly. To his left is former UUA president Dana McLean Greeley. Photo by Dan Bernstein. *UUA Now*/UUA Archives, Andover-Harvard Theological Library, Harvard Divinity School, Cambridge, Massachusetts.

The Black Affairs Council Disaffiliates from the UUA

[*1970*]

THE CRISIS THAT TRIGGERED the Walkout did not end with the vote of the 1969 General Assembly to give the Black Affairs Council another $250 thousand. Faced with a rapidly deteriorating financial situation, the Unitarian Universalist Association Board drastically cut the UUA budget at its November meeting. Those cuts affected every aspect of the Association including BAC, who would receive $1 million but over five years instead of four. Interest groups and regions across the country raised an outcry.

Bob West's new policy of open Board meetings led to a change of venue in order to accommodate the guests, observers, and protestors who flooded to Boston to attend the next UUA Board meeting in January 1970. The meeting was a powder keg waiting to explode.

That Sunday, January 25, the temperature in Boston hovered below 30 degrees, with just a dusting of snow whipped about by a gusty wind. Inside, everyone at the Board meeting looked grim—the Board members seated around the table, the representatives of BAC and of BAWA, and the forty members of the Fellowship for Renewal lining the wall in protest of the Board's November vote. When the Board reaffirmed its decision to fund BAC over five years instead of four, the protestors began singing the nineteenth-century protest hymn by James Russell Lowell.

> Once to every man and nation comes the moment to decide,
> In the strife of truth with falsehood, for the good or evil side....
>
> Then to stand with truth is noble, when we share her wretched crust;
> Ere her cause bring fame and profit, and 'tis prosperous to be just....
>
> Though the cause of evil prosper, yet 'tis truth alone is strong;
> Though her portion be the scaffold, and upon the throne be wrong....
>
> Then it is the brave man chooses, while the coward stands aside,
> Till the multitude make virtue of the faith they have denied.

This hymn tells us a lot about the lens through which FFR and BAC saw what had happened.

The UUA Financial Crisis Comes to a Head

In 1969, when Bob West took office as president, he knew the Unitarian Universalist Association was in difficult financial straits. Prior to consolidation, the Universalist Church of America had gone through the very painful exercise of bringing its expenses in line with its income, but the American Unitarian Association had not. Deficit budgeting was routine in the AUA and continued in the new UUA. The practice predated Greeley's term as the AUA's final president (1958–1961); in 1957, the AUA carried a deficit of $48,930, in 1958, it was $51,433, and in 1959, $46,778. That represented an average annual deficit of over 13 percent of the budget. Such deficits had reduced the unrestricted endowment funds the UUA inherited in 1961. In the UUA's first years, the overruns of the Greeley administration were somewhat higher in absolute terms, but lower percentages of the budget than before: between 1962 and

1966, the average deficit was $64 thousand, which was a little less than 8 percent of the total budget. However, during that time, the overall budget climbed from $630,000 to $1,069,000, and in 1967, it reached $1,226,000. And while the budget nearly doubled, the Annual Fund, apart from special gifts, had increased on average only $40 thousand a year; giving had not kept up with expenditures.[418]

Ever the optimist, Greeley saw the administration's expenditures as an investment in growing the movement. David Cole, coming to the UUA from the Universalist side, said, "Dana Greeley had a great need for money and all available monies went into his pet programs.... He wanted lots of departments and a big staff in Boston and he was out to save the world. And so as little money as possible was put into regional organizations and most of the resources went to ... [the] Continental Organization."[419] Raymond Hopkins, the UUA vice president under Greeley, objected to the portrayal of Greeley as the "villain." In his defense, Hopkins pointed out that the Finance Committee, Board, and General Assembly all approved the budgets, and they did this despite annual warnings from Hopkins himself and the UUA treasurer.

(This problem was not unique to the UUA. Denominations across America were struggling financially. In 1969, budget cuts were also made by the United Presbyterian Church, the United Methodist Church, and the National Council of Churches.[420])

In 1968, the UUA budget was $1.4 million and the deficit was $100 thousand. However, the Cleveland General Assembly made a number of other allocations alongside the $250 thousand it voted to fund BAC. The situation warranted comment in the British newsletter *The Inquirer:*

> The problem of theological education caused considerable discussion. Crane Theological School at Tufts closes this June leaving

two schools—at Meadville, Chicago and Starr King in California, with a presence in Harvard Divinity School which was founded by Unitarians. There is some feeling that only one school is required but for the moment at any rate two will be maintained and to enable this to be done an extra $65,000 was voted, making $160,000 total in the next year. There had been a proposal in the budget to reduce the aid to the Districts by $45,000 but the delegates voted to increase the aid by $60,000. All this meant that instead of achieving a saving there will have to be found an extra $375,000 next year, making a grand total budget expenditure of $2,580,000.[421]

Hopkins claimed that the financial situation was the main reason Harry Scholefield chose not to run for UUA president. Harold Hadley, John Ogden Fisher, Deane Starr, and Bob West, all candidates in 1969, ran on platforms prioritizing fiscal prudence. While the deficit in 1968 was $100 thousand, in 1969 it reached $572 thousand. The total encroachment on the UUA's unrestricted funds since the consolidation was $1,082,575. And as David Cole noted, millions given to the UUA by the Massachusetts Universalist Convention "got dissipated."[422] Expenditures in development funds and unrestricted endowment totalled $5 million.

This was the financial situation West inherited, a budget of $2.6 million and an income of $1.6 million.[423] Six months into his presidency, he discovered that the UUA's bank held an open demand note for $450 thousand. Board member Leon Hopper said he could imagine how Bob West felt when the bankers told him "they wanted to foreclose on the UUA account because of unpaid loans."[424] In January 1970, West promised the bank that the UUA "would apply the full amount of every unrestricted bequest the Association received until the note was retired."[425]

Going into the 1968–1969 budget year, there was concern that BAC would negatively impact the Annual Program Fund. That was not the case. There was more enthusiasm than opposition. With the help of BAC, BUUC, and FULLBAC, annual giving came in 16.7 percent higher than the year before.[426] However, an ongoing drain on UUA funds was Beacon Press. West wrote, "In 1970, the UUA board appointed a special committee to explore ways to ease the financial difficulties associated with Beacon. During the previous eight years, the average amount of annual UUA support for the press had been $90 thousand plus an additional $30 thousand for office space, heat, light, and personnel benefits."[427] One option was to sell it.

Despite the severe financial situation, the UUA had roundly rejected mandatory dues as a way to increase revenue. That left West only one option: cut. His plan put forward a level of austerity previous Boards had been unwilling to endorse. But this was a new Board, and its members, having labored on church and district boards and committees, were elected to represent their districts. Their institutional experience and frame of mind led them to support his proposal.

West proposed cutting all subsidies to the Unitarian Universalist Women's Federation, which voluntarily returned its allocation before the budget was presented to the Board, as well as to the Laymen's League and the Church of the Larger Fellowship, and reducing the money allocated to Liberal Religious Youth and Student Religious Liberals. The Department of Social Responsibility was absorbed into the Department of Education and Social Concern, where it had been before Greeley made it into a department of its own. The Office of Overseas and Interfaith Relations was eliminated and its responsibilities migrated to the vice president's office. The $50 thousand the Assembly had voted to support Chicano empowerment was eliminated. The publication of *UUA Now* was suspended, and the magazine was replaced by a biweekly newspaper.

Eighteen committees were eliminated. The twenty district executives were let go, and seven interdistrict offices created. Five of eight department heads were terminated, and in all, the UUA staff was reduced from 108 to 55. These changes led to a 40-percent reduction in the budget, bringing it down to $1.6 million.

The cuts were, in part, guided by a budget priority survey, which FULLBAC asked congregations to boycott. Nonetheless, nearly three hundred responded. The priorities they ranked highest were theological education and religious education. Not surprisingly given the boycott, BAC ranked low medium and social responsibility still lower. Theological education accordingly received additional funding despite the overall cuts. However, not all the budget allocations were guided by the survey. The Canadian Unitarian Council, which was not ranked at all on it, came to an agreement with the UUA under which it would collect its annual fund and split it 50/50 with the UUA. And in regard to BAC, West proposed maintaining the status quo, guaranteeing the $250 thousand per year over the next four years that the General Assembly had committed to. He said, "I felt this was more realistic and more in keeping with what I felt was a moral commitment to BAC."[428]

The UUA Board saw things differently, and in November it revised the commitment to BAC. It maintained the commitment to $1 million dollars in funding, but decided to spread it over five years rather than four, reducing each payment to $200 thousand. However, if the annual fund went over its goal the excess, up to $50 thousand, would be given to BAC.

The $200 thousand promised to BAC represented a significantly higher percentage of the reduced budget than the $250 thousand had been of the original; while the overall budget was cut by 40 percent, BAC's yearly allocation was reduced by 20 percent.

BAC and the FFR vs. the UUA Board — Round Three

On the whole, the UUA Board and Bob West saw the 1969–1970 budget as the first step toward financial solvency. As institutional stewards, they made fiscal prudence their guiding principle; General Assemblies had been committing money that was not there. West wrote, "Throughout my tenure, the Association depended on the annual program fund for most of its current operating income. The annual goal had not been met during the previous administration's last three years and wasn't achieved during my first six years. . . . [However,] by 1973, we were completely out of debt."[429] "The task of making such choices," he said at the time, "has not been easy. We have not enjoyed having to bring the budget into balance with our resources."[430]

Nevertheless, the money that was committed to BAC was available, and available on BAC's terms in regard to its control and distribution, at least. But BAC and the Fellowship for Renewal were outraged that its disbursal was to be slowed down. The Chicago Area Black UU Caucus (CABUUC) declared, "The Association has demonstrated that it, like most white institutions in America, is racist. We were the last significant program of the denomination to be added and, true to tradition, we are among the first to be eliminated."[431]

Jack Mendelsohn, who left the Arlington Street Church weeks after the Walkout to become the minister of the First Unitarian Society of Chicago, said, "At a time when the future of the country depends on whether or not we are able to come to terms with the issue of black empowerment, I think it is a tragic error for our denomination simply to rank that issue with problems of denominational house-keeping and feel that it can make a cut on that front just the way it would cut a departmental budget—as if the two were, in any sense, equal.... They simply don't understand the kind of crisis we are in." And George Sikes, the co-chair of the Midwest FFR, said, "This appears to be a clear rejection on the part of the UUA Board of the priorities set up at not one, but two, General Assemblies. The action must be reversed."[432]

Across the country, regional FFR groups proposed avenues for action. They disseminated contact information for all UUA Board members and encouraged FFR members to call or write. This produced a flood of letters. The FFR newsletter also suggested that congregations follow Brooklyn's lead and withhold their contribution to the UUA in what was called symbolic escrow; if a congregation did not withhold funds from the UUA, individuals should withhold their contributions from the congregation. Donald McKinney, the minister in Brooklyn and a member of BAC, echoed this call, saying, "If we hope to save our denomination from destroying itself and its historic new thrust in the racial crisis we must act, and act now." Five congregations would join Brooklyn in withholding their dues. The First Unitarian Church of Denver voted to send its contribution to BAC instead of the UUA. The Board of Chicago First voted to delay the congregation's $833 monthly contribution. In turn, a church member countered that he would be loath to lead a movement to withhold personal contributions from First Chicago because of its action—implying that he would.[433]

At the November Southeast District meeting, the funding of BAC did not come up, but its minutes record the dismay and anger of the district Board at the "drastic solution," which weakened the districts.[434] The reaction to the cuts to districts added to a widespread sense of betrayal and anger. At the UUA's January Board meeting, the Finance Committee reported that congregations were withholding funds for a range of reasons: "BAC wasn't cut this year; it wasn't funded enough; BAWA wasn't funded; the appropriation for Chicanos was cut," or because of the cuts to districts.[435]

As UUA president, West was committed to a new openness. Whereas Board meetings during the Greeley administration had been closed, they would henceforward be open to observers. Indeed, the January Board meeting was moved from UUA headquarters to the Statler Hilton Hotel in order to accommodate the many observers and participants, including those from BAC, BAWA, and the FFR. Other petitioners and protestors arrived, including a representative from the Pacific Northwest District seeking to opt out of the Interdistrict plan. Even in the new meeting room, there was not enough space, and so the observers lined the wall, two behind each Board member.

Larry Ladd described the Board as soulless "technicians" who lacked vision and placed preserving the UUA before principle. The protesters he designated the "New Calvinists" who claimed allegiance to more transcendent values.[436] And John Smith, a Chicago First and FFR member who had been to General Assembly in July, drove from Chicago with LRYer, John Gibbons, to attend the Board meeting and later wrote,

> Is it me that's crazy? Is it me that doesn't understand? Did we not make a commitment to an experiment in black empowerment? And does not empowerment mean unequivocally turning over part of our decision-making power—in this case money power—to blacks? But the Board obviously still believes that the ultimate decision rests with them. They believe that they have the right to dispose of that money in line with overall denominational priorities and financial crisis, not necessarily in terms of black priorities. There is one black face, one black presence on that Board. The transfer of power has never been made.[437]

Hayward Henry spoke for BAC; Glover Barnes and Max Gaebler for BAWA; and Wayne Arnason, from the Liberal Religious Youth Executive Committee, spoke for the Fellowship for Renewal. Arnason argued that the 1968 and 1969 General Assemblies had made a moral commitment to BAC that could not be altered without compromising the mutual good faith between black and white Unitarian Universalists. The funding of BAC represented a transfer of power that should have been implemented without reservation, but the Board's unilateral decision to alter it revealed that power had not really been transferred and thus ran contrary to the meaning of black empowerment.[438]

In the President's verbal report to the Board, Bob West said the UUA would run a $500-thousand deficit and had $500 thousand remaining in unrestricted funds. Scowling at a Board they were certain was made up of racists, members of the FFR and BAC endured a lengthy discussion of a budget about which they did not care. That afternoon, BAWA was to make a request for funding, and while the FFR members considered blocking BAWA, they realized doing so would only anger the Board and decided not to.

The Board declined to fund BAWA but agreed to support a "ghetto ministry" in Cleveland that the Veatch Committee of the North Shore Unitarian Universalist Society (Plandome, New York) would fund.[439] The UUA Board also joined Project Equality and approved a loan of up to $25 thousand to Emanuel Apartments, Inc., a low-income housing project in Roxbury, Massachusetts. (In July, it would approve a similar loan to the Neighborhood Commons Corporation in Chicago.) Edna Griffin, the only African American Board member, moved that "no other organization for black empowerment be funded except the Black Affairs Council," and this motion carried with only one negative vote and two abstentions. The tension had been building all afternoon, and just before 5

PM the vote to reinstate $50 thousand to BAC was taken. Garnering just four votes, it failed.

As they had planned, the protestors, led by "the one-man band" Paul Cole, sang "Once to Every Man and Nation," and for good measure they added "Turn Back, O Man, Forswear Thy Foolish Ways." Then all hell broke loose. They "screamed at us, and told us we were immoral and unfaithful to our ideals," Ralph Helverson wrote in his diary.[440] Angry denouncements flew across the room, tears flowed, a mother from Connecticut cried, "What shall we tell the children in Sunday School?"[441] Gibbons marched up to West, yelled, "I am quitting your damn church" in his face, and stormed from the room.[442] The following Sunday, in a fiery testimony from the pulpit, Richard Traylor resigned from Restoration Church.

This was the beginning of the end for BAC and the FFR.

The UUA Board was new and expanded, and for the first time it had to balance regional loyalties with continental ones. The West administration was under financial duress. The use of polarization as a tactic by BAC and BUUC, LRY and SRL, FULLBAC and the FFR had undercut any sense that differing groups could work together for racial justice. And BAC and FFR's main ally, Homer Jack—whom they did not trust but who had worked tirelessly in marshalling support for them—was one of the UUA staff let go. The outcome, as Ladd said, was "anticlimactic."[443]

By the time the power play of what David Parke called "the left wing of the UUA"[444] failed, the relationships between many people were damaged. Many had made little effort to understand the perspectives of others, preferring to denounce them, and there was no trust upon which to build. This left the sides with no covenantal way forward.

The Black Humanist Fellowship of Liberation

The racial situation was changing rapidly, often faster than UU congregations could adjust. Kim Beach and Jim Hobart, the urban ministry team working with the four congregations of the Cleveland UU Parish project (CUUP), returned to Cleveland from the 1967 Emergency Conference knowing the original plan for CUUP would not work. They could not be community organizers, as Ron Engel and Neil Shadle had been in Chicago.

The project was in a formative stage. That gave them breathing room—which they needed. During that 1967–1968 academic year, both were interning in the Clergy in Urban Ministry program at Case Western Reserve University. Beach was engaged with a nonprofit housing organization and Hobart with the Hough Tenant Union while they were simultaneously working with CUUP to define its ministry and what their role would be when the Clergy in Urban Ministry program ended in May.

CUUP's office was in the Cleveland Unitarian Society. In 1951, when the First Unitarian Church had moved out to suburban Shaker Heights, the Society had decided to remain in the city's Hough neighborhood and create a racially integrated church. Its new minister, Farley Wheelwright, was an outspoken activist and veteran of Selma, but now he was beginning to question whether the congregation could remain viable where it was.

Meanwhile, CUUP had become a point of contention in the suburban Cleveland West Shore congregation. In 1966, when Jim Curtis began his ministry there, he had advertised himself as an activist and had pushed to establish CUUP. The congregation, however, was closely split on the project. In addition, his style was markedly different from that of the minister who preceded him.

By March 1968, dissatisfaction with his ministry was such that the question of whether to retain him came to a vote. Curtis won the vote, but decided that he did not have the support necessary to carry on a successful ministry; he resigned. Then CUUP's other promoter, the minister of the church in Shaker Heights, found his ministry in difficulty and he, too, resigned. Thus by the summer of 1968, CUUP's two strongest supporters were gone.

This happened as Hobart and Beach were turning their attention toward redefining CUUP's mission. Working in the interfaith community and playing supportive roles with organizations like the local Poor People's Partnership and the Welfare Rights Organization, they built relationships in the black community. Doing so was one of their goals; the other and more challenging one was keeping enthusiastic Unitarian Universalists engaged in addressing urban needs about which volunteers were often ill-informed.

Hobart and Beach set up task forces with volunteers from the four sponsoring congregations. Each focused on a separate issue: housing, welfare, employment, and education. But, the Unitarian Universalist volunteers were there to do good works, not to learn about how they were implicated in urban blight and systemic racism. Educating CUUP's sponsors and financiers about these issues in a way they could hear and accept was a frustrating undertaking. Volunteers needed to develop new sensitivities if they, as white people, were to be able to bridge the urban-suburban divide and serve as allies in the context of Black Power and self-determination. Sometimes they resisted these new perspectives. An evaluation of CUUP concluded, "The congregations agreed to sponsor one thing, and then found out they were sponsoring something else."[445]

Then another complication arose. In January 1969, West Shore settled a new minister. David Cole had a different vision, only grudgingly supported CUUP, and wasn't sure the congregation could keep funding it. Hobart and Beach doubted that the real issue was financial; they felt Cole was undermining them because he had other uses for the money and wanted to see CUUP disbanded.[446]

Meanwhile congregational life at the integrated, middle-class Cleveland Unitarian Society was becoming untenable. Members were mugged. The house the society bought to use as a neighborhood center was burned down. Wheelwright had a bottle thrown at him. People were fearful, meetings could not be scheduled at night, and attendance was shrinking. In May 1969, Wheelwright recommended to the Board that it give the building—a century-old neo-Gothic edifice with a dark oak interior and Tiffany windows—to the local BUUC to start a black fellowship. The Board rejected the idea eight to one.[447] Undeterred, Wheelwright wrote to the UUA and proposed staffing the congregation with a black ministry to the community.

Rev. Joseph Barth, director of the Department of Ministry, saw an opportunity to secure funding for an "Experimental Ghetto Ministry." At no time during the ensuing deliberation and grant solicitation did Barth consult with Beach or Hobart or tell them what was going on. But he did meet with Hayward Henry, and Henry reported "our deliberations have proceeded rather smoothly."[448]

By September 1969, following the Boston General Assembly, twenty-eight-year-old Rev. John Frazier, a newly ordained African American, had moved to Cleveland to begin the Black Humanist Fellowship of Liberation (BFL) as a "congregation within a congregation."[449]

Soon thereafter, Wheelwright raised the issue of what to do with the building once again, and again suggested it be given to the local BUUC chapter. On October 5, Hayward Henry, the BUUC chair, preached at the Cleveland Society. Beach said that during the visit, Henry expressed disdain for CUUP.[450] According to Beach, his sermon advocated giving the building to BUUC and challenged the congregation to be "one of the few white institutions that has peacefully turned over power to Black People."[451]

A week later, Glover Barnes, BAWA co-chair, also spoke at the Cleveland Society. "There is no substitute in this multi-racial society for true integration," he said. "You can dilly-dally, you can avoid, you can retreat, you can rationalize, and I'm going to continue to look you in the eye, celebrate you in my blackness, and you had better celebrate me in your whiteness because we do it together or we all die." At those words, members of BUUC walked out, and Barnes responded, "I am no stranger to tyranny."[452]

Giving up the building was a very contentious decision. The Society hosted a series of speakers, meetings were set up to debate the issue, and flyers were distributed. When it came to a vote on November 2, 1969, the issue was widely covered by the local press. Those who were for giving the building away lost the first three votes by a margin as wide as 22 to 108, but eventually, late in the afternoon after many members had departed and some minds had changed, they won, 60 to 31.

On November 7, BFL applied for fellowship status in the UUA, and on November 17, it was accepted by the Board. By November 18, Hobart and Beach had been notified that because Cleveland BUUC wanted CUUP's financial support, their employment would end in June 1970.

Meanwhile a petition calling for another vote on the question of handing over the building to BUUC was circulated. When it took place on December 14, 1969, the congregation reaffirmed the decision to turn the building and $54 thousand of its $165 thousand endowment over to BUUC by a vote of eighty-four to sixty. A lawsuit to stop the handover failed, and on March 1, 1970, the deed was transferred. A week later, the Veatch Committee agreed that

Cleveland would be the site of an experimental urban effort. In June, Veatch voted to fund the "ghetto ministry" with $24 thousand in 1970–1971. It received $12 thousand in 1971–1972, as well as a grant of $3,960 in October 1972 for roof repair.

Frazier set out to build a black congregation. Asked why he did not want an integrated one, he said, "Because every black person, with no exception, has deep within him hatred of the white man. It may, in an individual, almost never show, but it's there.... And because [of that,] the black man cannot be himself in the presence of white people. When we're with white people, we play games."[453]

Frazier had plans for the BFL, but just surviving posed a formidable challenge. The members of the BFL were not from Hough; they were black professionals from Cleveland Heights and other middle-class neighborhoods. Frazier was warm and friendly, but he had grown up in the South and had just returned from a year studying at Oxford University; he was untutored in Northern big-city life and had never served a congregation before. Lacking substantial lay leadership, BFL became dependent on its minister. Hobart and Beach, who had developed relationships across the city as CUUP staff, were gone, and since CUUP had been undercut by Joe Barth, by the national and Cleveland chapter of BUUC, and by David Cole of the West Shore congregation, local money was not forthcoming.[454]

BFL had trouble finding a focus, struggled to raise funds, and never developed a sustaining worship life. Outside funding for it ceased in June 1972 after Joe Barth, its champion, retired; the UUA withdrew its support; and the fellowship's grant request to the Veatch Committee for $50,515 over five years was declined. BFL ceased meeting in 1973, when its funds ran out. In 1974 Frazier moved to North Carolina, and later in the seventies, following a fire, the building was torn down.

"Blacks, Get Your Guns"

On December 4, 1969, Black Panther leader Fred Hampton was assassinated by the Chicago police and the FBI. Renford Gaines, the minister at Urbana-Champaign, was in Chicago when it happened. That Sunday, he ended his sermon to his all-white congregation with the words "Blacks, get your guns." The reaction was such that on the next Sunday, he began his sermon by saying, "My closing words in last week's sermon should not have created misunderstanding by anyone living in this country in this year 1969." The title of that second sermon was "Blacks, Get Your Guns."[455]

From the beginning of his ministry there, in August 1968, Gaines had sensed it would be difficult. Before that church year began in September, Stephen Fritchman had invited him to submit his name to two Los Angeles congregations, and Gaines had told him, "I'm sure both the emotional and meteorological climate out there would suit Harriet and I better."[456] Four days later, he wrote to Father Neil Jordall, "I am *not* taking to this job like a duck to water—I see the storms on the horizon and church hasn't started yet. But the church should be the home of conflict, should it not?"[457]

With more African American music, drums, poetry, and arts, Gaines brought a different and creative religious culture to worship. But tension grew between him and the music director until she resigned in April 1969. "What shall we do for music? Shall it be *black* or *white*?" he wrote to her afterward. "My vocation in this denomination demands that I do my part to make our total institutional expression less racist. I cannot ignore the total absence of blackness in any social institution of America, and most especially I cannot ignore it as it expresses itself in our church."[458]

In May 1969, Gaines participated in a series of radio broadcasts entitled "Psychopathology of Racism." In these, he described racists as showing the earmarks of a disturbed mind. In replying to a letter from a listener, he said, "We have been concealing our social evils long enough. It's time to open the festering wound and keep it open until it heals properly."[459] After the third program, the backlash began.

In the mail, both at church and at home, he received cards showing the back of his head in the crosshairs of a sniper scope. He walked into a garage to ask for help and a guy yelled, "You're that son-of-a-bitch" and threw a tire iron at him. He went to the sheriff and asked for protection; his request was dismissed out of hand. He received messages saying that his home would be burned down with his children in it. Gaines knew that a group called the "White Hats" was behind the threats, but the police did nothing. Even the president of the congregation—like the rest of his middle-class, white flock—did not take his fears seriously, even though Gaines once took him to the window of the church office and pointed out the white men parked, as usual, in front of the church.[460]

This was the context when, in December of his second year of ministry, Gaines delivered "Blacks, Get Your Guns." His words were tough and terse. After talking about the license police had to shoot black men without consequence, he said,

> Middle class blacks have been too silent while young black people have been dying to bring humanity and justice to black people in this country. I have played the "button-lip game" along with the rest. I am through with that. From here forward our communication about race will be issued in person, from the pulpit and my pen, as I feel they should. I notice that ministers who advocate black moderation and black non-existence in our movement do not reserve their opinions exclusively for discussion groups, but use their pulpits and their newsletters to promulgate their racism.

> The black minister in the white church—how will the experiment run?
>
> ...Let us understand each other on this point. I, as a black man, live in two worlds. If you wish to retain me as minister you will have to share as much of both my worlds with me as I share your intimate life with you.
>
> I am not the only middle class black in the community eye speaking a "get-your-gun-when-attacked" benediction. Listen to your NAACP and Urban League chapters. All we as blacks affirm is our right to life. Whites negatively respond to this, often because it threatens their comfort and peace of mind.
>
> Time is running out for all black people. We are about the business of survival, not parliamentary debating points of romantic escapism.[461]

Gaines himself began carrying a gun.

By January 1970, he had accepted a part-time position as executive director of the Afro-American Studies Commission at the University of Illinois. This led him to request that the Urbana-Champaign Board allow him to reduce his ministerial duties and serve the congregation part-time. On March 1, the Board passed a motion permitting the change. Around that same time, Gaines agreed to be the candidate for the position of senior minister at the Arlington Street Church; on March 17, he withdrew his application, but a month later spent a week in Boston as the candidate. Arlington Street offered him the call on May 5, and on May 19, he accepted.[462] He had already submitted his resignation to the Urbana-Champaign congregation on April 21, to take effect on July 1, 1970.

His resignation letter to the membership did not mention Arlington Street. Instead he wrote, "You have weathered the storm of a difficult, unchartered water. Together, we have demonstrated that a Black man can minister to a white church without disaster, indeed with a great deal of creativity."[463] Years later, he said, "It was a wonderful time and the church was filled with wonderful people but we, like the rest of the nation, were caught in a fantasy of brotherhood and the realities of our history and the times dealt severely with us."[464]

BAC Bonds

At the Boston General Assembly, BAC planned to call for a $5 million "reinvestment" in its economic development programs. But the Assembly endorsed an alternative investment program outlined by the UUA Board of Trustees.[465] Hayward Henry said, "Frustrated by closed minds, administrative chicanery and a closed agenda—and wanting to preserve the integrity of our proposal—we withdrew our demands."[466] BAC decided to take a grassroots approach and go directly to local congregations for funding. Homer Jack had a different analysis of what happened. He said that the idea of reparational investment was innovative, but that Bob Hohler's fast at 25 Beacon Street had preempted BAC's agenda by forcing the UUA Board to accelerate its "pace in the whole area of social responsibility and investment."[467]

Soon after the 1969 Boston General Assembly, the effort to promote BAC bonds commenced. Richard Traylor preached at the Main Line congregation in suburban Philadelphia and gave them "hell." Then he asked for $200 thousand. However, since the congregation was already borrowing to pay its own operating expenses, Traylor's pitch was never "seriously considered."[468] Main Line had been struggling financially since General Electric laid off four thousand employees and the congregation had lost between twenty and thirty pledging members.

On January 12, there was a congregational meeting at the Community Church of New York. BUUC had asked to hold an investment workshop about BAC bonds on February 13–14, 1970, and members were to vote on whether or not to provide BUUC the meeting space. The motion to do so failed, thirty-five to twelve. The church newsletter reported it was the "majority feeling that the Black Caucus methods and approach are alien to the Community Church's historic position on integration, and the church did not want to sponsor this sort of presentation."[469] A counterproposal was made that the Board sponsor a BUUC/BAWA debate, and Harrington took it up with Richard Traylor.

The sale of BAC bonds kicked off on January 23, 1970, at a gathering in Boston. Meetings were held in New York City, Philadelphia, Washington D.C., Denver, Los Angeles, and the Bay Area with about forty societies or their representatives, in hopes of raising $5 million. The 5-percent bonds were due to mature on March 1, 1980, and the funds would be used for loans to and investment in black-controlled enterprises. Among the criteria used in choosing investments would be a business's potential to alleviate "the powerless and dependent status of Black communities."[470] In February, Liberal Religious Youth became one of the first groups to buy in, staging a ceremony and photo-op to mark its purchase of $50 thousand in bonds. Meanwhile, on January 25, the UUA Board had reaffirmed its decision to trim $50 thousand from BAC's 1969–1970 allocation in the UUA's budget.

On February 1, 1970, Rev. Clyde Dodder, the minister of the First Unitarian Society of Newton, Massachusetts, preached a sermon entitled "If Black Is Beautiful, What Is White?" After tracing BAC's history since the Emergency Conference in 1967, he said, "We have not acted innovatively, but rather tended to repeat outworn patterns which are no longer persuasive." He put forward an alternative. "I propose to you as a congregation that we instruct our Board of Investment to re-invest at least $125,000" in BAC bonds. A special parish meeting was held on March 15. Hayward Henry and Ben Scott were present as resources, and the proposal to purchase $125 thousand worth of bonds over five years was passed by a vote of fifty-five to forty-nine. The narrowness of the vote ensured the debate would continue.

The third annual meeting of BUUC was held in Washington D.C. February 20–23, four weeks after the UUA Board reaffirmed its reduction of BAC's allocation. Attending the BUUC meeting were 132 delegates and 33 observers.[471] Eighty-four of the delegates came from only eight urban areas—the greatest number from New York, and then Washington D.C., Boston, Chicago, Cleveland, Philadelphia, Detroit, and Cincinnati. Eight more came from California, and six from the Southern and border states. The distribution reveals how concentrated African American UUs were in urban areas. Among the delegates were five ministers, none of whom had been granted fellowship before 1968. They represented a new generation.

BUUC leadership was angry about the cuts to BAC's allocation. Since the commitments that two General Assemblies had made to BAC clearly meant nothing to the Board, they argued, BAC should cut its affiliation with the UUA. Disaffiliating would free it to solicit operating funds directly from Unitarian Universalist congregations, to make up for what it considered a budget cut. Some BUUC members were concerned that disaffiliating seemed tantamount to leaving the UUA, while others held that disaffiliation didn't mean leaving the UUA but rather being independent, like the Unitarian Universalist Service Committee. Unanimity on the issue was not reached, but a substantial majority voted in favor of disaffiliation.

On Tuesday, February 24, BAC announced that it was disaffiliating from the UUA. Its statement said, "We feel that the People have made known their collective will on this issue" and charged the UUA Board of Trustees with having "never favored the existence and funding of BAC.... *Blackamerican Uni-Uni's have put as much time and energy as we can into a process that had led simply to our being 'the last hired and the first fired.'* "⁴⁷² BUUC said that it would boycott the upcoming Seattle General Assembly and that it was "on strike against racism in this country—as demonstrated by the UUA."⁴⁷³ At the same time, Hayward Henry "made it clear that he still expected the UUA to come through with the entire $1 million as promised," and said "that his people would do 'whatever is necessary' to get it."⁴⁷⁴

The phrase *the people* appeared in BACs "Statement of Disaffiliation" ten times in five pages. BAC/BUUC believed that securing two majority votes at two GAs was synonymous with BAC embodying the "will of the People." That this idiom was repeatedly evoked indicates that their understanding of UU polity was flawed. It was a fatal misreading. The paramount authorities were individual conscience, the local congregation, and covenants reached by consensus rather than the majority votes BAC wielded as a mandate.

The next day, UUA president Bob West issued a statement expressing dismay and regret, but also arguing that it was unfair to call the Board racist after its agonizing effort to balance its "social vision with the practical fiscal realities."⁴⁷⁵ Hayward Henry went to West's office and "engaged him in debate for more than an hour," the *New York Times* reported. "The issue is not the $50,000 or the extension of the commitment to five years," Henry said. "The issue is that this is one more case in which whites decided for the blacks what they can do and what they cannot do. If we did not resist this action, we would be prostituting ourselves."⁴⁷⁶

BAC met in Eutaw, Alabama on March 6–7, at the home of Dr. John Cashin, the founder of the National Democratic Party of Alabama, which was a BAC grant recipient. Eight of nine BAC members were in attendance, plus two guests and three BAC staff members.⁴⁷⁷ After a chair was chosen and an agenda adopted, the first order of business was a motion to remove "Unitarian Universalist Association" from BAC's letterhead. It passed. Now, alongside grant-making and asset management, energies would have to turn to fundraising for both BAC's operating budget (called the May 26th Fund) and BAC Bonds sales efforts. Workshops on the bonds were already being widely offered by Ben Scott, Richard Traylor, and Hayward Henry.

In his report to BAC, Henry complained about BUUC's Chicago chapter, CABUUC. He said that the national office had "received a lot of flack from the Chicago Caucus" and that they had "made their in-house business quite public."⁴⁷⁸ Members of CABUUC were upset by a comment Henry had made that had appeared in the *New York Times:* "Some blacks may be induced to remain [in the UUA], but the association will know that it has some house niggers in residence.' "⁴⁷⁹ CABUUC heard this as a call for blacks to leave their congregations, but Henry protested that interpretation as inaccurate. Interviewed by the *First Church News*, an unofficial newsletter published by a white member of the First Unitarian Society of Chicago, Henry said that he was just pointing out that BUUC members would be "boycotting the [General] Assembly and any Afro-Americans who are in attendance there as delegates will not be members of our organization, and that if whites want to say they've got blacks there, in fact they will know that what they have is 'house niggers.' "⁴⁸⁰

The use of the epithet "house nigger" was not the only point of contention with CABUUC. Some of its members disagreed with BAC's disaffiliation, others were ambivalent about the GA boycott, and still others had reservations about the legality of the bond issue in its current form. Indeed, CABUUC had abstained from voting in support of the bond issue at the BUUC national meeting.⁴⁸¹

The support that BAC had worked to marshal during the two previous years was being eroded by its decision to disaffiliate and by the language and reasons it used in doing so, as well as by its strident critique of BAWA. On March 1, 1970, Henry had spoken at the "After Church Forum" of the May Memorial Unitarian Society in Syracuse. A week later, a white member of long standing said in the Society's newsletter that she had left the Boston General Assembly impressed with what BAC was doing, but she was now regretfully returning to her "former position of opposing BAC." She made this decision when, during Henry's presentation, she became aware of the effort he was "putting in (on his own admission), not on promoting . . . BAC, but on attempting to destroy the integrated Community Church."[482]

As president of the Albany congregation, Alfred Weissbard had gone to the Cleveland General Assembly set on voting against BAC and found himself persuaded to support it. Now he wrote in his own church's newsletter about the UUA's financial situation and its decision to restructure BAC's allocation. "Unfortunately, the silent majority, the folks in the church back home, did not put money where the delegates' mouths were." After describing Henry's comments in the *New York Times* article as "vilifying West and the Board," Weissbard concluded, "I believe it important that Bob West be assured of our support and I propose to submit a resolution to that effect to our trustees."[483] He did, and the resolution passed.

On March 21, the starkness of the difference between BAC and BAWA was explored in a forum at Community Church attended by three hundred people. Henry, Traylor, and Scott represented BAC, and Barnes, Seiden, and Harrington spoke for BAWA. It was reported that "the meeting was marked by clarity and candor, but with complete civility despite the sharp difference."[484] In decision after decision and debate after debate, the degree of polarization both between and within congregations was revealed.

In a sermon delivered on March 8, 1970, W. Edward Harris, acting senior minister at the Arlington Street Church, proposed that the congregation purchase $200 thousand in BAC bonds, and Renford Gaines supported the proposal after he was called as senior minister in May 1970. On November 19, the congregation voted to purchase $60 thousand in bonds, even though it had insufficient unrestricted endowment to do so and had to take out a loan. Gaines said, "Today Arlington Street Church has taken a revolutionary step. It has chosen to invest in human growth, perhaps at the cost of its own institutional survival. But this was an act of faith."[485]

The largest backer of the BAC bond issue was All Souls Church Unitarian in Washington D.C. In May 1970, Rev. Bill Gardiner mailed out a circular to church members about a request from the local BUUC chapter to apply $400 thousand from the congregation's unrestricted endowment toward the purchase of the bonds. The proposal was broadly discussed in church and neighborhood meetings both before and after the Board discussed it at its June 2 meeting. The Board endorsed a subscription of $250 thousand, with the understanding that most of it would be used in the nearby Fourteenth Street corridor, which had been destroyed during the riots following Dr. King's assassination in 1968. The purchase was approved at a special congregational meeting on June 7 by a vote of 201 to 56. On July 17, Hayward Henry wrote to thank the congregation, noting that "All Souls plays a vital symbolic role in our denomination" and hoping that others would follow its lead.[486] It was not to be; only one other congregation approached this level of support.

That congregation was the First Unitarian Church of Brooklyn. In 1965, Brooklyn had hired an assistant minister, Duke Gray, to focus on urban ministry. In 1966, it had established the Fulton Street Center; it also provided office space to FULLBAC and had made a loan of $20 thousand to BAC. It withheld its Annual Program Fund payments from the UUA and contributed them to BAC instead; its minister, Don McKinney, would serve on BAC longer than any other Euro-American, and its bond subscription had no strings attached.

McKinney later claimed, "We were just about the only church in the denomination that played a major role in support of BUUC and BAC that was NOT crippled by the experience, or found it best to fire the minister."[487] This was not quite true.

LeRoy Cole was the lay black minister of the Fulton Street Center. Involved with it from its beginning, he was an adept community organizer and ran the Center's programs of service, advocacy, and community improvement. He had attended the UUA Emergency Conference at the Biltmore and the annual national BUUC meetings. But because his form of community action did not fit the local BUUC chapter's idea of black self-determination, "Cole later found himself having to explain his decisions on Fulton Street to his black caucus colleagues, who were unwilling to recommend funding for his center programs. (Funding for them was also denied by BAC.) Sick of the power struggle and disillusioned with both BAC and his black caucus colleagues, Cole resigned as lay minister in the summer of 1970 to protest the purchase of $157,500 worth of BAC bonds by the church's Social Reinvestment Committee."[488]

That purchase was not the only point of contention in Brooklyn. In October 1969, Kenneth N. Whitlock, a fairly new African American member of the congregation, petitioned its Board, asking "that neither Black nor White apartheid shall be initiated, supported, condoned or financed by the church."[489] The Board took no action, so Whitlock collected the ten signatures necessary to call a special congregational meeting, which was held in January 1970. At that meeting, he brought forward four resolutions, including one that stated, "Until the organization of BAC, BUUC, FULLBAC and FFR, neither White NOR Black apartheid (separatism) existed in our Society or our Denomination."[490] In April 1971, "an altercation between a BAWA and a BAC supporter, which earlier had marred a board meeting, erupted as a shoving match at . . . the congregational meeting."[491] Whitlock left First Brooklyn and joined Community Church.

In November 1970, Richard Traylor made a tour of the West Coast, from San Diego to Seattle, to promote the May 26th Fund and BAC bonds. His report on the trip was positive, but his hopes were measured. Some ministers were engaged in support of the effort, and Fritchman (now retired) and Roy Ockert (at Fullerton) were able to work together in supporting the May 26th Fund. Traylor met with enthusiastic lay supporters and BUUC members. But, significantly, he did not meet with the ministers of two of the largest West Coast congregations: John Ruskin Clark in San Diego and Peter Raible in Seattle. Neither would have been supportive.

They were not alone in being wary. In San Francisco, Harry Scholefield, a BAC supporter, had already expressed his opposition to converting any of the congregation's $100 thousand in unrestricted endowment to BAC bonds. Alan Deale was brand new to Portland, had been disgusted by the Walkout, and had spent the winter of 1970 on leave from his old congregation while running a supplemental Annual Program Fund drive for Bob West. His meeting with Traylor was cordial, but he was noncommittal. The minister at the Berkeley Church said "the negative response on behalf of BAC" was because some of his members were "invested in the classical 'integrationist' style."[492] Among them was Betty Seiden, the executive secretary of BAWA.

225

The only congregation that responded to Traylor's visit with a firm commitment to purchase BAC Bonds was the Berkeley Fellowship, which raised $2,000 and eventually bought $1,750 in bonds. On a list drawn up in 1971 of those who committed to subscribing over $1,000, the Berkeley Fellowship is the only West Coast congregation.[493]

In its 1969–1970 Annual Report, BAC said that its goal was to raise $577,500 from 120 selected churches and fellowships. Of that, $50 thousand was to make up for what was cut by the UUA Board, $500 thousand for the final two years of the original proposal, and $27,500 to cover the cost of the campaign. The campaign to sell BAC bonds was moderately successful. It was also in line with what would have been raised in a capital campaign with a lead gift of $250 thousand.

The campaign sometimes also left strife in its wake. In Newton, Massachusetts, after the March 1970 vote to purchase BAC bonds using their endowment, conflict mounted and threats of legal action to stop the purchase were made. In April 1971, the annual parish meeting accepted the trustees' recommendation to cut the amount from $125 thousand to $62,500. The conflict divided the congregation and led its minister, Clyde Dodder, to resign in early 1973.

The bulk of the money pledged to purchase BAC bonds came from seven institutions: All Souls in Washington D.C. promised $250 thousand (of which $162 thousand was actually remitted); First Unitarian Church of Brooklyn $157,500; First Unitarian Society of Newton, Massachusetts $62,500; the Arlington Street Church $60 thousand; Liberal Religious Youth $50 thousand; the Delaware Valley District $30 thousand; and the Unitarian Universalist Women's Federation $25 thousand. A tally of the financial pledges in June 1970 came to $686,900, and by early in 1971, it reached about $770 thousand. The total in 1975 was approximately

$840 thousand, and the seven institutions named above who pledged in the beginning represented about 75 percent of the subscriptions. In June 1970, the list of commitments included individual commitments totalling $63,600, the largest of which, $25 thousand, came from Hilda and Charles Mason, an interracial couple who were members of All Souls in Washington D.C. Hilda, who would become a prominent political figure in D.C., was a leader of the local BUUC chapter and became a member of BAC; Charles, a lawyer, had in 1952 anonymously contributed the money that paid for the establishment of the Unitarian Commission on Intergroup Relations, and he had also served on it. Over a two-year period, the Commission carried out the first in-depth study of the American Unitarian Association's attitudes and practices regarding race.

. . .

THE EFFORT REQUIRED to solicit for the May 26th Fund on top of promoting and managing BAC bonds was substantial. BAC's small staff was made up of its administrative secretary, Richard Traylor; its administrative consultant, Louis Gothard; and its administrative assistant, LaVerne M. Jones. Much of the work relied upon volunteers, and foremost among them was Ben Scott, the treasurer of BAC. BUUC knew that its smaller groups were already stretched beyond their capacity, while some of the larger groups, like BURR and CABUUC, had broken ranks with the national BUUC organization. The pace BAC and BUUC leadership maintained— speaking, leading workshops, and attending meetings—was relentless. Why, then, walk away from a guaranteed $550 thousand and have to direct energy toward raising operating funds as well?

At the time BAC disaffiliated, it had already received $450 thousand from the UUA and full funding amounting to $1 million finally had been guaranteed by the UUA Board. If BAC had remained a UUA affiliate, the UUA would have fulfilled that commitment by 1973.

Subscription to BAC bonds would eventually grow to $840 thousand. My guess is that, without the ongoing skirmishes, BAC could have raised a total of a $1 million to carry it through the ensuing years. Furthermore, the Veatch Committee of the North Shore Unitarian Church established a Racial Justice Fund in 1972, with $180 thousand of an initial $250 thousand earmarked for BAC. It is not a stretch to imagine that between 1968 and 1977, $2.5 million dollars could have flowed from the UUA through BAC to the African American community. That did not happen and strategic missteps made by BAC/BUUC played a significant role.

It's not clear what was behind the BAC/BUUC claim that the UUA was deciding for "blacks what they can do and what they cannot do" when no effort was being made to control its programs? The impact of the UUA Board decision was on the timing of the distribution and in no way exerted control on its use.

For a short time after the 1968 GA vote to fund BAC, the future looked bright. There was some collaboration with the Unitarian Universalist Association, even if it wasn't close. There was a small cadre of new African American ministers. There was a significant increase in African American representation in elected and appointed positions. Planning had commenced on how to introduce more African American concerns and heritage into UU religious education curricula. But most importantly, BAC had developed two leading-edge responses to the black rebellion—a black-controlled grant-making program aimed at furthering black self-determination and a program promoting reparational investment. The perplexing question is: Why did BAC become sidetracked into attacking BAWA and the UUA?

Even though BAC had now left the UUA, the storm was not about to abate. Soon some congregations would find their pulpits taken over; one would come close to a physical confrontation. The upcoming General Assembly in Seattle would also witness a renewal of the conflict. The answer to the questions above, and to the conflicts about to overtake the Unitarian Universalist Association, is that it was never simply about money, racism, and black self-determination.

Pulpit Takeover at Cedar Lane

On Sunday, May 4, 1969, James Forman interrupted the worship service at Riverside Church in New York City to deliver the Black Manifesto. On Wednesday, he called the Community Church of New York; on being told that Donald Harrington wasn't there, he declined to leave a message, saying that Harrington would know why he called. Harrington had been planning to speak at the Unitarian Society of Germantown in Philadelphia on Sunday, but he canceled and remained in New York.[494] He said that if Forman showed up on Sunday, he would not give up the pulpit, nor would he leave as the minister at Riverside had. He would call for a hymn, and if the situation deteriorated further and became violent, he would not hesitate to call the police. Nonetheless, he said that "society owes its deprived citizens much more than the $500 million Forman is asking. 'In a sense Forman is a moderate except in his method.' "[495]

Later that May, Forman was invited to present the manifesto to the United Presbyterian Church General Assembly. In June, he occupied the Interchurch Building in Manhattan. At the First Unitarian-Universalist Church of Detroit, a member of the National Black Economic Development Conference (NBEDC) Board read the Black Manifesto aloud at the invitation of the minister. Later the member was told to stop pressuring the Unitarian Universalists because of BAC and the Unitarian Universalist Association's 1968 commitment to it. Nevertheless, the UUA staff had expected a takeover attempt or the like to happen during the Boston General Assembly. It did not, but similar tactics were used elsewhere.

At All Souls Church in Washington D.C., David Eaton, the first African American called to a historic Unitarian Universalist church, began his ministry on September 1, 1969. Eaton supported BAC but left UU-focused engagement to his white associate minister, Bill Gardiner. Indeed, throughout his ministry, Eaton's primary focus was on D.C.

It was a surprise when, on Sunday, October 12, 1969, a man saying he represented the Black United Front, of which Eaton had been a founding member, interrupted the service and asked to be heard. Eaton invited him into the pulpit. "My people know today their kids are hungry, they need food, better jobs, yes and better places to live," the man said. "They no longer listen to that religious current of 'pie in the sky.' ... What's wrong with them living now? ... Many of our people lived and died that this nation can exist as it is today. How can you sit there and ask us to wait until tomorrow while you are enjoying the full fruits of their labors today?" He ended by requesting $250 thousand for his cause. Eaton responded, "Regardless of how churches in America may fear demands coming to them from outside, we should welcome these demands in order to set our own house in order. We should fear no earthly power. We should fear only ourselves, if we negate our responsibility.... The day has come, the hour has come. I feel secure just with the few people that I have met in this church, old and young alike, that we have already started working in the area of economic development."[496] Within eight months, the congregation committed $250 thousand to BAC bonds, with the understanding that the investment would be directed at rebuilding the burned-out Fourteenth Street corridor.

On that same Sunday, about ten minutes before service began at the First Unitarian Church of Ann Arbor, Charles Thomas, a local black militant leader, demanded that he be allowed to read the Black Manifesto to the congregation. Refusing all alternatives, he delivered it during the service and closed by demanding $5 thousand in reparations: half to buy "clothing for the children of welfare mothers" and the other half to "help defray the cost for a campaign to recall Sheriff Harvey."[497] On October 26, Rev. Erwin A. Gaede, the minister in Ann Arbor, wrote in his newsletter column, "I had a vague and uneasy feeling Sunday when Charles Thomas demanded time to read the Black Manifesto then and there that not all was legitimate."[498] A call confirmed for Gaede that Thomas had not been there on behalf of the NBEDC. Gaede called his action "opportunism," but despite that, and because he and the Board were in agreement with the general appeal, they passed a resolution establishing a $5,000 fund (the most that the Board could grant without a congregational vote) for the use of the Washtenaw County Welfare Rights Committee.[499]

That did not save them from further disruptions. In September 1970, the Washtenaw County Black Economic Development League and the Washtenaw County Welfare Rights Committee began staging sit-ins. These spread to eleven Ann Arbor churches, all of which, except First Unitarian, joined in obtaining an injunction against the protestors.[500] Eventually First Unitarian's contribution, which grew to $7,000, would garner it a letter of appreciation from the Washtenaw County Black Economic Development League.

The Unitarian Society of Germantown in Philadelphia, where FULLBAC co-chair David Parke served as minister, had a reputation for filling its pulpit with internationally known speakers. On May 11 (the day that Harrington had been scheduled to speak there before he canceled because of Forman's threat to take over his pulpit), Parke spoke approvingly of Forman's demand for reparations and of his actions. "If Mr. Forman's action," said Parke, "can rouse us from inaction and mobilize our united strength for the establishment in fact of equal opportunity . . . it will not have been in vain."[501]

Nonetheless, the Germantown church Board thought it best to develop a formal policy on interruptions of Sunday services. "At all times the representatives and members of our church should conduct themselves with courtesy, dignity and restraint," the policy asserted. It went into detail about what the person conducting the service should do if it was interrupted. The recommendations amounted to a set of negotiating options. Finally, if there was a threat to person or property, the minister or the president of the Board should be notified, if possible, before the police were called.[502]

Cedar Lane Unitarian Church in Bethesda, Maryland, had no such policy on Sunday, June 7, 1970, when three members of Student Religious Liberals rushed the pulpit. The leader of the threesome was Eric Schuman. He had been the youth member on the Cedar Lane Board until he resigned after a confrontation with the Board the previous fall.

At the September 1969 Board meeting, the senior minister, Robert Zoerheide, had advised against including BAWA among their annual social action disbursements due to the sensitivity of the conflict. The Board, which was divided on funding BAWA, left the decision to the Finance Committee, which decided to include BAWA. Eric Schuman, who had missed the Board meeting, objected to the

Finance Committee's decision and published a letter of protest in the newsletter decrying the proposal as "untimely and unfortunate."

At its October meeting, the Board revisited the issue and decided that no funds would be allocated to BAWA. While several Board members told Schuman that they found it upsetting and unfair that he had aired his disagreement to the congregation without discussing it with them first, others defended his right to state his opinion in the newsletter. At the November meeting, he condemned the Board and resigned.

On June 7, Helen Petersberger took nine-year-old Clare to the worship service rather than to Sunday school because she wanted her daughter to experience an adult service, with the organ, hymns, meditation, and preaching. They sat in the front row, a few seats in from the left aisle, so that Clare would have a clear view. As a youth quartet was playing Haydn, Petersberger heard voices behind her. When she looked over her shoulder, she saw three college-age youth striding down the aisle. An older man got a hand on one of them, but the intruders pushed aside the effort and headed for the podium. As the interlude ended, Rev. Zoerheide, seemingly unruffled, observed, "This is an unannounced takeover."

Petersberger thought, "What is this about? Not enough support for conscientious objectors? How's this going to play out?"

People rose from their chairs, and confusion reigned. One member stood up and said, "This is nothing but Brown Shirt tactics," and another said he would leave if the students were allowed to take over. Ushers moved to take the trio away, and Petersberger worried that the situation would turn violent. She stood up, grabbed Clare's hand, said, "We're going," and bolted up the aisle.

There was a scuffle on the podium. "You get your dirty hands off!" one of the young men shouted. Petersberger heard Zoerheide ask everyone to sit down, saying, "These are Unitarian young people.

They are dissenters. They are militant and I believe we should hear them out." But with Clare in tow, she kept right on moving.

Zoerheide managed to calm the situation down and negotiate a deal with the three protestors: Schuman; John White, who was also white; and Anne Singleton, an African American woman who was the president of Student Religious Liberals at the University of Maryland. Zoerheide would shorten his sermon, which was about "the rights of youth in a rapidly changing world," and then give them time to speak, after which they would entertain questions. The congregation voted to accept the deal, the youth resumed their seats, and the service proceeded. Following Zoerheide's abbreviated sermon, a dozen people left and the SRL group got up.

Singleton, White, and Schuman made eleven demands. First was that the church support BAC and raise $10 thousand to purchase BAC Bonds. Second was that it work to end youth oppression, including by allowing Liberal Religious Youth to use the church building without an adult advisor present and by supporting the legalization of marijuana. Third was that the church oppose the Vietnam War and provide counseling to those facing the draft. When they had finished speaking, they left without answering any questions, leaving many church members irate. "We're done with talking," they said outside. "We want action, not discussion."

The following day, members of Cedar Lane discovered that Sunday's events had made headlines in the *Washington Evening Star*: "Students Present Demands: 3 Seize Unitarian Pulpit in Bethesda." The press had been alerted beforehand, a reporter and photographer had been there, and Student Religious Liberals had prepared a press release. Further statements followed from all sides: The congregation's president circulated a letter, Zoerheide published a newspaper article in which he responded to (and rebuffed many of) the trio's demands, and a congregational discussion was held on June 21.

Zoerheide also said that the congregation had already planned to purchase BAC Bonds anyway. A drive kicked off on October 4, 1970, and congregation members ultimately bought $13,640 in bonds.[503]

The takeovers, all of them, were political theater. The Student Religious Liberals were saying, "You adults talk everything to death and then make wishy-washy compromises. That does not work for us. This is urgent, and we are angry, and we want to be in control rather than placated." The other takeovers sent a similar message. For dissidents protesting racism, the Vietnam War, and youth oppression, it was not a time for dialogue (or reason or tolerance) but for action. It was not about persuasion, it was about the exercise of power, and not power *with* but power *over*.

The Seattle GA Boycott

Before the ninth General Assembly of the Unitarian Universalist Association convened on Monday, June 29, 1970, the deepening of political and personal polarization was already in evidence.

On Tuesday, June 2, Mason McGuinness, minister of Main Line Unitarian Church and a member of the UUA Board, wrote to David Parke, his colleague at the nearby Germantown congregation in Philadelphia. He said he had read, and been offended by, Parke's description of the Board in a sermon he had delivered at Chicago First in early May. In it, he called the Board "self-condemned" and implied that they were "morally irresponsible." "Your rhetoric begins to sound like the totalitarian righteousness of an angry God," McGuinness told him. He was writing to tell Parke that he and his wife would not be attending the dinner party scheduled for the coming Friday evening. He would "miss the fellowship," McGuinness said, "but that is better than pretending."[504] Theirs was one of many relationships damaged during that conflicted era.

Housing at the Seattle General Assembly was an issue for Liberal Religious Youth and Student Religious Liberals. The Olympic Hotel, where the Assembly was held, was too expensive for the youth. At the Boston General Assembly, youth had been able to crash at Second Church. In Seattle, there was no conveniently located church willing to shelter them. After a hunt, a member of the LRY Executive Committee discovered the Fremont Hotel, which was only a fifteen-minute drive from the Olympic. An old flophouse that was about to close down, the Fremont was beyond shabby. It was woebegone, largely stripped of furnishings, and full of trash. A deal was nonetheless struck to rent the entire hotel, using funds from Liberal Religious Youth and the Fellowship for Renewal, for the week of General Assembly. It was marketed to the Fellowship for Renewal as intergenerational housing, an alternative to the evil corporate culture and expensive hotel of General Assembly's official location; it also gave BAC's co-collaborators a base of operation.[505]

The ninth General Assembly of the Unitarian Universalist Association ran from June 29 to July 4. It took place three thousand miles away from Boston and was very different from the gathering there. Mt. Rainier stood in the distance but was rarely seen, as northwestern weather was typically cloudy. The temperature was more comfortable than it had been the year before; it started in the sixties and climbed into the eighties. The makeup of the Assembly was different as well, with 182 fewer societies represented, 763 fewer delegates in attendance, and a boycott by BAC/BUUC.

When the delegates arrived, there were piles of literature waiting for them that put forward the issues at hand. Much of it focused on the Unitarian Universalist Association budget and on BAC. A BAWA flyer announced that the guest speaker at BAWA's dinner dance would be Rev. Andrew Young, the executive vice president of the Southern Christian Leadership Conference who was running for Congress, and afterward members of the cast of the musical *Hair* would perform.

There was also a "fact sheet" from the Fellowship for Renewal. At the end of April, it had held its annual meeting at the First Unitarian Society of Chicago, where Mendelsohn was now the senior minister and where Parke had delivered the sermon that had offended McGuiness. Committed to monitoring and challenging the Association, it had begun planning its strategy for General Assembly. In Seattle, that also meant being the stand-in for BAC/BUUC. The fact sheet began, "The issue is whether the UUA can respond in new ways to a revolutionary national and world situation." It asserted that the UUA Board's reduction of BAC's funding ran counter to the principle of black empowerment, which meant "Black people controlling their own affairs," and that the UUA's "commitment" was "in jeopardy." And it called upon the delegates to reverse the "downward drift of do-nothing and despair which the board calls 'fiscal responsibility.' . . . It is time to free this movement from the money-changers and return it to the people."[506]

Indeed, one of the surprises that had emerged from the 1968 and 1969 General Assemblies was that the Assembly did not control the Unitarian Universalist Association budget. Few people had realized that the budget passed by a GA was essentially advisory because the ultimate fiduciary responsibility rested with the UUA Board. Those who wanted to change this put forth a resolution to give GA the authority to prioritize programs and make the Board responsible only for managing them. However, the inclination of the 1970 Assembly was to show support for the decisions Bob West and the Board had made, and the resolution was defeated.

On Wednesday, July 1, the General Assembly newsletter ran a column entitled "Bob Kaufmann's Mad World: An Irreverent Look at the G.A." Kaufmann wrote, "Small group discussions are being held to allow everyone to get a chance to speak before the larger meeting convenes, so as not to interfere with the delegates who regularly monopolize the microphone."[507] This was the first effort of the UUA Program Committee, which was trying to create more dialogue and less polarization in the wake of the 1969 Boston GA.[508] The plenary sessions were run according to Robert's Rules of Order, which set a tone of pro and con debate that was not conducive to listening to or hearing one another. Such sessions were not places for conversation or sharing; their nature was adversarial, inviting participants to talk at, rather than with, one another.

Kaufmann also wrote, "The Black Affairs Council is boycotting the G.A. For further information, visit their official boycott booth on the mezzanine floor of G.A. headquarters."[509] This was a humorous reference to the fact that, although they claimed to be boycotting, their presence was unequivocally felt. BAC convinced Rev. Andrew Young to cancel his appearance as the keynote speaker at the BAWA dinner; Young said he did not want to become "embroiled in intra-denominational tensions." In addition, the local chapter of BUUC seemed to have a hand in delaying the performance of *Hair* at that gathering until after midnight.[510]

BAC's influence was evident, but not in the way that counted most, votes on the plenary floor. After BAC disaffiliated, the Unitarian Universalist Association Board had removed its allocation from the 1970–1971 budget. A motion to reinstate full funding of it was defeated, 399 for to 462 against. The sixty-three-vote margin was almost the exact reversal of BAC's sixty-one-vote triumph in 1969, which raises questions about the intent and value of its boycott. BAC's boycott made it seem obstructionist, but what it did was leave the door open for an alternative motion.

After the defeat of the motion to fund BAC, one was offered to fund BAWA. What eventually passed was a substitute motion that did not provide funding but instead urged member societies and their individual members to support the efforts of BAWA, acknowledge that institutional racism degrades blacks and corrupts whites, and reaffirm the Unitarian Universalist Association commitment to black empowerment. It also applauded BAC for going directly to the people. The resolution concluded, "The Unitarian Universalist Association must take the initiative in urging our churches and fellowships to support the community action program of BAC. We have moved through the experience of being polarized. We must now be ready to initiate our role of renewed responsibility."[511] However, the tone of the resolution offered little to suggest that delegates understood and embraced the fact that it was they, as white people, and their congregational cultures that needed to change.

The General Assembly also passed a resolution on ethnic obligations, which urged that the $50 thousand voted by the 1969 Assembly for use by Chicanos be granted, but also that it be asked to make the Unitarian Universalist Service Committee distribution. The Service Committee, however, was wholly independent of the Association and not bound by its wishes. Together, these two resolutions seem to indicate that the delegates wanted to be on the right side of the issues and to affirm the Consensus on Racial Justice the 1966 Assembly had passed, but only if it didn't cost them anything. As one delegate said, "More than a handshake and a blessing [was] needed."[512]

How deep were the divisions? The same delegate said, "I would like to say that I, as a Black Unitarian, found it a sad commentary on the times that those who were instrumental in arguing against the Black Affairs Council were the Negro members of BAWA."[513] Max Gaebler, the white co-chair of BAWA, said, "It was a long time before I got back to feeling totally at home even in my own family—my own denominational family."[514] And one white participant described the mood in Seattle as somber.

The defeat of the motion to fund BAC and the cancellation of Andrew Young's address garnered much attention, but little was paid to the address delivered by Howard Thurman. Thurman, who was among the most prominent religious leaders in America, had been one of Martin Luther King Jr.'s mentors. He had been featured in *Life* magazine. He had delivered the 1956 Ware Lecture and, having sat on AUA and UUA commissions, was no stranger to the UUA. Yet this acclaimed African American preacher seems to have had little impact. This suggests that the predominantly humanist UUs were uninterested in someone rooted in liberal Christianity whose mode of expression was spiritual rather than political. It is ironic—and perhaps self-evident—that most Unitarian Universalists were not concerned with cultivating the spiritual depth and sense of solidarity that had sustained Dr. King and the civil rights movement. As usual, they didn't see racism as a spiritual crisis.

However, the issues that were to shape the Unitarian Universalist Association's social action priorities were in evidence in both the parish poll conducted before General Assembly and the General Resolutions passed at it. In the titles of those resolutions, we can see the Association's concerns shifting and note the themes that would dominate the next two decades: "Withdrawal of Troops from Southeast Asia," "Population Control," "Indian Rights," "Disarmament," "Equal Rights and Opportunities for Women," "Discrimination against Homosexuals and Bisexuals," "Legalization of Marijuana," "Police Repression," and "Self-Government for Washington D.C." In the near future, attention would turn toward those issues with the most direct impact on Euro-American Unitarian Universalists—the war in Vietnam, women's liberation, and gay rights.

Is This Really Democracy? Crunching the Numbers

During the 1969 General Assembly in Boston, the Black Affairs Council declared it represented *the people*. This was BAC's conviction, and those who shared it saw every action of the Unitarian Universalist Association that did not support BAC as reneging on the 1968 commitment as racist, and as a betrayal. The foundations of this certainty were the resolutions passed supporting BAC at the 1968 and 1969 Assemblies.

Notwithstanding, what do we discover if we consider, first, historical trends regarding GA attendance figures and vote tallies specifically concerning the Association's commitment to racial justice and, second, whether passing a resolution actually means a consensus has been reached?

When votes on the plan for consolidation came before the American Unitarian Association and Universalist Church of America in Boston in 1960, the 887 accredited Unitarian delegates voted 725 to 143 in favor, with some abstentions, and the Universalists voted 365 to 65 in favor; that is, 83 percent of the 1,317 delegates voted yes.

In 1961, when the General Assembly was again held in Boston, the vote to support integration of the public schools was 475 for and 34 against: a very strong affirmation (92 percent) from many fewer delegates.

In Chicago in 1963, there were 1,036 delegates, of whom 270 were ministers. A vote on amending the Unitarian Universalist Association's bylaws to require that affiliated congregations admit members "without discrimination" was 436 for and 379 against. That represented a 53-percent majority but fell short of the 75-percent majority required for passage. A substitute motion that encouraged compliance and did not require a bylaw change passed 583 for to 6 against.

In 1965 in Boston, with 1,300 delegates in attendance, the vote was 531 for and 256 opposed to a resolution protesting segregation in Boston schools, or 67 percent for.

The 1966 General Assembly in Hollywood, Florida, was smaller, with only 845 delegates. When the vote for the Consensus on Racial Justice was taken, those opposed were asked to stand; fewer than twenty-four did so.

In 1968 in Cleveland, attendance was 1,350. We know that BAC, BUUC, FULLBAC, and SOBURR all organized to bring their delegates to General Assembly that year. The vote to support BAC was 836 to 327, or 71 percent in favor among the 1,163 who voted.

At the 1969 General Assembly in Boston, the vote to support BAC and not BAWA was 798 to 737, a 52-percent majority of 1,785 delegates. The attendance was 32 percent higher than in Cleveland and more than twice as high as that of the 1966 Hollywood GA. In 1969, BAC, BUUC, FULLBAC, and LRY were organized, as were C.O.N.C.E.R.N. and, to a lesser degree, BAWA. In addition, it was an election year and the Assembly was held in the Unitarian Universalist heartland, New England.

In Seattle in 1970, the number of General Assembly delegates dropped to 1,022, 43 percent fewer than in Boston and 25 percent fewer than in Cleveland. Several factors contributed to this. BAC/BUUC boycotted that year, of course. In addition, Seattle was far away from the demographic center of Unitarian Universalism, which was still east of the Mississippi. Seattle had a small African American population and no significant African American population centers nearby to draw upon. When the Seattle Assembly was asked to reverse the defunding of BAC, the motion failed 399 for to 462 against. The sixty-three-vote margin suggests that the boycott worked against BAC and was a strategic mistake. Instead, the Assembly passed a resolution that supported both BAWA and BAC, and another to reinstate the $50 thousand to be given to Chicano empowerment.

What do these numbers suggest?

By 1966, Unitarian Universalists had reached an overwhelming consensus on civil rights. This was demonstrated in the General Assembly vote for the Consensus on Racial Justice and confirmed by the report of the Committee on Goals. Released in 1967, that report said that 94.4 percent of UUs considered racial integration either "very" or "somewhat important" and that 90.6 percent "approved" or "strongly approved" of denominational activities in the field of civil rights and race relations. This consensus was built upon dozens of resolutions dating back to 1942; broad participation by UUs, and particularly UU clergy, in civil rights and open housing activities; and a notable increase in African Americans joining urban UU congregations, particularly in the Northeast and Midwest.

In 1968, four things came together to increase attendance at General Assembly and produce the vote giving $1 million to BAC over four years. BUUC, BAC, SOBURR, and FULLBAC rallied their supporters before GA, and during it delegates "were subject to massive and continuing appeals."[515] Cleveland was a major black population center and was within driving range of others: Detroit, Chicago, Washington D.C., New York, Philadelphia, and Cincinnati. The Kerner Report, which had just been released, had warned of "two societies, one black one white—separate and unequal." And Martin Luther King Jr. had been assassinated seven weeks earlier. The resulting 71-percent vote in favor of BAC was the high-water mark of support for it.

In 1969, General Assembly was held in Boston. Several Unitarian Universalist surveys had shown that New England had the weakest support for civil rights and was, in general, more conservative than other areas of the country. In addition, there were few

African Americans living in the region, and other black population centers were farther away. The average driving time from the six cities listed above was 9.5 hours to Boston, compared to 5.3 hours to Cleveland. BAWA had time to organize, and it was an election year. Attendance was the highest it had ever been at General Assembly, 32 percent higher than it had been the previous year and 27 percent higher than in Boston four years earlier. The vote in favor of BAC in 1969 was much closer than it had been the previous year—52 percent instead of 71 percent. Homer Jack said it was obvious from the first vote that year that Boston was more conservative than Cleveland simply because there was "more representation from more conservative New England Churches." Moreover, after a year of enduring BAC/BUUC tactics, Bob Hohler's fast, and the occupation of the UUSC office by the Interdenominational Racial Caucus, conservatives were prepared to fight back.[516]

The 1970 General Assembly was held in Seattle. The Pacific Northwest is relatively isolated, compared to New England. There is no significant African American population within driving distance; the nearest, in the Bay Area, is a twelve-hour drive away. Also, BAC boycotted that General Assembly and the overall number of delegates was down. It is perhaps not surprising, then, that the motion to reinstate BAC's funding failed, while the 1966 Consensus on Racial Justice was reaffirmed with a nod of goodwill to BAWA, BAC, and Chicano empowerment.

It seems that the geographic location of a General Assembly can skew its decisions. While this has a democratizing effect upon the Unitarian Universalist Association over the long run, it also complicates decision making.

Leading up to the 1969 Boston General Assembly, Rev. Dorothy Spoerl wrote in a July 1969 *UUA Now* article entitled

"Delegate Voting," "Obviously this is going to be the largest General Assembly on record." Then she asked, "Is it large enough to be truly representative? How would the 40 percent of lay and ministerial delegates who were not present have voted?" And if it is not truly representative, "where does the fault lie?" Her question was rhetorical: "The answer is clear." Disappointing votes, she said, were the fault of those who did not attend. But her answer does not capture the complexity of the variables.[517]

The location of a General Assembly obviously had an impact on who attended and thus on its decisions. Economic class was another factor. Who could afford to go, even with congregational support and subsidies to equalize travel expenses? How many potential delegates had the freedom to take a week off work? Clearly, the decisions made at a General Assembly are made by Unitarian Universalists who have the time and resources to participate. Thus there is a built-in class bias.

The predominance of ministers at General Assembly is another factor. In the years between 1964 and 1970, ministers on average represented 25 percent of the delegates, ranging from 27 percent in Hollywood to 19 percent in Seattle. The proportion of delegates at the American Unitarian Association May Meetings who were ministers had been higher. This made a difference. Rev. Chris Raible, a long-time attender of both May Meetings and General Assemblies whose father and older brother were also Unitarian Universalist minsters, said, "Ministers were far more radical in their ideas than most of their members. I have heard more passionate advocacy [from them] at a GA microphone than I doubt I would have heard, without more caveats and qualifications, from their home pulpits."[518] In 1963, during the debate on whether to amend the bylaws to forbid discrimination in membership admission, the first five people to address the Assembly were ministers, and of the thirty-five people who spoke in all, twenty-six were ministers.

Because of the commitment and resources that attending a General Assembly required, it drew those who were most highly motivated. These fell into two categories—social activists and institutionalists. Members of BUUC, FULLBAC, and the FFR were among the former, while ministers and those involved in a Unitarian Universalist Association district or continental governance made up the latter. General Assembly resolutions would, then, naturally tend to reflect a somewhat more progressive stance than the Association's general constituency. Given all these factors, while it can be said that General Assemblies are representative, one cannot assume that the positions any one GA took on a given issue actually represented a Unitarian Universalist consensus.

For what kind of decisions should winning a simple majority in a single vote be sufficient, and when should it not? The Unitarian Universalist Association did differentiate. A change to a C bylaw required a two-thirds vote in favor at two consecutive General Assemblies. General resolutions and business resolutions (including the vote to allocate $1 million to BAC) did not.

In any case, a vote, whether carried by a simple majority or by two-thirds of the electorate, does not guarantee fairness, and democratic process, as the tyranny of the majority, can support oppression.

In "The Black Power Hang-up," a sermon delivered on November 26, 1967, John Ruskin Clark recalled the 1963 Chicago General Assembly when the resolution on nondiscrimination was debated. Although a majority voted in favor of requiring congregations to admit members without consideration of their race, the vote did not attain the two-thirds majority needed to make the necessary bylaw change. Clark said,

In a way, it was a small issue since only one or two societies did discriminate on a racial basis in membership. The defeating cry was the preservation of local society autonomy. But I remember seeing, as I sat in the back of the room, the dejection of the handful of Negro delegates when the open membership amendment was defeated. What do you do when you are a small minority among a majority which is not sensitive to the symbolic significance of such an amendment? The few Negroes couldn't out vote the majority of whites.[519]

That memory helped Clark understand the formation of a Black Caucus. "They had to get together to make their feelings heard." BAC and BUUC, however, wanted more. They wanted justice and the power to bring it about. But how does such a minority acquire and exercise power in the Unitarian Universalist Association?

The Society of Friends governs itself by consensus and the spirit; for Quakers, decision making is a spiritual practice. As a faith community, Unitarian Universalists are covenantal but our polity is democratic, and which holds sway depends on the situation. When dealing with an association of autonomous congregations, consensus is required to move forward on issues of self-definition. Between the 1942 Resolution on Race Relations and the 1966 Consensus on Racial Justice, a consensus was reached on civil rights and integration; that consensus made the rapid Unitarian Universalist response to events in Selma possible. A single vote in Cleveland in favor of Black Power, which few white Unitarian Universalists really understood in 1968, and a narrow victory in Boston did not significantly alter that consensus.

Looking back in 1978, Donald McKinney, the Euro-American with the longest tenure in BAC, wondered if the vision that so many were excited about in Cleveland, of the Unitarian Universalist

Association relating to the black community in a new, more significant way, ultimately failed because our "ideology is so ingrained and rigid that the institutions we have fashioned to nurture and protect our individualism are incapable of collective action."[520] As the Fellowship for Renewal broadened its scope beyond just supporting BAC, it took on the challenge of smashing the Unitarian Universalist idolization of individualism, which made the isolated person the "source of human essence" while denying "the humanness found in community."[521] There is a form of hyper-individualism within Unitarian Universalism that, added to a distrust of authority, has made nimble collective action difficult and rapid consensus hard to reach. This is not the result of white supremacy. Rather, it reflects a struggle over, and different understandings of, where the locus of power within the Association should reside.

Another possibility is that the vision failed because it was ideological rather than relational. To succeed it needed to be grounded in relationship: to one's own values, to others (in this case, specifically to African Americans), and between congregations. Since power in a covenantal community resides in this relationality, to the degree that BAC, BUUC, and FULLBAC were willing to sever relationships, they could not succeed.

The definitive example of reaching a hard-won consensus is the 1961 final vote on consolidation of the Universalist Church of America and the American Unitarian Association. A consensus emerged, but it took decades and was, in a sense, incremental. A joint Commission on Hymns and Services produced *Hymns of the Spirit* in 1937. Many ministers held dual fellowship, and Unitarian ministers served Universalist churches and Universalist ministers served Unitarian societies. The African American Jeff Campbell was one such example: The Universalists granted him fellowship in 1935 and the Unitarians in 1938. In 1939, Frederick May Eliot, the

AUA president, foresaw the two denominations uniting into "The Liberal Church of America." Although he died in 1958, before the full consolidation, he was witness to many of the events that led to it. A joint denominational committee was established in 1951, which led to the formation of the Council of Liberal Churches (CLC) in 1953. Universalist and Unitarian youth programs merged in 1954. In 1956, the CLC's limitations led to the formation of a Joint Merger Commission, an exhaustive process of congregational consultation, and multiple votes, the final one of which required participation by at least 75 percent of all congregations. In the end, fully 90 percent of the votes cast were in favor of the merger.[522]

Like consolidation, the effort to revise the Unitarian Universalist Association's Statement of Principles and Purposes (which were originally adopted at the time of consolidation in 1961) was time-consuming and reliant on group process alongside broad and sustained denomination-wide discussion. The current statement was adopted in 1984, in the first of two votes at consecutive General Assemblies, after a formal process spanning four years. However, the push for that change must be seen as the consequence of the 1977 Women and Religion resolution, which called on the Association to "avoid sexist assumptions and language in the future." This meant that the sexist idiom of the 1960 statement had to be exorcised. The change went beyond degenderization and ultimately created phrasing that has become fundamental to Unitarian Universalist identity, including "the interdependent web of all existence, of which we are a part." The resolution was just the beginning of a process that led to a degenderized hymnal supplement in 1979 and a new hymnal, *Singing the Living Tradition*, in 1993,[523] and to the religious education program *Cakes for the Queen of Heaven* in 1995. Meanwhile, the number of women in the Unitarian Universalist ministry grew to 199 in 1987. In 2000, 431 of 853 active ministers were women, and in 2017, Rev. Susan Frederick-Gray became the first elected female president of the Association.

Honoring process is crucial when addressing issues of identity and self-definition. This did not happen when the Unitarian Universalist Association struggled to come to terms with the meaning of Black Power and America's enduring racial wound. A denomination-wide process was needed, but there was no way for that to happen during those tumultuous years. Most Unitarian Universalists had no significant relationships to African Americans; in and of itself, that should have aroused a deeper concern. But BAC and BUUC saw the needs of the black community as urgent enough to preempt process. For FULLBAC and FFR, the need to be supportive of BAC often overrode pragmatism and friendships; nor was wise counsel accepted, as when Dick Nash told Hayward Henry it was a political mistake to push his anti-pluralistic "either, but not both" position in regard to BAWA. The Alinsky-style politics of polarization and confrontation of that era left little room for dialogue, tolerance, or consensus building. Yet dedication to process, consensus building, and patience were exactly why consolidation and the revision of the Principles and Purposes succeeded. They were rooted in the faith's covenantal tradition. Consensus building and real change require years, even decades, of patience and tenacity. Disaffiliation and boycotts (i.e. absence) killed an emerging opportunity before its roots had grown deep.

The high-water mark for BAC came in 1968 under unique conditions. Afterward, despite much political maneuvering, BAC won a barely affirmative vote to receive $250 thousand in Boston in 1969 and then narrowly lost a vote to have its funds reinstated when it boycotted the Seattle General Assembly in 1970.

The reason why BAC lost in 1970 and again in 1971 was that Unitarian Universalists never reached a consensus about Black

Power. BAC won two votes, but it did not have a mandate. Few ministers would accept a call to a congregation with such a split vote. But based on a narrow victory in 1969, BAC proclaimed *the people* of the UUA were behind them based on the stronger vote a year earlier. That was hyperbole rather than truth. The survey conducted by the Unitarian Universalist Association Committee on Goals had indicated there was consensus around "integration," but that was a misnomer most Unitarian Universalists used when, in truth, they meant assimilation. The kind of shift BAC, BUUC, FULLBAC, and the FFR were looking for would not have come about without an enormous, time-consuming exertion of energy, like that of the joint commissions that brought about consolidation over the course of ten years. But that was exactly what black Unitarian Universalists did not have time for when cities were burning; nor would converting white Unitarian Universalists into antiracists have been a responsible use of their energies.

FULLBAC/FFR needed to invest time in changing white hearts and consciousness rather than finding votes.[524] But they lacked the language, conceptual framework, and pastoral pedagogy to do so. There was no way for Euro-Americans to talk about white supremacy, or privilege, or systemic racism, much less understand their role in maintaining them. The concepts and language did not exist in 1968. Most Unitarian Universalists still thought that treating African American UUs as honorary white folks was an achievement.

At heart, Euro-American Unitarian Universalists wanted to be moral progressives on the right side of history. In doing good, they could feel ethical and in charge. They thought of others as in need of redemption. A values survey carried out in 1976 found that *salvation* came "close to being a disvalue for Unitarian Universalists."[525] In a liberal theological milieu averse to addressing sin—meaning the many ways we fall short of our aspirations—Unitarian

Universalists lacked practices like prayer and confession that could have helped them deal with feelings of confusion, guilt, and shame. Some understood it was necessary for them to support rather than lead. But they did not know how to be allies without kowtowing, concede authority while honoring their own voice, brave black rage with forbearance, or honestly confess that they feared change. This was a difficult path to walk, especially without spiritual resources.

For all the hope there had been, and despite the good work that was accomplished with BAC grants, the end of BAC and BUUC, and eventually BAWA, would be sad, tragic, and deflating.

The Washington D.C. General Assembly

[1971]

As THE 1971 GENERAL ASSEMBLY in Washington D.C. approached, some were trying to calm the waters. Many hoped for reconciliation, and a few worked toward it. The Black Affairs Council put forward what it saw as a compromise. But the undertow of competing loyalties, dissatisfaction, distrust, and anger was so strong that even people who had been allies came into conflict, and the organizations that activists had formed also began to splinter. The Assembly delegates passed a resolution that came to be known as the Ross Resolution, which they hoped would resolve the internal conflict and provide funding without worsening the Unitarian Universalist Association's financial situation, thus allowing for a renewed focus on black concerns. Black and White Action acquiesced, but when BAC and its supporters rejected the Ross Resolution, the effort foundered.

From Skirmish to Schism: The Chicago Area Caucus Breaks with National BUUC

"Chicago Caucus Votes Break with National" was the headline on the March 21, 1971 edition of *First Church News*. The Black

Unitarian Universalist Caucus had held its fourth annual meeting in February, and Chicago Area BUUC (CABUUC) had broken with it less than two weeks later.

BUUC's meeting was held in Cleveland at the Black Humanist Fellowship of Liberation on February 19–21, 1971. Beforehand, Hayward Henry sent out a letter saying that, in establishing a black caucus "firmly in the Black Movement," he had accomplished what he had set out to do. He proposed that BUUC would now be best served by decentralizing and focusing on its own internal development and that a new national chair was called for, someone whose primary concern would be the process of decentralization. Therefore, although he had held the position since BUUC's founding in 1968, he would not stand as a candidate in the coming election. He was not disassociating himself from BUUC, he said, but would serve as its "Ambassador-at-Large."[526]

What Henry did not mention in his letter was that he was already the chair of the Congress of African People (CAP). Hayward Henry had been attending the annual Black Power Conferences since their inaugural conference in Newark NJ in July 1967, three months before he came to the UU Emergency Conference as a member from Second Unitarian, Boston. In 1970, when the Black Power conferences shifted in focus to Black Nationalism with a pan-African vision, Henry became the chair of this successor organization, the Congress of African People. CAP held its first conference in Atlanta on Labor Day weekend, 1970. Twenty-seven hundred delegates were in attendance; 350 were from 35 African and third-world countries.

BAC had helped fund the annual Black Power conferences and continued funding their effort through the Congress of African People in 1970.

In addition, there was a significant leadership overlap between the two organizations: Hayward Henry was co-convener of CAP (with Imamu Amiri Baraka), Richard Traylor was its treasurer, and BAC member Robert Small was chief administrator. Louis Gothard would become its coordinator, and one of the presenters at its first meeting was Dr. John Cashin, founder of the National Democratic Party of Alabama, who attended the Unitarian congregation in Huntsville. BAC treasurer Ben Scott, who was on the CAP Executive Board,[527] also attended, as did Whitney M. Young Jr., the executive director of the National Urban League, and journalist Alex Poinsett.[528] Baraka was not a Unitarian Universalist, but the others were.

As with the Interreligious Foundation for Community Organization and the National Black Economic Development Conference, BAC funding of groups and involvement in their leadership were entwined. It is unlikely that many white Unitarian Universalists were aware that black Unitarian Universalists were playing central roles in the black liberation movement beyond the Unitarian Universalist Association. However, it did not go unnoticed by some black Unitarian Universalists.

"There was much displeasure at Hayward's organizing the Congress without consulting the BUUC Steering Committee," wrote Marjorie Jordan in the Cincinnati BUUC newsletter.[529] In the face of this displeasure, the BUUC leadership prepared an "issues brief" for use in workshops and to promote honest dialogue at its annual meeting. Eight areas of contention were outlined. Among the questions that it flagged were: Was CAP's ideology consistent with BUUC's? Did the BAC/BUUC staff have authority to make such a significant investment of time and resources in CAP? Did leading BUUC and CAP at the same time place Hayward Henry in a conflict of interest? Was further discussion required before BUUC's involvement in CAP continued? Should BUUC have an ideology, and if so, what should it be? What was the relationship of BUUC to Black Humanism? And should BUUC boycott General Assembly again?[530]

Other contentious issues were raised in a five-page position paper that was developed by the Washington-area chapter for presentation at the meeting. The paper praised the Black Caucus for its initial demand that the Unitarian Universalist Association end its paternalism. It then presented a vision of a national organization committed to building stronger connections to its local chapters, being aware of their needs and opinions, and giving more attention to developing "local leadership." It called for "a free exchange of ideas," "careful listening," and "an atmosphere of freedom in speech," as well as for a more democratic process and a commitment to carrying out the will of the general membership. It challenged Article 10 of BUUC's constitution, which allowed a person to be removed from membership, and especially questioned the Steering Committee's right to make such decisions. The new leadership, it cautioned, would need to "maintain the respect and trust of those whom it serves," and at one point it referred to members feeling "manipulated by their own leadership."[531] While careful not to attack or blame the current leadership, by the time the position paper asserted that BUUC could not "function effectively in a condition of oligarchy," its dissatisfaction with the Steering Committee's heavy-handed leadership was clear.

The practice of sitting on a board that funds another organization in which one is serving in a position of leadership is a clear conflict of interest, and this was what Henry and others were doing when BAC funded CAP, IFCO, and the NBEDC. The position paper was circumspect in the way it affirmed what was needed rather than criticizing what was wrong. Still, it made its concerns clear. The issues brief and the position paper pointed to divergent loyalties, priorities, and styles—and also to a hidden agenda, which led to a schism and a lawsuit two years later.

At the February 1971 annual meeting, Harold Wilson, vice-chair of BUUC, was elected national chair, and Hayward Henry was designated "chairman emeritus."[532] BUUC voted to continue to support CAP, endorsed the Continental Renewal Conference that the Fellowship for Renewal planned to hold in Chicago in April, and said it would send representatives to that conference. However, it declined to adopt Henry's "Basic Primer of Black Humanism" as an official ideology. This essentially repudiated the action of the December 1970 Steering Committee meeting, which had adopted it. BUUC also voted to once again boycott the General Assembly.

Chicago-area BUUC members, who already had a difficult relationship with BUUC, grew increasingly disenchanted. Henry had complained to BAC about CABUUC in March 1970, and a second Chicago chapter, which did support BUUC, was later formed and called the Society of Black Soul.[533] Henry's departure as chair did not end CABUUC's disagreements with the national organization, and on March 4, CABUUC disaffiliated. The reason it gave was that it wanted to focus its attention and resources on local projects, but it is obvious that its differences with BUUC ran deeper.

In mid-April, the First Unitarian Society of Chicago held a special congregational workshop to examine the congregation's outside giving, including to the Unitarian Universalist Association, BAC, and the Neighborhood Commons Corporation (NCC). The Society's Board had voted to serve as guarantor of a $10 thousand loan to the NCC. John Keohane, who had gathered the signatures required for the special meeting, was concerned about "the 'increasing alienation' of some members over the congregation's decision to give $4 thousand from its UUA pledge to the Black Affairs Council."534 This meant the congregation made no contribution at all to the UUA.535 Keohane said that Hansel Hall, the chair of CABUUC, had helped to draft the petition for the special meeting, which is an indication of where Hall stood on BAC.

The relationship between BUUC and First Chicago was not the only one fracturing. Such ruptures seemed endemic to the era.

The Fellowship for Renewal was planning a Continental Renewal Conference, to be held at First Chicago that April. Reaching agreement on its purpose and focus was the first challenge. The Organizing Committee sought feedback on a proposal to make the gathering serve as an "alternate General Assembly." White BAC member Don McKinney warned against the idea, and although Max Gaebler, the former BAWA co-chair, supported the focus on renewal, he agreed that billing the conference that way would be seen "as a potential assault on the denomination."536 David Parke, who by then had been terminated by the disgruntled Germantown congregation, saw it as the focal point of a nationwide fund drive for BAC. Victor Carpenter, the minister of First Philadelphia, said, "We're wondering about the need for a conference at all. We're most concerned about funding BAC.... BAC needs $30,000 right now [and] I just don't see how a conference of workshops talking about renewal can really do very much when we have this kind of need facing us." Ultimately, however, the narrow focus that Carpenter proposed did not prevail. The conference planners agreed with John Smith, chair of the Chicago Area Felllowship for Renewal (CAFFR), who was "concerned that this not be a one-issue conference."537 CAFFR had made its position clear the previous summer: "We accept the challenge of racism as the crisis issue of our church and society. But we are equally dedicated to the empowerment of youth [and] women."538

It also was striving in order to go beyond the stifling UU intellectualism that one of its position papers critiqued and to "feel our faith, rather than just talk, talk, talk."[539] That spring, it led worship services on "oppression and liberation" in seven area churches, and it would lead another four in the summer.

The Continental Renewal Conference ran April 22–25, 1971. There were eighty-six registered participants and many who just showed up.[540] There was a business meeting, which endorsed a resolution that the Unitarian Universalist Association should give 10 percent of its annual budget to BAC, and there were workshops that developed a series of position papers: "The Ministry," "White Racism," "Funding the Black Affairs Council," "Youth," and "Sexuality, Sexism, and the Family."[541]

Other elements of the conference exposed the different priorities that had become evident during the planning calls. There was to be a multimedia service on white racism on Friday morning. Several people advised one of the organizers that they were sure it would be worthwhile, but they wanted to know when they would get down to the "real business." She discovered how widespread that attitude was when only fifteen people were there when the service was to begin. The paltry turnout made clear to her why the weekend's efforts at renewal, in other words celebration and worship, were largely unsuccessful. She was left with the impression that the attitude of some attendees was "People and community are all very fine, but we came here to do business," and their attitude seemed to her "to be directly contradictory to the realities of how people functioned."[542]

During the Renewal Conference, it became clear that the agendas of the Fellowship for Renewal and of the champions of BAC were related, but different. The difference was great enough to prompt the formation of the BAC Support Group in April, which was ready to act at the Washington General Assembly.

Reconciliation between BAC and BAWA?

As the 1971 General Assembly approached, there were those who tried to tread the middle ground. Many hoped for, and a few actively sought, reconciliation.

On May 18, 1971, Dick Gilbert, minister of the First Unitarian Church of Rochester, New York, wrote to his congregation,

> When I first heard of the creation of a Black Caucus and a proposed Black Affairs Council in 1967, I tended to oppose it . . . but I became more and more convinced that our denomination needed to empower black people. . . .
>
> Not that I haven't differed with some of the rhetoric of white and black supporters of BAC. . . . [And I have not] become such a "true believer" that I can tolerate no criticism of BAC. . . . I have tried to be a moderating voice in the councils of BAC supporters.
>
> I have learned a great deal. . . . I have learned that my previous easy talk of integration has too often meant the assimilation of blacks into white culture without any real change in representation or power for black people. I have learned that the civil rights revolution is necessary but not a sufficient condition for the self-determination of black people. . . . I have learned that brotherhood based on the good consciences of whites is at best more difficult than we had thought, and that it is justice for blacks which will usher in brotherhood, not sentimental appeals for love.
>
> I detect a conciliatory tone in our movement after three years of strife.[543]

Closing his letter, Gilbert said he supported the resolution that BAC had placed on the agenda of the upcoming General Assembly.

BAC's resolution proposed that it become an official affiliate of the Unitarian Universalist Association again and be given 10 percent of the Association's budget each year until the promised $1 million was fully paid. Since the Association's budget was smaller now than in 1969, the disbursement would amount to about a 30-percent reduction from the original $250 thousand per year. In order to make the money available, the resolution proposed to reduce the Association's interdistrict representative program and shift its responsibilities to volunteers in local clusters, reduce the publication frequency of *UU World*, and cut administration expenses by 5.3 percent. This would make $173,600 available for BAC.

Gilbert was not alone in hoping for some sort of reconciliation. On May 10, Donald Harrington wrote to Glover Barnes to report on three conversations he had had with the new BUUC chair, Harold Wilson. Harrington had known and liked Wilson for years, despite their deep differences of opinion regarding BUUC/BAC and BAWA. They agreed that because of the conflict "real issues had somehow been lost." The second time they met, they sought common ground as a basis for establishing a "live and let live" situation. Harrington also said further conflict would make fundraising more difficult. His hope was that under Wilson's leadership, a more constructive approach might be possible, and while he could not speak for BAWA's leadership, he hoped the same would be true for them as well. He told Wilson that all he could do was to report on their conversation to BAWA. Hoping for healing, he brought a draft "Statement of Reconciliation" to their third meeting.[544] It put forward seven affirmations, of which the second was "The organization of Black People for their own self-determination and liberation from discriminatory practices is as important for them as it was for Jews, Italians, Irish."[545] This was something Harrington had said when he first preached about Black Power in 1966. The seventh was "The UUA must survive." Throughout the statement, which Harrington offered to Wilson as a starting point, he maintained the tone of an integrationist and institutionalist. Wilson agreed it was something he could work with and promised he would get back to Harrington. Telling Barnes about the meeting, Harrington said, "I feel that it might be a symbol of a turning point." Harrington, Wilson, and Bob West did subsequently meet in Chicago, but it seems there was enough resistance to reconciliation in both BAC and BAWA that nothing came of their efforts.[546]

. . .

TWO WEEKS BEFORE THE 1971 General Assembly was to begin, Paul Carnes, the minister in Buffalo and a member of the Commission on Appraisal, wrote in his newsletter column,

> We now have a new opportunity. The leadership of BAC recognizes that they have made mistakes, the biggest being their attitude and conduct in Boston. But the fact remains that BAWA made mistakes—namely, that in itself BAC would lead to "separatism." . . .
>
> The other fact is that we need the program of both organizations, *as the leadership of both are now willing to admit*. We need an organization of Blacks and Whites working together . . . on integration and racial attitudes. But we must have an organization which can help us relate to social change in the Black Community. This BAC is doing and we must find ways to support it.
>
> So what are we going to do? . . . Are we going to find our true identity, the identity of our ideals, our words . . . as we bring these two organizations together and then find our commitment in money to support them? We'll know in two weeks.[547]

The 1971 General Assembly and the Ross Resolution

The tenth General Assembly of the Unitarian Universalist Association was held in Washington D.C. June 7–12, 1971. "Tomorrow Is Now" was its theme and there were 1,022 delegates in attendance, exactly the same number as the year before. Of these, 226 were ministers, making 22 percent of the delegates, a slightly higher proportion than in Seattle. Again BUUC boycotted the gathering as an organization, but was represented by its white allies and by African Americans who were there as delegates from their home congregations.

With 1969 in mind, the Unitarian Universalist Association Program Committee was still trying to redesign the flow of General Assembly business. Small groups were instituted as places where factual information about the issues under consideration could be disseminated and where discussions could be more participatory. The topic about which the delegates most often requested more information was BAC. They asked for this 131 times—more than three times as often as they asked about the second issue of concern, the budget, which they did 39 times. To put this in context, they asked for information on the role of the Association seventeen times, BAWA twelve, draft resisters eight, youth and the Liberal Religious Youth concert three times each, women once, and gay rights not at all. Moreover, in every small group someone was there representing BAC.

These numbers indicate several things: First, BAC was organized and had a strategy. Second, the delegates, as was often the case, were unfamiliar with BAC. Finally, concern about feminism and gay rights had not yet coalesced.

It was a good sign for BAC when, early in the proceedings, the UUA Commission on Appraisal reported that it had urged the UUA Board to meet its commitment to BAC and explore "sacrificial ways by which the denomination may demonstrate the depth and sincerity of its commitment." After discussing BAC's history and the Association's seeming inactivity, polarization, and funding challenges, it said, "The issue of institutional racism is real and still with us. We may not have the money for a specific effort, but we still have a moral commitment to do something—as much as we can." Lastly, it announced it would hold a hearing on Thursday evening.[548] Nonetheless, two members of the Commission on Appraisal dissented from its report.

Given that at least four of the Commission on Appraisal's nine members were strong BAC supporters, the position it took was not surprising. The BAC supporters included ex-LRY president Larry Ladd, BUUC members Harold Wilson and Joe Samples, and Harry Scholefield, an early member of FULLBAC.[549]

Samples would go on to chair the Commission on Appraisal. His presence on it, along with the accession at General Assembly of Dr. S. J. Williamson Jr. to the chair of the Planning Committee and of Dr. Dalmas Taylor to the Unitarian Universalist Association's Board, indicates that African Americans were beginning to function as UUA insiders. This had a long-term impact beyond the crisis of that era.

Others saw BAC in a more critical light. The Neighborhood Commons Corporation, the wholly black-run housing project in Chicago that white UUs Neil Shadle and Ron Engel had helped to found in 1966, circulated a flyer denouncing BUUC/BAC. Headed "DON'T FUND B.A.C." in bold upper–case letters, the angry, caustic text (signed by the NCC's executive secretary) called BUUC "a bunch of money-hustling middle-class Brothers!" and charged it with "saying to the white folks, 'You give us the money, we'll handle the Niggers.'" It advised the Unitarian Universalist Association that it should be funding programs that were "concrete and meaningful, not simply voting a quarter million dollars to soothe the body politics' consciences."[550] Behind this missive was the rage of the program's leader, Dick Brown.

The letter spelled out how the Neighborhood Commons Corporation was addressing its community's basic needs and developing an affordable housing project. What it did not say was what triggered the tirade. In 1968, Brown had attended BUUC's founding meeting in Chicago and hoped BAC would support the kind of independent action that the NCC represented. BAC did indeed award the NCC $5,000 in 1968–1969, but now the NCC needed more funds as well as a cosigner for a mortgage (Nixon had cut off HUD funds for such projects shortly after taking office in 1969). This time, BAC brushed it off. Outraged, Brown planned on traveling to Washington to directly confront them.[551]

The BAC Support Group also circulated a series of flyers. Each was headed "B.A.C. Is Now" and ended with a large encircled "10%." One maintained, "The [UUA's] financial crisis has deeper roots. The cause is its own leadership, a leadership which has traded prophetic vision for the role of a technocratic caretaker—a curator of an ideological museum of past relevance."[552]

General Assembly opened with an address from UUA president Bob West, who said he regretted that the matter of funding BAC would come down to a Yes or No vote. He said, "Whether the measure passes or loses we all lose. There will be another splitting of the denomination." He feared that divisions between Unitarian Universalists would become deeper and that further cuts to a budget that was already honed down to essentials would cripple the Association.[553]

UU historian Conrad Wright writes, "There are times when churches and denominations must ask themselves how much they should compromise for the sake of survival, at the expense of moral integrity. Wherever there is a denominational bureaucracy, this ambiguity, this tension is built into the structure."[554] This was the dilemma West had faced since becoming president in July 1969.

A Resolution for Full Funding of the Black Affairs Council came early in the agenda. Immediately after its details were presented on

Thursday, a substitute resolution was offered by Warren Ross of New York. This Resolution on Joint Funding for Racial Justice, later known as the Ross Resolution, called for the establishment of a Racial Justice Fund and a denomination-wide fund drive that would fund BAC, BAWA, and other racial justice efforts. Whether it was or not, BUUC/BAC saw this proposal as chicanery on the administration's part that was meant to confuse people. Ironically, BUUC had used a similar parliamentary procedure in 1968 to preempt the UUA Board's effort to introduce a resolution that would have included funding for both BAC and BAWA.

The meeting broke into a committee of the whole to debate the substitute resolution. Homer Jack introduced an amendment that proposed a grant of $100 thousand to BAC: $50 thousand from the Unitarian Universalist Association and $50 thousand from fundraising. It was defeated. When the session reconvened, BAC's treasurer, Ben Scott, offered another amendment to the substitute resolution that said BAC would participate in the fund drive for the Racial Justice Fund if the Association committed to pay BAC at least 10 percent of its continental budget each year until its commitment was paid in full. That amendment was also defeated, with 318 in favor and 475 against. The Assembly then went on to adopt the original Ross Resolution by a vote of 467 to 404. The pro-BAC forces had lost by a vote margin almost identical to the one in 1970, when BUUC had also boycotted General Assembly.

A *Washington Post* article the next day was headlined "Unitarians Refuse to Fund Own Black Council." It reported that "a prominent minister in the denomination predicted that the action might lead to a schism," and quoted Jack Mendelsohn as saying, "I don't see how you can hold onto a denomination that completely disregards its own commitments."[555] When General Assembly reconvened that morning, Aron Gilmartin presented a statement, already endorsed by many, that said he would not participate in the fundraising campaign. Instead, he would send his money directly to BAC.

A motion to reconsider the Ross Resolution was then made and defeated. The Assembly went on to pass general resolutions on peace in Southeast Asia, civil liberties, the rights of the poor, a national health plan, childcare, penal reform, and the environment.

In a fundraising letter written right after General Assembly, Harold Wilson, the new president of BUUC, said that he had been approached by people who had unintentionally voted against BAC in a "confusing situation wherein the motion on which the Assembly was voting was not clear to many people."[556] They had expressed regret and wondered what could be done. This claim is certainly plausible. As usual, many delegates would have been new to both General Assembly and the issues under consideration. The large number of requests made for more information about BAC in the small group discussions indicates how uninformed they were.

Wilson interpreted the vote as a defeat for the Board rather than for BAC/BUUC in that it undercut the Unitarian Universalist Association's effort at renewal and relevance. The resolution that passed was not the administration's resolution, but the administration would strive to implement it over the next seven months.

John C. Godbey, a professor at Meadville Lombard Theological School who, like Mendelsohn, was a delegate from the First Unitarian Society of Chicago, concluded his report to his congregation about General Assembly by saying,

> I hope we can all avoid vindictiveness and insistence that we alone are right. Given our denomination's situation, we must support those with whom we largely agree AND those with whom we disagree. This church ... may, in fact, be split. But I shall do

what is in my power, personally and financially, to prevent that, and I call on each of you to do the same, each in his own way. Thank you.[557]

Urban Ministry Reconsidered

Professor Godbey's report on the 1971 General Assembly also noted and celebrated the award the Unitarian Universalist Association bestowed upon Rev. Christopher Moore, the minister of music at the First Unitarian Society of Chicago. In 1956, Moore had founded what would become the Chicago Children's Choir as it grew from the congregation's twenty-four-voice children's chorus to 4,600 voices. From the beginning, it was interracial and multicultural in membership and repertoire, and it quickly became ecumenical as well. Around 1963, it added a school program, which brought further diversity; the school program soon expanded explosively when it began collaborating with Urban Gateways, a program focused on enriching the lives of inner-city children.[558]

The impact of the Chicago Children's Choir on the lives of tens of thousands of children and on Chicago itself cannot be overstated. It brought children from all classes, races, cultures, and faiths together, trained their voices and taught them discipline, enabled them to befriend one another, and, in a sense, allowed them to minister to the city—especially following Martin Luther King Jr.'s assassination in 1968.

At first the Choir's roots spread broadly into the hundreds of UU congregations it performed in across North America, but over time those roots grew deep into dozens of Chicago neighborhoods. The Choir was mission driven and a form of community ministry. But because Moore did not think in those terms in 1956, it was never conceived of as such. And because it was interracial (children and staff) and did not self-consciously promote black consciousness (although it did in fact promote it), BAC would never have considered funding it.

One of the BAC flyers distributed at the 1971 General Assembly listed nine of the programs it was supporting. Among them were the Committee for a United Newark, which helped raise the consciousness of the black citizens of Newark and was instrumental in electing Kenneth Gibson as the city's first black mayor, and the Center for Black Education in Washington D.C., which promoted training in problem solving and community building in the black community. In Chicago, BAC gave the Afro-Arts Theatre a grant in 1970 and a loan the following year.[559]

BAC had a particular ideological bent toward organizations that promoted black political power or enhanced black consciousness. The Fulton Street Center in Brooklyn and the Neighborhood Commons Corporation in Chicago did neither but were UU-connected groups involved in grass-roots organizing. While each received BAC funding in the first year, each was left by the wayside in 1970 and felt betrayed.

At the 1968 Cleveland General Assembly, Hayward Henry had said to the delegates, "We have missed a very simple question and it is: Who will the black community follow? Those who believe in its own right to self-determination? Or those who offer paternalistic approaches? This is the most noble opportunity we will ever have to be the Unitarian Universalists we want to be."[560]

What seems to have been at issue with CABUUC, BAWA, and others was BAC/BUUCs monopolistic posture. It represented itself as the only legitimate voice representing African American Unitarian Universalists, tried to assert control over the entire Unitarian

Universalist racial agenda, and insisted that any recognition given to BAWA was meant to divide blacks and confuse whites. BAC/BUUC was also dismissive toward groups like the Cleveland UU Parish, Neighborhood Commons Corporation, and the Fulton Street Center, organizations that were doing community organizing but fell outside BAC's ideological worldview.

Yet there were other UU-related groups, in addition to the Cleveland Unitarian Universalist Parish and the Chicago Children's Choir, engaged in the African American community in significant ways.

In March 1968, the Unitarian Universalist congregations of the Greater Washington Area met to begin to formulate a response to Black Power and the call for black self-determination. A month later, the Greater Washington Area trustees voted to provide $15 thousand for the first year of an inner-city project. African American William D. Wright was hired, and Unity House was founded. Its statement of purpose, in which Wright, as director, addressed local Unitarian Universalists, outlined what Black Power was: "It is primarily a search for black self-identity, the quest for inner pride . . . [which is the] prerequisite for integration." It is also "a renunciation of white paternalism." He went on to explain what he expected from white supporters. "We require assistance, but we reject interference. . . . We want understanding, not suggestions and advice. . . . This is no outlet for do-goodism. . . . We are aware of the gap which has allowed distrust and suspicion to enter into [our] two very different communities. If I am successful, we will be able to break down some barriers."[561] By fall of 1968, the project had opened its office in southeast Washington D.C., assembled a black library, established a talent bank of consultants to assist with economic development (largely suburban Unitarian Universalist volunteers), and was counseling black youth who wanted to attend college.

In February 1970, the third annual BUUC meeting was held in D.C., and Wright attended as an observer. Unity House was featured in a November 1970 *Ebony* article because of its work in founding Black Efforts for Soul in Television (BEST).[562] BEST was acclaimed for the work it was doing in the communications industry promoting programs directed to blacks, increasing black employment across the industry, and challenging the Federal Communications Commission regarding policies that were unfair to minority broadcasters. The *Ebony* article mentioned that Unity House was funded by Unitarians, although by 1970, grants from foundations were exceeding the annual contribution of the Greater Washington Area Unitarian Universalists and BAC does not appear to have been among the funders.

In the South, a project was initiated by Janet Pomeroy and other members of the Unitarian Universalist Fellowship of Athens, Georgia, a small congregation that had only one black member, Dr. Richard M. Graham, who became the first full-time African American faculty member at the University of Georgia in 1968. Pomeroy was passionate about helping African Americans and poor people. In January 1969, the congregation's Social Responsibility Committee met at her home to explore the possibility of starting a credit union. In February, the fellowship put up the money to provide educational materials. Soon thereafter, the Clarke County Federal Credit Union was born, and it still exists. Its office was in the Bethel Homes, an African American housing project in Athens. Members of the Athens Fellowship made deposits in the credit union, and one member served for years as its treasurer.[563]

In many and varied ways, Unitarian Universalists responded to the urban American upheaval of the latter half of the sixties independently of BAC. But it was the battle between the UUA, BUUC/

BAC, FULLBAC, the FFR, and BAWA that garnered attention then and has attracted it since. This battle, and the attribution of it to racism, has led many to assume that the overriding source of conflict was a white supremacist culture that held sway in the Unitarian Universalist Association. This assumption has obscured the successes; indeed, most Unitarian Universalists know nothing about them. It also obscures the impact of other equally deep-seated institutional issues.

. . .

FOLLOWING THE DECISION of the Universalist Church of America and the American Unitarian Association to consolidate, the Unitarian organizational model was chosen. The Unitarian Universalist Association would be an association of congregations, existing primarily to serve them, rather than a denomination, calling its congregations to serve others. Every UUA administration felt the pull to serve those who elected them and funded the UUA, and that pull was reinforced in 1969, when most UUA Board members began to be elected by and accountable to UUA districts.

The Unitarian Universalist Association had become increasingly democratic as the autocratic style of American Unitarian Association president Frederick May Elliot and the willfulness of Dana McLean Greeley faded into the past and the anti-authoritarian and extremely individualistic tendencies of fellowships came to the fore.[564] However, putting congregational polity and needs at the center of Unitarian Universalism's associational body led to an array of problems. One of these was defining the Association's relationship to community-based ministry.

There was then, and still is, tension in regard to the place of community ministers within an association of congregations. In Unitarian Universalism, only congregations can offer ordination; no other body has that right. Ministers who functioned outside the parish, like James Reeb, were designated as being in associate fellowship. That status did not entitle them to a vote at General Assembly, an entitlement every settled parish minister received, nor to settlement or other support from the Department of Ministry. Because they were not congregationally based and not organized around congregational needs, community and public ministry were sidelined and little attention was paid to them.

If the Unitarian Universalist Association had chosen to be a denomination, its approach to community, public, and other extra-parochial ministries would have been different. A denomination is more than an association of congregations, and its call to serve is broader. At its most far-reaching, it asks, "How do we proclaim our 'Good News'? How do we serve God and the world? What is our mission?" Theologically, Unitarian Universalists tend to supplant the divine with principles. A Unitarian Universalist denomination could have made different choices than those of the UUA, which had to cater to the more parochial needs of its congregations.[565]

The difference between the Universalist Church of America, a denomination, and the American Unitarian Association, an association, was obvious. A Universalist "Mission to the Colored People" in the Tidewater region of Virginia ran from 1887 to 1983, nearly a hundred years, and the Universalist mission to Japan continued from 1890 until the white missionaries were expelled in 1942. These two efforts continued even though Universalism was in decline and its congregations dying. They did so because the UCA was functioning as a denomination in spreading the gospel of Universalism: God's enduring and unbounded love for humankind. These efforts were a missional calling rather than a congregational demand.

The UUA's associational structure created a problem. As congregations fled to the suburbs and their overlap with the inner city grew thin, Unitarian Universalist civic engagement languished without a strong tradition of extraparochial ministry.[566] There were few examples of ongoing community ministry apart from the Benevolent Fraternity of Unitarian Churches (now the UU Urban Ministry), which was founded in Boston in 1839.

The concentration of power in congregations not only made decision making and action as a body difficult, it made ministry that was not tied to congregations a challenge—as it proved to be for the Cleveland UU Parish, the Neighborhood Commons Corporation, and the Fulton Street Center. The Unitarian Universalist Association's refusal to recognize, much less support, such ministries contributed to their struggles. Had community-based ministries been a priority and been helped to thrive, the Association would have been more engaged with, and more relevant to, the African American community. It would also have been less dependent on BAC and opened up more opportunities for black ministers. And to the degree that some in the black community would have been drawn to liberal religion, it would have reached individuals outside white middle-class suburbs.

Fall 1971

At the end of the tenth General Assembly, Bob West announced that the Unitarian Universalist Association Board had begun the process of implementing the Ross Resolution by establishing a three-person committee. "Let us stick with it," he said, "and work hard to try to find ways, through our difference, that we can do it *together*. I believe we can."[567] In a fundraising letter addressed to "Supporters of BAC" two days later, Harold Wilson was also cautiously hopeful that "during the coming year we will see a shift in the Board of the U.U.A. and the President's office so that we may join with them in doing basic fund raising for the denomination with a budget that includes funding for B.A.C.'s program."[568]

The members of the Committee on Racial Justice were William N. Holway, Charles V. Briggs Jr., and BUUC member Dalmas A. Taylor. The chair, Holway, wrote to BAC and BAWA to say that the joint fundraising effort would respect each group's approach to black empowerment, preserve the autonomy of each, and enhance the Unitarian Universalist Association's Annual Program Fund. He expressed the Committee's desire to meet individually with each group in July and with both jointly after that.[569]

That glimmer of hope dimmed as consultations stretched into the fall. At its October meeting, the Board decided to expand the Committee to seven members; the Committee then held a hearing with all the concerned groups in November. BAC wanted to be involved in raising contributions to the Annual Fund and have its 10 percent allocated to it from the Association's budget rather than a Racial Justice Fund; BAWA's Board had voted unanimously to support the Racial Justice Fund but protested a recommendation that it receive less from the fund than BAC. West refused to consider any plan that drew directly from the UUA budget. They were at an impasse. In January 1972, the Board, on a closely divided vote (twelve against, ten for, and two abstentions), rejected both a majority proposal that guaranteed funds to BAC and a minority recommendation to establish a voluntary fund. Neither idea was fully acceptable to the organizations directly concerned, including the Board itself. The Board ended up passing a motion recommending that individual Unitarian Universalists and congregations support black empowerment and racial justice by giving to the organization of their choice.

The Board vote mirrored the divisions in the Unitarian Universalist Association; there was no consensus on how best to move forward on the issue of racial justice. After four years of battles and disappointment, the distrust BAC/BUUC and its supporters felt for the UUA Board and administration ran deep.

In mid-September, Stephen Fritchman distributed a fundraising letter through the Pacific Southwest District newsletter. It was caustic, but he knew his audience. The PSWD had organized delegates to go to General Assembly to vote in favor of the resolution to fund BAC. Now Fritchman wrote that congregations and individuals had to decide whether "to support BAC and send less to the UUA ... or to throw in the sponge and say we are indeed the white racist movement some have called us."[570] He agreed with a colleague who said of the Association, "Survival and identity, we are told, should be the current preoccupation of the UUA. Perhaps! But I wonder. Why should the UUA survive?" Fritchman had decided to contribute to BAC, and he invited others to do likewise.

In the October newsletter of the First Unitarian Society of Chicago, Jack Mendelsohn denounced the UUA administration for not telling the delegates, during the discussion of the budget and the $319 thousand debt, that it was anticipating an unrestricted bequest of $266 thousand. In January of 1970, West had discovered that the UUA owed its bank $450 thousand and had promised the bank that the UUA would direct all unrestricted bequests to paying down that debt.[571] His efforts to suppress the news included admonishing the editor of *UU World* about secrecy, perhaps because word of it would doubtless have created resistance to the commitment he had made to the bank.[572] "The suppression of the information," Mendelsohn said, "may or may not have been deliberate, but it is a classic example of what is meant by institutions operating, consciously and unconsciously, in racist ways."[573]

West's response to charges like those made by Fritchman and Mendelsohn was, "I have to disagree that black empowerment stands above every other issue, because for the people charged with the life of this Association, I don't think black empowerment does stand above the issue of whether or not we are going to have a viable continental program."[574] For him, the question was not about support for BAC or BAWA or his support for racial justice; it was about the survival of the Association and balancing a multiplicity of responsibilities and commitments.

On October 22, 1971, the day the UUA Board met to decide on its next action in regard to the Ross Resolution, Beacon Press published Senator Gravel's edition of *The Pentagon Papers: The Defense Department History of United States Decisionmaking on Vietnam*. Excerpts had already appeared in the *New York Times*, the *Washington Post*, and other papers, but Beacon published the entire report that defense analyst Daniel Ellsberg had given the senator despite the threatening telephone call President Nixon made to Beacon's director, Gobin Stair. Beacon had not had enough working capital to publish the *Papers*, but the Veatch Committee of the North Shore Unitarian Universalist Society had agreed to loan it up to $100 thousand. Following the book's release, the FBI subpoenaed the financial records of both Beacon Press and the Association, and the UUA had to seek a court injunction to stop the investigation. There were press conferences and testimony before a Senate committee; the time commitment and legal fees were substantial. By June 1972, expenses had mounted to $35 thousand, and West reported to the Board that the difference between income and expenses in the 1971–1972 budget could largely be attributed to legal expenses.

Yet another controversy demanded additional time and legal fees. In the spring of 1971, the UUA Board began considering the legal and other consequences of publishing the junior high religious education unit *About Your Sexuality*. The curriculum, released that fall, used pictures of naked female and male models of multiple races;

later a unit entitled *The Hidden Minority—The Homosexual in Our Society* was added. All of this made it explosively newsworthy, and articles about it ran in *Newsweek* and the *New York Times*, among other outlets. In Albany, New York, the police chief attacked the curriculum in the press. In Wisconsin, a county district attorney threatened to prosecute the Unitarian Church West in Brookfield if it used *About Your Sexuality*;[575] the church sought an injunction and taught it anyway. The impact of *About Your Sexuality* on sex education went far beyond the Association.

The controversies surrounding BAC/BUUC, FULLBAC, and the FFR, and the demands they placed on UUA resources, are magnified when viewed in isolation. The *Pentagon Papers* and *About Your Sexuality* were also justice issues. And given that the war in Vietnam and human sexuality were issues that affected the African American community as well, it is legitimate to question why BAC's work should preempt them. These publications were timely and consequential, and their publication and defense were expensive. Given the difficulty balancing these competing obligations posed, there is cause to question the moral certitude of those who so vociferously condemned Robert West and the UUA board.

Religious Education Labors

In the years leading up to the publication of *About Your Sexuality* in 1971, a quieter revolution had been taking place in religious education. What triggered it was not what was published but rather what was not.

When *The Free Church in a Changing World* was published in 1963, it included the report of the Commission on Education and Liberal Religion. Among the religious education materials of the day were a series of books for preschoolers about two children named Martin and Judy, and the Commission asked, "How meaningful are they and their neat white house in the suburbs to children whose world includes all the blood and thunder...of television?"[576] That same year, the Commission on Religion and Race challenged the UUA Department of Education to revise its curricula. The department responded apologetically, but took no action.

In 1965, Beacon Press published two booklets by Esther Bailey: *Won't You Miss Me?* and *A House for James*. The back covers of both explained, "Based on the experiences of young children who are part of the multi-ethnic, mobile populations of our towns and cities, the purpose of the stories is to help the child discover a concept of self and to identify with his peers." James, a main character, is a little black boy. His family is moving from an apartment in a diverse neighborhood to a house in a neighborhood that, from the illustrations, is obviously less diverse. Farley Wheelwright, in commenting on Bailey's stories, said that they "mostly illustrated black children playing with white in lovely white suburban settings."[577] Race was never mentioned, but the message was clear: Integration meant being nice to black kids as they assimilated into white culture. Both stories were included in the 1967 *When Brucie Came to Play, and Other Stories*.

Hugo J. Holleroth became director of curriculum and program development in 1965. "The educational world," he later recalled, "had moved from a didactic approach to approaches with names like 'the discovery method' and 'the inquiry method.'" Leading secular educators, who were also Unitarian Universalists, were "heaping scorn on the Department of Education for seemingly being unaware of contemporary approaches to progressive education."[578] Under his direction, the UUA department began implementing the discovery method in its new curricula.

Freedom and Responsibility, a program for junior high students, was one such effort. In September 1967, a group of directors of religious education gathered in St. Louis to evaluate an early draft of the curriculum and plan to test it in their congregations. Among them was Pauline Warfield Lewis, an African American who had been director of religious education at the First Unitarian Church of Cincinnati since 1956. She asked why the program did not address the "black/white crisis in America." This prompted considerable discussion, and the gathering agreed unanimously that it had to be included.

Apparently it was not. Nine months later, after field-testing the draft unit, Lewis wrote to Jack Mendelsohn explaining her dissatisfaction with the *Freedom and Responsibility* program. "I felt a great disappointment that the first unit of a new curriculum ... did not include a Negro. The French, the Asian, the English-American are all there ... but no Negro American."[579] She sent copies of her letter to, among others, Hayward Henry and Marjorie Jordan.

Holleroth responded immediately. The unit, he said, had been "an *incomplete first* draft of the very *first* course we began to develop."[580] Its primary focus had been on the new discovery method; subsequent drafts would include a biography of Malcolm X and "materials related to the current black/white crisis." He also said that the department was looking forward to working with the Black Caucus in developing a curriculum on black culture and identity. On that same day, he wrote to Hayward Henry saying he valued his judgment and would like to get together as soon as possible.

When *Freedom and Responsibility* was published in 1970, it included sessions on Malcolm X and Martin Luther King Jr. Subsequently two curricula for nine-to-twelve-year-olds were published. *Man, the Culture Builder I* was comprised of eighteen sessions about the Navajo, and *Man, the Culture Builder II* offered seventeen about the Kung of the Kalahari.

After the BUUC position prevailed at the 1969 General Assembly in Boston, Holleroth decided to ask Hayward Henry to take the lead in identifying people to serve on a team addressing racism in religious education curricula. During GA, he saw Henry standing in front of Beacon Press, surrounded by a group of people. As Holleroth walked toward him, two men stepped forward and said, "Hayward is not available now." Henry said, "Let him pass," and Holleroth and Henry agreed to meet in Holleroth's office in a week.

Henry identified a half dozen black Unitarian Universalists to serve on a curriculum team. They met for two and a half days, and their discussions of what needed to be presented in such a curriculum revealed many things to Holleroth that he had not considered. The major obstacle to proceeding, however, was that no one on the team was willing to write one. That would have required putting the material into an educational curriculum format, bringing it back to the curriculum team in three months for evaluation and suggestions, working on it for another three months, bringing it back to the team again, and then field-testing it. Developing a new curriculum was an eighteen- to twenty-four-month process, but it couldn't happen without an author.

About a month later, Henry came up with a solution. Mary L. Small (who was not a member of the team but had been the BUUC program coordinator) would write a curriculum entitled "American Values and Racism." When Small and Holleroth met, she said she did not want to work with the curriculum team, nor with him. She would give it to him when it was completed.

Holleroth cared deeply about the project and the possibilities latent within black empowerment. He thought of the project as one way the UUA community could speak out in support of racial justice. He felt proud of what had happened at General Assembly and wanted the curriculum to be a part of this new thrust. And he was not alone; many religious educators around the country were excited about the possibility. However, he had a process that worked, and having a team was part of that process. All the Association's programs were using the new pedagogy, but Small would allow no input on her work. Holleroth put his misgivings aside and agreed, hoping that, over time, he and Small would start to work together. It did not happen that way.

Holleroth had been on the Commission on Education and Liberal Religion that had critiqued the relevance of the Beacon Series curriculum in 1963, and his interaction with BUUC members on the curriculum team gave him a deeper understanding of the black perspective and the ways whites needed to change. By the time the tumultuous 1969 Boston General Assembly began, he was an even stronger supporter of BUUC. At that Assembly, Holleroth sat with the UUA staff. When Mendelsohn invited the delegates to join him at the Arlington Street Church, Holleroth wrestled for a moment with whether to leave or stay. He didn't want to lose his job, but in the end, he walked out with David Parke, with whom he had taught on the St. Lawrence University Theological School faculty. This act of protest did not cost him his job.

Knowing that Small was a BUUC activist, BAWA was concerned and began corresponding with Holleroth. In February 1970, Holleroth wrote to Max Gaebler to say that as soon as the team had signed off on Small's curriculum and revisions had been made, he would send it for BAWA to review. Quite naturally, he did not mention his own trepidations or the fact that there was no team.

For eighteen months, Holleroth frequently contacted Small to inquire if they could get together and go over what she was creating. She always said, "You can see it when it is finished." Finally she gave it to him. It was titled "Black America, White America: Understanding the Discord." Holleroth said, "It was a deeply profound and moving experience to sit and read what she had created ... but it was not a curriculum."[581]

At the 1971 General Assembly, a workshop on Small's proposed curriculum was offered. Betty Seiden, the executive secretary of BAWA, was also an educator and had written BAWA's first project paper, "Black History in Our Curriculum." The six-page booklet outlined broad goals in teaching black history and then discussed how the approach should vary from preschool through junior high; it also offered a list of resources. Seiden was shocked at the materials she received at the GA workshop, and early in September, she wrote Holleroth saying she found Small's methodology out of tune with the interests of children, a sort of indoctrination into black consciousness, and more suitable for an adult encounter group than for a children's program.

Nonetheless, Holleroth went against his better judgment and organized field tests of the program. He hoped for some kind of breakthrough. Perhaps the field-testers would convince Small that it couldn't work in its present form and she would agree to some restructuring, or at least that some of the material she had created might be used elsewhere. The field test began with a weekend training session in which fifteen congregations participated, after which each began teaching the curriculum. Initially each sent a report to Holleroth each week, but the reports tapered off as teachers became discouraged.

One of the tests took place in Des Moines, Iowa, in a class led by Edna Griffin, an African American UUA Board member and activist. There were six students in the class, all Euro-American adults. Holleroth and Renford Gaines attended one of the sessions. Carol Henderson, one of the participants, recalled that the class largely consisted of Griffin imparting knowledge. She did remember one exercise in which students brainstormed a list of meanings for the word *black* and another in which they were shown a picture of Frederick Douglass and asked if they knew who he was. They did not. They were then asked if he was black or white, and they could not tell. When asked if his race mattered, everyone except her said "no." She said "yes" and could tell from Gaines's response that her answer was the one he had wanted. At other times, she reported, it was just as clear when he was angry.[582]

This was the UUA Department of Religious Education's first substantive effort to respond to BUUC/BAC's demand that it produce materials that addressed the African American experience. But by fall 1972, the reports from field-testers had made it clear that Small's curriculum could not be published as it was. There had been no breakthrough. The material was still sitting in Holleroth's file cabinet when he left the position in 1980.

After it became clear that the Unitarian Universalist Association would not move ahead with "Black America, White America," Henry introduced Holleroth to Musa Eubanks. Eubanks was working on a curriculum about Africa, and together he and Holleroth completed his project. *Africa's Past: Impact on Our Present* was published jointly by Afro-Audio Visuals and the UUA in 1976. Meant for junior high, it was never widely used in Unitarian Universalist Sunday schools.

Later the charge would be made that racism was the reason "Black America, White America" was never published. The real story offers a different perspective. A willful, non-collaborative author produced a didactic thousand-page manuscript that would have been prohibitively expensive to produce and reflected a dated and inappropriate pedagogical approach. Trapped in the white liberal racial dilemma, Holleroth acquiesced. Blinded by hopefulness, paralyzed by white liberal guilt, committed to the cause of black empowerment, and driven by the urge to do good, he repeatedly ignored his better instincts. It kept him from saying the project could not possibly work. It is doubtful he would have allowed this to happen if Mary Small had been white. "That's how I felt and that's what I did," Holleroth said. "It was not a solution I was proud of nor was I proud of myself. It was one of the low moments—perhaps the lowest—in my 15 years at the UUA."[583]

Deadlocked

[*1972–1975*]

"BLACK CAUCUS UPSETS UNITARIAN GALA," read the headline in the *Wilmington Morning News* on Monday, January 10, 1972. The previous morning was to have been the farewell celebration for the senior minister of the First Unitarian Church of Wilmington, Delaware, Rev. Robert Doss. He was about to go on sabbatical, but that changed after a member of the congregation's newly formed Black Caucus took over the podium.

Norman Lockman, who would join the UUA Board eleven years later, walked up to the master of ceremonies and announced he was going to make a statement. When asked if he could wait until later, Lockman said, "No." His statement declared that the Caucus wanted the congregation to be more meaningfully involved in the black community. They welcomed white participation but not control. The Caucus would provide direction aimed at bringing more justice and equality to Wilmington.[584]

Exactly two weeks later, the congregation voted on a proposal to give office space and telephone service to the Black Caucus and its consultant, Louis Gothard. Gothard had made the original demand for space and $2,000 in December. Doss, who delayed his sabbatical, said that at first he had been "reluctantly in favor" of housing the Caucus but now was opposed. The issue was not racism, he said, as the Caucus insisted it was; rather, the demand was "a power grab." Responding, Gothard said, "The hour is late. First I have to get your attention, and I think at least I have your attention."[585] The proposal was defeated 184 to 112.

On January 18, 1972, Renford Gaines, who had left Urbana, Illinois, in September 1970 to become the senior minister of the Arlington Street Church in Boston, circulated a letter to his staff saying he had taken a new name, Mwalimu Imara, his "free name." The response of some parishioners was strong and racist, and a few simply refused to use his chosen name, continuing to call him Rennie.[586]

Two weeks after Imara announced his name change and a week after the Wilmington congregation voted not to house its Black Caucus, the UUA Board (stymied in its effort to implement the Resolution on Joint Funding for Racial Justice) passed its motion that congregations and individuals should support racial justice as they saw fit. It was a somber admission of defeat and changed nothing. The Unitarian Universalist Association was deadlocked, unable to move forward in regard to racial justice and black self-determination. Finally, the Veatch Committee of the North Shore Unitarian Universalist Society in Plandome, New York, made an offer that brought about peace—at least for a little while.

Veatch Committee to the Rescue

In the wake of the Washington General Assembly of 1971, hopeful but uncertain about future revenues, Harold Wilson, the chair of BUUC, sent out a letter soliciting contributions to BAC. In September, Stephen Fritchman sent out a regional appeal. By October 1971, a goal of $200 thousand was chosen for the May 26th Empowerment Fund and a continental campaign with regional committees was organized.

Bill Kohlbrenner, coordinator for BAC's northeast region, received a description of the campaign that included the goal, the regional expectations, and an outline of its organizational structure. Less than a month later, he resigned, saying that he was the "wrong man for the job" and that it would be better for him to resign than to "copout":

> Few of the (white) BAC supporters that I have met can explain BAC's position and aims and fewer still have the time or interest in pushing hard on BAC fund raising....
>
> Judging by the people I have met most of the money that can be raised is still guilt money or "integration" money. One cannot collect it by confronting people and trying to change their attitude, but by careful soft-sell that threatens no one, rocks no boats, and causes no substantial change. Even some of the best and most active in the BAC support group are still not thinking beyond the question "What is BAC doing with my money?" Rennie Gaines blasted a bunch of people one night at Adams' house on precisely this point.

Kohlbrenner said he was for rocking the boat, but someone had to be found who could do it "with charm, rather than aggressiveness."[587] Here was the problem: a mismatch of style and interest. BAC attracted activists eager to challenge the system, but it needed fund-raisers adept at persuasion. Denny Davidoff, the eastern region coordinator, recalled that they did not raise the money.[588]

As part of its 1971–1972 campaign, BAC sought special gifts from foundations and businesses. This section of the campaign was co-chaired by Hilda Mason and James Gunning. Gunning had accompanied Ben Scott and Richard Traylor when, on May 26, 1971, they made a presentation to the Veatch Committee, representatives of the Board of the North Shore Unitarian Universalist

Society of Plandome, and the congregation's Finance, Social Action, and Denominational Affairs Committees.

The congregation's leadership was familiar with the issues. Eleanor Vendig, the Veatch Committee program administrator, attended UUA Board meetings and had reported on the Board's effort to implement the Ross Resolution. Moreover, the church sent two members to the inaugural BUUC meeting in Chicago in 1968; Hayward Henry spoke at North Shore in May 1969; Harrington approached its minister about whether financial support would be available for BAWA in March 1970; Bayard Rustin, an advisor to Martin Luther King Jr., gave a talk entitled "The Failure of Separatism" in May 1970; and its Social Action Committee included liaisons to both BAWA and BAC. Following the presentation by Scott and Traylor, the discussion focused on BAC's finances and fundraising.

At its January 4 meeting in 1972, the Veatch Committee discussed a grant request from BAC. Members debated whether they wanted to direct funds to black empowerment and, if they did, whether they should do so through BAC or another group, like the NAACP or the Urban League. They were also worried that BAC might spend half of the grant on administration. A grant of $25 thousand, not to be used on administration, was proposed and then tabled until the UUA Board made a decision about the implementation of the Ross Resolution.[589] On January 31, Eleanor Vendig reported that the Board had made "a sincere and strenuous effort" but could not move it forward.[590]

On February 14, the Committee took up BAC's grant request again. It designated two of its members to consult with Bob West about the feasibility of setting up a racial justice fund with money from Veatch. This consultation triggered a series of meetings that led to the establishment of the Special Fund to Promote Racial

Justice and Combat Racism, with a $250 thousand grant from Veatch to cover its first eighteen months. BAC would be given $180 thousand and BAWA $45 thousand, with the remainder distributed at the discretion of the Fund's Standing Committee. That committee had six members, four of whom were African American and three of whom were members of BUUC.[591] The fund's guidelines required that grant money not be used for fundraising or administration; that any fundraising by grantees not compete with the UUA Annual Program Fund; that the fund be administered by a standing committee of the UUA Board; that recipients have full discretion in choosing programs and projects to benefit from the grants but define their expected results and report semiannually on outcomes; and that the funding program be comprehensively reviewed by the Standing Committee.

As a result of this arrangement, BAC became an associate member of the Unitarian Universalist Association and requested that its "Black Affairs Council Funding" motion be withdrawn from the final agenda of the 1972 Dallas General Assembly. This was not legally possible, but an alternate motion, recommending that BAC funding not be discussed in considering the annual budget, was developed.

While the new fund alleviated funding difficulties for BAC and BAWA, it created new problems. The most immediate was BAWA's protest that it was not an equal beneficiary; one BAWA Board member suggested wearing buttons to General Assembly that said "50/50." Meeting in advance of the 1972 Assembly, the UUA Board accepted BAWA as an associate member of the Association and clarified that its disproportionately low funding followed the recommendation of the Board's Racial Justice Committee, which had considered BAC's and BAWA's past fundraising efforts and their success. BAC, in turn, argued against aspects of the Racial Justice

Fund that undermined black self-determination. It came to an understanding with Veatch that there would be no "pre-program evaluation." Behind this agreement was concern over a loss of autonomy. BAC did not wish to be accountable to a white funding institution, which it had not been when the Association, rather than Veatch, funded BAC in 1968 and 1969.

The General Assembly was held in Dallas May 31–June 3. Its theme was "Affirm One Another." The attendance was down to 678, a third less than in 1971 and 1970 and 62 percent less than in Boston in 1969. Of the delegates, 168 were ministers, down 25 percent from the year before. In its ongoing effort to promote more considered discussion before issues were debated in plenary session, the Planning Committee introduced mini-assemblies.

The major issue to come before the Dallas General Assembly was whether to hold GA biennially instead of annually. The vote on the motion to switch to a biennial meeting lost 352 to 187. The alternate resolution regarding BAC funding passed, as did resolutions supporting integrated education, Project Equality, and the United Farm Workers' lettuce boycott. For the first time since 1968, there was no acrimonious debate pitting Black Power against integration.

Donald Harrington's thoughts on the new situation appeared in a church newsletter column entitled "An End to Conflict?"

> It looks as though there has begun a closing of the chasm ... on the question of the best way to move towards real equality of opportunity for all people in this land.... Now, for the first time, we begin to see signs of mutual tolerance, glimmers of understanding and a desire for reconciliation.... Both groups, I think, have concluded that those of us who want Black and White equality cannot afford to waste their strength fighting each other. The enemy is far too strong, and is the only one who can benefit from that.[592]

Perhaps the rapprochement between Harrington and Harold Wilson did make a difference. In April 1972, at a meeting at the North Shore Unitarian Universalist Society, Richard Traylor told the Veatch Committee and the other participants that BAC had decided the previous October that it and BAWA "could live together and they are no longer fighting BAWA." Reporting on this meeting, Edwina Ferguson, a BAWA Board member, said, "I guess they forgot to spread this info throughout their ranks—and/or to us!"[593]

BAC vs. the Black Humanist Fellowship— See You in Court

Over the years, differences within BUUC sharpened. The more radical, and somewhat younger, members of BUUC were attracted to a form of black nationalism that clashed with the principles of inclusiveness and pluralism that most Unitarian Universalists held dear. The more radical members also emphasized unity over individualism. These conflicting values played out stylistically, as well. More moderate BUUC members emphasized persuasion, while radicals rallied behind whatever means seemed necessary to achieve their goal. During spring 1972, while the details of the Special Fund to Promote Racial Justice and Combat Racism were being worked out by the Veatch Committee, the UUA, BAC, and BAWA, this division within BAC/BUUC deepened, triggering an identity crisis, a power struggle, and a lawsuit.

At the fourth annual meeting of BUUC, delegates had declined to adopt Hayward Henry's "Basic Primer of Black Humanism" as the group's official ideology. However, at the fifth meeting, in February 1972, a resolution passed that opened the way to explore Black Humanism: "Resolved—That the Religious Systems Workshop of this Fifth National BUUC Convention unanimously recommends the formation of a Black Humanist Fellowship in order to develop and further define Black Humanism, and to create the appropriate symbols and processes necessary for its expression."[594]

In November 1972, the BUUC Steering Committee created a subcommittee to make recommendations for a vote at the sixth annual meeting on whether BUUC should be renamed the Black Humanist Fellowship (BHF). In December 1972, the proposal to make the change was circulated. Shortly thereafter Gwendolyn Thomas, BUUC's vice-chair, circulated an alternate proposal: "I am asking the Steering Committee to reconsider their decision to recommend that the National Meeting transform BUUC into a new Black church known as the Black Humanist Fellowship.... Until we identify and *secure* another funding source, we cannot afford to alienate ourselves from Unitarian support." After describing the possible consequences of this proposed change, she put forth an alternative: "We advocate establishing BHF as an adjunct to BUUC while maintaining BUUC as it stands, *without constitutional changes* . . . as the organization which elects from its constituency the members of the BAC.... Recognizing that our reasons are practical and lack the idealism which makes BHF so attractive, I nevertheless offer them for your consideration."[595] Her language was conciliatory and supportive in recognizing Black Humanism as a timely ideal worth nurturing.

That those in favor of the change had already made a decision about the path forward became clear to BAC treasurer Ben Scott in November 1972. In his role as secretary of the BAC Investment Corporation (BIC), he asked Richard Traylor to transfer some bond funds. Instead of conveying them, Traylor told him that the funds had been deposited in the First Pennsylvania Bank and would remain there until after the next election of BAC trustees, at the end of February. Scott said later that he "expected that the obvious desire of the top paid executives of the two organizations to found a church... would not succeed" because it would put the Veatch funding at risk. Furthermore, BAC's tax-exempt status depended on its being a Unitarian Universalist group and its authorization to sell bonds depended on its being a denominational program. Therefore, he "thought they would not succeed because of the impracticality of the idea."[596]

Thomas was not so sanguine. For reasons that were not spelled out, she tried to move the annual meeting from Philadelphia to Cleveland. It may have been a maneuver to prevent the meeting from being packed with members of pro-BHF caucuses.

On February 20, Harold Wilson wrote to the members of BUUC, "Most of you have recently received a communication from our Vice Chairman, Gwen Thomas. This communication, to my knowledge represents the first attempt in our history to usurp the office of the National Chairman and to move outside of our constitution. This is very serious.... [The coming annual meeting] may be the hottest meeting we have ever had. It will, indeed, be the most serious as to the question of direction—one way or the other." He promised pro and con position papers and a full debate.[597]

A six-page handout entitled "From BUUC to BHF... Questions and Answers on the Issue" was distributed prior to BUUC's 1973 annual meeting. It listed the Boston, Philadelphia, Cincinnati, Brooklyn, and San Francisco Bay caucuses as sponsoring the renaming. Among members of the sponsoring caucuses, Hayward Henry and Mwalimu Imara were members of Boston BUUC, Traylor of Philadelphia, and Wilson of the Bay Area. The Greater Washington Area caucus was not a sponsor, nor was Black Unitarians for Radical Reform; nor was the caucus in Denver, where Gwen Thomas lived. The caucus in Chicago had disaffiliated from BUUC in 1971.

The first question in "From BUUC to BHF" was "What is the Black Humanist Fellowship?" The answer: "It is the institutional form which gives concrete expression to the spiritual, social, and cultural basis of black liberation."[598] And what is black liberation? Ben Scott, in his book *The Coming of the Black Man*, wrote, "The Black Power movement is aimed at removing blacks from colonial status in their native land."[599] This liberation was the overarching, universally affirmed goal of BUUC. The only question was how to balance that goal with other loyalties and practicalities.

Dalmas Taylor was reported to have called the BHF "anti-Unitarian." Richard Traylor rejected the allegation. Taylor based his charge on statements in the handout that said the name change was intended "to develop our own internal spiritual system that had nothing to do with anything founded in Unitarianism" and maintained, "Something basic [is] missing in our black experience as long as our identity is wedded to the Unitarian structure. Our direction, that is, our tactical necessity, may instruct us to operate in relationship to Unitarian structures to obtain resources to be used for the struggle, and for certain other alliances in areas of mutual concern, but to confuse our identity in this relationship is to court paranoid and schizoid behavior."[600] In other words, BUUC's relationship to the UUA was expedient and tactical, and not an identity marker or a source of black spirituality.

Black Humanism was not Unitarian Universalist humanism. Black Humanism argued for collectivism over individualism because it held there was no freedom for any individual black person until all black people were free. It proclaimed itself a holistic system rather than a pluralistic one. Some of its principles, including naturalism, overlapped with those of Unitarian Universalism, but it was a different belief system. Nonetheless, longtime African American Unitarian Universalists were by and large activists who had joined Unitarian Universalism because of its liberal religious values.

Black Humanism pointed toward a painful truth: Something was spiritually missing in Unitarian Universalism. BUUC's white allies in the Fellowship for Renewal also chafed at the lack of spirituality and were seeking new ways of being religious. The challenge for African Americans, however, was different because they had to expend so much energy managing their relationship to white folks and white institutions—the Unitarian Universalist Association, Veatch, and their local congregation and its members. Rather than being able to channel their energies into creating something that spoke from and to the black experience, they spent them dealing with white needs, reactions, fears, and need for control. African Americans found white desires, interests, and anxieties trumping their own, including the need of African American Unitarian Universalists to engage more authentically with the black community and have their faith community do likewise. BUUC began as a response to this urgent black need; the proponents of the name change saw it as the next stage. The Black Humanist Fellowship "would have a much broader black constituency that would be interested in Black institutional development."[601] Conveying a new identity would enable BUUC to reach people who would never join a predominantly white denomination.

To champions of the Black Humanist Fellowship, it looked like BUUC was dead. "Individuals exist that relate to BUUC, but as a group of people moving on the imperative of liberation, BUUC does not exist." They wanted something more. When the question was posed, "Is the BHF a new church?" the answer was, "No, it is not a church. It is a spiritual system based on Black Humanism. Black/African need and purpose is nationhood, the existential condition of our being a single people." It was pan-Africanism, which embraced a metaphysical understanding of blacks as a people and a positive, creative transformation of humanism.[602] For those stirred by such an *a priori* commitment to blackness, Unitarian Universalism was, of necessity a means to an end, not the end itself.

The sixth annual meeting of BUUC was held at the Germantown congregation in Philadelphia on February 24, 1973. BUUC members who were opposed to the name change "arrived at the meeting to find door guards who let only selected people enter. They noted many unfamiliar faces in the assembly."[603] The legality of the meeting was challenged, but the chair overruled the objection. At that point, a group including Gwen Thomas, Hilda Mason, Ben Scott, Dalmas Taylor, and Lou Gothard left and gathered separately. In their absence, the vote was taken to change the name of the Black Unitarian Universalist Caucus to the Black Humanist Fellowship. The vote was sixty-two for and two against, with two abstentions. On February 28, Harold Wilson sent a letter inviting the dissidents to return. On March 8, BAC Treasurer, Ben Scott, filed a law suit, *Black Unitarian Universalist Caucus, Inc., et al. v. Richard L. Traylor, et al.*

Scott's lawsuit argued that the name change and other actions, such as bylaw changes, taken at the meeting were invalid because there had been no quorum and some voters had not been members of BUUC. The preliminary hearing was held on March 13, with the vice-chair of All Souls Unitarian (Washington D.C.) testifying in support of the plaintiff. She presented a resolution on behalf of All Souls' Board: "WHEREAS: All Souls Church has purchased a BAC bond in the face value of $162,000; WHEREAS: the bond was purchased with the assurance that the funds would be utilized in accordance with our principles as Unitarian-Universalists; WHEREAS: the change to Black Humanist Fellowship deleted all references to Unitarian-Universalism and raises grave questions whether the principles and philosophy of this organization are compatible with ours; THEREFORE BE IT RESOLVED: that All Souls Church Unitarian supports the position of plaintiff in the pending litigation." Dalmas Taylor, a BUUC member and UUA trustee, also testified on behalf of the plaintiff, saying that the name change was "a withdrawal from the philosophy and the principles of Unitarian Universalism."[604]

On April 15, *UU World* published a statement by Dalmas Taylor, on behalf of Ben Scott and the other plaintiffs, and one by Richard Traylor, on behalf of the Black Humanist Fellowship.

The trial began on April 23.

On April 25, on the advice of the Unitarian Universalist Association's legal counsel, the managing editor of *UU World* declined to include the BAC supplement *BACgrounds* until after a court ruling was issued. The supplement had been scheduled to appear on May 1 and Mwalimu Imara later condemned this decision in the newsletter *Creative Interchange*. His article outlined the history of the BUUC-BHF conflict, noted that "the *UU World* carried a presentation on the issues" on April 15 and charged the Association with censorship.[605]

On May 18, Mwalimu Imara and Hayward Henry were among the witnesses for the defense. The prosecution witnesses included LaVerne Jones of the BAC staff and David Eaton, senior minister of All Souls. On May 21, the court ordered that all securities and certificates of deposit held by both BAC and BHF be placed in a safe deposit box under court supervision.

Amazingly, minutes of the UUA Board give no indication that it discussed the litigation before May 29, when Dalmas Taylor made a brief presentation.

Meanwhile, the white allies of what had been BUUC/BAC faced a quandary. What position should they take in regard to the BUUC-BHF conflict? On May 19, members of the Fellowship for Renewal and the BAC Support Group met in Brooklyn. While the issue at hand was the change to the name and bylaws, those present knew the legal case reflected a "gulf years in the making within the black empowerment movement around questions of goals, strategy, ideology and identity." Individuals leaned in different directions, but they came to consensus on "organizational neutrality." The outcome had to be left "to the process of black-self-determination." The larger Unitarian Universalist world should keep its "hands off" and not take sides or suppress information.[606]

The twelfth General Assembly convened in Toronto, Canada, on May 30, 1973. Its theme was "The Bonds of Love Keep Open the Gates of Freedom." There were 971 delegates, and 213 of them were ministers.

In the Unitarian Universalist Association, 1973 was an election year. Bob West was reelected president and African Americans were elected to all the major commissions and committees. Joseph B. Samples Jr., chair of the Commission on Appraisal, was reelected and joined by Norma R. Poinsett; Gwendolyn Thomas was elected to the Planning Committee, and Winnifred L. Norman and John O. Coleman to the Nominating Committee. The UUA Board already included Edna Griffin, who sat on the executive committee, and Dalmas Taylor. In addition, Mwalimu Imara's appointment to the Ministerial Fellowship Committee was renewed.

The business resolutions included one on corporate responsibility, one calling for the creation of an "Office on Gay Affairs," and one calling for equal opportunity in all levels of UUA employment, "particularly in key decision-making positions." This latter also required the administration to provide an annual statistical summary of staffing. By the time West's presidency ended in 1977, the proportion of employees who were people of color had grown to 17 percent. The general resolutions touched on an array of issues, including abortion, disarmament, and Indian affairs, but there was nothing about BUUC, BAC, or the BHF, and no acrimony. The Association was moving on—but from a new plateau where African Americans were on the major decision-making bodies, as they had not been in the 1960s. At the end of the Toronto General Assembly, BUUC distributed flyers that explained its need for operating funds: "The Black Affairs Council Funds are frozen because of our efforts to protect these funds."[607] Two weeks later, BUUC program director Lou Gothard sent out a fundraising letter that said that many were confused about the split between the Caucus and the Black Humanist Fellowship. "We feel," he wrote, "that while the Black Humanist Fellowship may have good reason for leaving—in effect—the Uni Uni church, we can see no reason that [BHF] should take the resources that we have *all* worked for."[608]

Donald W. McKinney, the minister in Brooklyn, the former co-chair of FULLBAC, and the longest standing Euro-American member of BAC, found himself in an untenable situation. He was a member of two BACs, one controlled by BUUC and the other by the BHF. Honoring what he had been taught over the years, he announced that he would refrain from participating in what he saw as an internal political struggle between them. "Such differences are not the business of white UUs," he wrote to James Luther Adams. "[But] we now are being told (by both sides) that we cannot refuse to choose between them."[609] Years later, he said, "It was terribly difficult for me to be the deciding vote on the BAC Board. I worked happily and closely with the board members but I would not be the white guy who made the decision."[610] On June 20, 1973, he sent out this letter to the "Members of the Black Affairs Councils, BUUC and BHF":

> After long reflection I have decided it is necessary for me at this time to resign my membership on the Black Affairs Council....

This is a difficult decision to reach. I find it impossible, however, to conscientiously choose between positions in which I find truths so evenly divided. While it might seem expedient to wait for the court ruling before making this decision, I have come to realize—whatever that ruling may be—the philosophic and programmatic divisions within the Black UU constituency are such that it would be impossible for me to effectively serve in a positive role as a member of either BAC.[611]

McKinney was more frank about his despair and his thoughts in a letter sent a week later to Duke Gray. Regarding the Black Humanist Fellowship, he said that he could not rid himself "of the fear ... that there is a potential for dogmatism (etc.) within BHF that—unchecked by the presence of the BUUC people," would be too much to deal with. Regarding BUUC, his concern was that "BAC, stripped of the vision, courage and understanding of BHF people," was not worth the effort.[612]

The case dragged on for three more years. Finally the court ruled that there had been no quorum and that, therefore, the name and bylaw changes were invalid. In June 1976, after All Souls intervened for the bondholders, a settlement agreement was approved by the court.[613] Throughout the legal battle, bondholders had received the 5 percent interest due on the bonds that Ben Scott and BUUC/BAC held, and in the end they retrieved about 60 percent of their face value. Little retrievable remained from the third that Traylor controlled. A letter sent to the bondholders by the Black Humanist Fellowship and signed by Harold Wilson, Henry Hayward, and Richard Traylor said, "The whole national climate is one of reaction and conservatism."[614] They asserted that the legal process and the Unitarian Universalist Association were manifestly racist.

The Special Fund to Promote Racial Justice and Combat Racism had given BAC $180 thousand in 1972. From this, BAC made grants of $28 thousand to the Center for Black Education in Washington D.C. (which developed materials for independent black learning centers), $30 thousand to assist Combined Black Publishers, and another $30 thousand to the Boston United Black Appeal. BAWA was given $45 thousand, with which it hired a director. Over the life of the Racial Justice Fund, it would award a total of $420 thousand.

In 1973, the Veatch Committee extended the Racial Justice Fund and awarded it an additional $70 thousand by July 1974. However, Veatch decided the following January that there would be no further allocations to those involved in the litigation until it was resolved. BAWA received an additional $10 thousand before funding for it also ceased. Lack of funding meant BAWA's director returned to being simply a member of the Board. BAWA went on to publish five more project papers, including one entitled "How to Integrate a Church" and another on Project Equality, continued sponsoring General Assembly workshops and speakers, published a newsletter, and ran two television public service announcements.[615]

BAWA wound down in 1981 with a whimper rather than a bang when it forfeited its associate status by failing to remit its dues on time. Kenneth Whitlock, its consulting administrative officer, said BAWA would carry on, but Marcia McBroom Landess, the co-chair, countered in a statement delivered at the General Assembly plenary session: "We do not wish to revive the debates that so intensely divided us. . . . We do wish however, to acknowledge that the 60s are behind us and the prophetic 80s have arrived." She continued on to say that BAWA would merge its "energies and resources with those of all Unitarian Universalists in the continuing struggle to achieve full equality for all.[616] Neither of their statements had been approved by the BAWA Board.

Although the Unitarian Universalist Association had taken a

leap forward from Dana Greeley's naive paternalism, it remained embedded in institutional racism. Furthermore, the concept of institutional racism was new and understood only by a few, and the will of Unitarian Universalists to engage with issues of race flagged. They were worn out after the turbulent decade that included the intense 1963 General Assembly debate, the establishment of the Commission on Religion and Race, Unitarian Universalist participation in the March on Washington, the 1965 voting rights protests in Selma, the formation of BAC in 1967 and BUUC in 1968, the General Assembly Walkout in 1969, BAC's disafilliation from the UUA in 1971, the 1972 breakdown of the Ross Resolution, and the creation of the Black Humanist Fellowship and the lawsuit that followed in 1973. The Association's executive vice president William F. Schulz shared the perception of many when he wrote in 1980 that "with the decision in 1970 to end UUA funding of the Black Affairs Council, all effective UUA attention to racial justice ended too. Our relief translated itself into inaction. Like children with hot stoves, we shunned the burner. For us, indeed, no 'fire next time.'"[617]

Schulz's summation amplified an element of the truth that Unitarian Universalist Association president William Sinkford saw as well. "As a movement we didn't engage, we pulled back, and it was caused by our fear," he said.[618] It would be more accurate to describe the mid-seventies as a pause, rather than a pulling back. After the turmoil, race relations needed to lie fallow. The crop had ripened and been harvested, the field ploughed up, and the next rotation awaited a different crop and harvest. During the hiatus, energy and concerns were redirected toward women's rights, gay rights, and urban ministry. The liberation of women and gay people (once they began to come out) had intimate and therefore immediate implications for most Unitarian Universalists. They were their mothers, sisters, and daughters, their uncles, aunts, and friends. These causes elicited a kind of response that white Unitarian Universalists' remote, beneficent hope for the well-being of black people did not.

The Revolution's Offspring

Women, gay people, and other oppressed groups could not help but see the impact of the civil rights and Black Power movements. Once awakened to the possibility of human liberation, they organized and asserted themselves. The sixties set the scene for the seventies, when other marginalized people in America and in the Unitarian Universalist Association began to caucus, speak out, claim space, and make demands. As Orloff Miller said, "The women's movement picked up where Black Power left off."[619] It was never easy going. After a director of the Office of Gay Concerns was hired, almost two years passed before she was invited to speak at a congregation. Groups experienced resistance, but the right of people to gather together to explore their identity, formulate strategy, and take a stand had been established. In the context of the Unitarian Universalist Association, one can see a direct connection.

Richard Nash marched in Selma, was deeply involved in supporting BAC, and was co-founder of the Gay Caucus, which was named after the Black Caucus.[620] Connie Burgess marched in Birmingham, was a member of BAC, and was the executive director of the Unitarian Universalist Women's Federation (UUWF). Denny Davidoff, another BAC supporter and regional coordinator for the May 26th Empowerment Fund, said that she "emerged during the BAC, BUUC, BAWA controversy in 1968."[621] She went on to become president of the UUWF and later Moderator of the UUA.

Don McKinney said, "I think there is no question that the women's movement was very, very deeply affected by what happened in the Black movement and the Gay Caucus was definitely there."[622]

Civil rights to black empowerment to women's liberation and gay rights—one followed the other. These were not tranquil streams meeting and merging. They were turbulent, often branching off on their own, sometimes intermingling, yet always moving toward greater human liberation.

The first same-sex services of union performed by a Unitarian Universalist in the U.S. were in 1957 and 1958.[623] In 1969, a police raid on the Stonewall Inn, a Greenwich Village gay bar, ignited riotous protest, and the following year, the Unitarian Universalist Association passed a general resolution condemning "discrimination against homosexuals and bisexuals." In 1971, the Unitarian Universalist Gay Caucus was founded.[624] In 1973, at the Toronto General Assembly, a resolution was passed calling for the creation of an "Office on Gay Affairs," its name deriving from the Black Affairs Council. In 1974, when the British General Assembly passed a resolution promoting "homosexual equality," it referenced the actions of the UUA.[625] When the UUA office was established in 1975, after a twelve to eleven Board vote, it was paid for from the grant section of the UUA budget funded by the Veatch Committee.[626] Between 1970 and 1984, when a resolution encouraging ministers to perform services of union passed overwhelmingly, General Assemblies passed seven resolutions that, in various ways, affirmed lesbian, gay, and bisexual rights.

Robert Reed, a FULLBAC member and long-time activist, delivered a sermon entitled "Gay People and the Liberal Church" in May 1972. It began with the story of Richard Nash, with whom he had attended Meadville Lombard Theological School in the 1950s. Reed said that it wasn't until more than a decade later, when Nash "surfaced," that he discovered that Nash was gay. Nash had gone to Selma in 1965, had been a group leader at the Emergency Conference in 1967, and had served as chair of the Boston-area

FULLBAC when it challenged the hiring practices of the Statler-Hilton Hotel prior to the 1969 General Assembly. Reed also spoke of a woman who was active in the Gay Liberation Front and had told him she "fully expects Gay Liberation to be the sort of civil liberties issue in the 70s that racial justice has been in the 60s."[627]

Although the 1970 resolution condemned discrimination against homosexual and bisexual people, Unitarian Universalists were not lining up to support them in the years leading up to it. In 1968, the UUA Committee on Goals reported that 7.7 percent of Unitarian Universalists believed that homosexuality should be discouraged by law, and fully 80.2 percent said it should be discouraged by education. The Committee had also asked whether being "a woman" or "a Negro" would "hamper [the] effectiveness" of a minister; it did not even think to ask about sexual orientation.[628] Despite the many General Assembly resolutions, Unitarian Universalists repeatedly faltered in their willingness to live up to their espoused values. Just as they had balked at calling African American ministers to serve their congregations, they also balked at ministers who were not straight.

One of the first openly gay ministers, Mark Belletini, was not yet "out" when he went before the Ministerial Fellowship Committee in 1976, or when he began to search for a settlement in 1978. He was turned away by six ministerial search committees when questions they asked led him to reveal he was gay. None of them were prepared to consider a gay man. After these rejections, he revised his ministerial packet to speak openly about his personal life so that a search committee could discuss the issue before inviting him to interview. Anticipating that a call would never come, he decided to keep sending out packets anyway as a small, personal effort to educate Unitarian Universalists. Then a moment of grace arrived. Rev. Diane Miller invited him to serve as her interim assistant minister at the First Unitarian Universalist Church of San Francisco, and in 1979 he was settled and ordained.[629]

In June 1973, immediately following General Assembly, Donald Harrington preached a sermon entitled "Hope despite Disillusion: Unitarian Universalists and the Homosexual." He began by confessing it "to be the most difficult sermon of my ministry." He went on to talk about how the Fellowship For Renewal, an all-white support group, had supported BUUC, and now the Black Humanist Fellowship was "trying to take itself completely out of the Unitarian Universalist Association." "This year, a resolution came to the Assembly, vigorously supported by the Fellowship For Renewal, and sponsored by the Gay Caucus of the UUA, calling for the creation . . . of an Office on Gay Affairs. . . . I was the only minister to speak against this resolution." He then asked, "Is homosexual behavior a norm?" His sermon trod an intellectually tortuous path that did not condemn homosexuality but did pathologize it.[630]

Around the same time, Daniel G. Higgins, BAWA's minister for human unity and its program director, wrote an editorial in its newsletter entitled "Where Does It End?" He questioned the legitimacy of focusing on a particular experience of otherness and oppression and warned that the next group to organize would be the "UU Caucus for Left-Handed Persons." He asked, "When will reason . . . compel us to recognize that continued fragmentation contributes to the deterioration of the dialogue, about [concepts] that create and sustain the religious community?"[631]

. . .

THE PAUSE IN THE Unitarian Universalist Association's emphasis on racial justice did not last. In 1978, the year after Paul Carnes was elected president, the Religious Education Department released *The Adventures of God's Folk*, a curriculum that included sessions about Sacajawea and Harriet Tubman.[632] In 1979, there were three African Americans on the UUA Board and two on the Commission on Appraisal. Whatever plan Carnes may have had to reopen the issue of racial justice, however, was cut short by his illness and death that March. Eugene O. Pickett became president, and he moved promptly. In June 1979, the UU Urban Church Coalition met in Detroit, Rev. Jesse Jackson was the Ware Lecturer at General Assembly in East Lansing, and Dr. Loretta Williams, one of the African American Board members, was hired as the Association's director of social responsibility. In October, at a meeting of all the active African American ministers in Boston, Pickett "emphasized the high priority his Administration place[d] on racial issues and his desire to see renewed attention focused on this area."[633] In April 1980, the UUA Board hired Community Change, Inc., to work with the UUA Institutional Racism Audit Team, and in April 1981, they delivered the "Institutional Racism Audit." In 1980, Skinner House Books, the publishing imprint of the Association, published *Black Pioneers in a White Denomination.* In 1981, the UUA Committee on Urban Concerns and Ministry, under the leadership of Jack Mendelsohn, created a new source of grants, the Whitney M. Young Jr. Urban Ministry Fund. Pickett himself joined the Board of the National Urban League. Also in that year, Yvonne Seon became the first African American woman ordained into the Unitarian Universalist ministry. She was joined by Adelle Smith-Penniman in 1982, the year Michelle Bentley, who would become the third African American woman to be ordained, enrolled at Meadville Lombard Theological School. A new chapter had begun.

Black Power Was the Trigger, Not the Cause

An exploration of power within the Unitarian Universalist microcosm during these years must take into account the environment in which it was embedded—the massive resistance to the American status quo that arose during the latter half of the sixties. A farmworkers' strike in 1965 became the Delano Grape Boycott and lasted five years. The Black Panther Party and National Organization of Women were founded a year later. The Free Huey Campaign and the March on the Pentagon took place in 1967. In 1968, Dr. Martin Luther King Jr. and Robert F. Kennedy were assassinated; riots once again erupted across America; the Poor People's Campaign marched on and camped out in Washington D.C.; and women protesting the Miss America pageant threw bras, girdles, and other symbols of oppression into a "freedom trash can." The Yippies (Youth International Party), having gathered in Chicago during the Democratic National Convention to protest the war in Vietnam, were attacked by rioting police on Michigan Avenue. The counterculture surfaced, along with encounter groups and sexual liberation. The Stonewall riots in Greenwich Village and the iconic Woodstock Festival on a farm in upstate New York marked 1969. Among hippies, weed was as common as booze. In 1970, the

Kent State massacre shocked the nation. Baby boomers roamed the country in VW vans, explored transcendental meditation, and experimented with communes. America, a mass of contradictions, was in turmoil, and so was the Unitarian Universalist community.

Amidst this cultural realignment, Unitarian Universalism tried to reconcile itself with the implications of Black Power. That effort set off an upheaval, but Black Power was not the cause of the upheaval, only its trigger. African American Unitarian Universalists were few in number; no survey has ever been taken, but in the late sixties, they were probably around 1 percent of all Unitarian Universalists. Not quite two hundred black Unitarian Universalists attended the inaugural meeting of BUUC in Chicago; 165 came the next year in Detroit; and about 150 when it met in Washington D.C. There is no way to know how many came to the General Assemblies in 1968 and 1969. A realistic estimate is that several hundred African Americans were actively involved in BUUC. They were enough to serve as a reagent, the reaction to which lingers to this day.

Hemorrhaging Members?

Between 1968 and 1974, membership in Unitarian Universalist congregations declined by 75,646, or 26 percent. Some attributed this drop to the failure of the Unitarian Universalist Association to support the Black Affairs Council. But this explanation is too simplistic. All religious organizations saw declines in membership, and among mainline denominations, the drop was even more precipitous than in the UUA.[634] Administrative decisions contributed to the UUA's losses. In 1970, in the midst of a recession, the West administration established the Annual Program Fund, for which dues were based on congregational membership numbers. It also launched *UU World* and mailed it directly to members' homes, meaning that churches and fellowships needed to supply members' names and addresses. These two changes led congregations to trim their membership rolls. Membership figures dropped across all congregations and seemed to have nothing to do with which way a congregation leaned during the conflict. Between 1968 and 1974 at the First Unitarian Church of Los Angeles, the birthplace of Black Unitarians for Radical Reform, membership fell from 953 to 681, a nearly 30-percent decline. Black and White Action began at the Community Church of New York, a congregation which saw its membership fall more than 50 percent, from 2000 to 934. The First Unitarian Church of Brooklyn and its minister, Donald McKinney, were so deeply supportive of black empowerment that BAC presented it with the All Souls Award in 1971. However, its membership dropped from 547 to 220, which is a loss of 60 percent. The Arlington Street Church, a congregation that was financially and institutionally troubled following Jack Mendelsohn's charismatic ministry, saw membership decline from 632 to 398, or 37 percent. Cedar Lane Unitarian Church in Bethesda, which had seen its pulpit taken over, saw membership drop from 1,056 to 765, or 28 percent. Even University Unitarian Church in Seattle, far from the center of strife, saw a decline from 877 to 320, a dramatic 63-percent fall.

There were exceptions. In Walnut Creek, California, where UUA presidential candidate and BAC supporter Aron Gilmartin was minister, the congregation grew from 351 to 475. Urbana-Champaign, where Mwalimu Imara was from 1968 to 1970, added 10 members, growing from 342 to 352, while at the First Unitarian Society of Chicago, where Mendelsohn went in 1970, the membership figure remained essentially unchanged.

Why membership figures went down is open to speculation. Some of the declines were due to particular local circumstances like the departure of a long-serving and charismatic minister, as when Stephen Fritchman stepped down in 1970. Some losses were due to unrelated changes in the region, as when Boeing laid off 65 thousand people in 1970–1971. This would account for the large drop in membership in Seattle.

But the overall downward trend suggests more universal causes. Many of the congregations that lost members were urban and were affected by the ongoing flight to the suburbs. More broadly, an increasing proportion of the U.S. population was unaffiliated with a religious institution or did not attend religious services. In addition, the political landscape shifted within America and in Unitarian Universalism during the sixties. Finding Republicans in a Unitarian Universalist congregation was normal in the first half of the twentieth century. But during the sixties and seventies, the percentage of Unitarian Universalists who identified themselves as Democrats increased, while the percentage who identified as Republicans decreased precipitously. By 1990, only 18 percent of Unitarian Universalists identified as Republican, and by 2008, 6 percent. This shift reflected a larger cultural and political realignment that began in 1964, when Southern Democrats voted Republican and carried the South into the Republican Party. The mirror image of that change happened within Unitarian Universalism. Unitarian Universalist values were, and have remained, consonant with emerging progressive political trends. Civil rights was the first in a series of issues that grew to include Vietnam War resistance, Black Power, abortion rights, women's liberation, and gay rights. These movements reshaped and polarized the American political landscape, and at the same time made Unitarian Universalist congregations inhospitable to those of a more conservative bent. Some African Americans, who can be quite socially conservative, would have been among them.

There is no way to know how many African Americans were Unitarian Universalists at the beginning of this period, how many left, or why they left; nonetheless, some who lived through those years have pointed to a supposed exodus of black people as proof that the Unitarian Universalist Association failed in its response to Black Power. William Sinkford, former president of the UUA, wrote, "It was a time when dreams of integration were challenged by demands for black empowerment, days when it got too hard and painful for our congregations to stay involved.... And when our faith withdrew from the racial justice conversation, more than a few people of color withdrew, too. Feeling betrayed, we left UUism. I was one of them, but there were many others."[635] Others tell a similar story. Joe Samples, chair of the Commission on Appraisal and member of the First Unitarian-Universalist Church of Detroit, said, "Blacks became disillusioned about what the hell was going on and started leaving the church." And Larry Ladd, who followed Sinkford as president of Liberal Religious Youth, said, "So many people who had had their spirits raised by the 1968 and 1969 General Assemblies had effectively given up by then [1970]. Particularly the African Americans who had been part of BUUC and supported BAC. The disappointment and disillusionment was rampant."[636]

Disappointment was rampant, but not universal. All Souls Church in Washington D.C. is a case in point. David Eaton said that when he became minister in 1969, the congregation was 90–95 percent Euro-American, but he and the Board decided together that becoming an all-inclusive, multiracial, pluralistic congregation was the church's mission. Between 1968 and 1974, membership at All Souls declined from 1,563 to 990, and it finally stabilized at 800, a drop of 49 percent. But at the same time, All Souls became one of the most diverse congregations in the Unitarian Universalist Association. Similarly, membership at the First Unitarian Society of

Chicago fluctuated between ministries (although it never reached the inflated five hundred that was reported to the UUA during Kent and Mendelsohn's ministries), but the proportion of people of color increased from one-tenth in 1962 to about one-third. Chicago had embraced diversity and begun integrating in 1948.

All Souls hired Bernice Just, an African American, as its director of religious education in 1957. In 1962, Rev. Andrew Kuroda founded the first and only Japanese Unitarian fellowship outside Japan as a Japanese-language congregation within All Souls. In 1970, Chicago First hired Marshall C. Grigsby, an African American, to serve as assistant minister. The music programs of both congregations were active and diverse; one had the Chicago Children's Choir, the other the Jubilee Singers. Both Eaton and Mendelsohn were well known and controversial figures engaged in public ministry. The congregations were located in vibrant urban settings that included a substantial and established black middle class. By 1970, both of the congregations included significant numbers of long-tenured black members and leaders who were middle-class professionals. These were also the congregations from which National BUUC experienced the most pushback. Their black members represented a different generation; they were progressives rather than radicals. In 1971, the Chicago Area BUUC, which was made up largely of First Church members, disaffiliated from National BUUC, and the Greater Washington Area BUUC submitted a five-page critique of how national BUUC was being run. In 1973, All Souls supported Ben Scott in his suit against Richard Traylor and the Black Humanist Fellowship. However much some African Americans despaired of the UUA, All Souls and Chicago First, bolstered by the loyalty and tenacity of their black members, offered reason to be hopeful.

Claims that the empowerment controversy led to an exodus of African Americans from Unitarian Universalism suggest that the flow was one-way when it was not. Beyond All Souls and Chicago First, middle-class African Americans continued to join Unitarian Universalist congregations. In Athens, Dr. Richard M. Graham, the first full-time African American faculty member at the University of Georgia, joined; at Fourth Universalist in New York City, Donald Ryder, an acclaimed architect, and Shauneille Perry, a noted theater director, became members. In Harrisburg, William H. Harris Jr., an engineer, joined and eventually went on the Joseph Priestley District Board and was later recognized with the UUA Unsung Hero Award. In Pittsburgh, Alan and Jacqui James joined First Unitarian in 1972. She went on to become the congregation's director of religious education, and in the eighties and nineties, she was a pivotal member of the Unitarian Universalist Association's staff as it struggled to become an antiracist institution.[637]

African Americans did leave. Sinkford was one. Joe and Pearl Samples saw others depart. Their personal experiences cannot be denied, but there were also many who did not leave, including the Samples. Sinkford left, but his mother, Kathryn, did not. Ministers Harold Wilson and Mwalimu Imara moved on, but Thomas Payne, Bill Jones, David Eaton, Jeffrey Campbell, and Lewis McGee remained. How many departed is not known. Alex Poinsett, who left, estimated 1,000 other "disgruntled African Americans" left as well.[638] However, this is unlikely given that the combined black membership of Community Church of New York, All Souls D.C., First Chicago, and the predominantly African American All Souls First Universalist on the city's Southside would have been at least six hundred. Indeed, even if all 1,500 or so African American Unitarian Universalists had left, they would have represented just 2 percent of the UUA's total loss in membership over the six-year period engulfed by the empowerment controversy. Testimonies from Sinkford, the Samples, and Ladd are personal and anecdotal, and so they represent a facet of the truth. The larger picture is more complex.

Following Dr. King's assassination in 1968, African Americans were inevitably swept up in a cascade of emotion. Full of rage, which is one of grief's stages, and heartache, and in reaction rather than by choice, many held white people collectively accountable for his death. His murder was seen as another act of violence and intimidation in the ongoing history of white terrorism. Alongside their anger and despair, African Americans felt a renewed sense of urgency and impatience with white foot-dragging. The rebellions that erupted in urban America multiplied, and attitudes shifted. African Americans had to lead this struggle for black self-determination and identity. Within the Unitarian Universalist Association, this struggle first manifested in BURR, then BUUC, then BAC, and later still in the BHF.

Middle-class African Americans had been part of a vanguard when they joined liberal white Unitarian Universalist congregations in the forties, fifties, and sixties, but even before Dr. King's death, that was changing. With his assassination, it became suddenly (and painfully) clear how disconnected and isolated many of them had become from the black community. Some probably felt a sense of guilt and needed to reestablish that connection. Proving that their Unitarian Universalist community could be relevant was one way of doing so, which is why both blacks and whites hung so many hopes on BAC and on the $1 million commitment that was made to it.

When internecine struggles brought BUUC to its end, some blamed the Unitarian Universalist Association's 1970 decision to reduce its annual support of BAC for the decline in African

American membership. Sinkford described it as a betrayal and said he left broken-hearted. Sinkford said he "did not enter one of our churches for more than a dozen years [and] didn't join another church or even attend one."[639] On the other hand, Hayward Henry went on to attend Sojourner Truth Presbyterian in Berkeley and a Christian Methodist Episcopal church in Houston. The bottom line for Henry was whether a church could be an agent of change and transformation for the African American community; if it could not, he would direct his attention elsewhere. His loyalty was not to Unitarian Universalism but to black liberation and whatever institutions could best support liberation in its fullest sense.

Some African Americans left for reasons akin to Henry's. Some told their ministers, "Sorry, I feel torn, but right now I have to put my time into the black community." David Bumbaugh had such a conversation in 1969, when he became the minister of the Mount Vernon church in Alexandria, Virginia. An African American family came to him to explain that they had been attending Mount Vernon's early service and then going to the 11 AM service at a black church, and had come to the realization that this compromise was not sustainable. They felt that the black church and the community it served needed their time, their energy, and their resources, so they were withdrawing from the Unitarian church. But they wanted Bumbaugh to know that they made the decision with reluctance and that they were not unhappy with the Mount Vernon congregation. Bumbaugh assured them he understood and thanked them. Later he said, "I must admit that I felt it was an inevitable consequence of the growing influence of the Black Power movement, and indeed, within a year or so, the congregation had no more African Americans participating."[640]

Others certainly drifted away quietly as they sought to reconnect to the African American community. The balance shifted.

Affirming one's black identity became more important than nurturing one's liberal religious identity. For some, the energy required to transform a Unitarian Universalist congregation was energy diverted from the pressing needs of the African American community. For others, integration had lost its sheen. Perhaps black radicals made black moderates feel like Uncle Toms. How many turned to the church seeking comfort rather than turmoil? Or maybe their reasons for departing were the same as those of the Euro-Americans who also left, as overall membership in Unitarian Universalist congregations declined.

To assert that African American attitudes and reasons for leaving were monolithic is a form of racism. African Americans were not in complete accord then, and never are.

The Past as Prelude

Surveying the conflict that arose in Unitarian Universalism in its attempt to respond to Black Power without reference to the institutional tensions that persisted following the consolidation of the Universalist Church of America and the American Unitarian Association guarantees that the events of those years will be misinterpreted.

In 1967, when the Emergency Conference took place and the Black Caucus made its demands, the Unitarian Universalist Association was organizationally only six years old. The history of Universalism and Unitarianism in America went back much further, but at that moment, the movement was still working through a merger of cultures, administrative styles, and ways of distributing power. The matter of who held power was not yet resolved.

In the American Unitarian Association and the Universalist Church of America, power was located in different arenas. Power in the UCA was situated in state conventions, state superintendents, and, of course, the congregations. The superintendents in Maine, New Hampshire, Vermont, New York, the Midwest, the South, and California were responsible to their state conventions rather than to the UCA's general superintendent. They met together annually in a Council of Superintendents and worked, by and large, cooperatively with the general superintendent.[641] Fellowship committees were state-run and held financial resources. It was a structural arrangement that kept power dispersed and made collaboration a necessity.

After the merger, several state conventions refused to allot their endowments to the Unitarian Universalist Association. Donald Harrington said the question was whether it would be possible to get "the State Conventions to give up their power to a national organization, which the Unitarians really felt was absolutely essential."[642] In the American Unitarian Association, power had been centralized during the reigns of three strong presidents: Samuel Atkins Eliot (1900–1927), Frederick May Eliot (1937–1958), and Dana McLean Greeley (1958–1961). While the Universalist general superintendent was accountable to the UCA Board, the AUA president was only accountable to the annual assembly, called the May Meeting.

The Universalist Church of America was less than half the size of the American Unitarian Association, and the structure that was chosen for the new, merged Unitarian Universalist Association more or less followed the Unitarian model. However, it remained in flux, and battles continued after consolidation. They were still evident in the candidates' election platforms in 1969 and periodically surfaced in succeeding administrations.

The first major battle was one of many that left the Universalists feeling betrayed. Dana Greeley decided to run for president even though the UCA was opposed to the head of either body running. Philip Giles, the UCA general superintendent, declined to stand for election and tried to convince Greeley to do likewise. Greeley would not hear of it and ended up running against William Rice, who had been the masterful chair of the Merger Commission. Rice was in favor of a weak presidency, which the Merger Commission had recommended. Greeley was for growth and maintaining all the power he had had as AUA president.

Greeley won with 54 percent of the vote, but that did not end the battle over the power of the presidency. The first moderator of the UUA was Marshall Dimock. Dimock came from Bethel, Vermont; was a professor of public administration; and had been on the Mode of Organization Committee as the two institutions prepared for the massive reorganization merger would require. "Dimock was always of a mind that the Moderator of the UUA would be the dominant factor," said UUA Board member William A. Donovan, who had been on the committee with him.[643] As moderator, Dimock insisted on having an office at headquarters and pushed a plan he called the "CBS Plan" (Collect Before Spending). It was over that issue that he crossed swords with Dana Greeley. Donald Harrington, who was also on the Board, said, "Marshall Dimock wanted to have a board that was dominant.... Dana felt very strongly, no, it should be an elected president and the president should be elected by the whole denomination in General Assembly and should have to work with the board but should be subject only to the General Assembly." "It was a tug-of-war between the two of them over the character of the UUA," he continued. "It was pretty frightful at times."[644]

The contest came to a head in June 1964. "Moderator Announces He Will Resign" was the lead headline in that month's *Register-Leader Spotlight*. The article quoted Dimock as saying, "During the nineteenth century the tendency for executives was to rule things with roughshod, dictatorial methods.... The decision you want to make is whether the power should be concentrated in the president or diffused."[645] Upon seeing the article, Raymond Hopkins, Greeley's vice president, withdrew that edition of the *Register-Leader* and fired the editor.

Dimock's departure did not end the disagreement over whether power should rest with the president or the Board. In 1969, it was an issue in the election to choose Greeley's successor. John Ogden Fisher, one of seven who ran, declared, "Centralism has gone too far and it is time for a drastic revision of our organizational structure."[646] Fisher's platform stated he would be a one-term president, after which the Board would appoint the chief executive officer.

Fisher's platform also called for reorganizing the districts and giving them responsibility for religious education, extension, social responsibility, and fundraising. William Donovan said, "The original feeling of the [Mode of Organization] Committee was that the field organization ought to be larger [and] somewhat more autonomous with a greater responsibility."[647] The Committee wanted to make regions responsible for more service delivery, but that was not implemented until it had to be, during the downsizing when the interdistrict regions were created. Deane Starr said, "I support the notion of curtailing the activities of continental headquarters in favor of stronger districts."[648] Indeed, four of the candidates favored decentralization.

In 1969, the Unitarian Universalist Association moved to a model in which trustees were elected from the districts rather than at large. Expanding the Board to include district representatives was an effort to empower the districts or, at least, to make the Board more responsive to them. It also represented a distribution of power along a new line.

When the districts began to elect national Board members, Rev. Marvin Evans was chosen by the Pacific Northwest District (PNWD). "The PNWD voted to not participate in the new inter-district arrangement and this resulted in long, difficult negotiations as to the future of our district," Evans explained. "My job as district trustee was to take a leading and decisive role in those negotiations, leading to establishing our own district office in Vancouver, BC, Canada with Rod Stewart as [district executive]. I have lived in the west for fifty-one years and easterners, including the UUA staff, still do not understand that the Left Coast is a different country."[649]

The Pacific Northwest District was noted for its independence, the strength of its cross-border relations, and the collegiality of its ministers. However, it was not the only region to be outraged by the Association's decision in 1969 to cut district staff. On the opposite side of the country, an announcement of the annual meeting of the Southeast District (SED) explained, "This drastic solution, appearing as it did to be an emasculation of the district and contrary to priorities established by the two previous General Assemblies, both dismayed and angered the SED Board."[650]

In 1960, a newly created Midwest Universalist Conference merged with the Western Unitarian Conference to create the Midwest UU Conference, mere weeks in advance of continental consolidation. Prior to the Midwest gathering, an informal meeting of several members of the Conference Board took place. They knew "how Dana was with money" and held the opinion "that if the money were sent to Boston it would disappear." They recommended joining the merger but also creating a Midwest UU Foundation to maintain their combined assets and ensure they were used locally.[651] The proposal to supplant the regional organization by creating districts naturally "aroused conflict."[652] Although the Midwest UU Conference did not survive, the Association did not get its funds either. Regions were another cradle of resistance to the consolidation of power.

Regions resisted centralization while Unitarian Universalist fellowships, wary of centralized power in any form, fiercely protected their own prerogatives. In *The Fellowship Movement*, Holley Ulbrich identifies four cultural characteristics that, while not universal, are broadly typical of fellowships. One is "resistance to authority." The positive side of fellowships' tug-of-war over who was in charge was the empowerment of laity—the membership of the community rather than the clergy or denomination. This emphasis on what James Luther Adams called the priesthood and prophethood of all believers can be credited with fueling an engagement with social action. But on the other hand, as Ulbrich wrote, "Resistance to authority often extends to distrust of denominational leadership.... Many fellowship members express a mixture of disdain, ignorance, and indifference to the Unitarian Universalist Association."[653] Fellowships were not about to accede to the demands of either the UUA or BAC; doing so ran counter to their antiauthoritarian culture.

Prior to merger, the Universalist Church of America met biennially, while the American Unitarian Association met annually at its May Meetings. Year in and year out, there were perhaps 150 ministers who were almost always in attendance at the May Meetings, and another hundred who attended intermittently. Lay delegates came and went, and each year perhaps a third were first-timers, but there were perhaps two hundred who caught the bug and attended most assemblies. These were delegates who might have worked their way through the leadership positions in their churches and welcomed the opportunity to participate in a larger circle. In terms of governance, the AUA, despite its bylaws, was in practice less an association of churches than an association of ministers with substantial lay support. It was largely ministers who attended conferences and conventions, ministers who spoke from the floor in general meetings, and ministers who led the various factions. It was ministers whose careers and livelihood were at stake, and ministers who held much of the power. With merger this changed in two ways.

First, a process of "democratization" began, in which lay influence grew. This occurred, in part, because the new Unitarian Universalist Association continued the Universalist pattern of holding General Assembly in June, or occasionally July, and in different cities around the country, rather than the Unitarian practice of always meeting in May in Boston. More laypeople could attend in summer months than in May, and varying the location drew heavier regional participation. The percentage of delegates who were ministers dropped from above 30 percent at May Meetings during the fifties to less than 25 percent at General Assemblies during the sixties; it was lower still in Dallas in 1972 (24.8 percent) and Toronto in 1973 (21.9 percent). Meanwhile, the total number of delegates attending General Assemblies grew.

Second, in the American Unitarian Association, all Board members were elected at large. The Nominating Committee made sure that regions were represented and that the Board included both ministers and laypeople. In consultation with the president, it also nominated the next Nominating Committee. The Board always met in Boston. This meant the AUA Board was strongly weighted toward New England, malcontents were rarely elected, and, with the exception of Errold D. Collymore, included no members of color. This changed after merger when each district elected a Board member. Only four members were directly elected at large, and it was agreed that one of these would be Canadian and another African American. Districts rarely elected ministers to the Unitarian Universalist Association Board because, while most ministers saw districts as useful sources of programming, they were rarely involved with district boards and committees save in advisory capacities.[654]

Comparing the American Unitarian Association with the Unitarian Universalist Association shows that the overall effect of merger was the dilution of ministerial power, a reassertion of regionalism,[655] and a shift of power toward laity and districts. Moreover, there was a built-in tension within the governance structure between the moderator and the president; whether this led to conflict or collaboration depended upon their relationship and temperaments.

. . .

AT THE EMERGENCY CONFERENCE in 1967, the Black Caucus asked the participants "to concur in the establishment of a Black Affairs Council to implement the specific recommendations of the Black Caucus and to insure a vehicle to express the interests, feelings and aspirations of Black Unitarian Universalists for power within the denomination," and then demanded an up or down vote, without debate, after which they would deal directly with the group who held power, the UUA Board of Trustees. "That's where the power of change lies," BAC member Barbara Jackson said, "not here."[656]

But the power was not where the Caucus assumed it was. BAC and BUUC, FULLBAC and FFR could organize, disrupt, polarize, and boycott all they wanted, but none of this would force those with power to negotiate, because the way power was distributed within the UUA is confounding in its complexity. Unitarian Universalists, in general, were wary and distrustful of power; therefore, the loci of power were often in tension with one another. The UUA's administration was led by a president elected by and accountable to the General Assembly—a transitory body. Moderators were also elected by and accountable to the General Assembly rather than the Boards they led. Most members of the Board of Trustees were accountable to a district. Delegates to the General Assembly elected the president, the moderator, some at-large trustees, the Nominating

Committee, and some other committees, and delegates were accountable to their home congregations. Congregations were accountable solely to their membership—not to the General Assembly, the UUA Board, or their district. The Board, moderator, and president did not always agree; the General Assembly could vote on budget items but the Board had ultimate fiduciary responsibility; the Planning and Nominating Committees were autonomous from, but collaborated with, the administration and the Board. Regions defended their turf, and congregations guarded their autonomy. In 1968, when ministers saw the resolution proposing mandatory dues as a threat to congregational autonomy, Fritchman, Harrington, and others on all sides of the conflict denounced it so vehemently that it was resoundingly defeated. Although there are many areas of Unitarian Universalist governance in which democracy is the rule, there are other major areas that are effectively consensual and covenantal. In regard to social action, the freedom of the individual conscience and radical congregational polity regularly clashed with the imperative to take moral stands and act on those as a body.

In 1968, the Cleveland General Assembly chose BAC's proposal over the Board's. In the weeks leading up to the 1969 GA, the administration recommended fulfilling the $250 thousand commitment to BAC, but the Board's Finance Committee recommended allotting it only $200 thousand. The administration's position carried, but the Board then added a $50 thousand allotment to BAWA, which angered BAC. At the Boston GA, the ordering of the agenda was not within the Board's purview but was under the auspices of the GA's Business Committee and ultimately of the Assembly; BAC's inability to reorder the agenda resulted in the Walkout. GA voted to give BAC $250 thousand and BAWA nothing, and the West administration concurred. But in the fall of 1969, the Board voted otherwise. In 1970, GA voted against funding BAC or BAWA from the UUA's operating budget, and in 1971, it passed the Resolution on Joint Funding for Racial Justice to create a separate fund relying on voluntary donations.

This points to the truth of what Al Weissbard wrote following the 1968 Assembly: "Now the denomination needs your help. You'll have to help me 'put *our* money where *my* mouth was.'" A General Assembly could pass any resolution it wished, but unless congregations were willing to provide the financial wherewithal, and they often were not, the Association was hamstrung. In this case, and others, it proved too true.[657]

Because of the dispersed nature of power in the Unitarian Universalist Association, it was impossible to marshal its energy in service of any particular effort without a significant, association-wide effort. Investing that kind of effort in a white institution and its membership was not what BAC was called into being to do. But without such an undertaking, there was no way to build the moral and financial support required to fulfill its mission.

Vying for Power

"Power was at the center of the problem as it always is in relationships of marginality," Mtangulizi Sanyika (née Hayward Henry) has said. "Power was all right for white folks to have, but it was an alien concept for black folks to have."[658] Maintaining that what took place was a reaction to black people's insistence on being in control of the decisions and financial resources that effected them was on target. But this binary view of the world promotes the assumption that whites were a monolithic entity in Unitarian Universalism. It did not exist except metaphorically; indeed, within the Unitarian Universalist Association, many groups felt marginalized and were vying for power.

BAC allied itself with LRY, which sought and gained control of $100 thousand and its own programming. Canadian Unitarians felt marginalized; at the 1969 annual meeting of the Canadian Unitarian Council, a vote to withdraw from the UUA, on the grounds that the CUC's budget allocation had been reduced and its needs ignored, failed only narrowly. The largest group to feel marginalized were those who identified as Universalist. The remnants of the Universalist Church of America's state conventions had money but no power within the new administrative structure. The Universalist Service Committee was gobbled up by the Unitarian Service Committee; the Massachusetts state convention's endowment was spent; the two Universalist theological schools were closed; Dana Greeley, former president of the American Unitarian Association, was now president of the Unitarian Universalist Association; and although the merged denomination was officially "Unitarian Universalist," both black and white Unitarians often left out the second word. The Universalists, having lost out in the division of power, were wary and distrustful of BAC's attempt to seize it.

Hayward Henry said that blacks "who have the greatest expertise in blackness" needed to be in charge of developing the black community.[659] In other words, they knew how to serve the community's needs and should have been given the power and resources to do so. Liberal Religious Youth said the same thing about youth programming, and Rev. Marvin Evans said it about the needs of the Pacific Northwest District. The Canadians felt the same way about the Unitarian Universalist Association and doubted whether BAC had the ability to assess Canadian programs. This insistence that a group's special circumstances should be recognized and respected and that it should control the decisions and resources affecting it was not unique to BAC. Many groups expressed it, feeling themselves at a disadvantage either because they were regional or because their members were oppressed, and most of them felt that the UUA Board had reneged on commitments made to them at General Assemblies.

As to the claim of special status BAC made because of the votes at the 1968 and 1969 Assemblies, the Southeast District made a similar claim when it said in 1969 that the UUA Board, in reducing the twenty-one district offices to seven interdistrict offices, was acting "contrary to priorities established by the two previous General Assemblies." It was an administrative rather than a moral complaint, but it was nonetheless true.

Prejudice and institutional racism were, of course, components of the response to BAC. However, to point to them as the primary reason BAC's funding came to an end does not accurately portray what happened or explain the volatility or lingering impact. Walking into the Unitarian Universalist cultural arena, where a multiplicity of marginalized and resentful groups were vying for power, and demanding $1 million dollars and complete autonomy in its use was like walking into a powder keg and lighting a match.

What fueled the conflict within the Unitarian Universalist Association was not simply BAC's reaction to white supremacist culture, or BAWA's distrust and alternative vision, or regionalism, although New England and Universalist provincialism were significant factors. Nor was the only problem that many groups felt marginalized and were vying for power. The truth is that an era in which power had been exercised in paternalistic and patriarchal ways was coming to an end.

Paternalism and patriarchy are both about exercising power over others; nonetheless it is important to distinguish between them. They look similar but are different. The UUA administration was paternalistic. But BAC, BUUC, BAWA, and FULLBAC, like the UUA, were all patriarchal.

Paternalism and Patriarchy

Theorizing about the role that paternalism and patriarchy played during this era is a more speculative endeavor than chronicling what happened, but the effort leads to the most cogent explanation for why the empowerment tragedy played out as it did.

It is worthwhile to return to the question Hayward Henry asked during the plenary at the 1968 Cleveland General Assembly: "Who will the Black community follow—those who believe in its own participation and right to self-determination as our caucus have attempted to investigate or those who offer paternalism?"[660] Paternalism, with its munificent, aloof, "father knows best" mindset, was insufficient, patronizing, had already failed, and could in no way meet the demands of that moment.

In 1969, looking ahead to the election of the next president of the Unitarian Universalist Association, David Parke asserted, "In the next administration we seek neither a 'father figure' who will determine our goals nor yet a catalyst who will seek consensus. Rather, we seek for a man who will be a beloved friend and colleague, who will assist each of us, including himself, to become more than he presently is."[661] In rejecting the father figure, Parke could only be referring to Dana McLean Greeley. Greeley, a Boston patrician who was John F. Kennedy's mentor at the Boston Rotary Club, sat on the UUA Board with others of that rarified class. Among them were diplomat and MIT professor Lincoln P. Bloomfield and Judge Lawrence Brooks. Like Greeley, both had graduated from Harvard. When Greeley ran for the UUA presidency, it had been anticipated that James Killian, who had been president of MIT and was the American Unitarian Association's moderator before the consolidation, would run for moderator. When Killian did not, Dimock was nominated. The AUA's lineage embodied New England provincialism and patriarchy—upright and privileged.

Greeley tried to understand the civil rights movement. But from the remove of his New England upbringing and Harvard education, he never really understood it, much less Black Power. In his moist-eyed, heartfelt invitation to those who had walked out of the 1969 General Assembly to return, the reason he offered was that families didn't settle arguments that way. This tells us how he saw the Unitarian Universalist community; it was a family and he, the father, was inviting the prodigal back home.

Greeley was known to be generous to a fault. He routinely reached out to those who had reason to dislike him, like Ernst Kuebler and Bill Rice (whom he defeated in the 1958 and 1961 elections, respectively). He hired Ray Hopkins as his vice president even though Hopkins had endorsed Rice. Hopkins came to consider Greeley "the kindest, most honest and loyal individual I have ever known," and said, "His biggest weakness is that he found it impossible to let anyone dislike him."[662] Thus it was characteristic that, before the 1968 Cleveland General Assembly, Greeley tried to befriend Ben Scott, Richard Traylor, and Hayward Henry. It was also typical that, following the vote in Cleveland to give $1 million to BAC, he said, "I want to thank BAC for leading us in new directions and winning converts to an evolving great cause. I hope that what we call losers will keep their conviction and be magnanimous in defeat, and I know they will."[663]

His memoir *25 Beacon Street* shows how deep-seated Greeley's paternalism was. Although it was published in 1971, he still wrote, without a hint of chagrin, "In a large number of speeches in the spring [of 1968] I compared the blacks of the Black Caucus ... to young people who might rebel against their own families to achieve their identity and then join them later as coequals." The phrasing is unambiguous in revealing his attitude. He saw Black Caucus members not as adults but as adolescents.

Patriarchy, being less benevolent than paternalism, manifested itself throughout the empowerment conflict in displays of male posturing, verbal aggression, defenses of honor when principle and power were at stake, and a sense of prerogative.

David Parke rejected Greeley as a father figure, but was himself embedded within the patriarchal paradigm. He did not forsake the will to control but rather sought a "man" (colleague-oligarch) who would lead in a direction consonant with the radical, uncompromising moralism that led Parke himself to disdain consensus. After walking out of the Boston General Assembly, Parke declared that the Moral Caucus should "foster a new movement which pre-exists in the hearts of all of us."[664] In other words, the protestors should break away from Unitarian Universalism. Metaphorically killing both the father, Greeley, and the organization he had invested his life in was an act of *patriarchy* rather than *paternalism*. Patriarchy turns to violence to depose the leader when it must, because patriarchy is about the exercise of power. In this case, it was also transracial and manifested in both the generational conflict within the UUA and in BAC/BUUC's overthrow of the African American old guard.

"Patriarchy calls for and legitimates the traumatic disruption of intimate relationships.... [and] the effect of such trauma on the human psyche is precisely to suppress personal voices and relationships," write Carol Gilligan and David A. J. Richards.[665] That is what transpired. Ben Scott was not alone in recalling how "lifelong friendships crumbled, marriages dissolved ... and congregations [were] factionalized."[666]

Racism was a factor in the empowerment controversy. But to develop a comprehensive understanding of what happened and why the bitterness has endured, we must examine the role played by patriarchy. Through the sixties and into the early seventies, the Unitarian Universalist Association was a social system in which power was primarily held by adult men and in which cultural norms and customs favored men over women. This patriarchy, in its immoderation and rigidity, magnified differences and disagreements. It was also in the early stages of its end. Yet the first battle in its overthrow was fought not over sexism but ostensibly over black empowerment. As factions polarized and protagonists verbally clashed, they rent the communal bonds and disrupted relationships throughout the Association.

The American Unitarian Association and the Universalist Church of America were both patriarchies. Within the upper echelon of leadership, there were few examples of women except Aurelia Henry Reinhardt, who was the AUA's moderator from 1940 to 1942, and Emily Taft Douglas, who held the position from 1958 to 1960. In regard to ministry, twenty-one Unitarian women ministers formed the Iowa Sisterhood prior to the turn of the century, but the AUA leadership eventually opposed the group. In Universalism, it is evident that women were recognized from the second half of the nineteenth century until around 1920. In the years around the turn of the century, the Ohio Universalist Convention alone had nearly twice as many women licensed to preach as the entire Unitarian Universalist Association did in 1965,[667] and in 1910, of a total of 689 ministers recognized by the Universalists, 67 were women.[668] The influence of Olympia Brown, Phebe Hanaford, and Augusta Chapin was denomination-wide. But from the twenties until after consolidation in 1961, patriarchy in both Unitarianism and Universalism limited women in ministry. In 1955, when Greta W. Crosby told Frederick May Eliot that she wanted to abandon her career in law for ministry, he told her, "It's as hard to be a woman in the

Unitarian ministry as to be a Negro."[669] Women's power was circumscribed, largely limited to women's alliances and religious education.[670]

As merger approached, the anxieties of white male leaders had to be placated in order to get their political buy-in, especially that of the Universalist state superintendents and Unitarian district executives. Raw politics came into play. Malcolm Sutherland, Dana McLean Greeley's vice president, said that he promised that those regional staff who supported consolidation would have work.[671] That is what happened. By 1964, four of the thirteen former state superintendents were settled in parishes and four were in administrative positions (including Philip Giles, the former Universalist Church of America general superintendent, and Raymond Hopkins, who became Greeley's vice president when Malcolm Sutherland moved on to become the president of Meadville Lombard Theological School). In addition, all eight Unitarian regional executives who wanted to continue ended up on staff, some others retired, and three died. Under the new patriarchy, those who had been in power—all white men—remained in power.

In 1967, months before Unitarian Universalists were forced to come face to face with Black Power, the *Report of the Committee on Goals* was released. It revealed that women made up 56.3 percent of all Unitarian Universalists, and two-thirds of them were housewives not employed outside the home. Women's liberation went unmentioned in reports on controversial social issues, and when asked how a woman minister's sex would affect her ministry, 47.2 percent of those polled said that "her sex might hamper her effectiveness." However, when asked whether abortion should be allowed in each of six scenarios positing a difficult or unwanted pregnancy, the majority of those polled answered yes in every one. Percentages in favor ranged from 61.8 percent "if she is married and does not want any more children" to 99 percent "if the woman's own health is seriously endangered."[672]

During this era, the Unitarian Universalist Association was still a patriarchy. There were no female interdistrict representatives or department directors.[673] Of the nine officers of the Association, two were women, and they held the positions of vice-moderator and recording secretary. Four of twenty-five Board members were women. Of the Board standing committees, two of the eleven members of the Ministerial Fellowship Committee were women, and no women served on the Finance or Investment Committee; on the Committee of Committees, which made committee assignments, one member out of five was female. Among the standing committees and commissions of General Assembly, one stood out. The Nominating Committee was comprised of eleven members, five of whom were women. And of seven hundred ministers listed in full fellowship in the 1971 directory, twenty were women.[674]

Patriarchy was visible not only in numbers but in process. In the 1963 General Assembly debate over whether to pass a bylaw change that would overturn the traditional practice of radical congregational polity by requiring congregations to admit members regardless of race, thirty-five people spoke. Twenty-six of them were white male ministers.

Bluster and bravado, patriarchy's companions, were in evidence at ministers' meetings. Colleagues sat around in smoke-filled rooms bragging about their congregations' attendance figures, growth in membership, endowment size, and latest building expansions. Posturing was commonplace, as were drinking copious amounts of hard liquor and boasting about sexual liaisons.[675]

Patriarchy was pervasive in Unitarian Universalist institutions, as it was in the larger culture. In 1963, when he was a senior at Meadville Lombard Theological School, Jim Hobart attended the annual ministers' study group called the Prairie Group. The stories of sexual conquest told by those whose ranks he was about to join surprised him. In the fall of 1964, the state of affairs became even clearer to him when he attended an orientation for new ministers. All the participants were male ministers, and the director of the Department of Ministry advised them, "Keep your girl friends at least 50 miles from church and home." Hobart was startled by the assumption "that we would have girl friends in addition to wives."[676] In 1966 in one East Coast congregation, partner swapping was sanctioned by the minister. A generation later, his successor was told that one woman had felt forced to participate by her husband. In Colorado Springs, a minister was "run out of town after an experiment in 'Extended Families' (multiple open marriages resulting in multiple divorces) failed spectacularly."[677] A similar situation arose in Canada at the congregation in South Peel, Ontario, when its minister started a commune. By 1969, his ministry was over and the congregation so traumatized it didn't call another minister for twenty years. As Richard Kellaway said, "Back then there was sex all over the place."

Such events highlight two things. First, the effects of the cultural revolution were broad, including not just the black revolution but also the youth movement, women's liberation, gay rights, and sexual liberation. It was a toppling of old mores that continues today. Second, even as this revolution was underway, society remained embedded in a patriarchal system. In that context, no one understood what was wrong about unequal power dynamics in sexual relationships. Male sexual prerogative was just one of the ways power was exercised. Indeed, the emergence of sexual liberation and experimentation, combined with the tendency of laity and ministers alike to deny that a power differential existed, hid what now would be recognized as boundary violations.

The Committee on Goals had asked about Unitarian Universalist attitudes toward extramarital sex in 1967: 43.4 percent of respondents said it was never justifiable, 18.3 percent responded that it was justifiable if the marriage partner agreed, and 38 percent said it should be left to free choice.[678] Four years later, in the midst of the sexual revolution, a Fellowship for Renewal position paper said, "We are compelled to respond with increasing openness to the issues of sexuality in our society.... We affirm and encourage the acceptance of all non-exploitive sexual experience between mutually consenting persons as natural experience."[679] In the early seventies, it was not yet as clear as it was to become where free love ended and abuse began. No one understood the subtle coercion all power differentials ensure. The language of clergy sexual misconduct and boundary violation did not exist, and the Unitarian Universalist Association, despite its progressive political and moral attitudes, remained embedded in patriarchy and male domination.

Liberal Religious Youth had a different president each year of the sixties. Two were women: Maria Fleming (1961–1962) and Ruth Wahtera (1966–1967). The male presidents included Bill Sinkford, Larry Ladd, and Rob Isaacs, and in 1965, during Sinkford's presidency, the treasurer was Toni Reed, an African American woman. In the 1969 presidential election, all five candidates were men. LRY was a little more gender-balanced than the rest of the Unitarian Universalist Association, but it was no bastion of feminism.

In 1973, Meadville Lombard Theological School had no female faculty and one female seminarian. In 1974, there were two women students, and in 1975 three.

In the fall of 1974, when Carol Henderson was serving as co-director of religious education at the Unitarian Universalist Congregation of Princeton, she mistakenly arrived at a ministers' meeting that Homer Jack was hosting at the United Nations. She walked into a room full of white male ministers and later said, "I couldn't miss the sharp intake of breath."[680] A couple of ministers of religious education came to her rescue by taking her under their wings.

However, sexism is only one aspect of patriarchy; at its core is a culture that rewards men for acting in a dominating way. Both Harrington and Fritchman were known for this. In 1978, the Community Church of New York was in search for a new senior minister to succeed Donald Harrington. In line with the model that John Haynes Holmes and Harrington had followed, Harrington wanted a "colleague successor." It would have required the candidate to spend several years under Harrington's tutelage before becoming the congregation's senior minister. After interviewing William F. Schulz, the Committee voted fourteen to three to ask him to be the candidate. Schulz accepted, but only as the senior minister rather than as minister-successor, an offer that was declined. Later it was passed on to Schulz by a member of the committee that Harrington had vetoed the invitation.[681] He had "a tight grip on everything," said a long-time congregation member.[682]

Harrington's domination of the Search Committee is akin to the control his nemesis, Stephen Fritchman, exercised over his own Board at First Unitarian Church of Los Angeles. Fritchman's "professional ego" had been hurt because of the attention Roy Ockert earned for his ardent support of BURR and his membership on BAC, as well as by Ockert's lack of appreciation for Fritchman's pioneering efforts. As Fritchman admitted, they were both stubborn. Fritchman insisted that the Board fire Roy Ockert, and it did.

Fritchman, Harrington, and the other major players in BAC, BUUC, FULLBAC, and BAWA were almost all male. Their attitudes and the organizations themselves manifested patriarchy replete with sexism, herculean efforts to control, uncompromising stances, and hyperbolic condemnations. It was men who took over the mikes at General Assembly, pushed one another out of the way, and used intimidation. Intoxicated by the nobleness of their cause, they carried on in the only way they knew how, using and perpetuating the value system of male domination.

At the Emergency Conference, one in five delegates was a woman. When the Commission on Religion and Race dissolved in November 1967, one of its eight members was female. Following the inaugural meeting of BUUC in February 1968, its Steering Committee included one woman. Coming out of the 1968 General Assembly in Cleveland, BAC had nine members: six were black, three were white, and all were male. Twelve officers and Board members of BAWA were elected at that General Assembly; four of them, including the secretary, were women. At the Cleveland GA, thirteen members of the FULLBAC Steering Committee were elected; only one was female.[683] At its second annual meeting, in February 1969, BUUC adopted a constitution that required two "sisters" be on BAC and two on the Nominating Committee. Prior to the 1969 GA, FULLBAC expanded its Steering Committee to twenty-six, of whom three were women, including the treasurer, Ann Raynolds. Decades later, in reviewing the list of BAWA Board members, Betty Seiden said she had forgotten how dominated by men it had been.[684]

These people were all, with two exceptions, volunteers. The demands on them were substantial. Women were making key organizational contributions, but most often in support roles: Betty Seiden as secretary for BAWA, Ann Raynolds and Bette Sikes for FULLBAC and FFR, and executive secretary Leona Light for SOBURR are just some examples.

These women worked for either a white support group or an integrated one. For black women supporting black groups, the situation was more complex and nuanced. Lillian Jenkins, an African American who attended BUUC's inaugural meeting as a representative of the Unitarian Universalist Women's Federation, said, "I think women should be generous to a fault in any circumstance where the oppressed and more or less disenfranchised attempt a worthwhile program.... It would give Blacks a chance to prove themselves in leadership roles."[685]

The gender imbalance between black women and men needs to be understood in context. In the face of racism, black women felt called to support black men. "There was a resistance to stepping up in front of our men or to compete for power," said Betty Reid Soskin.[686] Black women were in a difficult situation. They wanted to support black men and certainly not undercut them in front of whites, and yet they also wanted to be included in meaningful ways. Too frequently this did not happen. They were overlooked or taken for granted, as when Hayward Henry, in his address at the inaugural meeting of BUUC, mentioned that the Board member from the Laymen's League was there but failed to mention that a Board member of the UUWF was also in attendance.

Soskin's description of the victory party the women of BUUC prepared for the men following the triumph at the 1968 Cleveland General Assembly captured the predicament in which black women found themselves. The women waited and waited for the men, their companions and co-conspirators, to arrive, and they did not. "Our men had opted for the 'white' parties in other places in the hotel where the young white women they'd charmed during the week were waiting." She said that when they later confronted the men, the men "were petulant, defensive in the face of the brutal honesty of the women, and on an ego-centric high from their conquests.... it was a prelude to the many break-ups of relationships and marriages over the following decade."[687] At the second annual gathering of National BUUC, in February 1969, eight months after that painful victory party that the men had not bothered to attend, there was a workshop in which women expressed what was "bugging" them about their relationship to BUUC. They wanted to know: Who are we? What is our role in our family, in our community, and in BUUC? How can we best contribute to BUUC? Such dissatisfaction would spread.

By February 1971, when National BUUC met in Cleveland, dissatisfaction with its Steering Committee's leadership style led Greater Washington BUUC, which Hilda Mason chaired, to submit a five-page position paper. After praising BUUC's insistence that Unitarian Universalists "be liberal and stop being paternalistic," the paper warned that BUUC needed to avoid reducing "the role of the general membership to that of simply going on record in support of or opposition to a policy which is all but made," and said that it should be "receptive," "sensitive," "seeking consensus," a "cohesive force" "capable of working *with* the people." The implication was, of course, that this was not the current reality. The closest the paper came to calling BUUC's leadership patriarchal was when it said the organization could not "function effectively in a condition of oligarchy."[688] The message was clear and not new.

From BAC's beginning, there had been complaints about how BAC exercised power. Lillian Jenkins noted how, despite the diversity of opinion at the founding BUUC conference in Chicago, votes went the way the "movers of the caucus" wanted them to. Betty Reid Soskin spoke of "power plays," and Walter R. Jones did not like the "self-serving power politics." Such attention to control is emblematic of patriarchy. In April 1971, the Fellowship for Renewal linked its critique of sexism to that of racism. In its position paper, it avowed, "We challenge ourselves and our denomination to struggle with our involvement with the oppression of women." It recognized that "racism and sexism are the primary methods of social control," and that the repression of women circumscribes their right to self-determination. In addition, it said, "women carry the burden of restoring and sustaining men's self-image, which is repressed and restricted by the world outside the home."[689] This was exactly the situation that confronted black women and was, in a way that has been overlooked, a factor in the split that was to come.

. . .

IN FALL 1972, the UU Center City Church Conference met in Philadelphia. There were white and black delegates to the conference, and a few BAWA supporters alongside members of BUUC, BAC, and the FFR. By then, it was becoming evident that there were philosophical divisions within BUUC between those who wanted to continue within a Unitarian Universalist context and those who wanted to depart to form an independent organization.

In the 1970s communes were generally associated with hippies, but in Philadelphia a communal housing arrangement of black men, women, and children was formed. Some of those involved were members of BUUC and BAC. Richard Traylor was one of them. During the conference, Traylor invited several white allies to hear a presentation about their concept for this communal living arrangement. Jim Hobart, Jack Mendelsohn, George Sikes, who had all been faithful allies of the Black Caucus from the beginning, were among those invited.

In explaining how their extended family living arrangement worked, Traylor said that gender roles were clearly defined. At home, Hobart was experiencing major changes as he and his feminist wife re-negotiated their "traditional" family arrangements, so he asked Traylor, 'But suppose a woman in your community decides she does not accept solely gender-assigned roles? How does the community deal with that?' Traylor simply replied, "That is not an issue we face," and the conversation went in another direction.

The next morning, as people gathered before the conference program began, Hobart was standing near the bottom of a staircase next to Mwalimu Imara, now in his third year as senior minister of the Arlington Street Church. They were long-time allies, and so Hobart was startled when Imara turned to him and said in a loud and angry voice, "Man, what were you up to last night? What kind of trouble are you trying to cause? You have no right to question the way we live our lives."

The room fell silent as everyone turned their attention to the two of them. Hobart felt humiliated, ashamed, and speechless. Finally he offered a stumbling apology, adding that he had not meant to cause trouble. Without responding, Imara walked away. As Hobart stood there wrapped in silence and confusion, a black friend walked over to him and said, "Jim, this is not about you." Hobart found some comfort in those words but remained confused. Later, Mendelsohn pulled him aside and said, "I knew before the words were out of your mouth that you were in trouble. There are some questions that white people don't have the right to ask."

Later Hobart interpreted the encounter with Imara as theater meant for everyone there,[690] an act of intimidation, which is itself another sign of a patriarchal environment.

· · ·

IN THE LEAD UP to the climactic 1973 meeting in which BUUC changed its name to the Black Humanist Fellowship, Gwen Thomas first tried to negotiate creating BHF within BUUC. When a compromise could not be reached, she made an effort to move the meeting. This provoked a charge from BUUC national chair Harold

Wilson that she was trying to usurp his office. At the meeting, guards were stationed at the door who let only selected people enter. The series of events had all the markings of patriarchy: an unwillingness to compromise and a strategy to guarantee control backed up by intimidation.

There was a gender twist to the ensuing lawsuit as well. All the defendants were male: Richard Traylor, Harold Wilson, Mwalimu Imara, Jerry Jones, and Hayward Henry. Half of those who supported the BUUC plaintiff Ben Scott were women: Meredith Higgins and Hilda Mason from Washington D.C., Elizabeth Young from Cleveland, and Gwen Thomas from Denver. In fact, if we look at who moved into leadership in the years leading up to BHF splitting from BUUC, we see women stepping forward and trying to negotiate and ameliorate the situation with suggestions and non-confrontational language. In the face of male domination, it was to no avail, and after most of the men left the UUA these and other black women carried on.

Endings and Beginnings

A CONFESSIONAL TONE WAS SET by the black Unitarian Universalists who gathered at the First Unitarian Church of Los Angeles in August 1967 to form the group that became Black Unitarians for Radical Reform. They opened a space in which they could be honest about their pain, disappointment, and anger. When the group invited Stephen Fritchman into their circle, they talked about the slights they had endured from white members of this ultra-liberal congregation. Their anger poured forth. For them it was cathartic; for Fritchman it was enlightening, and he was thankful.

This confessional quality was also in evidence two months later, when many of the black participants in the Emergency Conference on the Unitarian Universalist Response to the Black Rebellion gathered in their own space to talk. Henry Hampton spoke of how transformative it was "just hearing other black people talking about themselves and about the turmoil and pain and isolation sometimes of being black." He said, "It was so much simpler and cheaper than therapy and, for me, it was church."[691]

It seems that this process of transformation quickly turned political. Strategizing superseded sharing, and ideology supplanted discovery. A patriarchal value system asserted itself. That value system prized control over compromise, domination over relationship, cooptation instead of cooperation, winning over persuading, and power over rather than the relational power that developes from building consensus.

Once an adversarial model was embraced, sharing and willingness to be vulnerable ended. Immediately after the 1968 General Assembly voted to give BAC $1 million, Dana Greeley, hoping to build on the enthusiasm, asked Dayton Yoder to arrange a small meeting with the BAC leadership to seek their cooperation in fundraising. Accounts of what happened at the beginning of that meeting vary, but each describes how the chairs were arranged and that BAC rearranged so that they faced one another as opposing parties. Greeley had assumed this was the beginning of a collaboration, but the way the chairs were repositioned said otherwise. Perhaps in the face of Greeley's paternalism there was no other way, but once the relationship devolved into power versus power, the tragedy that played out could not be avoided.

The conflict that embroiled the UUA between 1967 and 1976 marked a collision of worldviews and loyalties that left all sides feeling misunderstood and battered, victimized and betrayed. Everyone stood on principle. Caring deeply, they did what they felt called to do. Each claimed the moral high ground and over the years spun a narrative in which they defended the good cause and suffered for it. Having constructed a sense of integrity out of righteous hubris, the recitation of ancient justifications became the bulwark of their defense. Everyone saw themself as having defended principles while others betrayed them. Contrition was for the guilty, and they were not.

Integrationists felt they were being asked to repudiate their earlier struggle for civil rights and long-term commitment to equality for all. They were shocked to see pluralism cast aside and themselves called racists. It seemed there was no longer room to hold a different opinion, choose another path, and still be in fellowship.

Institutionalists felt they had staved off financial ruin and preserved the democratic process and the respect for pluralism that is fundamental to a covenantal faith, all while making the wrenching choices necessary to balance the moral imperative with institutional survival.

BAC and BUUC felt the time was now. Dr. King was dead. Cities were burning. No more waiting. But whites were unwilling to put justice first or to trust African Americans with power. The "familiar denominational racial routine" that had delivered little institutional change was the Unitarian Universalist version of forty acres and a mule, the empty promise made to the freed slaves.

The white allies in FULLBAC, SOBURR, and FFR were among those most committed to radical change in the UUA, yet because they tended to feel angry, impatient, and righteous, they were unsuited for the task of persuasion and conciliation that are fundamental to a covenantal faith. Their decisions and actions were ideologically, rather than spiritually, grounded. What enlivened them was the feeling that they were on the side of the oppressed. In responding to the imperative to make justice the preeminent value, they fell into seeing other UUs as either helpers and companions or obstacles and enemies. They pushed, and the harder they pushed the greater the resistance. Relationships could not bear it and shattered.

Standing outside the controversy, Gene Reeves, a UU minister and a white professor at historically black Wilberforce University, said, I had "both bigger and smaller fish to fry . . . and it was best for me to avoid what I felt was an ego-driven denominational squabble."[692] Ostensibly they were forwarding a cause, but it was done in a way that fed ego.

Hubris fuels tragedy; it does not lead to spiritual health.

African American Unitarian Universalists needed an expansion and deepening of the confessional space in which they could continue to process and heal from the ongoing experience of white racism they endured within and beyond their congregations. They needed a context in which to develop a religious language, liturgy, and ritual more consonant with their experience. They needed to channel their energies into creating something that spoke from and to the black experience, rather than perpetually having their own concerns diverted by the needs, desires, and fears of white folks. They also wanted power and that, to a degree, they acquired.

White Unitarian Universalists needed a place to bring white guilt over slavery, Jim Crow, the prejudice they had witnessed, inculcated, and acted upon; their fear of black people and black rage; and their anxiety about change and the end of Euro-American male dominance. They needed to be free to utter such thoughts without being shamed or having to defend their honor. Normally people turn to the church for help in coming to terms with their transgressions, but within Unitarian Universalism, there was no process for acknowledging the ways in which one had fallen short, and there were no spiritual or liturgical mechanisms to aid people in this quest. They could not bear to look at their privilege and come face-to-face with their shadow when Unitarian Universalism offered no resource to help move them toward atonement, self-acceptance, and reconciliation with others. The rage with which they accused others was the energy it took to deny their own feelings of pain and guilt.

In response to the upheaval, some Unitarian Universalists departed, never to return. Some remained but were never reconciled. Some simply carried on because that is what they were called to do, while others left and unexpectedly found their way back. The pain of a few was such that afterward they refused to discuss it. All of these responses are fine, and in the *Sturm und Drang* of life inevitable.

In January 1968, Jeff Campbell wrote in his congregation's newsletter that he questioned caucuses. He said that perhaps, "in the hurly burly of the great political protest, [caucuses are] essential. They may even play some political role, but never can this be the case in a fellowship. To me there can be no fellowship from which the religious quality is absent. Friendship and oneness in mind and spirit are the gifts of God. I can call them none other. To the extent that the Unitarian Universalist movement has attained fellowship, it is religious and not one whit beyond that."[693]

Power in the context of fellowship is held mutually, and the greater good is not fixed; instead, it emerges from the process of striving together toward justice. As a deeply relational undertaking, striving for the good requires trust. Without trust, power and resources are husbanded and defended rather than shared. An adversarial model, by definition, is not mutual and not efficacious in the context of religious community. The spiritual sanctuary to which people bring their longings (including for justice) and doubts, to which they come in search of relief from insecurity and pain, is a place for them to let down their guard. It welcomes all who have fallen short and are broken. And we all are. Some who remained in the bonds of fellowship were chastened by the events of the empowerment controversy and looked back with regret and acceptance. There were paths to reconciliation. Many did not or could not travel them, but some did.

In spring 1970, while the conflict was still at full throttle, Homer Jack was traveling through Europe and Asia. From Austria, where he was attending a conference on world peace, he wrote to Orloff Miller in Colorado Springs:

I am sorry, Orloff, about the differences that grew among us during the Black Power controversy. I say this as if the controversy is over, but from what I learn from the states, it is very much continuing and even more bitter than before. I use the past tense because, happily for me, I am at least out of it. Others can fight the battles. I tried and now others can take my place.... But I am sorry that deep differences grew between us. I hope this chapter can soon be forgotten, for we have much in common, quite apart from common experiences for several crucial years, and I want on my part to consider you a close friend—no matter what.[694]

Among the most important of the common experiences to which Jack was referring took place on Monday, March 8, 1965, when Dr. Martin Luther King Jr.'s telegram announcing a clergy march arrived at the Unitarian Universalist Association headquarters. Both Jack and Miller were then working for the UUA; they consulted together and then began calling ministers across the country. On Tuesday morning, Miller joined Jack in Selma, and after the march they went to Walker's Café. Jack left before Miller and turned left; Miller, accompanying Clark Olsen and James Reeb, turned right. Soon they were attacked by white racists and two days later, James Reeb died of his injuries.

Jack and Miller had been through too much together to let what was really a disagreement over strategy stand between them. They were reconciled, and their correspondence continued until Jack's death in 1993. When Jack was sick, Miller ended every letter he sent to him with "Courage, Jack."

"I lived through the period . . . as a young Unitarian Universalist," wrote Bill Sinkford. "I experienced my own family of origin divided as a result, and a deep sense of betrayal as my faith community 'withdrew from commitment to racial justice.'"[695] Sinkford left Unitarian Universalism and was churchless for over a decade.

When his mother became ill, he returned to Cincinnati with his young family. She died in 1984. A few days after her death, an old friend of his mother from his home congregation showed up on his doorstep with a casserole and stories of his mother that helped him begin to grieve. Before she left she said, "We want to be your church." And that was the beginning of his return to the First Unitarian Church of Cincinnati, where he had found Unitarian Universalism as an adolescent, and where, as a man, he began to reclaim his faith.

Steadfast, Ben Scott remained until the Black Affairs Council Investment Corporation (BIC) was dissolved and its assets distributed to the BAC bondholders but then, after moving to South Carolina, severed his ties to Unitarian Universalism.

Others never left, like Black and White Action members Betty Seiden, Glover Barnes, and John Cornethan, and Black Unitarian Universalist Caucus members Hilda Mason, Dalmas Taylor, Gwen Thomas, Joe and Pearl Samples, Winnifred Norman, and Norma Poinsett.

Poinsett said she remained not because she disagreed with those who left "but to continue addressing covert and overt racism within the UUA." She said she "literally came out of the kitchen" and, through BUUC, rediscovered her leadership ability. That led her to spend the next thirty years serving on the UUA Planning Committee, Commission on Appraisal, Board of Trustees, Racial Justice Curriculum Committee, and Black Concerns Working Group, and also on the boards of the UU Service Committee and Meadville Lombard Theological School. Of this work, she said, "I refuse to abandon it . . . because I believe the UUA is truly committed to the worth and dignity of all persons, strives for justice, equity and compassion in human affairs, encourages spiritual growth, and envisions a world community with peace, liberty and justice for all."[696] Alex, her husband, had walked away from the UUA, and eighteen years later, he returned to support her.[697]

UUA president Bob West was so traumatized by his experience in the role that after his term ended in 1977, he did not attend a General Assembly until 2003, and only set foot in 25 Beacon Street twice, attending the memorial service for a long-time staff member and having his picture taken with other presidents in preparation for the Association's fiftieth anniversary in 2011. Yet he, too, found a measure of reconciliation, as is made clear in this recollection by John Gibbons:

> In 2000, Bob West and I worked together to create a Massachusetts chapter of the Interfaith Alliance. At a time of increasing hate, Bob was passionately committed to encouraging civility, respect, and interfaith understanding. Meetings were often at our UU church in Bedford, and Bob noted that these were among the first times he'd been in a UU church in more than 20 years, since leaving the UUA presidency.
>
> When I was alone with Bob, he and I talked about the difficult years of his presidency. In particular, I recalled my participation in the emotional protest of the UUA Board decision to cut BAC funding. Then, in January of 1970, standing at the perimeter of the room, surrounding the Board, we BAC supporters angrily responded to the vote by tearfully and self-righteously singing, "Once to Every Man and Nation," culminating in a denunciation of "the faith they have denied." In the chaos afterward, I made my way to where Bob sat alone at the head of the Board table. Seething, in his face, spitting my words, I said to him, "I'm quitting your damn church!" and I turned and stomped out of the room.
>
> Recalling this tumult with Bob, in the Bedford church more than two decades later, I [said to] him that I now regret and am embarrassed by my long-ago words and actions. "You were treated

rudely and I was rude to you. You deserved better." Sincerely, my voice cracking and with tears in my eyes, I said, "I'm sorry."

He listened to me carefully, then said, "After all these years, I never thought I'd hear such words." And in a soft and wistful drawl, Bob said, "I thank you."

On at least two public occasions, I heard Bob speak of these traumatic events. Each time, in a quiet tone of surprise and gratitude, he said, "And, you know, one of the LRYers later apologized to me."[698]

. . .

THE LINES MOST OFTEN QUOTED from the African American abolitionist, Frederick Douglass, were delivered during a speech on August 3, 1857, in Canandaigua, New York, on the twenty-third anniversary of the "West India Emancipation":

> If there is no struggle there is no progress. Those who profess to favor freedom and yet deprecate agitation are men who want crops without plowing up the ground; they want rain without thunder and lightning. They want the ocean without the awful roar of its many waters.
>
> This struggle may be a moral one, or it may be a physical one, and it may be both moral and physical, but it must be a struggle. Power concedes nothing without a demand. It never did and it never will.[699]

The struggle that transpired within the UUA and the United States during the Civil Rights and Black Power eras was necessary. African Americans wanted and needed to acquire and exercise power. Addressing the issue of power in 1964 Bill Jones, African American UU minister, speaking several years before the split in the African American activist community spoke to the meaning of this shift:

No matter what segment of the Negro community you focus upon, the view is the same: force is necessary. The burning question among Negroes today is no longer force or no force, but *how much* and *what kind* of force. The alleged rift among civil rights leaders is not a conflict over the desirability or necessity of force but a difference of opinion as regards what types of force are legitimate and *effective* expressions of *non-violent* coercion.[700]

Broadly within the UUA there was little question that seeking justice was an imperative and the end was equal rights and opportunity. Broadly it was acknowledged that this would require black empowerment, the affirmation of Blackness, and an end to white racism. The disagreement was over strategy. In this struggle, the church had to hold in balance two responsibilities. Alongside justice-seeking, it was also called to serve as a spiritual and emotional resource for those engaged in that effort and for those who were not, to be not only a moral bellwether but a balm for the wounded and haven for the weary. The prophets were not embodiments of the pastoral, but the church itself had a duty to maintain this difficult balance. Holding these in equilibrium, while neither succumbing to righteous moralism nor sanctioning avoidance, was a challenge the UUA did not meet.

During 1966 and 1967, I was deeply involved in the First Unitarian Society of Chicago. In addition to being the president of its sixty-member Liberal Religious Youth group, I was the assistant janitor and Sunday morning office manager. That came to an end in late August 1967 when my father dropped me off at college. I would not be involved in Unitarian Universalism again until I entered Meadville Lombard Theological School in September 1974. My absence began when the planning for the Emergency Conference had just begun and continued through the formation of

BUUC, the assassination of Dr. Martin Luther King Jr., the UUA's $1 million commitment, and the Boston "Walkout" and did not end until the suit between Benjamin Scott and BUUC, Richard Traylor, and the Black Humanist Fellowship had been in court for a year and a half. I missed the turmoil that gripped the UUA but not the trauma that upended America nor later the repercussions of this tragedy that lingered on in Unitarian Universalism and lingers still.

After the black student rebellion hit my college campus, I flunked out and slunk back home to Chicago. Not knowing where to turn, I went to church. They were glad to see me, and very quickly, and not surprisingly, I was recruited to teach in the Sunday School kindergarten. Something happened there that made a disheartened nineteen-year-old drag himself to church every Sunday morning. The kids, and particularly a developmentally delayed African American boy named Dickie, thought I was great. I was broken but their unconditional regard began to restore my self-esteem. And six months later, I moved from Southside Chicago to the south end of Columbus, Ohio, off the Parson Avenue corridor where the smoke stack haze from the Buckeye Steel plant never lifted, to begin working with African American youth as a Volunteer in Service to America (VISTA).

I returned to church because it was my spiritual home. It was a place where I had been nurtured, and because I was nurtured I grew; having grown, I could give, and having given I grew more. It was a place where in pain I could go; where, having gone, I was cared for; where cared for, I could heal and go on. It was a place that was concerned with the world, and in showing me that I was connected to others taught me to care, and that caring demanded that I act.

So be it.

Notes

Introduction

1 "Tuesday—A Day of Decision," *UUA Now*, Newsletter Issue, July 28, 1969, p. 6.
2 Jack Mendelsohn, in Ronald M. Cordes, producer, *Wilderness Journey: The Struggle for Black Empowerment and Racial Justice within the UUA, 1967–1970* (Bedford Common Productions, 2003).
3 *Register-Leader*, Midsummer 1965, p. 19.
4 Until this time, the group was actually called the International Association for Liberal Christianity and Religious Freedom, a name it had adopted in 1932; it renamed itself the International Association for Religious Freedom at the 1969 conference. For simplicity, however, I use the latter name throughout.
5 "Boston Diary," *Inquirer*, August 23, 1969, p. 4.

Before and After Selma

6 Robert Hohler, collected by Jack Mendelsohn for use in Richard D. Leonard's *Call to Selma: Eighteen Days of Witness* (Boston: Skinner House, 2002).
7 *Report on Departmental Programs* (Unitarian Universalist Association, 1962). This forty-six-page booklet reviewed the work of the seven UUA departments. Nowhere in the sections on Extension, Adult Program, Ministry, or Education is race, culture, or gender mentioned. The section on Department of Service Projects, which would merge with the UU Service Committee in 1963, mentions "brotherhood in one world" as its mission.
8 Arthur Wilmot, letter to the Commission on Religion and Race, n.d., paraphrasing a local minister in Chico, CA (Andover-Harvard Theological Library [hereafter AHTL], Harvard Divinity School, Unitarian Universalist Association Board of Trustees [hereafter UUA Board Records], Special Commissions, Commission on Race and Religion Records, 1963–1968, bMS 1026/9, and Selma, Church Response, 1965–1966.

9 *Report of the Committee on Goals* (Unitarian Universalist Association, 1967), p. 45 (table 68), uua.org/sites/live-new.uua.org/files/documents/board trustees/6703_goals_report.pdf

10 *UUA Directory* (Boston: Unitarian Universalist Association, 1966), pp. 68–69.

11 Joan Singler, Jean Durning, Bettylou Valentine, and Maid Adams, *Seattle in Black and White: The Congress of Racial Equality and the Fight for Equal Opportunity* (Seattle: University of Washington Press, 2011), pp. 157, 161, 165.

12 Robert B. McKersie, *A Decisive Decade: An Insider's View of the Chicago Civil Rights Movement during the 1960s* (Carbondale: Southern Illinois University Press, 2013), p. 55.

13 *Register-Leader*, Midsummer 1965, p. 19.

14 "The Fulton Street Center: A Report to the Congregation of the First Unitarian Church of Brooklyn," November 1966 (Archive at First Unitarian Church of Brooklyn, NY, Fulton Street Center file).

15 *Anvil: Working Papers of the Center for Urban Ministry*, vol. 1, no. 1 (March 1966): pp. 7, 8 (University of Chicago Library, Special Collections Research Center, Neil Shadle Papers, box 6).

16 J. Ronald Engel, emails to Mark Morrison-Reed, September 1, 2013; October 1, 2013; February 13, 2014; September 13, 2016.

17 J. Ronald Engel, email to Mark Morrison-Reed, June 28, 2015.

18 Warren R. Ross, "Becoming Multicultural: How One Church Points the Way," *The World*, March–April 1993, p. 32.

19 William Dikeman, ed., *A History of the Unitarian Universalist Church of the Restoration at 175: Milestones and Landmarks* (Philadelphia: The First Unitarian Universalist Church in Mt. Airy, 1995), p. 42.

20 William G. Sinkford, "The Dream of White Innocence," sermon delivered at Unitarian Universalist Association General Assembly, Columbus, OH, June 23, 2016, uua.org/ga/program/highlights/slt

21 Martin Luther King Jr., "Don't Sleep through the Revolution," Ware Lecture delivered at the Unitarian Universalist Association General Assembly, Hollywood, Florida, May 18, 1966, in *Witnessing for the Truth: Martin Luther King, Jr., Unitarian Universalism, and Beacon Press* (Boston: Beacon, 2014), p. 19.

22 Ibid., p. 21.

23 Ibid., p. 27.

24 Ibid., p. 32.

25 Ibid., pp. 32, 36.

26 Richard S. Gilbert, email to Mark Morrison-Reed, June 9, 2015.

27 King, "Don't Sleep Through the Revolution," pp. 30–31.

28 Stephen H. Fritchman, "The Churches and Watts: A Report Seven Months Later," sermon preached at the First Unitarian Church of Los Angeles,

March 27, 1966, pp. 13–14 (Archive at First Unitarian Church of Los Angeles, Fritchman Files).

29. Farley W. Wheelwright, "The Unredeemed Legacy of Martin Luther King, Jr.," in *Twice-Told Tales: A Collection of 21 Sermons* (Laredo, TX: Shelfstealer, 2014), p. 22.
30. Martin Luther King Jr., *Where Do We Go from Here? Chaos or Community* (New York: Harper and Row, 1967), p. 9.
31. Wheelwright, "Unredeemed Legacy," p. 22.
32. *Report of the Committee on Goals*, pp. 28 (table 15), 29 (table 18), 39 (table 48).
33. J. Ronald Engel, email to Mark Morrison-Reed, June 12, 2015.
34. Julius Lester, *Look Out, Whitey! Black Power's Gon' Get Your Mama!* (New York: Grove, 1968), p. 97.
35. Martin Luther King Jr., *Where Do We Go, from Here?* pp. 30–31.
36. J. Ronald Engel, email to Mark Morrison-Reed, June 12, 2015.
37. McKersie, *A Decisive Decade*, p. 68.
38. "After Selma Committee," April 14, 1965, pp. 1–3 (UUA Board Records, 1961–1981 [hereafter UUA Board Records], bMS 1032/2 (8)).

The Emergency Conference on the UU Response to the Black Rebellion

39. Peter H. Samson, "If I Where a Negro" (Archive at West Shore Unitarian Universalist Church, Cleveland).
40. Stephen H. Fritchman, "Is There an Alternative to Black Power for the American Negro Today?" sermon preached at the First Unitarian Church of Los Angeles, August 7, 1966 (Archive at First Unitarian Church of Los Angeles, Fritchman Files); Donald S. Harrington, "What's the Matter with Black Power?" sermon preached at the Community Church of New York, October 3, 1966 (Community Church of New York, bound sermon books).
41. In 1968, the Community Church of New York reported a membership of 2,000 and the First Unitarian Church of Los Angeles reported membership of 953. *UUA Directory* (Boston: Unitarian Universalist Association, 1969).
42. Stephen H. Fritchman, *Heretic: A Partisan Autobiography* (Boston: Skinner House, 1977), pp. 121–123.
43. Ibid., pp. 312, 298.
44. Fritchman, "Is There an Alternative," p. 7.
45. Donald S. Harrington, "The White Problem," *Community News* (newsletter of Community Church of New York), November 17, 1946.
46. Donald Szantho Harrington, "Odyssey: I Sing a Life; Manhattan Ministry," speech delivered at the annual meeting of the Metropolitan New York Ministers' Association, Stamford, Connecticut, 2002, pp. 31, 21 (Meadville Lombard Theological School [hereafter MLTS], Sankofa Collection [hereafter

Sankofa Collection], Mark Morrison-Reed Papers [hereafter Morrison-Reed Papers]). Jack Greenberg, the general counsel of the NAACP, was also a member of Sigma Pi Phi.
47 Fritchman, "Is There an Alternative," p. 6.
48 Harrington, "What's the Matter with Black Power?" pp. 15, 17.
49 Fritchman, "Is There an Alternative," p. 8.
50 Ibid., p. 9.
51 Harrington, "What's the Matter with Black Power," pp. 17–18.
52 Fritchman, "Is There an Alternative," p. 11
53 Harrington, "What's the Matter with Black Power," pp 21–22, 18–19, 12.
54 Fritchman, "Is There an Alternative," p. 12.
55 Harrington, "What's the Matter with Black Power," p. 25.
56 Fritchman, "Is There an Alternative," p. 13.
57 Fritchman, "The Churches and Watts," p. 1.
58 Ibid., pp. 12, 16.
59 Frank James, "Martin Luther King Jr. in Chicago," *Chicago Tribune*, January 20, 2018, chicagotribune.com/news/nationworld/politics/chi-chicagodays-martinlutherking-story-story.html
60 "Thirty Arrested in Election Protest," *Troy (NY) Record*, November 9, 1966, p. 39.
61 McKersie, *A Decisive Decade*, p. 147.
62 Archive at First Unitarian Society of Albany, NY, Cardell file.
63 "Pool Pickets," *Rochester (NY) Democrat and Chronicle*, November 8, 1967, p. 2.
64 "SR at Sixth General Assembly," newsletter of the Department of Social Responsibility, Unitarian Universalist Association, June 1967, p. 1.
65 Leon Hopper and Max Gaebler, in Cordes, *Wilderness Journey*.
66 Fritchman, *Heretic*, p. 311.
67 Black Unitarians for Radical Reform, "The New Black Revolution" (Archive at First Unitarian Church of Los Angeles).
68 King, "Don't Sleep through the Revolution," p. 33.
69 Roy A. Ockert, "Conflict: Function and Dysfunction," sermon delivered at the First Unitarian Church of Los Angeles, October 1, 1967, pp. 1–6 (Archive at First Unitarian Church of Los Angeles).
70 *Report of the Committee on Goals*, p. 45 (table 67).
71 Ockert, "Conflict," p. 3.
72 Singler et al., *Seattle in Black and White*, p. 198. McKissick's undated comment was recorded by Jean Adams.
73 Ibid., p. 200.
74 Maura O'Brien, interview by Mark Morrison-Reed, September 20, 2014.
75 Singler et al., *Seattle in Black and White*, p. 201.

76 Ibid., pp. 202–203.
77 Ibid., p. 203.
78 "After Selma Committee," April 14, 1965, 1–3 (UUA Board Records).
79 Benjamin F. Scott, "Thoughts on the Occasion of the Tenth Anniversary of the Vote to Fund the Unitarian Universalist Black Affairs Council," First Unitarian Society, Chicago, June 11, 1978.
80 Whitney M. Young Jr., *Beyond Racism: Building an Open Society* (New York: McGraw Hill, 1969), p. 102.
81 Homer A. Jack, "A Letter to My Unitarian Universalist Colleagues on the Black Caucus," October 18, 1967, p. 1.
82 Jeffrey W. Campbell to Dana MacLean Greeley, March 26, 1968 (AHTL, Unitarian Universalist Association, Records of the Commission on Religion and Race, Records, 1968–1969 [hereafter Records of the Commission on Religion and Race], bMS 1148).
83 Jesse A. Reed, letter to Homer Jack, December 3, 1967 (Records of the Commission on Religion and Race, bMS 1148/4).
84 A conference roster appears in *Special Report: The Emergency Conference on the Unitarian Universalist Response to the Black Rebellion; Proceedings* (Boston: Department of Social Responsibility, Unitarian Universalist Association, 1967) that lists thirty-three "leaders." To arrive at 34, one needs to include the registrar, Susan Granger, who is listed among the conference staff. The list of participants numbers 140, but 1, Jack Kent, also appears on the leaders list.
85 The *Special Report*, ibid., says that five African Americans studying for the ministry were invited. However, only four appear: John Frasier Jr., Renford Gaines (later Mwalimu Imara), Thomas E. Payne, and Howard Traylor. Harold A. Wilson did not attend.
86 Ann Holmes Redding, "Here I Am, Lord," unpublished memoir, August 8, 2015.
87 Henry Hampton, "Last Exit to Grosse Point," *Respond*, Fall 1967 (UU Laymen's League).
88 Redding, "Here I Am, Lord."
89 *Special Report*, p. 2.
90 Ibid.
91 "UUA 1967—Goals Report and Survey," (MLTS, Archives and Special Collections, Jim D. Hunt Papers, MLTS.US.4006, box 1).
92 Redding, "Here I Am, Lord."
93 Scott, "Thoughts on the Occasion of the Tenth Anniversary."
94 Henry Hampton, interview by Carol Dornbrand, 1985 (Sankofa Collection, MLTS.US.5018).
95 Hampton interview.
96 Redding, "Here I Am, Lord."

97 Alex Poinsett in Alicia McNary Forsey, ed., *In Their Own Words: A Conversation with Participants in the Black Empowerment Movement within the Unitarian Universalist Association, January 20, 2001* (Berkeley: Starr King School for the Ministry, 2001), p. 50.
98 James Hobart, email to Mark Morrison-Reed, December 7, 2016.
99 Harrington, "Odyssey," p. 355.
100 Tony Perrino, "Random Ruminations," newsletter of the Unitarian Society of Schenectady, November 1967.
101 Roy Ockert, in Alicia McNary Forsey, ed., *In Their Own Words*, p. 15.
102 Jeanette Hopkins, in *Special Report*, p. 31.
103 Thaddeus B. Clark, "Black Power in Unitarianism," *St. Louis Unitarian* (newsletter of First Unitarian Church of St. Louis).
104 Jeanette Hopkins, in *Special Report*, p. 31.
105 David Parke, email to Mark Morrison-Reed, September 5, 2015.
106 James Hobart, email to Mark Morrison-Reed, December 7, 2016. The woman he describes was Barbara Jackson, from Syracuse, New York.
107 Only thirty people appear on the official list; Renford Gaines is omitted. Given the depth of his involvement in all subsequent BAC undertakings, this is most likely an oversight, so I use the number thirty-one.
108 Eugene Sparrow, letter to Homer Jack, October 20, 1967 (Records of the Commission on Religion and Race, bMS 1148/4).
109 Max Gaebler, letter to Joseph Fisher, October 12, 1967 (Records of the Commission on Religion and Race, bMS 1148/4).
110 Winnifred Norman, interviewed by Lisa Ward, February 5, 1991 (Sankofa Collection).
111 Scott, "Thoughts on the Occasion of the Tenth Anniversary," p. 2.
112 Ann Black, email to Sharon Dittmar, April 9, 2014.
113 Bette Sikes, email to Mark Morrison-Reed, January 23, 2018.
114 Wallace P. Rusterholtz, *The First Unitarian Society of Chicago: A Brief History* (Chicago: First Unitarian Society of Chicago, 1979), p. 21.
115 Homer A. Jack, "A few reactions to the Unitarian Universalist Black Caucus," February 19, 1968 (Records of the Commission on Religion and Race, bMS 1148/2 (1)).
116 Rusterholtz, *First Unitarian Society of Chicago*, p. 21.
117 Sikes email, January 23, 2018.
118 Sankofa Collection, George and Lee Reed file, box 4, folder 5, MLTS. US.5000.01.B4.
119 Peggy McIntosh, "White Privilege: Unpacking the Invisible Knapsack," 1989, nationalseedproject.org/white-privilege-unpacking-the-invisible-knapsack
120 Neil Shadle, email to Mark Morrison-Reed, December 14, 2016.

121 James Hobart, email to Mark Morrison-Reed, December 14, 2016.
122 Ernest Dunbar, "The Black Revolt Hits the White Campus," *LOOK Magazine* vol. 131, no. 22 (October 31, 1967), p. 27.
123 "'Black Power' Statement by National Committee of Negro Churchmen," *New York Times*, July 31, 1966.
124 Alongside white and integrated denominations, the National Council of Churches included the traditionally black denominations like African Methodist Episcopal, and denominations like the United Methodist that had black conferences.
125 Samuel Beecher, letter to Joseph Fisher, October 11, 1967 (Records of the Commission on Religion and Race, bMS 1148/4).
126 Dan Ackron, letter to Homer Jack, October 19, 1967 (Records of the Commission on Religion and Race, bMS 1148/7).
127 "Memorandum to Committee members, CMD Board and staff, From Robert Reed, Social Action Committee Chair, Subject: Initial report on the U.U.A. Black Power Conference held in New York City, October 6–8, 1967," October 25, 1967 (Sankofa Collection, Black Empowerment Collection [hereafter Black Empowerment Collection], Series IV, Selina Reed, box 3, folder 7, MLTS.US.5011-B3F7-001).
128 Kenneth B. Clark, "Racism for the UUA?" *Register-Leader*, May 1968, p. 12.
129 Selina E. Reed, letter to Homer Jack, November 3, 1967 (Records of the Commission on Religion and Race, bMS 1148/7, Set VI).
130 Commission on Religion and Race, "Agenda and Conference Proposal Summary," November 4 (Records of the Commission on Religion and Race, bMS 1148/4, Set V).
131 William R. Jones, "Black Power and Unitarianism: A Personal View," sermon delivered at All Souls Church, Unitarian, Washington DC, November 5, 1967 (Records of the Commission on Religion and Race, bMS 1148/4 (5)).
132 Jack Mendelsohn, "Black Power and the Liberal Church," sermon delivered at Arlington Street Church, Boston, November 5, 1967 (Morrison-Reed Papers).
133 Hayward Henry, "Report to the Black Caucus," 1968 (Black Empowerment Collection, Box 3, Folder 7, MLTS.US.5011).
134 Horace Westwood, "The Black Unitarians Search for Identity," sermon delivered to First Unitarian Church of Houston, November 26, 1967 (Records of the Commission on Religion and Race, bMS 1148/4 (5)).
135 Ibid.
136 In his doctoral thesis, "Unitarian Universalism and Black Empowerment in the United States: A Nationwide Survey of UU Attitudes toward Black

Power and Participation in Militant Civil Rights Activities" (Loyola University, 1974), Michael McCloskey writes that the second most influential factor in determining support for Black Power was age (p. 87). Of those under fifty years old, 62.6 percent gave it high support, while of those over fifty years old, 60.1 percent gave it low support (p. 77).

137 "A Statement from the Steering Committee of the Unitarian Universalist Black Caucus," November 13, 1967, in *Special Report*, p.11.
138 "Statement by Dr. Dana McLean Greeley, President, Unitarian Universalist Association," November 13, 1967, p. 10 (Records of the Commission on Religion and Race, bMS 1148/7, Set III).
139 Henry, "Report to the Black Caucus."
140 Robert Jones, letter to Homer Jack, November 17, 1967 (Records of the Commission on Religion and Race, Black Rebellion Conference, bMS 1148/2 (2)).

The Formation of the Black Unitarian Universalist Caucus

141 Homer A. Jack, "Repercussions from the Black Caucus," November 30, 1967 (Records of the Commission on Religion and Race, bMS 1148/4 (13)); Henry, "Report to the Black Caucus."
142 "Prudential Committee Acts on Black Caucus," *Spotlight* (Arlington Street Church newsletter), February 1968, p.1.
143 Betty Bobo Seiden, email to Mark Morrison-Reed, February 22, 2016. Charles Patterson, who had attended the Unitarian Church of Fort Wayne, Indiana, in the late forties and then the Cleveland Unitarian Society during the fifties before joining a congregation in San Francisco, directed the Oakland Economic Development Administration before becoming vice president of World Airways.
144 Leon Dash, "Splinter Movement Discussed: Negro Unitarians Probe Future," *Washington Post*, February 17, 1968, p. C5.
145 Dwight Brown and Philip Giles, "Memo: To all DEs, Re: Black Caucus," January 26, 1968 (Morrison-Reed Papers).
146 Homer A. Jack, letter to Leona Light, November 25, 1968 (Records of the Commission on Religion and Race, bMS 1148/2 (2)); Homer A. Jack, "Memorandum to Dwight Brown and Phil Giles, Re: your memo to 'all DEs' dated January 26," February 16, 1968 (Records of the Commission on Religion and Race, bMS 1148/4 (2)).
147 Jeffrey Campbell, "I Question Caucuses," *Amherst Unitarian* (newsletter of the Unitarian Society of Amherst, MA), vol. 15, no. 19 (January 17, 1968); Homer A. Jack, letter to Jeffrey Campbell, February 14, 1968 (Records of the Commission on Religion and Race, bMS 1148/4 (2)).
148 Susan Backer, email to Mark Morrison-Reed, March 7, 2017.

149 "Plan for a Unitarian Universalist Social Responsibility Office in Ottawa" (City of Ottawa Archives, First Unitarian Congregation of Ottawa, A 2010-1568 (75 D 86), box 8).
150 Joseph Samples, in Cordes, *Wilderness Journey*.
151 Ibid.
152 [Grant] Delbert Venerable II, "The Black Caucus: Racism or Not?" March 22, 1968 (First Unitarian Society of Chicago, Venerable Papers).
153 Benjamin Scott, "Report to the Congregation," *Spotlight* (newsletter of Arlington Street Church, Boston), March 1968 (Records of the Commission on Religion and Race, bMS 1148/2 (6)).
154 Hayward Henry, "National Caucus of Black Unitarian-Universalists" (AHTL, Unitarian Universalist Association, Black Empowerment Controversy, Records, 1968–1979 [hereafter Empowerment Controversy Records], bMs 531/5 (34)).
155 Hayward Henry, "The Caucus Story, National Conference of Black Unitarian Universalists, Chicago, IL, February 23, 1968," in *Caucus* (Black Unitarian Universalist Caucus, May 1968), pp. 4–7.
156 "Report on the Activities of the Commission on Religion and Race of the UUA, UUA General Assembly, May 9–16, 1964, San Francisco," p. 3 (MLTS, Richard S. Gilbert Papers [hereafter Gilbert Papers], Commission on Religion and Race).
157 The program included Dr. Kenneth Clark's book *The Negro Protest*, which contained interviews with Dr. Martin Luther King Jr., Malcolm X, and James Baldwin.
158 Hayward Henry, "The Caucus Story," op cit.
159 Ibid.
160 Ibid.
161 Ibid.
162 "The National Caucus of Black Unitarian Universalists: A Preliminary Report from a Non-Participant," February 29, 1968 (Records of the Commission on Religion and Race, bMS 1148.2). The report is anonymous, but the style seems like that of Homer Jack.
163 Joseph Samples, in Cordes, *Wilderness Journey*.
164 "National Caucus of Black Unitarian Universalists: A Preliminary Report."
165 Betty Seiden, in Cordes, *Wilderness Journey*.
166 Lillian W. Jenkins, memo to Unitarian Universalist Women's Federation Board, March 13, 1968 (Empowerment Controversy Records, bMS 531/5 (37)).
167 Betty L. Reid (Soskin), "A Letter from Home," in *Caucus* (Black Unitarian Universalist Caucus, 1968), pp. 18–19.
168 Scott, "Report to the Congregation."

169 "Problem Solving Session Group 8, Cultural Development," February 25, 1968.
170 Scott, "Report to the Congregation." The phrase was used by Hester Lewis, treasurer of the Greater Boston Black Caucus.
171 "The National Caucus of Black Unitarian Universalists."
172 Jenkins, memo to UUWF Board.
173 Venerable, "The Black Caucus: Racism or Not?"
174 Betty Reid Soskin, *Cbreaux Speaks* (blog), April 12, 2015, https://cbreaux.blogspot.com/
175 Betty Seiden, in Cordes, *Wilderness Journey*.
176 Richard Boeke, email to Mark Morrison-Reed, February 21, 2018.
177 Betty L. Reid (Soskin), "A Letter from Home."
178 Scott, "Report to the Congregation."
179 For example, Ben Scott and Lee Reed were as light-skinned as Jeffrey Campbell.
180 Jeffrey W. Campbell, letter to Dana MacLean Greeley, March 26, 1968 (Records of the Commission on Religion and Race, bMS 1148/4 (2)).
181 "The Feast of Absalom Jones/Black History Month," Episcopal Church, episcopalchurch.org/files/bi020815half.pdf
182 "A Black Schism," *Newsweek*, March 4, 1968, p. 90; Harold Schachern, "Priests Call Church 'Racist,'" *National Catholic Reporter*, April 24, 1968.
183 "National Caucus of Black Unitarian Universalists."
184 Grant Delbert Venerable II, email to Mark Morrison-Reed, January 27, 2017.
185 According to the 1967–1968 UUA Commission on Religion and Race Annual Report (Records of the Commission on Religion and Race), the contributions to the Freedom Fund were $19,286 in 1965–1966, $14,869 in 1966–1967, and $4,902 in 1967–1968 (until March 30).
186 Philip Giles, letter to Dana Greeley, March 25, 1968 (Records of the Commission on Religion and Race, bMS 1148/4 (2)).
187 Homer A. Jack, letter to Dana Greeley, March 29, 1968 (Records of the Commission on Religion and Race, bMS 1148/4 (2)).
188 David Parke and Jack Mendelsohn, in Cordes, *Wilderness Journey*.
189 McCloskey, "Unitarian Universalism and Black Empowerment," p. 87.
190 Included among the ninety-five initial sponsors are Robert Reed (the chair of the Central Midwest District Social Action Committee, which gave BAC $1,000 to finance the BUUC conference), Ron Engel and Neil Shadle, Jim Hobart and Kim Beach, Duke T. Gray and Donald McKinney, Victor Carpenter, Orloff Miller, David Weissbard (the chair of the Massachusetts Bay District Social Action Committee), Stephen Fritchman, Jack Mendelsohn, David Parke, Rudi Gelsey, and James Luther Adams.

191 James Luther Adams, letter to Homer Jack, March 15, 1968 (Records of the Commission on Religion and Race, bMS 1148).
192 Martin Luther King Jr., "I've Been to the Mountaintop," sermon delivered at Mason Temple, Memphis, April 3, 1968, https://en.wikipedia.org/wiki/I%27ve_Been_to_the_Mountaintop
193 Jack Mendelsohn, in Cordes, *Wilderness Journey*.
194 Robert Eller-Isaacs, "Are You Worth It?" sermon delivered at All Souls Church, Unitarian, Washington DC, 1998, pp. 5–6 (Eller-Isaacs Personal Papers).
195 Homer A. Jack, letter to Dana Greeley, April 15, 1968 (Records of the Commission on Religion and Race, bMS 1148/4).
196 W. E. B. Du Bois, "John Haynes Holmes, the Community Church and World Brotherhood," in *Dedication Book in Celebration of the New Building of the Community Church of New York, October 17, 1948* (New York, 1948), p. 36.
197 John Haynes Holmes, "The Minister's Corner," *Community News*, Community Church of New York, November 31, 1946.
198 David H. Cole (project administrator) and Iska Cole (assistant), *An Oral History of the Consolidation of the American Unitarian Association and the Universalist Church of America and the Creation of the Unitarian Universalist Association* (Unitarian Universalist Historical Society, 1997), p. 136.
199 Homer Jack, letter to Stephen Fritchman, as quoted in Charles W. Eddis, *Stephen Fritchman: The American Unitarians and Communism—A History with Documents* (Lulu.com, 2011), p. 94, and "Homer Jack Replies to Fritchman Complaint," October 23, 1953 (Unitarian Church of Evanston [IL], Eddis Papers, FULLBAC/Fritchman file).
200 Harrington, "Odyssey."
201 Donald S. Harrington, letter to Mark Morrison-Reed, March 1, 1982.
202 Donald McKinney, interview by Mark Morrison-Reed, March 3, 2015.
203 *Community News*, Community Church of New York, February 18, 1968, p. 3.
204 Donald S. Harrington, *Community News*, Community Church of New York, February 25, 1968, p. 2.
205 Harrington, "Odyssey."
206 Homer Jack to Donald S. Harrington, April 23, 1968; Donald S. Harrington to Homer A. Jack, April 26, 1968; Jack to Harrington, April 29, 1968; Harrington to Jack, April 30, 1968 (Records of the Commission on Religion and Race, bMS 1148/4 (2)).
207 Donald S. Harrington, letter to Mark Morrison-Reed, March 1, 1982.
208 Elizabeth Garvais, "Congregational Meeting of May 12, 1968," *Community News* (newsletter of Community Church of New York), May 19, 1968.
209 *BAWA Newsletter*, vol. 1, no. 5 (December 1969), p. 3.
210 Harrington, "Odyssey," pp. 32–33.

211 At its inception, BAWA was named Black and White Alternative, in clear reference to BAC. Its name was changed at the 1968 Cleveland GA.
212 Congregational discussion with Mark Morrison-Reed, Community Church of New York, NY, February 2015.
213 Stephen H. Fritchman, to "Members and Supporting Friends," July 12–15, 1968 (Archive at First Unitarian Church of Los Angeles).

The Cleveland General Assembly and Its Aftermath

214 Robert Zoerheide, "Black Power and the White Liberal," sermon delivered at Cedar Lane Unitarian Church, Bethesda, MD, March 3, 1968, p. 4 (Archive at Cedar Lane Unitarian Universalist Church).
215 John Wolfe, "Black Power Comes to Unitarianism," sermon delivered at All Souls Unitarian Church, Tulsa, OK, May 5, 1968 (Archive at All Souls Unitarian Church).
216 Dana McLean Greeley, letter to Ann Raynolds, May 13, 1968 (Records of the Commission on Religion and Race, bMS 1148).
217 Wade McCree, letter to Dana McLean Greeley, May 17, 1968 (Wayne State University, Walter P. Reuther Library of Labor and Urban Affairs, Wade H. McCree Jr., Papers, UUA: Board of Trustees—correspondence, box 44 (24)).
218 Al Weissbard, "From the President," newsletter of the First Unitarian Society of Albany, NY, May 1968.
219 The campaign goal remained the same, $300 thousand per year, but $50 thousand would be distributed to BAC as an advance by June 15, 1968.
220 Dana McLean Greeley, in "Program—Seventh Annual General Assembly, Unitarian Universalist Association, May 23–30, 1968, Cleveland, Ohio" (MLTS, Orloff Miller Papers, 1968 GA Program file).
221 Homer A. Jack, "Black Power Confronts Unitarian Universalists," *Christian Century*, June 26, 1969.
222 The resolutions were recorded in the UUA's General Assembly minutes as follows:

BE IT RESOLVED:

1. That the Unitarian Univeralist Association Board of Trustees and Administration recognize and finance a Black Affairs Council which will serve to suggest and implement programs to improve the conditions of black Unitarian Universalists and black people in America.
2. That the Black Affairs Council be accorded associate or affiliate membership status with the Association, similar to that now maintained by the Unitarian Universalist Women's Federation, the Laymen's League (Unitarian Universalist) and the Unitarian Universalist Service Committee, Inc.

3. That the Unitarian Universalist Association contribute annually for four years, for the support of the Black Affairs Council, a total of $250,000. This annual contribution should be made in the following manner:
  (1) $150,000 should be contributed to the Black Affairs Council no later than July 1, 1968.
  (2) The remaining $100,000 will be raised by the Unitarian Universalist Association with the cooperation of the Black Unitarian Universalist Caucus during the eight month period beginning July 1, 1968. In the event that the fund raising effort is unsatisfactory, the Unitarian Universalist Association would make up the deficit. This process will be continued throughout the four year period beginning July 1, 1968.

223 Glover Barnes, in Cordes, *Wilderness Journey*.
224 The eventual officers of BAWA were Glover Barnes and Rev. Max Gaebler as co-chairs, Betty Seiden as secretary, and Dore Schwab as treasurer.
225 Harry S. Nachman, letter to Dave N. Bortin, July 13, 1982, reporting on interview of Max Gaebler, (Empowerment Controversy Records, Commission on Appraisal papers, bMS 531).
226 David H. MacPherson, in *Kairos: An Independent Quarterly of Liberal Religion*, no. 12 (Autumn 1978).
227 "Stokes' Ware Lecture: Action beyond Power," *UUA Now*, supplement, June 1968, p. 6.
228 Hayward Henry, in Cordes, *Wilderness Journey*.
229 Norma Poinsett, in Cordes, *Wilderness Journey*.
230 Vincent Silliman to Elizabeth Silliman, May 27, 1968 (MLTS, Vincent Brown Silliman Papers, MLTS.US.2022).
231 Fritchman, *Heretic*, p. 321.
232 Miriam Barnes, in Cordes, *Wilderness Journey*.
233 Marcia McBroom, "A BAWA Identity Concept," *UUA Now*, supplement, June 1968, p. 7.
234 "BAC to Get $1 Million," *UUA Now*, supplement, June 1968, p. 1.
235 Robert Nelson West, *Crisis and Change: My Years as President of the Unitarian Universalist Association, 1969–1977* (Boston: Skinner House, 2007), pp. 15–16.
236 This is a summation of Ronald Cordes's review of the 1968 UUA General Assembly financial reports, which he did in preparing *Wilderness Journey*. Ron Cordes, interview by Mark Morrison-Reed.
237 "BAC to Get $1 Million," p. 1.
238 Gordon Gibson, in Cordes, *Wilderness Journey*.
239 Albin A. Gorisek, "Unitarians Put OK on Negro Council," *Cleveland Plain Dealer*, May 27, 1968, p. 11.

240 Walter Donald Kring, "Is There a Phoenix among Unitarian Universalist Ashes?," sermon delivered at Unitarian Church of All Souls, New York City, June 16, 1968; Jack Hume, "Unitarians Told Black Council Violates Its Constitution," *Cleveland Press*, May 27, 1968, p. G5.
241 Weissbard, "From the President," June 1968.
242 Betty Reid Soskin, *Cbreaux Speaks* (blog), April 12, 2015, https://cbreaux.blogspot.com/
243 Jack, "Black Power Confronts Unitarian Universalists."
244 "BAC to Get $1 Million," p. 2.
245 Kring, "Is There a Phoenix among Unitarian Universalist Ashes?" p. 3.
246 Del Tweedie, "Recollections around the 1969 UUA General Assembly" (Morrison-Reed Papers, Main Line Unitarian Church File).
247 Ralph Helverson, diary, June 10, 1968 (AHTL, Ralph Norman Helverson Papers, bMS 601/5 (6) [hereafter Helverson Papers]).
248 Homer A. Jack, "The Role of the Division of Social Responsibility and Race Relations after the Cleveland General Assembly," June 13, 1968 (Records of the Commission on Religion and Race, bMS 1148).
249 "Amendments to the Constitution and By-Laws," Minutes of the Seventh General Assembly, pp. 4–6 (Unitarian Universalist Association).
250 Max Gaebler, to "Friends (of BAWA)," August 1968 (MLTS, BAWA file, David H. MacPherson Papers [hereafter MacPherson Papers], MLTS. US.2056).
251 Dana McLean Greeley, letter to Donald S. Harrington, July 16, 1968.
252 Walter Donald Kring, *Safely Onward*, vol. 3 of *The History of the Unitarian Church of All Souls, New York City*, 1882–1978 (New York: Unitarian Church of All Souls, 1991), p. 163.
253 BAC's officers were James Clark, chair; Jack Mendelsohn, vice-chair; Richard Traylor, secretary; Benjamin Scott, treasurer; and Samuel Beecher, Louis Gothard, Hayward Henry Jr., Chester Lewis, and Roy Ockert, with Althea Alexander and Barbara Jackson as alternates.
254 "Black Empowerment in the UUA: A Progress Report," prepared by David B. Parke in consultation with Mason F. McGuinness and Richard Traylor, October 15, 1968 (Records of the Commission on Religion and Race, bMS 1148/2 (3)).
255 Richard L. Traylor, "Secretary's Report on the Developing Program of the Black Affairs Council" (Morrison-Reed Papers).
256 Minutes of the Task Force on the Black Affairs Council, November 4 and 25, 1968 (Records of the Commission on Religion and Race, bMS 1148/4).
257 Traylor, "Secretary's Report."
258 H. J. Muller, to "Fellow Members," July 12, 1968 (Archive at First Unitarian Church of Los Angeles).

259 Stephen H. Fritchman, to "Members and Supporting Friends," July 12–15, 1968 (Archive at First Unitarian Church of Los Angeles).
260 Commission on Appraisal, *Empowerment: One Denomination's Quest for Racial Justice, 1967–1982* (Unitarian Universalist Association, 1984), pp. 112–14.
261 Gordon D. Gibson, email to Mark Morrison-Reed, January 2012.
262 "Dayton T. Yoder," in "The Black Rebellion and the UUA: What Happened at Cleveland?" *Kairos*, no. 12 (Autumn 1978), p. 7.
263 Minutes of the Task Force on the Black Affairs Council.
264 Al Weissbard, "From the President," June 1968.
265 Paul Carnes, quoted in "Dayton T. Yoder."
266 Minutes of Task Force II on White Racism, December 12, 1968 (Records of the Commission on Religion and Race, bMS 1148/4).
267 Homer A. Jack, memo to Division Advisory Committee, "Re: Black/White Relations in the Denomination since Cleveland," November 6, 1968 (Records of the Commission on Religion and Race, bMS 1148).
268 Hayward Henry, letter to Homer A. Jack, October 30, 1968 (Records of the Commission on Religion and Race, bMS 1148).
269 Minutes of Task Force on the Black Affairs Council, November 25, 1968 (Records of the Commission on Religion and Race, bMs 1148).
270 Donald S. Harrington, "Is Integration Dead?" sermon delivered at Community Church of New York, October 20, 1968 (Archive at Community Church of New York).
271 Harold Wilson, in Forsey, *In Their Own Words*.
272 Minutes of the Unitarian Universalist Association Board, November 9–10, 1968 (Unitarian Universalist Association).
273 "M-REIT," *Register-Leader*, May 1968, p. 41. The UUA legal counsel said that the Board could not buy shares in M-REIT as an investment but could use unrestricted funds and purchase them as an "asset."
274 Bob Cromie, "Deerfield Builder Still Active" (archives.chicagotribune.com/1969/12/04/page/31/article/bob-cromie). George W. Reed Jr., a member of the First Unitarian Society of Chicago, was on the Board of the Progressive Development Corporation that was behind the housing project.
275 Dana MacLean Greeley to Robert J. Small, June 22, 1968 (AHTL).
276 Richard Traylor, "1968–1969 Report of the Black Affairs Council," February 1969 (Gilbert Papers).
277 Lillian Jenkins to Connie Burgess, "Report from BUUC Meeting, Detroit, 2/14/69–2/16/69," March 7, 1969 (Empowerment Controversy Records, bMS 531/5 (37)).

Prelude to Controversy

278 Robert Reed, "Racism's Darker Ways: Toward a Deeper Understanding of Racism," sermon delivered at First Unitarian Church of Louisville, March 25, 1969 (MLTS, Robert Reed Papers, MLTS.US.2026).

279 Homer A. Jack, "The 'Non-Violent Act of Witness and Conscience' of Robert Hohler," April 7, 1969 (Empowerment Controversy Records, bMS 531/6).

280 Homer A. Jack, letter to Bob Hohler, April 5, 1969 (Empowerment Controversy Records, bMS 531/6).

281 "Hohler Calls for Immediate Moral Audit," *UUA Now*, April 28, 1969, p. 1.

282 Cornelius McDougald, Donald Gutstein, and Donald S. Harrington, "Racial Policies of the Community Church," Community Church of New York, November 20, 1969, p. 3 (Gilbert Papers).

283 David C. Pohl, "UUA General Assembly in Cleveland," First Unitarian Congregation of Ottawa newsletter, May 1969 (City of Ottawa Archives, A 2010-1569 (75 D 86), Box 9).

284 Cole, *An Oral History of the Consolidation*, pp. 99–100.

285 Paul H. Beattie, "The UUA *Still* in Crisis," sermon delivered at All Souls Unitarian Church, Indianapolis, March 9, 1969, pp. 3–5 (Morrison-Reed Papers).

286 Dorothy Spoerl, "Poor Return on Board Surveys," *UUA Now*, June 19, 1969, p. 7.

287 Homer A. Jack, "Like It Was," International Affairs Workshop, Star Island, New Hampshire, August 4, 1969, in *Respond*, vol. 4, no. 1 (September 1969), pp. 6–8.

288 It was called the Continental Study Conference on the Religious Imperative of Unitarian Universalist Social Action.

289 Mary Lu MacDonald, "Periscope on Punderson Lake," *UUA Now*, June 19, 1969, p. 18.

290 Larry Ladd, "The Youth Agenda (1969)," in Dan McKanan et al., eds., *A Documentary History of Unitarian Universalism, Volume II: From 1900 to the Present* (Boston: Skinner House, 2017), pp. 295–297.

291 Wayne Arnason, email to Mark Morrison-Reed, May 13, 2017.

292 George K. Beach, "Some Personal Reflections," *CUUP Newsletter*, vol. 2, no. 6 (May 1969).

293 David Parke, memo to FULLBAC Steering Committee, "Re: Concerns of 18 April Meeting in Boston," April 16, 1969 (Unitarian Universalist Association, FULLBAC Records, 1967–1971, bMs1146 box 3).

294 "Statement from the Black Caucus, Continental Study Conference on the Religious Imperative of Unitarian Universalist Social Action, Newbury, Ohio, May 10, 1969" (Richard Kellaway Papers).
295 The signatories to the statement were Marsh Agobert, John Young, Ed Lee, Harold Wilson, Ann Redding, Thomas Payne, Thomas Haley, and George Johnson.
296 Mary MacColl, "The Politics of Revolution, or How FULLBAC'ers Got Shafted," Delaware Valley FULLBAC, April 1969 (Unitarian Universalist Association, FULLBAC Records, 1967–1971, Box 3).
297 Nathan Wright, *Black Power and Urban Unrest* (New York: Hawthorne Books, 1967), pp. 147–149.
298 Beach, "Personal Reflections."
299 MacDonald, "Periscope on Punderson Lake," p. 18.
300 David H. MacPherson, "To Friends," May 7, 1969 (MacPherson Papers).
301 Parke memo to FULLBAC Steering Committee. The quotation from Larry Ladd's letter of April 4 is part of the memo.
302 George Dulury, Gertrude Entemann, Walter Royal Jones, David Hicks MacPherson, Howard Waterhouse, "To All UU Societies," May 16, 1969 (MLTS, MacPherson Papers).
303 "UUSC Occupied in Protest," *UUA Now*, supplement, June 19, 1969, pp. 1, 7.
304 Betty Seiden, letter to Richard S. Gilbert (Empowerment Controversy Records, bMS 531/6 (33)), quoted in Commission on Appraisal, *Empowerment*, pp. 76–78. The papers amassed during this study are held in this collection.
305 *The Uniter* (newsletter of the Unitarian Universalist Church of Urbana-Champaign, IL), July 1969.
306 Rhys Williams, "A Journal of a Trial by Fire, and of Subsequent Dialogs with 'The Fellowship for Renewal' and 'The People's Development Group,' March 29, 1968, through April 14, 1970," p. 8.4, cited in Linda Simmons, "The Burning of First Church and the Congregation: When Rebuilding Is More Than Bricks and Mortar" (Congregational History Project, Harvard Divinity School), December 15, 2010. I have drawn extensively from the work of Linda Simmons.
307 Jack Mendelsohn, letter to Rhys Williams, October 18, 1968 (AHTL, Rhys Williams Papers, 1951–2003 [hereafter Williams Papers], bMS 178/2 (21)), cited in Simmons, "The Burning of First Church and the Congregation," ibid.
308 Jack Mendelsohn, letter to Theodore Jones, October 7, 1960, cited in Simmons, "The Burning of First Church and the Congregation," ibid.

309 Duke Gray, letter to Rhys Williams, February 20, 1969 (Williams Papers, bMS 178/2 (23)).
310 Simmons, "The Burning of First Church and the Congregation."
311 G. Robert Hohler, letter to Aron Gilmartin, July 22, 1968 (Empowerment Controversy Records, bMS 531/6).
312 G. Robert Hohler, address delivered to Arlington Street Church, Boston, MA, September 22, 1968 (Empowerment Controversy Records, ibid.).
313 Duke T. Gray, to "All the Delegates to the Boston General Assembly of the Unitarian Universalist Association," July 10, 1969 (AHTL, General Assembly Administrative Subject Files, Presidential Campaign Records 1969 [hereafter Presidential Campaign, 1969], FULLBAC, bMS 1397/1).
314 Alma L. Howard, *Reflective Light: The 75-Year Story of the University Unitarian Church of Seattle, 1913–1988* (Seattle: University Unitarian Church, 1988), p. 14.
315 *UUA Now*, June 19, 1969, p. 13.
316 Ralph N. Helverson, letter to UUA Board Members, June 26, 1969 (AHTL, Records of First Parish in Cambridge [MA], bMS 604/2).
317 Richard Nash, letter to FULLBAC Steering Committee, ca. May 30, 1969 (Presidential Campaign 1969, General, bMS 1397/1).
318 Frederick May Elliot, "Our Chief Glory as Unitarians," in Alfred P. Stiernotte, ed., *Frederick May Elliot: An Anthology* (Boston: Beacon Press, 1959), p. 32.
319 Walter Royal Jones to Aron Gilmartin (Presidential Campaign 1969, Gilmartin, bMs 1396-1).
320 Ibid.
321 Rudi Gelsey to Aron Gilmartin, June 21, 1969 (Presidential Campaign 1969, Gilmartin, bMS 1397/1).

Boston General Assembly

322 "Reporter's Notebook," *Inquirer*, August 2, 1969.
323 Grant Delbert Venerable II, email to Mark Morrison-Reed, September 25, 2016.
324 Tweedie, "Recollections."
325 Alan Rosenthal, interview by Mark Morrison-Reed, September 10, 2015.
326 "Boston Diary," *Inquirer*, August 23, 1969, p. 4.
327 John Cummins, interview by Mark Morrison-Reed, October 10, 2014.
328 Dana MacLean Greeley, welcoming address, UUA General Assembly, 1969, p. 5 (AHTL, bMS 1030/3).
329 Fritchman, *Heretic*, p. 321.
330 Tweedie, "Recollections."
331 John Gibbons, email to Mark Morrison-Reed, May 10, 2015.

332 Fritchman, *Heretic*, p. 322.
333 Jules Ramey, "Boston Unitarian Universalist Assembly Delegate Reports," August 10, 1969, pp. 10–10a (Archive at First Unitarian Church of Los Angeles).
334 Tweedie, "Recollections."
335 Fritchman, *Heretic*, 322.
336 Nina Grey, email to Mark Morrison-Reed, March 14, 2015.
337 Jeremy Taylor, "What Was the Fight All About?" *Respond: What Happened in Boston*, 1969 (Empowerment Controversy Records, bMS 531/7 (27)).
338 Til Evans, "Boston Unitarian Universalist Assembly Delegate Reports," August 10, 1969, p. 12 (Archive at First Unitarian Church of Los Angeles).
339 Ramey, "Boston Unitarian Universalist Assembly Delegate Reports," p. 9.
340 Ann Maupin, in "Boston Unitarian Universalist Assembly Delegate Reports," p. 2.
341 "Tuesday—A Day of Decision," *UUA Now*, July 28, 1969, p. 6.
342 Ibid.
343 Forsey, *In Their Own Words*, p. 30.
344 Fritchman, *Heretic*, p. 323.
345 "Tuesday—A Day of Decision."
346 Fritchman, *Heretic*, p. 324.
347 Richard Kellaway, interview by Mark Morrison-Reed, July 22, 2015.
348 Victor Carpenter, interview by Mark Morrison-Reed, July 22, 2015.
349 Nina Grey, email to Mark Morrison-Reed, March 17, 2015.
350 Rudi Gelsey, in Cordes, *Wilderness Journey*.
351 Gordon Gibson, in Cordes, *Wilderness Journey*.
352 Wayne Arnason, email to Mark Morrison-Reed, December 8, 2016.
353 Larry Ladd, "Youth: '. . . but the children wept,'" *UUA Now*, September 26, 1969, p. 19.
354 Marsh Agobert, email to Mark Morrison-Reed, August 12, 2015.
355 W. Edward Harris, email to Mark Morrison-Reed, June 30, 2008.
356 Alan Deale, email to Mark Morrison-Reed, April 21, 1915.
357 Alan Rosenthal, interview by Mark Morrison-Reed, September 10, 2015.
358 Jack, "Like It Was."
359 Ibid.
360 Betty Seiden, in Cordes, *Wilderness Journey*.
361 Rob Eller-Isaacs, in Cordes, *Wilderness Journey*.
362 John Gibbons, email to Mark Morrison-Reed, May 10, 2015.
363 The estimates on how many walked out range from 150, in "Tuesday—A Day of Decision," to more than 200 according to Louis Garinger in the *Christian Science Monitor*, July 17, 1969, to 400+ according to Victor Carpenter in *Long Challenge: The Empowerment Controversy, 1967–1977* (Chicago:

Meadville Lombard Theological School, 2003), p. 52. Several others say 300. In addition to those who joined the first walkout, others joined the protestors at Arlington Street Church later, and not all of those who walked out were delegates.
364 "Tuesday—A day of Decision."
365 Glover Barnes, in Cordes, *Wilderness Journey*.
366 Betty Seiden, "Lest We Forget," newsletter of the First Unitarian Church of Berkeley, CA, April 1970.
367 The group was made up of Dana Greeley; Joseph Fisher, the moderator; Homer Jack; Jack Kent and Jeffrey Campbell, the originators of the motion; Phillip Hewett for the Program Committee; Chris Raible, representing Robert West; and David Weissbard, representing Deane Starr.
368 Mtangulizi Sanyika (formerly Hayward Henry), Starr King School for the Ministry President's Lecture at General Assembly, 2003, reported by Dan Harper, edited by Lisa Presley, uua.org/ga/past/2003/169491.shtml
369 "Tuesday—A Day of Decision."
370 Commission on Appraisal, *Empowerment*, pp. 130–131.
371 Leon Hopper, email to Mark Morrison-Reed, March 2015. In the summer of 1965, Hopper spent two weeks in Selma as part of the UUA's "Selma Witness."
372 "Tuesday—A Day of Decision."
373 Ibid., p. 7.
374 Rob Eller-Isaacs, in Cordes, *Wilderness Journey*.
375 Holley Ulbrich, *The Fellowship Movement: A Growth Strategy and Its Legacy* (Boston: Skinner House, 2008), p. 42.
376 "The Church and the Black Community," *UUA Now*, July 28, 1969, p. 27.
377 Ockert, "Conflict."
378 David Weissbard, email to Mark Morrison-Reed, March 23, 2015.
379 Fritchman, *Heretic*, p. 325.
380 Louis Garinger, "Unitarian Universalist Split Avoided over Funds-for-Blacks Controversy," *Christian Science Monitor*, July 18, 1969.
381 Seiden, "Lest We Forget," p. 4.
382 Hayward Henry, "BAC: '... greatly disturbed,'" *UUA Now*, September 26, 1969, p. 13. Election results are reported in "List of BUUC Nominees for UUA Offices" (AHTL, UUA General Assembly 1969, bMS 1030/3), although Edna Griffin and Cornelius McDougald (honorary chair of BAWA) were not included on BUUC's list.
383 Michael Schofield, "An Encounter with Change," *UUA Now*, September 26, 1969, p. 8.
384 Henry, "BAC: '... greatly disturbed,'" p. 13.
385 Jack, "Like It Was," pp. 2–3.

386 "FFR Programming," *UUA Now*, September 17, 1969, p. 2.
387 *On Renewal* (newsletter of the Fellowship for Renewal), November 1969 (MLTS, John Gibbons Black Empowerment Papers [hereafter Gibbons Papers]).
388 *On Renewal*, December 1969 (Gibbons Papers).
389 Simmons, "The Burning of First Church," p. 19.
390 MacDonald, "Periscope on Punderson Lake," p. 18
391 Connie Burgess, "UUWF: '... a more *radical* role," *UUA Now*, September 26, 1969, p. 18.
392 "Blacks Demand Purse Strings," *Boston Globe*, July 15, 1969.
393 Til Evans, "Boston Unitarian Universalist Assembly Delegate Reports" (Morrison-Reed Papers).
394 Ralph Stutzman, email to Mark Morrison-Reed, September 10, 2014; David Weissbard, email to Mark Morrison-Reed, March 23, 2015; Stutzman and Weissbard email to Mark Morrison-Reed, June 4, 2017.
395 Ralph Stutzman, email to Mark Morrison-Reed, September 10, 2014.
396 Jules Ramey, "Boston Unitarian Universalist Assembly Delegate Reports," pp. 6, 10a (Morrison-Reed Papers).
397 A. Phillip Hewett, "Tearing Down the Temple," sermon delivered at First Unitarian Church of Vancouver, October 2 and 5, 1969 (Morrison-Reed Papers).
398 John Gibbons, email to Mark Morrison-Reed, May 10, 2015.
399 Ladd, Youth: '... but the children wept.'"
400 "Apollo Mission—Dr. Reed One of 142 Principle Researchers," *Chicago Defender*, July 23, 1969, p. 1.
401 Russell E. Miller, *The Larger Hope: The Second Century of the Universalist Church in America, 1870–1970* (Boston: Unitarian Universalist Association, 1985), pp. 119–20. A. J. Canfield of St. Paul's Universalist Church was on the World Parliament's Planning Committee, and Universalist Augusta J. Chapin chaired the Women's Committee.
402 In 1928, the British and Foreign Unitarian Association merged with a wider, more ecumenical group of churches and became the General Assembly of Unitarian and Free Christian Churches.
403 A. Phillip Hewett, email to Kathleen Parker, June 1, 2010.
404 Jack, "Like It Was," p. 5.
405 General Assembly of Unitarian and Free Christian Churches, *Annual Report 1969* (London), 1969, p. 18.
406 Max A. Kapp, "Overseas Relations: 'Toward a new isolationism,'" *UUA Now*, September 26, 1969, p. 16.
407 Jack, "Like It Was," 6.
408 Kapp, "Overseas Relations."

409 Hewett, email to Kathleen Parker, June 1, 2010.
410 Michael Scholefield, "CUC Defeats Separatist Resolution," *UUA Now*, June 19, 1969, p. 2.
411 Hayward Henry Jr. was the fifth Workman Lecturer. The lecture held annually by the First Unitarian Congregation of Toronto began in 1965 with an address by Dr. Linus Pauling, and in the second year, Dr. Ashley Montague spoke. The lecture was named after the nineteenth-century founding members Joseph and Samuel Workman and their brother, Benjamin.
412 "That the CUC Board present a full report to the UUA Board of Canadian dissatisfaction with UUA along with a request for higher priority in budget allocation to permit the CUC to do more effectively those services which they agree are suitable to be handled by the CUC for Canadians." From "Delegates Reject Separation But Ask That Canadian Grievances be Aired with UUA," *Canadian Unitarian*, Toronto, Summer 1969, Vol. 11 No. 3, p. 2.
413 Phillip Hewett, *Unitarians in Canada*, 2nd ed. (Toronto: Canadian Unitarian Council, 1985), p. 271.
414 "Musings," A Phillip Hewett, *Canadian Unitarian*, Winter 1969, p. 5.
415 Dana McLean Greeley, *25 Beacon Street and Other Recollections* (Boston: Beacon, 1971), 103.
416 John May, "Encounter with Change," *Canadian Unitarian*, Toronto, Autumn 1969, p. 1.
417 A. Phillip Hewett, "Musings," *Canadian Unitarian*, Toronto, vol. 12, no. 2, Winter 1969, p. 5.

The Black Affairs Council Disaffiliates from the UUA

418 "Since consolidation the total Annual Fund increase has been only $377,000 of which roughly $150,000 to $170,000 had come from special gifts. The giving level has increased only by about $200,000 or an average of $40,000 a year. Over five years of giving from member societies has not produced sufficient income to support additional expenses for districts." From the Minutes of the Unitarian Universalist Association Board of Trustees, November 10–12, 1967 (UUA Board Records).
419 Cole, *An Oral History of the Consolidation*, p. 22.
420 "Church Financing Poses Major Problem," *UUA Now*, December 24, 1969, p. 5.
421 "Assembly Lines—Training for the Ministry," *Inquirer*, June 29, 1968, p. 6.
422 Cole, *An Oral History of the Consolidation*, p. 20.
423 These are the figures that Robert West used in his *Crisis and Change* and in Cordes's film *Wilderness Journey*; the figure $2.6 million appears in the

November 3, 1969, *Fitchburg* (MA) *Sentinel*, as well. However, in the December 24, 1969, edition of *UUA Now*, the figures $2,841,897 and $1,871,000 appear on a front-page article entitled "West Gets Board-Backed Reorganization Underway." A March 19, 1970, article in the *Christian Science Monitor* uses the figures $2.8 million and $1.8 million. I have no explanation for the difference.

424 Leon Hopper, email to Mark Morrison-Reed, March 2015.
425 West, *Crisis and Change*, 12.
426 Dayton T. Yoder, "Report on Annual Fund, UUA General Assembly," 1969 (AHTL, bMS 1030/3).
427 West, *Crisis and Change*, pp. 56–57.
428 "An Interview with Robert West," *First Chicago News*, January 11, 1970 (Empowerment Controversy Records, bMS 531/8 (36)).
429 West, *Crisis and Change*, p. 19. West is mistaken; the Annual Fund met its goal in 1968.
430 "West Gets Board-Backed Reorganization Underway."
431 "An Interview with Robert West."
432 Ibid.
433 "First Church 'Delays' Payments to UUA Pending Study of Black Affairs Cut," *First Chicago News*, January 11, 1970 (Empowerment Controversy Records, bMS 531/8 (36)).
434 "The Southeast District of the UUA, December, 10, 1969—Notice of Annual Meeting" (Archive at Unitarian Universalist Fellowship of Athens, Georgia).
435 Michael Scholefield, "UUA Board of Trustees Wrestles with Dollar Dilemma," *Unitarian Universalist World*, vol. 1, no. 1 (March 1, 1970), p. 1.
436 Larry Ladd, "Report on the UUA Board Meeting held January 24–25, 1970, to the Commission on Appraisal," pp. 1–2 (Ladd Papers).
437 John Smith, "A Bad Trip," distributed at the First Unitarian Society of Chicago and reprinted by the Fellowship for Renewal, February 7, 1970 (Empowerment Controversy Records, bMS 531/7 (41)).
438 Larry Ladd, "Report on the UUA Board Meeting," pp. 2–3.
439 The Veatch Committee was established by the North Shore Society in 1959, using funds from a bequest the congregation received in 1953. It was a major funder of UU programs, and the UUA routinely turned to it for funding.
440 Ralph Helverson, diary, January 26, 1970 (Helverson Papers, bMS 601/6 (1)).
441 Ladd, "Report on the UUA Board Meeting," p. 4. The woman he mentions is Denny Davidoff. She and her husband, Jerry, were comparatively new to

Unitarian Universalism, but her husband nonetheless served as BUUC/FULLBAC parliamentary consultant. She went on to serve as president of the UUWF and moderator of the UUA.
442 John Gibbons, email to Mark Morrison-Reed, March 28, 2017.
443 Ladd, "Report on the UUA Board Meeting," p. 4.
444 David Parke, memo to FULLBAC Steering Committee, "Re: Concerns of 18 April Meeting in Boston, April 16, 1969" (Morrison-Reed Papers).
445 Ruth Bercaw (note taker), "CUUP Evaluation," May 26, 1970 (Archive at West Shore Unitarian Universalist Church, Rocky River, OH).
446 James Hobart, email to Mark Morrison-Reed, April 9, 2017. Comprehensive descriptions of CUUP can be found in George K. Beach, "New Ministers," *Journal of the Liberal Ministry*, vol. 9, no. 2 (Spring 1969), pp. 42–54, and George K. Beach, "Final Report, Cleveland Unitarian Universalist Parish," July 1970 (Archive at West Shore Unitarian Universalist Church, Rocky River, OH).
447 Donald Harrington, letter to Farley Wheelwright, January 7, 1970.
448 Hayward Henry, letter to David Eaton, George T. Johnson, Harold Wilson, John Frazier, Thomas Payne, and Renford Gaines, August 25, 1969 (Archive at All Souls Church, Unitarian in Washington DC, Black Affairs Council file).
449 Colin Bossen, "The Black Humanist Fellowship of Liberation," in *Darkening the Doorways*, edited by Mark Morrison-Reed (Boston: Skinner House, 2011), p. 208. This section draws extensively on Bossen's essay and research.
450 George K. Beach, email to Morrison-Reed, April 11, 2017.
451 Hayward Henry, "The Case for Black Unitarianism," October 5, 1969 (Archive at UU Society of Cleveland, Cleveland Heights, OH).
452 Glover W. Barnes, "The Case for Integrated Unitarianism," October 12, 1969 (Betty Seiden Papers).
453 "Changes in the Black Ghetto—II," *SR*, Department of Social Responsibility, Unitarian Universalist Association, August 1, 1970, p. 14.
454 Minutes of the Veatch Committee, May 5, 1971 (Archive at Unitarian Universalist Congregation at Shelter Rock, Manhasset, NY [formerly North Shore Unitarian Church], NSUS, RG VIII B1).
455 Renford Gaines, "Blacks, Get Your Guns," sermon delivered at Unitarian Universalist Church of Urbana-Champaign, IL, December 13, 1970 (Empowerment Controversy Records, bMS 531/5 (29)).
456 Renford Gaines, letter to Stephen Fritchman, August 19, 1968 (Archive at Unitarian Universalist Church of Urbana-Champaign, IL [hereafter UUCUC Archive].)
457 Renford Gaines, letter to Father Neil Jordall, August 23, 1968 (UUCUC Archive).

458 Renford Gaines, letter to Lorraine Weber, April 2, 1969 (UUCUC Archive).
459 Renford Gaines, letter to Mary Altenbernd, May 23, 1969 (UUCUC Archive).
460 Renford Gaines, interview by Mark Morrison-Reed, August 2009.
461 "Blacks, Get Your Guns."
462 Beth Robbins, "The Ministry of Mwalimu Imara at Arlington Street Church," paper submitted for UU History and Polity class, Meadville Lombard Theological School, April 24, 2017.
463 Renford Gaines to Unitarian Universalist Church of Urbana-Champaign members, April 21, 1970 (UUCUC Archive).
464 Mwalimu Imara (formerly Renford Gaines), email to Mark Morrison-Reed, October 26, 2010.
465 "An Encounter with Change," *UUA Now*, September 26, 1969, vol. 50, no. 15 (Autumn 1969), p. 10.
466 Henry, "BAC: '...greatly disturbed,'" p. 13.
467 Jack, "Like It Was," p. 4.
468 Tweedie, "Recollections."
469 "Congregational Meeting," *Community News* (Community Church of New York newsletter), February 1, 1970.
470 "Offering Circular—$5,000,000 The Unitarian Universalists Black Affairs Council, Inc." (Morrison-Reed Papers).
471 Minutes of the Black Affairs Council, March 6–7, 1970 (Empowerment Controversy Records, bMS 531/1 (5)). The attendance list shows a different count: 124 and 31.
472 "Statement of Disaffiliation of the Black Affairs Council, Inc. from the Unitarian Universalist Association," revised March 30, 1970 (Empowerment Controversy Records, bMS 531/1 (13)).
473 Black Unitarian Universalist Caucus, "Days of Absence—No Blacks to Attend UUA Meetings," (Gilbert Papers).
474 Louis Garinger, "When Is a Church 'Racist'? Black Unitarians Assail Fund Cut," *Christian Science Monitor*, March 19, 1970.
475 "Statement of Rev. Robert N. West, president of Unitarian Universalist Association, re Black Affairs Council of UUA," (Empowerment Controversy Records, bMS 531/1 (12)).
476 John H. Fenton, "Black Council Disaffiliated from Unitarian Church," *New York Times*, February 28, 1970, p. 17.
477 The BAC members in attendance were: Althea Alexander, Samuel Beecher Jr., Hayward Henry Jr., Carol Hull, Chester I. Lewis, Hilda Mason, Benjamin F. Scott, and Gwendolyn A Thomas. The unrecorded absent member was Donald McKinney. The staff were Richard Traylor (administrative

secretary), Louis Gothard (administrative consultant), and La Verna M. Jones (administrative assistant). The guests were Matt Green and Fred Sparks.
478 Minutes of the Black Affairs Council, March 6–7, 1970.
479 Fenton, "Black Council Disaffiliated."
480 "BUUC Will Boycott Seattle General Assembly," *First Church News*, March 22, 1970 (Empowerment Controversy Records, bMS 531/8 (36)). *First Church News*'s publisher was Dick Fireman.
481 It is likely that this abstention was recommended by the chair of the Chicago First board, Kenneth Gibson. He was at the Washington DC BUUC meeting, and as an employee of the Internal Revenue Service, he would have been concerned.
482 Joyce Ball, "A Letter on the Black Affairs Council," newsletter of the May Memorial Unitarian Society, Syracuse, New York, March 10, 1970.
483 Al Weissbard, "From the President," March 1970.
484 "Black Affairs Forum," *Community News* (newsletter of Community Church of New York), April 12, 1970.
485 "Church to Invest Funds in BAC Bonds," *Boston Globe*, November 20, 1970.
486 Hayward Henry to David Eaton and Dr. Julius Mack, July 17, 1970 (Archive at All Souls Church, Unitarian, Washington DC, Black Affairs Council file).
487 Author unknown, draft, p. 10 (William Gardiner Papers [hereafter Gardiner Papers]). Gardiner guessed that it may be a draft of Victor Carpenter's *Long Challenge*.
488 Olive Hoogenboom, *The First Unitarian Church of Brooklyn: One Hundred and Fifty Years—A History* (New York: The First Unitarian Church of Brooklyn, 1987), p. 346.
489 Kenneth N. Whitlock, Resolution, October 22, 1969 (Archive at First Unitarian Congregational Society of Brooklyn, New York, BAC/BAWA file).
490 Kenneth N. Whitlock and David Schwarz, "Reaffirmation of the Principles of 'A Community Church for All Races of Men': and Rejection of Racial Apartheid," January 15, 1970 (Archive at First Unitarian Congregational Society of Brooklyn, NY, BAC/BAWA file).
491 Hoogenboom, *First Unitarian Church of Brooklyn*, p. 347.
492 Richard Traylor, memo to Stephen Fritchman, November 30, 1970.
493 "1971 list of those 'committed' to purchase BAC bonds over $1,000, October 1975" (Archive at First Unitarian Congregational Society of Brooklyn, New York, BAC/BUUC file).
494 David B. Parke, "The Church and the Black Community," newsletter of the Unitarian Society of Germantown, Philadelphia, May 11, 1969.

495 Albin A. Gorisek, "Minister Would Call Police if Forman Disrupted Service," *Cleveland Plain Dealer*, May 10, 1969.
496 Allison Blakely, "A Leader for the Second Reconstruction: David Hilliard Eaton" (unpublished), 1998 (Archive at All Souls Church Unitarian Archive, Washington DC).
497 Meredith Klaus, "The Black Manifesto Comes to Our Church," newsletter of the First Unitarian Church of Ann Arbor, MI, October 14, 1969 (University of Michigan, Bentley Historical Library, First Unitarian Universalist Church records, 86918 Ba 2, box 3).
498 Newsletter of the First Unitarian Church of Ann Arbor, October 20, 1969.
499 Minutes of the Board, First Unitarian Church of Ann Arbor, MI, October 26, 1969 (University of Michigan, Bentley Historical Library, First Unitarian Universalist Church records, 86918 Ba 2, box 3).
500 "2nd Church Yields in Ann Arbor Sit-in," *Detroit News*, September 5, 1970, p. 5A.
501 Parke, "The Church and the Black Community."
502 "Statement of Church Policy concerning Interruptions to Religious Services or Other Actions in Support of Civil Rights Demands" (draft), September 2, 1969 (Archive at Unitarian Society of Germantown in Philadelphia, Board Files).
503 This description of the SRL pulpit take over at Cedar Land Unitarian Church draws from a compilation of sources: Washington DC Student Religious Liberals, "Why We Are Here," June 7, 1970; "Washington SRL Seizes Unitarian Pulpit," *SRL News Release*, June 7, 1970; William Willoughby, "Students Present Demands: 3 Seize Unitarian Pulpit in Bethesda," *Washington Evening Star*, June 8, 1970; Alan S. Rosenthal, to "Fellow Members of Cedar Lane," June 10, 1970; "Minister Makes Response to Sunday's Pulpit Seizure," *Montgomery County Sentinel*, June 11, 1970; Helen Petersberger, email to Mark Morrison-Reed, March 10, 2015; and Alan Rosenthal, interview by Mark Morrison-Reed, September 10, 2015. Most of these sources are available in Archives at Cedar Lane Unitarian Universalist Church, Bethesda, MD. Clare Petersberger went on to become a UU minister.
504 Mason McGuiness, letter to David Parke, June 2, 1970 (AHTL, David B. Parke Papers, 1945–2005, bMS 543/29 (12)).
505 Wayne Arnason and John Gibbons, email to Mark Morrison-Reed, June 8, 2017.
506 "Fact Sheet: Questions and Answers," 1970 (Morrison-Reed Papers).
507 Bob Kaufman, "Bob Kaufman's Mad World ... ," *Puget Sounds* (General Assembly Newsletter), July 1, 1970, p. 2 (AHTL).

508 For this General Assembly, the UUA Program and Business Committees were merged to form a Planning Committee that had overall responsibility for GA.
509 Kaufman, op cit.
510 Commission on Appraisal, *Empowerment*, pp. 86–87.
511 "Action on Items of Business," Minutes of the Ninth General Assembly, p. 2.
512 Fred Houghteling, Dick Gardner, Perry PremDas, "More Fun and Games (Report from Seattle G.A.)," July 26, 1970 (Morrison-Reed Papers).
513 Ibid.
514 Max Gaebler, interview by Mark Morrison-Reed, June 27, 1986.
515 Scott, "Thoughts on the Occasion of the Tenth Anniversary," p. 2.
516 Jack, "Like It Was," p. 2.
517 Dorothy Spoerl, "Delegate Voting," *UUA Now*, July 28, 1969, p. 8.
518 Christopher G. Raible, email to Mark Morrison-Reed, November 9, 2014.
519 John Ruskin Clark, "The Black Power Hang-up," First Unitarian Church of San Diego, November 26, 1967 (Archive at First Unitarian Church of San Diego).
520 Donald W. McKinney, "The Black Rebellion and the UUA: What Happened at Cleveland?" *Kairos*, No. 12 (Autumn 1978), p. 6.
521 Continental Renewal Conference, "This Way to Renewal" (position paper), April 21–25, 1971, p. 2 (Gibbons Papers).
522 Raymond C. Hopkins, "Recollections, 1944–1974: The Creation of the Unitarian Universalist Association and the Administrations of Dana Greeley and Robert West," *Journal of Unitarian Universalist History* 31 (2006–2007), p. 10.
523 Paul Carnes was elected president of the UUA in 1977, the same year that the Women and Religion resolution was passed. He subsequently established the Commission on Common Worship. *Familiar Hymns in New Forms* was published in 1979 and *Hymns in New Forms for Common Worship* in 1982. It included fifty-three recast and degenderized hymns from *Hymns for the Celebration of Life* (Unitarian Universalist Association, 1964).
524 Jack Mendelsohn, in Cordes, *Wilderness Journey*: "We had to win votes."
525 Robert L'H. Miller, "The Religious Value System of Unitarian Universalists," *Review of Religious Research*, vol. 17, no. 3 (Spring 1976), p. 208.

The Washington D.C. General Assembly

526 Hayward Henry, "The Fourth Annual Meeting of the Black Unitarian Universalist Caucus—Open Letter to the Membership," February 10, 1971 (AHTL, Unitarian Universalist Association, Black Affairs Council Records, 1958–1983 [hereafter Black Affairs Council Records], bMS 1144/1 (5)).

527 Marjorie Jordan, "Congress of African People," Cincinnati BUUC Newsletter, January 17, 1971, p. 1 (Morrison-Reed Papers, Clemmie R. Wylie file).
528 Alex Poinsett, "It's Nation Time," *Ebony*, December 1970.
529 Jordan, "Congress of African People," p. 1.
530 "Issue Briefs," 1971 (AHTL, Unitarian Universalist Association, Black Affairs Council Records, 1958–1983, bMS 1144/1 (5)). The topic headings were Restructuring and Retrenchment, BUUC-BAC and CAP, Elections, Financial Survival, BUUC Ideology, BUUC and Black Humanism, Family Roles and Relationships, and Denominational Affairs.
531 "Position Paper of Greater Washington Area BUUC, February 18, 1971" (Black Affairs Council Records). Also see Commission on Appraisal, *Empowerment*, pp. 38–39, 48, footnotes 35, 55.
532 "BUUC Elects New Chairman," *First Church News*, March 21, 1971 (Empowerment Controversy Records, bMS 531/8 (36)).
533 Ibid.
534 "Block Move to Reconsider Current Commitments," *First Church News*, March 21, 1971 (Empowerment Controversy Records, bMS 531/8 (36)).
535 Bette Sikes, email to Mark Morrison-Reed, August 21, 2017.
536 "Max Gaebler Voices 'Benevolent Neutrality' toward Chicago Meeting," *First Church News*, March 21, 1971 (Empowerment Controversy Records, bMS 531/8 (36)).
537 "Conference Planners Split over Goals," *First Church News*, March 21, 1971, ibid.
538 Chicago Area Fellowship for Renewal, "Oppression and Liberation," order of service for Third Unitarian Church of Chicago on June 7, 1970 (Gibbons Papers).
539 Continental Renewal Conference, "This Way to Renewal" (proceedings), Chicago, April 21–25, 1971, p. 2 (Gibbons Papers).
540 "Continental Renewal Conference," *CAFFR News*, May 1971 (Gibbons Papers). Among the participants were Christopher Raible, Aron Gilmartin, James Luther Adams, Paul Carnes, Harry Thor, Harold Wilson, Emil Gudmundson, Lou Gothard, Harry Nachman, Jerry Jones, John Smith, George and Bette Sikes, and Joyce Marco.
541 "This Way to Renewal."
542 Joyce M. Marco, in "Continental Renewal Conference."
543 Richard S. Gilbert, to "Fellow Unitarian Universalists," May 18, 1971 (Gilbert Papers).
544 Donald S. Harrington, letter to Glover Barnes, May 10, 1971 (Empowerment Controversy Records, bMS 531/4 (37)).

545 Donald S. Harrington, "Statement of Reconciliation—BUUC and BAWA," ca. April 1971, ibid.
546 David N. Bortin, draft paper for the Commission on Appraisal's Empowerment study (Black Affairs Council Records, 1958–1983, bMS 1144).
547 Paul N. Carnes, "Strictly Personal," newsletter of the First Unitarian Universalist Church of Buffalo, May 25, 1971 (Empowerment Controversy Records, bMS 531/6 (20)).
548 "Report of the UUA Commission on Appraisal," June 1971 (Black Affairs Council Records, bMS 1144).
549 The Commission on Appraisal members in 1970–1971 were Wilson C. Piper (former UUA Board treasurer), John Cummins, Larry Ladd, Harry B. Scholefield, Harold Wilson, Joseph B. Samples Jr., Mrs. Frank E. Buell, and Frank E. Faux. Piper and Cummins were not in complete agreement with the statement issued by the Commission.
550 Pat Creer, "Don't Fund B.A.C.," Neighborhood Commons Corp., June 5, 1971 (Gilbert Papers).
551 Neil Shadle, email to Mark Morrison-Reed, June 13, 2017.
552 Black Affairs Council Support Group, "B.A.C. Is Now—The Issue Is Deeper Than Black vs White [or Black vs Red]" (Gilbert Papers).
553 John C. Godbey, "Brief Report to the First Unitarian Church of Chicago," June 13, 1971, p. 2 (Empowerment Controversy Records, bMS 531/6 (35)).
554 Conrad Wright, *Walking Together: Polity and Participation in Unitarian Universalist Churches* (Boston: Skinner House, 1989), p. 94.
555 Betty Medsger, "Unitarians Refuse to Fund Own Black Council," *Washington Post*, June 11, 1971.
556 Harold Wilson, to "Supporters of BUUC," June 14, 1971 (AHTL).
557 Godbey, "Brief Report to the First Unitarian Church of Chicago," p. 6.
558 Sarah Dennis, *The First Forty Years of the Chicago Children's Choir (1956–1996): Changing the World with Anti-bias Immersion through Music* (unpublished), 2017.
559 "The Black Affairs Council (BAC) and the Black Unitarian Universalist Caucus (BUUC): How They Function and What They Support" (General Assembly flyer), May 12, 1971 (Gilbert Papers).
560 Hayward Henry, in Cordes, *Wilderness Journey*.
561 William D. Wright, "Statement of Purpose—Unity House," September 23, 1968 (Archive at Cedar Lane Unitarian Church, Bethesda, Maryland).
562 Phyl Garland, "Blacks Challenge the Airwaves," *Ebony* 26, no. 1 (November 1970), p. 35.
563 Horace Montgomery, *In Pursuit of the American Birthright: A Quarter-Century of Unitarian-Universalist Involvement in Athens, 1954–1979*

(Athens, Georgia: Unitarian Universalist Fellowship of Athens, 2003), p. 5; Jane King (UUFA member and former treasurer of the Clarke County Federal Credit Union), interviewed by Mark Morrison-Reed, November 18, 2016.
564 Ulbrich, *The Fellowship Movement*, pp. 34–44.
565 Putting congregational polity and needs at the center of Unitarian Universalism's associational body has led to an array of problems beyond missional paralysis. In 1963 at the Chicago General Assembly, the major debate was over which should take precedence: congregational polity or nondiscrimination. Congregational polity won out.
566 See Kathleen R. Parker, *Sacred Service in Civic Space: Three Hundred Years of Community Ministry in Unitarian Universalism* (Chicago: Meadville Lombard Press, 2007), for a full exploration of the breadth and struggles of those who found their primary calling to ministry outside the parish.
567 "Statement by Dr. Robert Nelson West, President, Unitarian Universalist Association, Made to the General Assembly, June 12, 1971" (Empowerment Controversy Records, bMs 531/7 (47)).
568 Wilson, to "Supporters of BUUC."
569 William N. Holway, to "BAC c/o Richard Traylor and BAWA c/o Morton R. Kenner and Glover Barnes," June 16, 1971.
570 Stephen Fritchman, "The Black Affairs Council and the Washington UU Assembly," September 1971 (AHTL).
571 The amount on the $450 thousand demand note was reduced to $413 thousand by April 1970 and to $323,500 by January 1971. The bequest of $266,726.15 from George W. Boyle of Little Falls, NY, which appears in the October 1971 Board minutes, may have been received any time between March 15 and September 30, 1970.
572 Denny Davidoff, email to Mark Morrison-Reed, July 20, 2016.
573 Jack Mendelsohn, "Meanwhile, Back at Denominational Headquarters," newsletter of First Unitarian Society of Chicago, October 1971 (Archive at First Unitarian Society of Chicago).
574 West, *Crisis and Change*, p. 28.
575 Ibid., pp. 53–54.
576 *The Free Church in a Changing World: The Reports of the Commissions to the Churches and Fellowships of the Unitarian Universalist Association* (Boston: UUA, 1963), p. 56.
577 Farley W. Wheelwright, "Up Unitarian Black Power!" sermon preached at the Cleveland Unitarian Society, May 26, 1968, p. 4 (Morrison-Reed Papers).
578 Hugo Holleroth, email to Mark Morrison-Reed, April 26, 2012.
579 Pauline Warfield Lewis, letter to Jack Mendelsohn, May 13, 1968 (AHTL).

580 Hugo Holleroth, letter to Jack Mendelsohn, May 16, 1968.
581 Hugo Holleroth, email to Mark Morrison-Reed, April 26, 2012.
582 Carol Henderson, interview by Mark Morrison-Reed, November 7, 2015.
583 Much of the story regarding Holleroth's work in developing curricula is taken from his email correspondence with Mark Morrison-Reed, April 26, 2012; May 13, 2012; and July 6, 2017.

Deadlocked

584 Eileen C. Spaker, "Black Caucus Upsets Unitarian Gala," *Wilmington (Del.) Morning News*, January 10, 1972, p. 26.
585 Eileen C. Spaker, "Unitarians Reject Black Caucus Demands," *Wilmington (Del.) News Journal*, January 24, 1972, p. 21.
586 Beth Robbins, "The Ministry of Mwalimu Imara at Arlington Street Church" (paper submitted for UU History and Polity class), Meadville Lombard Theological School, April 24, 2017, 19.
587 Bill Kohlbrenner to Lou Gothard, November 3, 1971 (Empowerment Controversy Records, bMS 531/2 (4)).
588 Denny Davidoff, email to Mark Morrison-Reed, July, 20, 2016.
589 Minutes of the Veatch Committee, January 4, 1972 (Archive at North Shore Unitarian Society, Plandome, NY, RG VIII B1).
590 Minutes of the Veatch Committee, January 31, 1972.
591 The Committee members were William N. Holway (chair), Edna Griffin, Rev. Raymond Hopkins (UUA vice president), Marjorie Jordan, Mildred McDougald, and Jack O. Le Flore Sr.
592 Donald S. Harrington, "An End to Conflict?" *Shipmates* (newsletter of the Unitarian Universalist Fellowship of Lexington, Kentucky), September 13, 1972.
593 Memo to "All Board and DSH, From Edwina (Ferguson), Subject: Sequel to Exec. Board Meeting—4/28/72, May 4 1972," (Empowerment Controversy Records bMs 531/4 (40)).
594 "From BUUC to BHF . . . Questions and Answers on the Issue," February 1973 (Gardiner Papers).
595 Gwen Thomas, memo to BUUC Steering Committee, "Re: Changing the BUUC into the Black Humanist Fellowship," (Gardiner Papers).
596 Ben Scott, memo, March 26, 1973 (Gardiner Papers).
597 Harold Wilson, to "Members of the BUUC," "Subject: Meeting Site, February 20, 1973" (Gardiner Papers).
598 "From BUUC to BHF."
599 Benjamin Scott, *The Coming of the Black Man* (Boston: Beacon, 1969), p. 29.
600 "From BUUC to BHF," pp. 1, 3.
601 Ibid., p. 3.

602 Ibid., pp. 3, 4–5.
603 Commission on Appraisal, *Empowerment*, p. 50.
604 Mwalimu Imara, "UUA Censors BAC Insert to the *UU World*," *Creative Interchange*, no. 31 (Arlington Street Church, Boston, April 30, 1973).
605 Ibid.
606 "Position Paper on the BUUC/BHF Controversy," *RENEWS: Fellowship for Renewal*, May 29, 1973, pp. 2–3 (Gibbons Papers).
607 Black Unitarian Universalist Caucus, "S.O.S. Help Save Our Ship," June 2, 1973 (Gilbert Papers).
608 Louis J. Gothard, circular letter, June 17, 1973 (Gilbert Papers).
609 Donald W. McKinney, letter to James Luther Adams, April 18, 1973 (Archive at First Unitarian Church of Brooklyn, NY, BAC/BUUC/BHF file).
610 Donald W. McKinney, interview by Mark Morrison-Reed, January 17, 2015. See also Commission on Appraisal, *Empowerment*, p. 49.
611 Donald W. McKinney, to "Members, Black Affairs Council, BUUC, and BHF," June 20, 1973 (Gardiner Papers).
612 Donald W. McKinney, letter to Duke Gray, June 27, 1973 (Archive at First Unitarian Church of Brooklyn, NY, BAC/BUUC/BHF file).
613 For details, see West, "Black UU Caucus Court Proceedings," in *Crisis and Change*, pp. 35–48.
614 Richard Traylor et al., to "Members of All Souls Church of Washington D.C.," in *Empowerment: One Denomination's Quest for Racial Justice, 1967–1982: Report of the Unitarian Universalist Commission on Appraisal to the General Assembly, UUA, June 1983* (Boston: Unitarian Universalist Association, 1984), p. 52.
615 BAWA Project Papers (Empowerment Controversy Records, bMS 531/4 (16), and "BAWA TV Spots," (Empowerment Controversy Records, bMS 531/5 (16)).
616 Marcia McBroom Landess, "Statement Made at General Assembly Plenary Session," June 18, 1981. BAWA did not officially cease to exist until July 1991, when it discontinued its status as a nonprofit organization.
617 William F. Schulz, preface to *Black Pioneers in a White Denomination*, by Mark D. Morrison-Reed (Boston: Skinner House, 1980), p. ix.
618 William Sinkford, response to Mtangulizi Sanyika (formerly Hayward Henry), Starr King School for the Ministry President's Lecture, 2003 (Morrison-Reed Papers).
619 Orloff W. Miller, email to Mark Morrison-Reed, March 24, 2015.
620 Frank Robertson, letter to Tandi Huelsbeck, December 12, 1994 (Abhi Janamanchi Papers).
621 Denny Davidoff, interview by Nicole Kirk, Chicago, Fall 2013 (MLTS).

622 Don McKinney, in Forsey, *In Their Own Words*, p. 41.
623 The first documented Unitarian same-sex wedding was conducted by Rev. Ernest Pipes in 1957 at the Community Church of Santa Monica, California. The next year, Rev. Harry Scholefield conducted a same-sex wedding at the First Unitarian Society of San Francisco. See Jeff Wilson, "'Which One of You Is the Bride?' Unitarian Universalism and Same-Sex Marriage in North America, 1957–1972," *Journal of Unitarian Universalist History* 35 (2011–2012), pp. 160–61.
624 Rev. James Stoll, Elgin Blair, and Richard Nash founded the Unitarian Universalist Gay Caucus in 1971. Jeff Wilson, "'Fear, Trembling, and Joy': Unitarian Universalists and Same-Sex Marriage in the U.S. and Canada, 1973–1984," *Journal of Unitarian Universalist History* 36 (2012), p. 85.
625 Ann Peart, "Of Warmth and Love and Passion: Unitarians and (Homo) Sexuality," in George D. Chryssides, ed., *Unitarian Perspectives on Contemporary Social Issues* (London: Lindsey, 2003).
626 West, "Office of Gay Concerns," in *Crisis and Change*, pp. 139–143.
627 Robert Reed, "Gay People and the Liberal Church," sermon delivered at First Unitarian Church of Louisville, May 28, 1972 (MLTS, Reed Papers, MLTS.US.2026).
628 *Report of the Committee on Goals*, p. 30 (tables 19, 20).
629 Mark Belletini, email to Mark Morrison-Reed, July 7, 2017.
630 Donald S. Harrington, "Hope despite Disillusion: Unitarian Universalists and the Homosexual," sermon delivered at Community Church of New York, June 10, 1973 (Archive at Community Church of New York).
631 Daniel G. Higgins, "Where Does It End?" *BAWA Newsletter*, vol. 6, no. 3, summer 1973.
632 *The Adventures of God's Folk* was created by the teaching team at All Souls Church, Unitarian in Washington DC, tried out by a few teams in the area, and welcomed by the UUA. Harriet Tubman was not in the field test version. Betty Jo Middleton, email to Mark Morrison-Reed, November 1, 2017.
633 "UU President," *UU World*, December 15, 1979. The meeting, which was sponsored by Thomas E. Payne, was held at the Benevolent Fraternity of Unitarian Congregations. In addition to Payne, the group included Jeffrey Campbell, David H. Eaton, Marshall Grisby, John Frazier Jr., Grayland Hagler, William R. Jones, Mark Morrison-Reed, and Ronald White.

Black Power Was the Trigger, Not the Cause

634 West, *Crisis and Change*, p. 79.
635 Sinkford, "The Dream of White Innocence."
636 Larry Ladd and Joseph Samples, in Cordes, *Wilderness Journey*.

637 James was the UUA's director of worship resources and liaison to the Hymnbook Commission that produced *Singing the Living Tradition* (Boston: Unitarian Universalist Association, 1993). She co-authored *Weaving the Fabric of Diversity* (Boston: Unitarian Universalist Association, 1996) and co-edited *Been in the Storm So Long* (Boston: Skinner House, 1991) and *Voices from the Margins* (Boston: Skinner House, 2012). She was central to the founding of the African American Unitarian Universalist Ministries and the Diverse Revolutionary Unitarian Universalist Ministries. She coordinated the Beyond Categorical Thinking program and served as the UUA's affirmative action officer.

638 Alex Poinsett, in Forsey, *In Their Own Words*, p. 53.

639 Sinkford, "The Dream of White Innocence."

640 David Bumbaugh, email to Mark Morrison-Reed, March 2, 2015.

641 Philip Giles, in Cole, *An Oral History of the Consolidation*, p. 121.

642 Donald S. Harrington, in ibid., p. 140.

643 William A. Donovan, in ibid., p. 51.

644 Donald S. Harrington, in ibid., pp. 156, 138.

645 "Moderator Announces He Will Resign," *Register-Leader Spotlight*, June 1964. p.1.

646 John Ogden Fisher, to "Leaders in our Churches and Fellowships," January 1, 1969 (Presidential Campaigns, Presidential Campaign 1969—Fisher, John, bMS 1397/1).

647 William A. Donovan, in Cole, *An Oral History of the Consolidation*, p. 55.

648 "Rev. Deane Starr," *UUA Now*, June 19, 1969, p. 14.

649 Marvin Evans, email to Mark Morrison-Reed, September 19, 2014.

650 Southeastern District of the Unitarian Universalist Association, "Notice of Annual Meeting," December 10, 1969 (Archive at Unitarian Universalist Fellowship of Athens, Georgia).

651 Alan Deale, email to Mark Morrison-Reed, April 21, 2015.

652 Cole, *An Oral History of the Consolidation*, p. 129.

653 Ulbrich, *The Fellowship Movement*, p. 42.

654 Christopher G. Raible, emails to Mark Morrison-Reed, August 26–September 5, 2014. Raible is a lifelong Unitarian who served as the UUA's director of communications in 1970–1971 and as director of extension in 1972–1976 during the West administration.

655 The formation of the Conference of Western Unitarian Churches in Cincinnati in 1852 is an early and well-known example.

656 *Special Report*, p. 12.

657 Weissbard, "From the President," June 1968.

658 Mtangulizi Sanyika (formerly Hayward Henry), Starr King School for the Ministry President's Lecture, reported by Dan Harper, edited by Lisa Presley, 2003, uua.org/ga/past/2003/169491.shtml
659 Henry, "The Caucus Story."
660 Hayward Henry, in Cordes, *Wilderness Journey*.
661 Deane Starr, "An open letter to professional leaders in the Unitarian Universalist Association," June 10, 1969 (Presidential Campaign, Starr, Deane, bMS 1397/1).
662 Hopkins, "Recollections, 1944–1974," p 14.
663 "Cleveland: 1968," *UUA Now*, supplement, June 1968, p. 2.
664 "Tuesday—A Day of Decision," p. 6.
665 Carol Gilligan and David A. J. Richards, *The Deepening Darkness: Patriarchy, Resistance, and Democracy's Future* (New York: Cambridge University Press, 2009), p. 21.
666 Scott, "Thoughts on the Occasion of the Tenth Anniversary."
667 During the fifty years between 1872 and 1922, twenty-nine women in the Ohio Convention were listed as licensed, ordained, or preaching. In *The Universalist Church in Ohio* (1923), Elmo Arnold Robinson notes that in 1877, Lucinda White Brown was a prominent figure in the Convention. By comparison, in 1965 there were fourteen women in final or associate fellowship in the UUA.
668 Barbara Coeyman, email to Mark Morrison-Reed, September 3, 2017: "I note a total of 144 Universalist women in ministry through 1920, most of them born 1847–1867. The peak of their numbers of the total Universalist ministers was around 1910: in 1910 67 of the 689 Universalist ministers were women. . . . That's not saying anything about the type of ministry they served. . . . Often women were in part-time, lower paid roles, etc. . . . Unitarians were also ordaining women but at about half the rate of Universalists."
669 Greta W. Crosby, interview by Mark Morrison-Reed, August 3, 2013.
670 The Universalist women raised money for the Universalist Centennial; they later refused to hand over the remainder of the funds, using them instead for their own work. In Canada during the Second World War, Lotta Hitchmanova, a founder and executive director of the Unitarian Service Committee of Canada, made the Committee a major focus in most Canadian Unitarian congregations.
671 In email correspondence with Mark Morrison-Reed, October 23–25, 2013, John A. Buehrens recounted this conversation with Malcolm Sutherland. Ken Hurto concurs that a deal was cut. The figures in this paragraph were arrived at by comparing the final Universalist Church of America yearbooks to the 1964 Unitarian Universalist Association Directory.

672 *Report of the Committee on Goals*, 41 (table 54), 44 (table 64), 30 (table 20), 31–32 (table 24). In regard to ministry, 47.6 percent said a women's sex would make little difference, and 5.2 percent said it would improve her effectiveness.

673 In 1972, Doris Pullen became the editor-in-chief of *UU World*, and in 1975, she also became director of the Department of Communications and Development. She was the first female UUA department director and the first woman on the executive staff.

674 "This Way to Renewal," p. 7.

675 This statement is based on the author's experience of attending ministers' meetings since 1977 and witnessing the described behavior wane as the number of female ministers dramatically increased.

676 James Hobart, email to Mark Morrison-Reed, July 24, 2016.

677 "Orloff Wakefield Miller at Selma with His Son Orloff Garrik Miller, March 2015" (unpublished), March 2016 (MLTS, Orloff Garrick Miller Papers).

678 *Report of the Committee on Goals*, p. 32 (table 26).

679 "This Way to Renewal," p. 6.

680 Carol Henderson, interview by Mark Morrison-Reed, November 7, 2015.

681 As told to William F. Schulz by a member of the Community of New York Search Committee. Schulz email to Mark Morrison-Reed, July 21, 2017.

682 Congregational interview by Mark Morrison-Reed, Community Church of New York, February 2015.

683 "Self-Determination: BAC," "Black and White Together: BAWA," "The Revolution Is US: FULLBAC," *UUA Now*, supplement, June 1968, p. 7.

684 Betty Seiden, email to Mark Morrison-Reed, April 30, 2015.

685 Lillian W. Jenkins, memo to Unitarian Universalist Women's Federation Board, March 13, 1968 (Empowerment Controversy Records, bMS 531/5 (37)).

686 Betty Reid Soskin, *Cbreaux Speaks* (blog), April 12, 2015, https://cbreaux .blogspot.com/

687 Ibid.

688 "Position Paper of Greater Washington Area BUUC," February 18, 1971.

689 "This Way to Renewal," p. 6.

690 "A Reflection on the Center City Church Conference: Held at the First Unitarian Church of Philadelphia," email from Jim Hobart to Mark Morrison-Reed, March 28, 2015.

Endings and Beginnings

691 Henry Hampton, interview by Carol Dornbrand, 1985 (Sankofa Collection, MLTS.US.5018).

692 Eugene Reeves, email to Mark Morrison-Reed, November 3, 2014.
693 Campbell, "I Question Caucuses."
694 Homer A. Jack to Orloff Miller, April 4, 1970 (AHTL).
695 William Sinkford, Introduction to Victor H. Carpenter, *Long Challenge: The Empowerment Controversy (1967–1977)* (Chicago: Meadville Lombard Theological School, 2003), p. vii.
696 Norma R. Poinsett, August 26, 1986 (Sankofa Collection, Norma R. Poinsett, General Assembly, MLTS.US.5001.1) and 1996 (MLTS, Sankofa Collection, Norma R. Poinsett, General Assembly, MLTS.US.5004).
697 Forsey, *In Their Own Words*, p. 53.
698 John Gibbons, email to Mark Morrison-Reed, March 28, 2017.
699 Frederick Douglass, "West India Emancipation," speech delivered at Canandaigua, New York, August 4, 1857, in Philip S. Foner, ed., *The Life and Writings of Frederick Douglass*, vol. 2, p. 437.
700 William R. Jones, "The Negro's Image of White America: Its Influence on Integration Strategy," sermon delivered at First Unitarian Church, Providence, RI, May 10, 1964, p. 2 (William R. Jones Papers, acquired from Robert Schacht Jr.).

Index

25 Beacon Street, 188, 331

abortion, 30, 300, 312, 334
About Your Sexuality, 277–278
Abyssinian Baptist Church (New York), 92
Accreditation of Directors of Religious Education Committee (UUA), 176
Ackron, Dan, 60
Adams, James Luther, 86, 87, 103, 114, 118, 148, 288, 300, 323
Adams, Jean, 42, 143
Adams, Margaret, 87
Adventures of God's Folk, The, 307
Advisory Committee for the Washington Office for Social Concern (UUA), 131
Advisory Panel on Integration of the Public Schools (Chicago), 6, 7
Africa's Past: Impact on Our Present, 284
Afro-Arts Theatre, 269
Afro-Audio Visuals, 284
After Selma Committee (UUA), 21, 43
Agency for International Development (AID), 147
Agobert, Marsh, 143, 168

Alabama Democratic Party, 133
Albany, NY, 4, 31–32, 105, 115, 125, 172, 222, 278
Alexander, Althea, 176, 195
Alexandria, VA, 317
Alinsky, Saul, 33, 52, 63, 174, 182, 250
All Souls Church Unitarian (Washington DC), 9, 62, 70, 89, 223, 226, 227, 230, 297–298, 301, 313, 314, 315
All Souls First Universalist Society (Chicago), 45, 100, 315 *See also* All Souls Free Religious Fellowship (Chicago)
All Souls Free Religious Fellowship (Chicago), 109 *See also* All Souls First Universalist Society (Chicago)
All Souls Unitarian Church (Indianapolis), 139
All Souls Unitarian Church (Tulsa, OK), 104
American Committee on Africa, 25, 91–92
American Federation of Labor (AFL), 37
American Friends Service Committee, 9
American Jewish Committee, 27
American Jewish Congress, 27

395

American Metal Climax Corporation, 137
American Unitarian Association (AUA), 1, 5, 108, 132, 138, 173, 184, 199, 227, 241, 245, 248, 272–273, 318–319, 323–325, 328, 330, 333
American Values and Racism, 281
Ann Arbor, MI, 231
Annual Program Fund (UUA), *See* Unitarian Universalist Association, Annual Program Fund
antiwar movement, 33, 42, 117, 123, 160
Arlington Street Church (Boston), 43, 62, 69, 88, 106, 130, 149–151, 153, 168–171, 194, 204, 216, 223, 226, 282, 287, 311, 343
Arlington, VA, 61
Arnason, Wayne, 142, 167, 180, 207
Arnold, Mel, 129
assimilation, 15, 49, 92, 251, 260, 279
Athens, GA, 72, 271, 315
Atlanta, GA, 89, 254
AUA, *See* American Unitarian Association

BAC, *See* Black Affairs Council
BAC bonds, 217–219, 221, 223, 225–228, 231, 234–235, 297
BAC Investment Corporation, 293, 351
BACgrounds, 298
Bagnall, Powhatan, 109
Bailey, Esther, 279
Baptists, 3, 16, 132
Baraka, Imamu Amiri, 255
Barnes, Glover, 110, 113, 115, 166–167, 170, 177, 193, 207, 212, 222, 261–262, 351
Barnes, Miriam, 113
Barr, James Madison, 7
Barth, Joseph, 21, 211, 213

"Basic Primer of Black Humanism" (Henry), 257, 292
Beach, George K. (Kim), 9, 58, 103, 142, 145, 209–213
Beacon Press, 52, 129, 131, 176, 202, 277, 279, 281
Beacon Series curriculum, 282
Beattie, Paul, 139
Bedford, MA, 108, 352
Beecher, Samuel, 60, 64
Belletini, Mark, 306
Bellevue, WA, 6
Benevolent Fraternity of Unitarian Churches, 274
Bennington, VT, 66
Bentley, Michelle, 308
Berkeley Fellowship of Unitarian Universalists (CA), 226
Berkeley, CA, 69, 92, 225–226
Bethel, VT, 320
Bethesda, MD, 102, 159, 232–235, 311
Beverly Unitarian Church (Chicago), 93
Beyond Selma Committee (UUA), *See* Unitarian Universalist Association, After Selma Committee
BIC, *See* BAC Investment Corporation
Biltmore Hotel (New York), 46, 93
Birmingham, AL, 168, 304
Black "P" Stone Nation (Chicago), 133
Black Affairs Council (BAC), 11, 48, 52, 55, 62, 78–80, 83, 85–86, 97–99, 102–108, 110–129, 131–133, 137–141, 146, 150, 153–155, 157, 159–161, 164–166, 169, 174, 176–180, 183, 186–187, 189, 191, 192, 195, 196, 198–208, 217–230, 234, 236–244, 246–248, 250, 252–267, 269, 271, 274–278, 284,

INDEX

287–293, 297–298, 300–301, 303–305, 310–311, 313, 316, 323, 325–329, 331–332, 338–339, 341–342, 346–347, 351–352
Black America, White America: Understanding the Discord, 283, 284
Black and White Action (BAWA), 30, 42, 99, 110–114, 117–120, 124, 126–128, 132, 137, 141, 148, 150, 154–157, 160–161, 164–166, 169–170, 172, 174, 177, 179, 183, 193, 195, 196, 198, 206, 207, 212, 218, 222, 225, 228, 232–233, 236, 238–239, 242, 244, 250, 252, 253, 258, 261–263, 266, 269, 272, 275, 277, 282–283, 289–290, 292, 302, 304, 307, 311, 326, 329, 338–339, 342, 351
Black and White: Power Subreption, 129
"Black Caucus" (Traylor), 83
Black Caucus, 36, 44–46, 49–55, 60–66, 68–72, 79, 86, 94, 218, 224, 247, 254, 260, 287, 304, 318, 325, 342 *See also* Black Unitarian Universalist Caucus
"The Black Caucus and Black Rebellion: A White Perspective" (Carpenter), 83
Black Caucus Fund, 65, 69
"The Black Caucus: Racism or Not?" (Venerable), 83
Black Concerns Working Group (UUA), 351
Black Efforts for Soul in Television (BEST), 271
"Black History in Our Curriculum," 148, 283
Black Humanism, 293, 295–296
Black Humanist Fellowship (BHF), 293, 295–298, 300–301, 303, 307, 314, 316, 343–344, 355

Black Humanist Fellowship of Liberation (BFL), 211–213, 254
Black Manifesto, 141, 229–231
Black Nationalism, 15, 254
Black Panthers, 141, 153, 214, 309
Black Pioneers in a White Denomination, 308
Black Power, 13, 20, 23–30, 33, 41, 44–45, 48, 51, 56, 59, 62, 78, 83, 86, 93, 96, 103, 118, 123, 126, 127, 135, 157, 160, 174, 189, 210, 247, 250–251, 254, 261, 270, 291, 295, 304, 310, 312–313, 317, 318, 331, 334, 350, 353
"Black Power and the Liberal Church" (Mendelsohn), 62–63
"Black Power and the White Liberal" (Jack), 86
"Black Power and the White Liberal" (Zoerheide), 102
"Black Power and Unitarianism: A Personal View" (Jones), 62
"Black Power Comes to Unitarianism" (Wolfe), 104
"The Black Power Hang-up" (Clark), 246
Black Stone Rangers, 78
Black Unitarian Universalist Caucus (BUUC), 4, 51, 53, 54, 68, 71, 80–85, 87, 93–95, 97–99, 102–105, 110, 111–112, 115, 118, 121, 122, 124, 126–127, 133–134, 139, 141–142, 152–153, 159, 160, 162, 166, 170, 174–175, 177–178, 183, 185, 189, 194, 202, 208, 211–213, 217, 219–221, 223–225, 227–228, 236–237, 238, 242–243, 244, 246–248, 250–252, 254–258, 261, 263–267, 271, 275–276, 278, 280–282, 284, 286–290, 292–301, 303–304, 307, 310, 313, 314, 316, 325, 329 (*cont.*)

397

Black Unitarian Universalist Caucus (BUUC) (*continued*) 331–332, 338–344, 347, 351, 355
See also Black Caucus
Black Unitarian Universalist Caucus (BUUC) Women's Caucus, 133–134
Black Unitarian Universalist Caucus, Inc., et al. v. Richard L. Traylor, et al., 297
Black Unitarians for Radical Reform (BURR), 30, 34–36, 38–39, 45–46, 50–51, 55, 64, 94, 122, 141, 160, 162, 173, 227, 294, 311, 316, 338, 345
Black Unitarians of the Bay Area (BUBA), 70
Black United Front, 230
Black, Ann, 55
Blackburn, Charles, B., 40
Blacks and Whites Together, 97
"Blacks, Get Your Guns" (Gaines), 214
Blackside, Inc., 131
Blattman, Margaret, 167
Bloomfield, Lincoln P., 330
Board of Trustees (UUA), *See* Unitarian Universalist Association, Board of Trustees
Bontemps, Arna, 129
Boston, 1, 3, 5, 6, 7, 8, 9, 21, 24, 43, 45, 46, 62, 64, 69, 72, 73, 81, 88, 109, 119, 121, 130, 139, 140, 145, 146, 148, 149, 150, 151, 152, 153, 154, 157, 158, 159, 160, 161, 163, 168, 169, 170, 171, 173, 174, 175, 179, 180, 181, 182, 183, 184, 186, 187, 188, 189, 198, 200, 204, 211, 216, 217, 218, 219, 222, 223, 226, 230, 236, 238, 241, 242, 243, 244, 247, 250, 254, 262, 274, 281, 282, 287, 291, 294, 302, 306, 308, 311, 324, 326, 330, 331, 332, 343, 352
Boston United Black Appeal, 302

Boston Walkout, *See* General Assembly, walkout
Boulé, The, 26, 92
boycotts, 5–7, 42, 178, 203, 220–221, 236, 238, 242, 250, 256–257, 291, 309, 325
Bozeman, MT, 72
Brahmo Samaj, 90
Brewer, James, 141
Briggs, Charles V. Jr., 275
British and Foreign Unitarian Association, 184
British General Assembly of Unitarians, 184, 305
Brookfield, WI, 278
Brooklyn Heights, NY, 8
Brooklyn, NY, 8, 33, 46, 94, 120, 151, 205, 223–226, 269, 270, 274, 294, 299–300, 311
Brooks, Lawrence, 330
Brothers, The, 31–32, 105
Brown v. Board of Education, 5, 61
Brown, Dick, 10, 19, 21, 58, 264–265
Brown, Dwight, 70–72, 195
Brown, Ethelred, 109
Brown, Olympia, 333
Buddhists, 185
Buffalo, NY, 43, 262
Bumbaugh, David, 317
Burgess, Connie, 5, 304
BURR, *See* Black Unitarians for Radical Reform
Burton, Harold, 5
Business Committee (UUA), 76, 176, 181
BUUC, *See* Black Unitarian Universalist Caucus

Cakes for the Queen of Heaven, 249
Cambridge, MA, 86–87, 118
Cambridge, MD, 43
Campbell, Jeffrey W., 45, 46, 71–72, 75, 81–82, 113, 161, 170, 172–173, 248, 315, 349

INDEX

Canada, 73, 131, 163, 186–189, 324, 328, 336
Canadian Unitarian, 186–187
Canadian Unitarian Council (CUC), 131, 141, 186–189, 203, 328
Canandaigua, NY, 353
Cardell, Nick, 4, 32, 105
Carmichael, Stokely, 15, 20, 23, 41
Carnes, Paul N., 125, 262, 307–308
Carpenter, Victor H., 83, 103, 167, 258
Carter, James, 66, 127
Carter, William H. G., 109
Carver, George Washington, 76
Case Western Reserve University, 209
Cashin, John, 133, 220, 255
Catholic Workers, 9
Catholics, 82
Cedar Lane Unitarian Universalist Church (Bethesda, MD), 102, 159, 232–235, 311
Center for Black Education (Washington DC), 269, 302
Central Brooklyn Citizens Union (Brooklyn, NY), 8
Central Midwest District (UUA), 10, 60
Challenger, Thomas V., 98
Chapin, Augusta, 333
Chemical Bank New York Trust, 137
Chicago, 2, 6, 7, 8, 10, 19, 21, 31, 43–46, 53–58, 61, 69, 71–73, 83, 88, 93, 96–97, 100, 102, 108, 109, 117, 133, 151, 158, 162, 163, 172, 204–207, 209, 214, 219, 221, 227, 235, 237, 241, 243, 246, 253–254, 257–258, 262, 264–270, 274, 276, 289, 294, 303, 309–311, 313–315, 335, 341, 354–355
Chicago Area Black UU Caucus (CABUUC), 55–57, 204, 221, 227, 254, 257–258, 269, 294, 314

Chicago Area Felllowship for Renewal (CAFFR), 258
Chicago Children's Choir, 268, 270, 314
Chicano empowerment, 178, 186, 202, 206, 239, 243, 244
Chico, CA, 3
Christian Methodist Episcopal Church (Houston, TX), 317
Christian Register, 24, 93, 100
Church of the Larger Fellowship, 202
Church of the Unitarian Brotherhood (Cincinnati), 109
"The Churches and Watts: A Report Seven Months Later" (Fritchman), 25
Cincinnati, 33, 43, 55, 57, 64, 73, 108–109, 121, 163, 219, 243, 255, 280, 294, 351
Citizens Alert Patrol, 25
civil disobedience, 5, 17, 33
civil liberties, 267, 306
civil rights, 5, 7, 13, 18, 40, 58, 243, 247
Civil Rights Act, 4
civil rights movement, 11, 14, 15, 18, 21, 60, 78, 103, 240, 260, 304, 331, 346, 353
Clark, John Ruskin, 225, 246–247
Clark, Joseph S., 4, 130
Clark, Kenneth B., 44, 61, 63, 65, 72, 95–96
Clark, Peter H., 108
Clarke County Federal Credit Union (GA), 271
Clarke, John Hendrik, 129
Clergy in Urban Ministry program, 209
Cleveland, 5, 22, 31, 32, 46, 58, 59, 60, 67, 83, 85, 86, 89, 94, 97, 102, 105–107, 110–115, 117, 119, 121, 125, 128, 132, 135, 137–139, 141, 142, 148, 155, 158, 160, 163, 166, 179, 200, 207,

Cleveland (*continued*)
    209–211, 212–213, 219, 222,
    242–244, 247, 254, 269–270,
    274, 294, 326–327, 330, 331,
    339, 340, 341, 344, 346
Cleveland Heights, OH, 213
Cleveland Unitarian Society, 209,
    211–212
Cleveland Unitarian Universalist
    Parish (CUUP), 32, 58–59, 142,
    209–213, 270, 274
Cole, David H., 200–201, 210–211,
    213
Cole, LeRoy, 224
Cole, Paul, 208
Coleman, John O., 299
Collyer, Robert, 9
Collymore, Errold D., 91, 109, 324
Color and Race, 129
Colorado Springs, CO, 336, 349
Columbus, OH, 355
Combined Black Publishers, 302
Coming of the Black Man, The, 129,
    295
Commission for Action on Race,
    (UUA), 83, 107
Commission on Appraisal (UUA),
    See Unitarian Universalist
    Association, Commission on
    Appraisal
Commission on Education and
    Liberal Religion (UUA), 278,
    282
Commission on Hymns and Services
    (AUA and UCA), 248
Commission on Religion and Race
    (UUA), *See* Unitarian
    Universalist Association,
    Commission on Religion and
    Race
Committee for a United Newark,
    (NJ), 269
Committee of Committees (UUA),
    335

Committee on Civil Rights (East
    Manhattan, NY), 91
Committee on Goals (UUA),
    See Unitarian Universalist
    Association, Committee on Goals
Committee on Racial Justice (UUA),
    275
Committee on Urban Concerns and
    Ministry (UUA), 308
Community Change, Inc., 308
Community Church (New York), 10,
    23–24, 54, 90–92, 95–100, 110,
    113–114, 117, 120, 126, 130,
    137, 217–218, 222, 225, 229,
    311, 315, 338
Community News, 95
Community School Committee
    (Brooklyn Heights, NY), 8
C.O.N.C.E.R.N., 147, 156, 160–161
"Conflict: Function and Dysfunction"
    (Ockert), 36
Congress (U.S.), 237
Congress of African People (CAP),
    254–257
Congress of Racial Equality (CORE),
    4, 6, 19, 20, 25, 27–28, 38, 40–42,
    44, 62, 129, 143–144
Consensus on Racial Justice (1966),
    12–13, 17, 77, 106, 239, 242–
    244, 247
consolidation of the AUA and UCA,
    2, 24, 104, 138, 153, 173–174,
    199, 201, 241, 248–249, 250,
    272, 318–320, 322–325, 330,
    333–334
Continental Committee on
    Development and Fundraising
    (UUA), 138
Continental Conference, 141
Continental Renewal Conference,
    257–259
Cooper, Ida Cullen, 91
CORE, *See* Congress of Racial
    Equality

Corelator, 42
Cornethan, John, 6, 40–41, 351
Council of Churches (Seattle), 6
Council of Liberal Churches (CLC), 1, 249
Council of Superintendents (Universalist Church of America), 319
covenant, 247–248, 250, 326, 347
Crane Theological School at Tufts University, 130, 200
Creative Interchange, 298
Crisis, 95
Crosby, Greta W., 190,, 333
Cullen, Countee, 91
Cummins, John, 160
Cunningham, James, 109
curricula, 12, 52, 76, 108, 125, 148, 277, 279–284, 307
Curtis, James, 32, 58, 59, 209

Daley, Richard, 88, 117
Dallas, TX, 290–291
Dalton, Gloster, 108
Davidoff, Denise (Denny), 288, 304
Dawkins, Maurice A., 24–25, 91
Deale, Alan, 168, 225
decentralization, 153, 254, 321
Deerfield, IL, 130
Delaware Valley District (UUA), 226
Democratic National Convention, 117, 133, 309
democratic process, 66, 94, 97, 125, 162, 182, 246, 256, 272, 326, 347
Denver, 32–34, 40, 72, 121, 158, 163, 205, 218, 294, 344
Department of Adult Programs (UUA), 76
Department of Education (UUA), 76, 279
Department of Education and Social Concern (UUA), 202
Department of Fundraising and Development (UUA), 139
Department of Ministry (UUA), *See* Unitarian Universalist Association, Department of Ministry
Department of Overseas and Interfaith Relations (UUA), 2, 111
Department of Religious Education (UUA), 52, 284, 307
Department of Social Action (UUA), 97, 142
Department of Social Responsibility (UUA), *See* Unitarian Universalist Association, Department of Social Responsibility
Des Moines, IA, 72, 283
desegregation, 14–15
Detroit, 43, 73, 133, 163, 219, 229, 243, 308, 310, 313
Devon, PA, 118, 159, 161, 217, 235
Dimock, Marshall, 320–321, 331
disaffiliation, 220, 222, 227, 238, 250, 303
disarmament, 300
Discrimination against Homosexuals and Bisexuals (GA Resolution), 305–306
Division of Communication and Publications Advisory Committee (UUA), 131
Dodder, Clyde, 218, 226
"Don't Sleep through the Revolution" (King), 13
Donovan, William A., 320–321
Dorchester, MA, 9
Doss, Robert M., 286
Douglas, Emily Taft, 333
Douglas, Paul, 4
Dow Chemical, 137
draft resistance, 30, 106, 123, 150, 234, 263
Du Bois, W.E.B., 91

401

East Bay Project (Oakland, CA), 58, 75
East Mount Airy Neighborhood Association (Philadelphia), 11
East Shore Unitarian Church (Bellevue, WA), 6
Eastman Kodak Company, 33, 154
Eaton, David H., 230, 298, 313–315
Ebony, 271
Eliot, Frederick May, 156, 248, 272, 319, 333
Eliot, Samuel Atkins, 319
Eller-Isaacs, Rob, 88, 169, 172, 337
Ellsberg, Daniel, 277
Emanuel Apartments, Inc. (Roxbury, MA), 207
Emergency Conference on the Unitarian Universalist Response to the Black Rebellion, 36, 39, 44–45, 53–55, 57–58, 59–61, 63–64, 68–71, 93–96, 100, 102, 120, 122, 125, 129, 143, 144, 145, 152–153, 191, 209, 218, 224, 254, 305, 318, 325, 339, 345, 354
Engel, J. Ron, 8–10, 19, 21, 57, 103, 209, 264
Eno River Unitarian Universalist Fellowship (IN), 109
Eno River, IN, 109
environmental movement, 42, 267
Episcopalians, 82, 144
Eubanks, Musa, 284
Eutaw, AL, 220
Evans, Marvin, 321
Evans, Til, 181
Evanston, IL, 43, 64

Fair Housing Ordinance (Racine, WI), 72
fascism, 183, 186
Federal Bureau of Investigation (FBI), 93, 214, 277
Fellowship for Renewal (FFR), 179–181, 198–199, 204–208, 225, 236–237, 246, 248, 250–251, 257–259, 272, 278, 296, 298, 307, 325, 337, 341–342, 347
Fellowship Movement, The, 173, 323
feminism, 30, 123, 263, 337, 342
  See also patriarchy and women
Ferguson, Edwina, 292
FFR, *See* Fellowship for Renewal
FIGHT (Freedom, Independence, God, Honor, Today), 33, 154
Finance Committee (UUA), *See* Unitarian Universalist Association, Finance Committee
First Church (Boston), 149–151, 180
First Church News (Chicago), 221, 253
First Nations people, Canada, 73, 186, 187
First Parish Church (Bedford, MA), 352
First Parish in Cambridge Unitarian Universalist (Cambridge, MA), 86–87, 118
First Pennsylvania Bank, 293
First Unitarian Church (Berkeley, CA), 69, 92, 225
First Unitarian Church (Cincinnati), 55, 108, 280, 351
First Unitarian Church (Los Angeles), 16, 23–24, 34, 36, 38, 69, 99–100, 122, 130, 167, 183, 311, 338, 345
First Unitarian Church (Louisville, KY), 106, 135
First Unitarian Church (Oakland, CA), 69
First Unitarian Church (Philadelphia), 83, 167, 258
First Unitarian Church (Pittsburgh), 315
First Unitarian Church (Portland, OR), 225
First Unitarian Church (Rochester, NY), 175, 260

First Unitarian Church (Shaker Heights, OH), 209–210
First Unitarian Church (Vancouver, BC), 183
First Unitarian Church (Wilmington, DE), 286–287
First Unitarian Congregation (Ottawa, ON), 73, 130, 137–138, 188
First Unitarian Congregation (Toronto, ON), 186
First Unitarian Congregational Society (Brooklyn, NY), 8, 33, 94, 120, 151, 205, 223–226, 300, 311
First Unitarian Society (Chicago), 7, 21, 31, 45, 55–56, 83, 88, 100, 151, 158, 172, 204–206, 221, 235, 237, 257–258, 267–268, 276, 311, 313–315, 354
First Unitarian Society (Denver), 205
First Unitarian Society (Madison, WI), 110
First Unitarian Universalist Church (Richmond, VA), 53
First Unitarian Universalist Church (San Diego), 225
First Unitarian Universalist Congregation (Ann Arbor, MI), 231
First Unitarian Universalist Society (Albany, NY), 4, 32, 105, 115, 125, 172, 222
First Unitarian Universalist Society (Newton, MA), 218, 226
First Unitarian Universalist Society (San Francisco), 103, 225, 307
First Unitarian-Universalist Church (Detroit), 229, 313
First Universalist Church (Minneapolis), 160
First Universalist Society (Philadelphia), 108
Fisher, Carlton, 65, 152, 153, 154, 155, 161, 166

Fisher, John Ogden, 153–154, 157, 158, 201, 321
Fisher, Joseph, 60, 165, 170
Fleming, Maria, 337
Flint, MI, 64
Flowers, Clayton, 96
Flushing, NY, 80, 109
Forman, Charles, 232
Forman, James, 140, 229
Fort Myers, FL, 72
Fort Wayne, IN, 152
Forth Worth, TX, 42
Fourth Universalist Society (New York), 99, 315
Franklin, John Hope, 129
Frazier, John, 130, 211, 213
Frederick-Gray, Susan, 250
Free Church in a Changing World, The, 2, 278
Free Huey Campaign, 309
Free Religious Fellowship (Chicago), *See* All Souls Free Religious Fellowship (Chicago)
Freedom and Responsibility, 280
Freedom Fund (UUA), *See* Unitarian Universalist Association, Freedom Fund
freedom riders, 40
Freeman, Sid, 190
Fremont Hotel (Seattle), 236
Fritchman, Frances, 167
Fritchman, Stephen H., 4, 16, 23–24, 26–30, 34, 93, 99–101, 103, 112, 122–123, 139, 145, 148, 162–163, 167, 169, 171, 178, 193, 214, 225, 276, 287, 312, 326, 338, 345
Front de libération du Québec (FLQ), 188
Full Recognition and Funding of the Black Affairs Council (FULLBAC), 85–87, 97, 99, 103, 104, 105, 110–111, 118, 121, 124, 126, 127, 137, 139, 142, 144–146, 150–151, 152–153,

Full Recognition and Funding of the Black Affairs Council (FULLBAC) (*continued*)
    155, 159, 160, 169, 171, 178, 179, 183, 193, 202, 203, 208, 224, 225, 232, 242, 243, 246, 248, 250–251, 264, 272, 278, 300, 305–306, 325, 329, 338, 339, 347
FULLBAC, *See* Full Recognition and Funding of the Black Affairs Council
Fullerton, CA, 225
Fulton Street Center (Brooklyn, NY), 8, 224, 269, 270, 274
fundraising and development, 124–125, 136–138, 155, 221, 261, 267, 274–276, 289–290, 300, 321, 346

GA, *See* General Assembly
Gaebler, Max, 33, 54, 110–111, 120, 141, 162, 193, 207, 239, 258, 282
Gaede, Erwin A., 231
Gaines, Renford G., 53, 129, 131, 142, 148, 151, 176, 214–216, 223, 283–284, 287–288 *See also* Imara, Mwalimu
Gardiner, William J., 223, 230
Gardner, William E., 138
Gary, IN, 78
Gay Liberation Front, 306
"Gay People and the Liberal Church" (Reed), 305
Gehr, Harmon, M., 160
Gelsey, Rudolph, C. (Rudi), 10–11, 85, 103, 123, 157, 167, 169
General Assembly (UUA), 241–252, 320, 324–325
  1961 (Boston), 241
  1963 (Chicago), 2, 6, 241, 246, 303, 335
  1965 (Boston), 5, 7, 242
  1966 (Hollywood, FL), 11, 13–18, 190, 242–243, 245
  1967 (Denver), 32–34

General Assembly (UUA) (*continued*)
  1968 (Cleveland), 60, 67, 83, 85–86, 94, 97–98, 102–119, 119, 121, 125, 128, 133, 135, 137–139, 148, 160, 163, 166, 179, 200, 222, 242–243, 247, 269, 326–327, 330–331, 339–340, 346
  1969 (Boston), 4, 81, 119, 139–141, 145–146, 148, 151–154, 157, 158–189, 191–196, 198, 203, 211, 217, 222, 230, 236, 238, 241–244, 250, 281–282, 291, 306, 326, 331–332
  1970 (Seattle), 220–221, 229, 235–240, 242, 244–245, 250, 263
  1971 (Washington, DC), 253, 256, 257, 258, 259–260, 262–268, 269, 274, 276,, 282–283, 287
  1972 (Dallas), 290–291
  1973 (Toronto), 299–300, 305, 307
  1981 (Philadelphia), 302
  1994 (Fort Worth, TX), 42
  2003 (Boston), 352
  Business Committee, 164, 326
  Program Committee, 182
  Resolution "To Bear Witness," 5, 7
  Resolution on Joint Funding for Racial Justice, 266, 287, 327 *See also* General Assembly Ross Resolution
  Ross Resolution, 253, 266–267, 274, 277, 289, 303 *See also* General Assembly, Resolution on Joint Funding for Racial Justice *and* General Assembly Ross Resolution
  Resolution on Women and Religion, 249
  walkout, 147, 158, 166–172, 194, 198, 204, 225, 303, 326, 331, 355
General Electric, 217
General Investment Fund (UUA), 136
Gibbons, John, 162, 169, 172, 183, 206, 208, 352–353

Gibson, Gordon D., 114, 124, 167, 169
Gibson, Kenneth, 269
Gilbert, Richard S. (Dick), 161, 260
Giles, Philip R., 70–71, 72, 84, 86, 103, 160, 319, 334
Gilligan, Carol, 332
Gilmartin, Aron S., 152–154, 156–157, 169, 170, 175, 195, 266, 311
Glenview, IL, 10
Gloucester, MA, 108
Godbey, John C., 267–268
Gold, William, 53
Gordon, Hershel, 10, 91
Gordon, Roger, 10, 91
Gothard, Louis J., 34, 51–53, 64, 71, 94, 141, 173, 227, 255, 286–287, 297, 300
Grace Baptist Church (Chico, CA), 3
Graham, Richard M., 271, 315
Grand Rapids, MI, 75
Gravel, Mike, 277
Gray, Duke T., 8–9, 11, 53, 103, 144–145, 149, 151–152, 179, 223, 301
Great Slave Narratives, 129
Greater Washington Area Unitarian Universalists, 270–271
Greater Washington Association of Negro Unitarian Universalists Concerned with Race, 70
Greeley, Dana McLean, 34, 47, 65–66, 68, 81, 83–84, 86–87, 89, 104–105, 107, 111, 114, 119, 120, 124, 125, 130–131, 136–137, 158, 161, 166–167, 169–170, 172–174, 177, 184–185, 187–188, 190, 199–200, 202, 206, 272, 302, 319–322, 328, 330–332, 334, 346
Grey, Nina, 163–164, 167
Grier, Bob, 96
Griffin, Edna M., 176, 207, 283–284, 299
Grigsby, Marshall C., 314
Gunning, James, 288

Hadley, J. Harold, 153, 176, 201
Haley, Thomas L., 131, 143, 186
Hall, Hansel, 258
Hammond, Jack, 150
Hampton, Fred, 214
Hampton, Henry, 47–48, 116, 131, 195, 345
Hanaford, Phebe, 333
Harding, Vincent, 131, 176
Harlem Unitarian Church (NY), 109
Harlem, NY, 26, 92, 109
Harrington, Donald S., 23–30, 50, 91–101, 103, 110–111, 114, 119–120, 126–127, 130, 139, 156, 161, 174, 195, 218, 222, 229, 232, 261–262, 289, 291–292, 307, 319–320, 326, 338
Harrington, Vilma, 25, 91
Harris, W. Edward, 168, 223
Harris, Howard, 190
Harris, William H. Jr., 315
Harrisburg, PA, 4, 315
Harrison, William H., 4
Hartford, CT, 167, 171
Harvard Divinity School, 86, 130, 201
Hatcher, Richard G., 78
Hayward, CA, 40
Helverson, Ralph, 87, 118, 155, 208
Henderson, Carol, 283, 337–338
Henry, Hayward, Jr., 4, 45, 53, 64, 65, 69, 75–78, 80, 84, 98, 105, 110, 112–114, 117, 124, 126, 128, 141–142, 148–151, 155–156, 161–162, 165–166, 170, 174, 177–179, 186, 193, 196, 207, 211, 217, 219–223, 250, 254–257, 269, 280–281, 284, 289, 292, 294, 298, 301, 317, 327–331, 340, 344 *See also* Sanyika, Mtangulizi
Heretic: A Partisan Autobiography, 34, 100

Hewett, A. Phillip, 183–185, 189
Hidden Minority, The—The Homosexual in Our Society, 278
Higgins, Daniel G., 307
Higgins, Meredith, 344
Hobart, James A., 9, 50, 52, 58, 103, 190, 209–213, 335–336, 342–343
Hoffman, Clifton, 94, 131–132, 190
Hohler, G. Robert, 1, 5, 136–137, 152, 174, 178, 180, 217, 244
Holleroth, Hugo J., 279–284
Hollywood, FL, 11, 13, 17, 190, 242–243, 245
Holmes, John Haynes, 24, 90–91, 120, 338
Holway, William N., 275
"Hope despite Disillusion: Unitarian Universalists and the Homosexual" (Harrington), 307
Hopkins, Jeannette, 96
Hopkins, Raymond, 161, 200–201, 321, 331, 334
Hopper, C. Leon, 33, 171, 201
Hough Riot, 32
Hough Tenant Union, 209
House for James, A, 279
House of Representatives (U.S.), 4
House Un-American Activities Committee, 93
housing, 4, 11–12, 16, 31, 55, 72, 130, 152, 181, 207, 209–210, 243, 264–265, 271, 342
Housing and Urban Development (HUD), U.S. Department of, 265
Housing Opportunities Made Equal, 55
Houston, TX, 317
Howard University, 62, 75, 130
Howlett, Duncan, 62
Hruska, Roman, 4
Human Relations Council (Grand Rapids, MI), 75
Human Relations Council (Greater Harrisburg, PA), 4
Human Relations Councils, 3–4, 75–76
Huntsville, AL, 255
Hymns for the Celebration of Life, 76
Hymns of the Spirit, 248

"I Have a Dream" (King), 15
"If Black Is Beautiful, What Is White?" (Dodder), 218
"If I Were a Negro" (Samson), 22
IFCO, *See* Interreligious Foundation for Community Organization
Imara, Mwalimu, 287, 294, 298–299, 311, 315, 343–344 *See also* Renford G. Gaines
Indian affairs, 300
Indianapolis, 139
individualism, 248, 292, 295
Inquirer, The, 200
Institutional Racism Audit Team, (UUA), 308
integrated schools, 268
integration, 4, 7, 9, 11, 12, 14–17, 24, 26, 36–37, 41, 48–49, 55, 57, 61–62, 66, 71, 75–77, 90–92, 97–98, 118–120, 126–127, 130, 132, 148, 209, 211–213, 218, 222, 241, 243, 247, 251, 260–262, 268, 270, 279, 291, 313, 318, 339, 346 *See also* segregation
Interchurch Building (New York), 229
Interdenominational Racial Caucus (IRC), 147–148, 153, 244
Interfaith Alliance, 352
Interim Study Committee on Fund Raising (AUA), 138
International Association for Liberal Christianity and Religious Freedom, 185

INDEX

International Association for Religious Freedom (IARF), 160, 184–187, 189
International Council of Unitarians and Other Liberal Religious Thinkers and Workers, 184
Interreligious Foundation for Community Organization (IFCO), 141, 173–174, 255–256
Investment Committee (UUA), 137, 176, 335
Iowa Sisterhood, 333
IRC, *See* Interdenominational Racial Caucus
"Is Integration Dead?" (Harrington), 126
"Is There an Alternative to Black Power for the American Negro Today?" (Fritchman), 23, 25
Isaacs, Rob, *See* Eller-Isaacs, Rob

Jack, Alex, 147
Jack, Homer A., 40, 43–46, 50, 54, 60–61, 64–67, 71–72, 83–84, 86, 89, 93–94, 95, 97, 103, 117–118, 126, 130, 136–137, 140–141, 144–145, 147–148, 162, 169, 179, 184, 187, 190, 208, 217, 244, 266, 337, 349–350
Jackson, Barbara, 325
Jackson, Jesse, 78, 308
Jackson, Jimmie Lee, 16
Jackson, MS, 18–19, 21
Jackson, William, 108, 132
James Reeb Civil Rights Worker, 11, 58
James Reeb Memorial Fund, 3, 7, 47
James, Alan, 315
James, Jacqui, 315
Japanese Unitarian Fellowship at All Souls Church Unitarian (Washington DC), 314
Jenkins, Joseph, 53

Jenkins, Lillian W., 79–80, 134, 340–341
Jenkins, Maude, 96
Jews, 27, 92
John Birchers, 162
Johnson, George T., 58, 75
Johnson, J. Rosamond, 90
Johnson, Lyndon B., 43, 82, 90, 107
Joint Merger Commission (AUA and UCA), 249
Jokel, Victor, 147, 153
Jones, Jerry, 128, 344
Jones, LaVerne M., 227, 298
Jones, Robert, 66–67, 72, 120, 190
Jones, Walter Royal, 156–157, 190, 341
Jones, William R., 46, 53, 62, 75, 131, 315, 353–354
Jordall, Neil, 214
Jordan, Cornelius Van (Van), 55
Jordan, Joseph, 108
Jordan, Marjorie, 54–55, 64, 80, 255, 280
Joseph Priestley District (UUA), 11, 315
Jubilee Singers (All Souls Church, Unitarian, Washington DC), 314
Just, Bernice, 314

Kansas City, MO, 89
Kapp, Max A., 185
Kaufmann, Bob, 237–238
Kellaway, Richard, 167, 183, 336
Kennedy, Robert F., 117, 309
Kent State Massacre, 310
Kent, Jack A., 21, 45, 56, 83, 170, 314
Keohane, John, 257
Kerner Report, 82, 85, 243
Killian, James, 330
Kimball, Alice, 181
Kimball, Robert, 145
King, Coretta Scott, 89
King, Martin Luther, Jr., 1, 3, 7–8, 13–18, 20, 23, 31, 36, 41, 75,

407

King, Martin Luther, Jr. (*continued*)
  86–89, 90, 104, 112, 129, 136,
  145, 154, 190, 223, 240, 243, 268,
  280, 289, 309, 316, 347, 350, 355
Kohlbrenner, Bill, 288
Konko Church of Izuo, 185
Kring, Walter Donald, 118, 120, 138
Ku Klux Klan (KKK), 115, 162
Kuebler, Ernst, 331
Kurlew, Bill, 80
Kuroda, Andrew, 314

labor, 37, 121, 123, 174
Ladd, Larry, 141–142, 146, 161, 168,
  179–180, 183, 206, 208, 264,
  313, 316, 337
Lake Shore Unitarian Universalist
  Society (Wilmette and
  Glenview, IL), 10
Lal, Amrit, 131
Landess, Marcia McBroom, 302
  See also Marcia McBroom
LaPorte, Pierre, 189
Larson, Philip, 153–154, 157
Latimer, Lewis, 109
Lauriat, Nathaniel, 167, 171
lawsuits, 5–6, 212, 257, 292, 297, 303,
  344, 355
Lazaras, Kathy, 171
LeFlore, Jack O., 176
Leonard, Richard, 103
lesbian, gay and bisexual rights, 30,
  123, 240, 263, 303–305, 312, 336
Lewis, Pauline Warfield, 280
Liberal Party of New York State,
  24, 92
Liberal Religious Youth (LRY), 15,
  40, 46, 55, 60, 88, 142, 146, 160,
  162, 167–169, 171, 178, 202,
  207, 208, 218, 226, 234, 236, 242,
  263, 264, 313, 328, 337, 353, 354
Life magazine, 240
Light, Leona, 103, 148, 339
Liuzzo, Viola, 7

Lockman, Norman, 286
Los Angeles, 16, 23–24, 34, 36, 38,
  69, 72–73, 85, 99–100, 122, 130,
  163, 167, 183, 214, 218, 311, 338,
  345
Louisville, KY, 106, 135
Lovely, Brandock L. (Brandy), 168
Lowell, James Russell, 199
LRY, *See* Liberal Religious Youth
Lutherans, 82, 95

MacDonald, Mary Lu, 141, 145, 181
MacPherson, David Hicks, 145–147,
  161
Madison, WI, 54, 110
Main Line Unitarian Church (Devon,
  PA), 118, 159, 161, 217, 235
Malcolm X, 80, 92, 280
Man, the Culture Builder I and II, 280
March Against Fear, 18–21, 23
  See also Meredith March
March on Washington for Jobs and
  Freedom, 2, 15, 22, 303
March to Montgomery, 1–2, 7, 19
marginalization, 304, 327–329
Marshall, Ken, 190
Martin and Judy series, 279
Martinez, Guillermo, 178
Mason Temple (Memphis, TN), 86
Mason, Charles, 227
Mason, Hilda, 227, 288, 297, 341,
  344, 351
Massachusetts Bay District (UUA),
  5, 85, 87
Massachusetts Council of Churches,
  159
Massachusetts Universalist
  Convention, 201, 328
May 26th Empowerment Fund, 221,
  225, 227, 287–288, 304
May Meetings, 86, 173, 245, 319,
  323–324
May Memorial Unitarian Society
  (Syracuse, NY), 222

INDEX

McBroom, Marcia, 113 *See also* Marcia McBroom Landess
McCree, Wade H., 63–65, 74, 105
McDougald, Cornelius (Neil), 26, 46, 53, 65, 74, 76, 91–94, 96, 98, 110–111, 176, 190
McGee, Lewis A., 3, 24, 45, 46, 74–75, 89, 109, 315
McGee, Marcella Walker, 109
McGuinness, Mason, 235, 237
McIntosh, Peggy, 57
McKee, Henrietta, 176
McKersie, Robert, B., 21, 31
McKinney, Donald W., 8, 11, 94–95, 120, 205, 224, 247, 258, 300–301, 304, 311
McKissick, Floyd, 20, 41, 44–45, 48, 78
McNatt, Isaac, 176
Meadville Lombard Theological School, 8, 9, 10, 40, 93, 103, 130, 148, 152, 201, 267, 305, 308, 334, 335, 337, 351, 354
Melrose Unitarian Universalist Church (Melrose, MA), 7
Melrose, MA, 7
Memphis, TN, 7, 18, 86, 87, 89
Mendelsohn, Jack, 5, 62–63, 72, 85, 87, 123, 148, 149–150, 156, 158, 161, 166–174, 180, 194, 204, 237, 266–267, 276, 280, 282, 308, 311, 314, 342–343
Meredith March, 23, 41, 59 *See also* March Against Fear
Meredith, James, 18–20
Merger Commission (AUA and UCA), 320
merger of the AUA and UCA, *See* consolidation of the AUA and UCA
Mero, Ralph, 6
Methodists, 75, 82, 95, 200
Metropolitan Low Income Housing Program (Boston), 9

Midwest Unitarian Conference (AUA), 322
Midwest Unitarian Universalist Conference, 69, 322
Midwest Unitarian Universalist Foundation, 322
Midwest Universalist Conference (UCA), 322
Milgram, Morris, 130
Miller, Diane, 306
Miller, Mary Jane, 166
Miller, Orloff, W., 86, 103, 166, 304, 349–350
Milwaukee, WI, 43
Ministerial Fellowship Committee (UUA), 176, 299, 306, 335
Minneapolis, 43, 72–73, 160
Mississippi Delta Project, 2
Mississippi Summer Project, 2
Mode of Organization Committee (AUA and UCA), 320–321
Montgomery, AL, 3
Montreal Stock Exchange, 189
Montreal, QC, 187, 189
Moore, Christopher, 268
Moore, Matilda, 190
Moral Caucus, 170, 174, 179, 332
Mount Vernon Unitarian Church (Alexandria, VA), 317
Mountain Desert District (UUA), 86, 121, 171
Mt. Diablo Unitarian Universalist Church (Walnut Creek, CA), 130, 152, 311
Murray, John, 108
Mutual Real Estate Investment Trust (M-REIT), 130

Nash, Richard, 155–156, 179, 250, 304–305
Nashua, NH, 173
National Advisory Commission on Civil Disorders, 43, 82

409

National Association for the Advancement of Colored People (NAACP), 4, 6, 24, 27, 62, 76, 90, 95, 152, 216, 289
National Black Economic Development Conference (NBEDC), 141, 229, 231, 255, 256
National Black Power Conference, 133
National Committee for Free Elections In Mississippi, 92
National Committee of Negro Churchmen, 59
National Conference of Black Unitarian Universalists, 69, 73–75, 78–79, 81, 95–96
National Conference on New Politics, 44, 95
National Council of Churches, 59, 200
National Democratic Party of Alabama, 133, 220, 255
National Memorial Universalist Church (Washington DC), 161
National Organization of Women, 309
National Unitarian Conference, 108
National Urban Coalition, 118
Near North Fellowship, Old Town (Chicago), 10
"The Negro Protest", 76
"Negroes Consider Breaking Away", 66
Neighborhood Commons Corporation (Chicago), 57–58, 207, 257, 264, 269–270, 274
"The New Black Rebellion" (McKissick), 48
"The New Black Revolution", 35
New England Fellowship for Renewal, 150
New Orleans, 64

New York, 10, 23, 24, 26, 39, 43, 54, 73, 82, 90–93, 95–100, 104, 110, 113–114, 117–118, 120–121, 126, 130, 137–138, 141, 163, 217–219, 222, 225, 229, 243, 311, 315, 338
New York Times, 23, 220–222, 277, 278
Newark, NJ, 43, 45, 254, 269
Newsweek, 278
Newton, MA, 218, 226
Nixon, Richard M., 265, 277
Nominating Committee (UUA), *See* Unitarian Universalist Association, Nominating Committee
Norfolk, VA, 108
Norman, Winnifred L., 54, 96, 99, 299, 351
North Shore Unitarian Church (Plandome, NY), 228 *See also* Unitarian Universalist Congregation at Shelter Rock (Manhasset, NY), North Shore Unitarian Universalist Society (Plandome, NY), *and* Veatch Committee
North Shore Unitarian Universalist Society (Plandome, NY), 130, 277, 287–292 *See also* North Shore Unitarian Church (Plandome, NY), Unitarian Universalist Congregation at Shelter Rock (Manhasset, NY) *and* Veatch Committee

Oakland, CA, 41, 58, 69, 75
Ockert, Roy, 36, 38–40, 50, 69, 72, 103, 122–123, 145, 174, 225, 338
Office of Gay Concerns / Office on Gay Affairs (UUA), 299, 304–305, 307
Office of Overseas and Interfaith Relations (UUA), 185, 202

Ohio Universalist Convention, 333
Ohio-Meadville District (UUA), 32
Oklahoma City, 72
Olsen, Clark B., 171, 350
Olympia Brown Unitarian
 Universalist Congregation
 (Racine, WI), 72
Olympic Hotel (Seattle), 236
Oneonta, NY, 72, 163
Ottawa, ON, 73, 130–131, 137–138,
 143, 186, 188

Pacific Central District (UUA), 75
Pacific Northwest District (UUA),
 206, 321–322, 328
Pacific Southwest District (UUA), 69,
 106, 276
pan-Africanism, 254, 296
Paris Peace Accords, 107
Parke, David B., 52, 85, 103–104, 110,
 123, 142, 146, 166, 171–172, 208,
 232, 235, 237, 258, 282, 330, 332
Pasadena, CA, 34, 160
paternalism, 68, 79, 100, 112, 118,
 256, 270, 302, 329–332, 341, 346
patriarchy, 174, 329–335, 337–339,
 341, 343–345 *See also* feminism
 and women
Patterson, Charles, 70, 72, 74
Payne, Thomas E., 49, 54, 72, 130–
 131, 143, 161, 315
Penn, Nolan, 176
Pentagon Papers, The, 277, 278
People's Temple Church Colored
 Unitarian (Chicago), 108
Perrino, Anthony R., 50
Perry, Shauneille, 315
Petersberger, Clare, 233–234
Petersberger, Helen, 233–234
Philadelphia, 10–11, 64, 83, 85, 87,
 91, 103, 108, 121, 144, 146, 163,
 167, 208, 217, 218, 219, 229, 232,
 235, 243, 258, 294, 297–298,
 302, 342

Pickett, Eugene O., 308
Pinderhughes, Charles, 131
Pittsburgh, 315
Plainfield, NJ, 43
Plandome, NY, 130, 207, 212–213,
 228, 277, 287–289, 291, 292,
 294, 302, 305
Planning Committee (UUA), 264,
 299, 326, 351 *See also* Unitarian
 Universalist Association,
 Program Committee
pluralism, 105, 111, 112, 118, 128,
 154, 155–157, 179, 292, 295,
 313, 346–347
Poage, William R., 4
Pohl, David, C., 137
Poinsett, Alex, 55, 255, 315, 351–352
Poinsett, Norma R., 112, 299, 351
police brutality and harassment, 12,
 25, 31, 55, 117, 214–215, 305,
 309
polity, 139, 156, 220, 247, 272, 326,
 335
Pomeroy, Janet, 271
Poor People's Campaign, 117–118,
 309
Poor People's Partnership, 210
Portland, OR, 225
Powell, Adam Clayton Jr., 92
Prairie Group, 336
Presbyterians, 200, 229, 317
Princeton, NJ, 337
Principles and Purposes, 249–250
privilege, 16, 57, 103, 251, 348
Program Committee (UUA), *See*
 Unitarian Universalist
 Association, Planning
 Committee, *and* Unitarian
 Universalist Association,
 Program Committee
Project Equality, 159, 207, 291, 302
"Psychopathology of Racism," 214
Punderson Lake conference, 141–
 143, 145–146, 181

Quakers, 247
Quebec, QC, 188

Racial Justice Committee (UUA), 290
Racial Justice Curriculum Committee (UUA), 351
Racial Justice Fund (UUA), *See* Unitarian Universalist Association, Special Fund to Promote Racial Justice and Combat Racism
Racine, WI, 72, 163
racism, 13, 16, 50, 58, 70, 78–82, 92, 105, 135, 145, 163, 171, 177, 179, 204, 210, 215, 220, 229, 239, 251, 258, 263, 272, 276, 281, 284, 286, 301, 303, 318, 329, 332, 340–341, 351
"Racism for the UUA?" (Clark), 95
Raible, Christopher G., 172, 245
Raible, Peter, 6, 225
Ramey, Jules, 34, 53, 162–164, 183
Randolph, A. Philip, 92
Ray, James Earl, 87
Raynolds, Ann, 104, 174, 180, 339
Readout, 95
Redding, Ann Holmes, 46–49, 143
Reeb, James, 1, 3, 5, 7–9, 13, 15, 19, 25, 47, 273, 350
Reed, George W., Jr., 56, (ca. 373 and ca. 382)
Reed, Jesse A., 45
Reed, Selina E. (Lee), 7, 45, 51, 54–56, 61
Reed, Robert, 60, 135, 169, 305–306
Reed, Toni, 337
Reeves, Eugene, 347
regionalism, 325, 329
Register-Leader, 61, 95, 320–321
Reinhardt, Aurelia Henry, 333
religious education, 1, 12, 24, 52, 76–77, 91–92, 108, 125, 148, 167, 203, 228, 249, 277–284, 307, 314–315, 321, 334, 337–338

Religious Education Action Clearing House, 76
Render, Sylvia Lyons, 109
Report of the Committee on Goals, 18, 47, 334
Resolution on Joint Funding for Racial Justice, *See* General Assembly Resolution on Joint Funding for Racial Justice
Resolution on Race Relations, 247
Resolution on Women and Religion, 249
Rice, William B., 190, 320, 331
Richards, David A. J., 332
Richmond, VA, 53
Ricks, Willie, 20
riots, 16, 18, 31, 33, 43, 55, 82, 88–89, 117, 223, 309
Rissho Kosei-kai, 185
Riverside Church (New York), 141, 229
Robeson, Eslanda, 24
Robeson, Paul, 24
Rochester, NY, 4, 154, 175, 260
Rose, Ken, 40
Rosenthal, Alan, 159, 164, 169
Ross, Warren, 266
Ross Resolution, *See* General Assembly, Resolution on Joint Funding for Racial Justice *and* General Assembly, Ross Resolution
Roxbury, MA, 207
Rush, Benjamin, 3
Rustin, Bayard, 44, 289
Ryder, Donald, 315

Sacajawea, 308
Saltonstall, Leverett, 4
Samples, Joseph B. Jr., 73–74, 78, 141, 176, 264, 299, 313, 315–316, 351
Samples, Pearl, 315–316, 351
Samson, Peter H., 22, 32

INDEX

San Diego, 73, 225
San Francisco, 69–70, 72–73, 103, 121, 218, 225, 244, 294, 307
sanctuary congregation, 106
Sanyika, Mtangulizi (formerly Hayward Henry), 327
Schenectady, NY, 50, 105
Scholefield, Harry B., 103, 201, 225, 264
School Board (Chicago), 6
School Board (Seattle), 6
school boards and committees, 5–8
School Committee (Boston), 5, 7
school integration, 4, 7, 9, 241
school segregation, 5–9, 31, 242
schools, 4–9, 31, 121, 133, 241–242, 268
Schuchter, Arnold, 129
Schulz, William F., 303, 338
Schuman, Eric, 232–234
SCLC, *See* Southern Christian Leadership Conference
Scott, Amy, 108
Scott, Benjamin F., 43, 48, 53, 54, 64, 74, 79, 81, 94, 129, 133, 174–176, 196, 219, 221–222, 227, 255, 266, 288–289, 293, 295, 297–298, 301, 314, 331–332, 344, 351, 355
Scott, Joyce, 43
Scott, William M., 176
Seattle, 6, 40–42, 144, 152, 220–221, 225, 229, 235–237, 239, 242, 244–245, 250, 263, 311–312
Second Unitarian Church (Boston), 45, 64, 149–151, 180, 236, 254
Second Unitarian Church (Chicago), 10
segregation, 5–6, 9, 12, 14–15, 38, 61, 91, 94, 98, 119, 242 *See also* integration
Seiden, Betty Bobo, 69–70, 79, 80, 91, 148, 169–170, 175, 193, 222, 225, 283, 339, 351

Selma, AL, 1–3, 7, 11, 15, 19, 25, 26, 43, 46, 64, 71, 77, 86, 91, 102, 152, 169, 171, 209, 247, 303–305, 350
Senate (U.S.), 4
Seon, Yvonne, 308
sexism, 333, 338, 341
sexual liberation, 309, 336
sexual revolution, 337
sexuality education, 278
Shadle, Neil, 8–10, 19, 57–58, 103, 209, 264
Shaker Heights, OH, 209–210
Shinto, 185
Shreveport, LA, 7
Sigma Pi Phi, 26, 92
Sikes, Bette, 339
Sikes, George, 55–56, 205, 342
Silliman, Vincent, 112
Singing the Living Tradition, 249
Singleton, Anne, 234
Sinkford, Kathryn, 55, 315
Sinkford, William G., 15, 55, 303, 313, 315–317, 337, 350–351
Sitka UU Fellowship (Sitka, AK), 109
Sitka, AK, 109
Skinner House Books, 308
Small, Mary L., 281–285
Small, Robert, 255
Smith, John, 206, 258
Smith-Penniman, Adelle, 308
Social Implication Subcommittee of the Investment Committee (UUA), 137
Social Responsibility Advisory Committee (UUA), 131
Social Responsibility Committee (UUA), 176
Society for the Abolition of Slavery, 3
Society of Black Soul, 257
Society of Friends, 247
Soskin, Betty Reid, 79–80, 116, 340–341

South Africa, 137
South Peel, ON, 336
Southeast District (UUA), *See* Unitarian Universalist Association, Southeast District
Southern Christian Leadership Conference (SCLC), 21, 27, 62, 104, 236
Sparrow, Eugene, 46, 53, 74–75
Special Fund to Promote Racial Justice and Combat Racism (UUA), *See* Unitarian Universalist Association, Special Fund to Promote Racial Justice and Combat Racism
Special Report: The Emergency Conference on the Unitarian Universalist Response to the Black Rebellion, 191
Spoerl, Dorothy, 244
St. Lawrence District (UUA), 110
St. Louis, MO, 280
Stair, Gobin, 277
Starr King School for the Ministry, 130, 145, 201
Starr, Deane, 153–154, 157, 175, 201, 321
Statler-Hilton Hotel (Boston), 159, 306
Steiner, Ruth, 40
Stewart, Rod, 322
Stokes, Carl B., 112
Stonewall Inn riots, 305, 309
Student Nonviolent Coordinating Committee (SNCC), 20, 40, 45, 140
Student Religious Liberals (SRL), 46, 146, 178, 202, 208, 232, 234–236
Stuztman, Ralph, 182–183
Suffolk, VA, 109
Supporters of Black Unitarians for Radical Reform (SOBURR), 69, 71–72, 85, 103, 122, 160, 242–243, 339, 347

Sutherland, Malcolm, 103, 334
Syracuse, NY, 73, 222

Taft, William Howard, 5
Tampa Bay, FL, 33
Task Force II on White Racism (UUA), 125, 128, 144
Task Force on Black Affairs Council (UUA), 125–126
Task Force on the Urban Church and Inner City Ministry (UUA), 34
Taylor, Dalmas A., 131, 264, 275, 295, 297–299, 351
Third Unitarian Church (Chicago), 162, 172
Thomas, Charles, 231
Thomas, Gwendolyn, 176, 293–294, 297, 299, 343–344, 351
Throop Memorial Church (Pasadena, CA), 34, 160
Thurman, Howard, 190, 240
Time magazine, 23
"To Bear Witness" (GA Resolution), *See* General Assembly Resolution "To Bear Witness"
tokenism, 92
Topeka, KS, 61
Toronto, ON, 72–73, 186–187, 299–300, 305, 324
Towson, MD, 145, 147
Traylor, Richard, 11, 53, 64, 70, 83, 122, 132–133, 141–142, 161, 177, 208, 217–218, 221–222, 225–227, 255, 288–289, 292, 293–295, 298, 301, 314, 331, 342–344, 355
Tubman, Harriet, 308
Tuckerman, Joseph, 9
Tulsa, OK, 104
Tuskegee Institute, 131–132
Tweedie, Del, 161–163

UCA, *See* Universalist Church of America
Ulbrich, Holley, 173, 323

INDEX

union movement, 37
Union of Black Clergy and Laity, 82
Unitarian Church of Harrisburg (PA), 4, 315
Unitarian Church of Flushing (NY), 109
Unitarian Church of All Souls (New York), 118, 120, 138
Unitarian Commission on Intergroup Relations (AUA), 227
Unitarian Fellowship of Huntsville (AL), 255
Unitarian Service Committee, 328
Unitarian Society of Cleveland, 31, 89
Unitarian Society of Hartford (CT), 167, 171
Unitarian Society of Fort Wayne (IN), 152
Unitarian Society of Germantown (Philadelphia), 85, 87, 229, 232, 235, 258, 297
"Unitarian Universalism and Black Empowerment in the United States," 85–86
"Unitarian Universalism: Yesterday, Today and Tomorrow" (Harrington), 24
Unitarian Universalist Association
  Accreditation of Directors of Religious Education Committee, 176
  Advisory Committee for the Washington Office for Social Concern, 131
  affiliate group status, 80, 83, 98, 119, 124, 228, 260
  After Selma Committee, 21, 43
  Annual Program Fund, 69, 150, 188, 201, 204, 224, 275, 290
  associate group status, 302
  Black Concerns Working Group, 351

Unitarian Universalist Association (continued)
  Board of Trustees, 17, 33, 51, 52, 53, 60, 61, 63–65, 68–69, 75, 83–84, 96, 106–107, 111–113, 119, 125–126, 128, 130–131, 136, 139, 142, 144, 154–155, 171, 172, 176, 178, 180, 181, 198, 200, 201, 203–208, 217, 218, 219, 222, 226–228, 235, 237, 238, 263–264, 266, 272, 274–277, 283, 286–287, 289–290, 298, 299, 308, 320, 324, 325–326, 329, 330, 335, 351, 352
  Business Committee, 76, 176, 181
  bylaws, 106, 140, 153, 156, 241, 245–246, 297–298, 301, 335
  Central Midwest District, 10, 60
  Commission for Action on Race, 83, 107
  Commission on Appraisal, 76, 140, 176, 262–264, 299, 308, 313, 351
  Commission on Education and Liberal Religion, 278, 282
  Commission on Religion and Race, 2, 5, 11, 12, 39, 43–45, 51–52, 61–64, 66, 69, 71, 76–78, 80, 83, 92–94, 111, 125, 137, 156, 190, 279, 303, 339
  Committee of Committees, 335
  Committee on Goals, 17–18, 40, 243, 251, 306, 337
  Committee on Racial Justice, 275
  Committee on Urban Concerns and Ministry, 308
  Constitution, 119
  Continental Committee on Development and Fundraising, 138
  Delaware Valley District, 226
  Department of Adult Programs, 76
  Department of Education, 76, 279
  Department of Education and Social Concern, 202

415

Unitarian Universalist Association (*continued*)
  Department of Fundraising and Development, 139
  Department of Ministry, 21, 128, 211, 273, 336
  Department of Overseas and Interfaith Relations, 2, 111
  Department of Religious Education, 52, 284, 307
  Department of Social Action, 97, 142
  Department of Social Responsibility, 2, 33, 43, 118, 191, 202
  district executives, 70, 86, 94, 103, 131, 203, 322
  districts, 44–46, 60, 106, 114, 153, 201, 202, 205, 246, 272, 321–322, 324–325
  Division of Communications and Publications Advisory Committee, 131
  elections, 2, 76, 96, 103, 133, 139, 152–157, 158, 160, 164, 165, 175–176, 241–252, 254, 272, 299, 319–322, 330, 337
  extension model, 132
  Finance Committee, 155, 200, 205, 326, 335
  Freedom Fund, 3, 47, 63, 69, 84, 125
  General Assembly, *See* General Assembly (UUA)
  General Investment Fund, 136
  Institutional Racism Audit Team, 308
  Investment Committee, 137, 176, 335
  Joseph Priestley District, 11, 315
  Massachusetts Bay District, 5, 85, 87
  Ministerial Fellowship Committee, 176, 299, 306, 335

Unitarian Universalist Association (*continued*)
  Mountain Desert District, 86, 121, 171
  Nominating Committee, 76, 176–177, 299, 326, 335
  Office of Gay Concerns, / Office on Gay Affairs, 299, 305–305, 307
  Office of Overseas and Interfaith Relations, 185, 202
  Ohio-Meadville District, 32
  Pacific Central District, 75
  Pacific Northwest District, 206, 321–322, 328
  Pacific Southwest District, 69, 106, 276
  Planning Committee, 264, 299, 326, 351 *See also* Unitarian Universalist Association, Program Committee
  Program Committee (UUA), 76, 176, 181, 183, 238, 263 *See also* Unitarian Universalist Association, Planning Committee
  Racial Justice Committee, 290
  Racial Justice Curriculum Committee, 351
  Social Implication Subcommittee of the Investment Committee, 137
  Social Responsibility Advisory Committee, 131
  Social Responsibility Committee, 176
  Southeast District, 94, 131, 205, 322, 329
  Special Fund to Promote Justice and Combat Racism, 83, 228, 266, 275, 289–292, 301–302
  St. Lawrence District, 110
  Task Force II on White Racism, 125, 128, 144

Unitarian Universalist Association
  (*continued*)
   Task Force on Black Affairs
    Council, 125–126
   Task Force on the Urban Church
    and Inner City Ministry, 34
   Urban Church Coalition, 8, 308
   Washington Office for Social
    Concern, 66, 72, 120, 131
Unitarian Universalist Center City
  Church Conference, 342
Unitarian Universalist Center for
  Urban Ministry (Chicago), 8, 10,
  19, 57
Unitarian Universalist Church in
  Fullerton (CA), 225
Unitarian Universalist Church of
  Buffalo (NY), 262
Unitarian Universalist Church of
  Nashua (NH), 173
Unitarian Universalist Church of
  Urbana-Champaign (IL), 130,
  148, 151, 214, 216, 287, 311
Unitarian Universalist Church of the
  Restoration (Philadelphia),
  10–11, 64, 91, 208
Unitarian Universalist Church West
  (Brookfield, WI), 278
Unitarian Universalist Congregation
  of Princeton (NJ), 337
Unitarian Universalist Congregation
  at Shelter Rock (Manhasset,
  NY), *See* North Shore Unitarian
  Church (Plandome, NY), North
  Shore Unitarian Universalist
  Society (Plandome, NY) *and*
  Veatch Committee
Unitarian Universalist Congregation
  of Queens (NY) *See* Unitarian
  Church of Flushing (NY)
Unitarian Universalist Fellowship of
  Athens (GA), 271
Unitarian Universalist Fellowship of
  Bozeman (MT), 72

Unitarian Universalist Gay Caucus,
  304–305, 307
Unitarian Universalist Laymen's
  League, 1, 46, 76, 136–137, 146,
  176, 180, 202, 340
Unitarian Universalist Service
  Committee (UUSC), 46, 76, 147,
  176, 219, 239, 244, 351
Unitarian Universalist Society for
  Community Ministries
  (UUSCM), 8
Unitarian Universalist United Nations
  Office (UU-UNO), 2
Unitarian Universalist Urban
  Ministry, 274
Unitarian Universalist Women's
  Federation (UUWF), 5, 46, 76,
  79, 134, 181–182, 202, 226, 304,
  340
Unitarian, The, 158
United Black Church, 95
United Church of Christ, 95, 159
United Farm Workers, 291
United Methodist Church, 200
United Presbyterian Church, 200,
  229
Unity House (Washington DC),
  270–271
Universalist Church of America
  (UCA), 1, 103, 108, 160, 199,
  241, 248, 272–273, 318–319,
  323, 328, 333–334
Universalist Service Committee, 328
University Unitarian Church
  (Seattle), 6, 40, 42, 152, 225,
  311
Urban Church Coalition (UUA), 8,
  308
urban concerns, 8, 16, 34, 58–59, 71,
  99, 102, 105, 109–210, 219, 243,
  271, 312, 314, 316
Urban Gateways, 268
Urban League, 4, 6, 44, 62, 76, 152,
  216, 255, 289, 308

417

urban ministry, 8–9, 11, 32, 46, 57, 103, 132, 207, 209, 211, 213, 224, 303
Urbana-Champaign, IL, 130, 148, 151, 214, 216, 287, 311
UU World, 261, 276, 298, 310
UUA, *See* Unitarian Universalist Association
UUA Now, 113, 154, 189, 191, 202, 244
"The UUA *Still* in Crisis" (Beattie), 139

Vancouver, BC, 183, 322
Veatch Committee, 212–213, 294, 302, 305 *See also* North Shore Unitarian Church (Plandome, NY), North Shore Unitarian Society (Plandome, NY), *and* Unitarian Universalist Congregation at Shelter Rock (Manhasset, NY)
Vendig, Eleanor, 289
Venerable, Grant II, 74, 80, 83, 158
Vietnam war, 17, 30, 33, 71, 107, 137, 147, 185, 234–235, 240, 277, 278, 309, 312
Volunteers in Service to America (VISTA), 355
voting rights, 12, 31, 303
Voting Rights Act, 11, 16

Wahtera, Ruth, 337
Walkout, *See* General Assembly Walkout
Walnut Creek, CA, 130, 152, 311
Ware Lecture, 13, 15, 16, 17, 18, 20, 33, 75, 112, 190, 240
Washington DC, 3, 9, 62, 66, 70, 72, 73, 89, 117, 120–121, 131, 161, 163, 218–219, 223, 226–227, 230–231, 243, 253, 257, 259, 262, 265, 266, 274, 287, 297, 302, 303, 309, 310, 313, 315, 344

Washington Evening Star, 234
Washington Office for Social Concern (UUA), 66, 72, 120, 131
Washington Post, 266, 277
Washington, Joseph, R., 129
Washtenaw County (MI) Black Economic Development League, 231
Washtenaw County (MI) Welfare Rights Committee, 231
Watts Riot, 16, 25, 99
Webb, Theodore, A., 103
Weissbard, Alfred, 105, 115–116, 125, 222, 327
Weissbard, David, 172, 174, 182
Welfare Rights Organization, 133, 210
Wells, John, 157, 175
West Shore Unitarian Universalist Church (Cleveland), 22, 32, 58, 59, 209, 210, 213
West, Robert Nelson, 4, 113, 153, 154, 157, 175, 176, 198–204, 206–208, 220, 222, 225, 237, 262, 265, 274–278, 289, 299, 310, 326, 352, 353
Westwood, Horace, 63
"What's the Matter with Black Power?" (Harrington), 23
Wheelwright, Farley W., 17, 89, 209, 211
When Brucie Came to Play, and Other Stories, 279
Where Do We Go from Here: Chaos or Community?, 17, 129
white flight, 9–11, 312
white guilt, 348
White Plains, NY, 91
White Power, Black Freedom, 129
"White Privilege: Unpacking the Invisible Knapsack" (McIntosh), 57
"The White Problem" (Harrington), 25

INDEX

white terrorism, 316
White, John, 234
Whitlock, Kenneth N., 224–225, 302
Whitney M. Young Jr. Urban Ministry Fund, 308
Wilkins, John Bird, 108
Wilkins, Raymond L., 176
William Styron's Nat Turner: Ten Black Writers Respond, 129
William, Wesley S., 176
Williams, Carroll, 195
Williams, Loretta, 308
Williams, Margaret, 176
Williams, Rhys, 148, 149, 150, 151, 180
Williamson, S.J. Jr., 176, 264
Wilmette, IL, 10
Wilmington Morning News, 286
Wilmington, DE, 286, 287
Wilmot, Arthur, 3
Wilson, Harold A., 127, 130, 142, 152, 166, 176,, 195, 257, 261–262, 264, 267, 274, 287, 292, 294, 297, 301, 315, 343–344
Wolfe, John, 104
women, 42, 240, 250, 303–305, 312, 334, 336 *See also* feminism and patriarchy

Women and Religion resolution, 249
Won't You Miss Me?, 279
Woodstock Festival, 309
Workman Lecture, 186
World Parliament of Religions, 184
Worshipping Together with Questioning Minds, 76
Wright, Conrad, 265
Wright, Nathan Jr., 144
Wright, William D., 270–271

Yippies, *See* Youth International Party
Yoder, Dayton T., 124, 346
Young Afro-Americans, 121
Young, Andrew, 236, 238, 240
Young, Elizabeth, 344
Young, Whitney M. Jr., 44, 130, 255
youth, 2, 136, 142, 146, 163, 174, 234, 336
"The Youth Agenda 1969" (Ladd), 141
Youth Caucus, 51, 141–142
Youth International Party, 117, 309

Zoerheide, Jack, 5
Zoerheide, Robert, 102, 232–234

419

Also by Mark Morrison-Reed from Skinner House Books

Been in the Storm So Long (co-edited with Jacqui James)
  More than 40 selections from the spirited voices of 29 African Americans. Contributors include David H. Eaton, Marjorie Bowens-Wheatley, Rosemary Bray McNatt, Thandeka, Egbert Ethelred Brown, and more.

Black Pioneers in a White Denomination, 3rd edition
  This portrait of racism in liberal religion tells the stories of two pioneering black ministers. Includes accounts of some of today's more integrated UU congregations and biographical notes on past and present black Unitarian, Universalist, and UU ministers.

In Between: Memoir of an Integration Baby
  Frank personal account of growing up black during the era of the civil rights movement. The author wrestles with racism, the death of Martin Luther King, black radicalism, his interracial family, and his experience as one of the first black Unitarian Universalist ministers.

*Darkening the Doorways: Black Trailblazers and
Missed Opportunities in Unitarian Universalism*
  Both a tale of systemic paternalism and one of idealism, courage, intrepid allies, dogged determination, and steadfast loyalty in the face of rejection. Profiles and essays are supplemented by archival documents.

Voices from the Margins: An Anthology of Meditations
(co-edited with Jacqui James)
  Spiritual reflections from Unitarian Universalists of color remind us of what we miss when we don't listen to marginalized voices and of the insights we stand to gain when we do.

*The Selma Awakening: How the Civil Rights Movement
Tested and Changed Unitarian Universalism*
  Selma represented a turning point for Unitarian Universalists. In answering Martin Luther King Jr.'s call to action, they shifted from passing earnest resolutions about racial justice to putting their lives on the line for the cause. Morrison-Reed traces the long history of race relations among the Unitarians and the Universalists leading up to 1965.